MILITARIZATION AND DEMOCRACY IN WEST GERMANY'S BORDER POLICE, 1951–2005

German History in Context

Series Editor
Bill Niven, Nottingham Trent University

Editorial Board
Stefan Berger, Ruhr-Universität Bochum
Atina Grossman, Cooper Union
Andrew I. Port, Wayne State University

DAVID M. LIVINGSTONE

MILITARIZATION AND DEMOCRACY IN WEST GERMANY'S BORDER POLICE, 1951–2005

CAMDEN HOUSE
Rochester, New York

Copyright © 2024 David M. Livingstone

All Rights Reserved. Except as permitted under current legislation, no part of this work may be photocopied, stored in a retrieval system, published, performed in public, adapted, broadcast, transmitted, recorded, or reproduced in any form or by any means, without the prior permission of the copyright owner.

First published 2024
by Camden House

Camden House is an imprint of Boydell & Brewer Inc.
668 Mt. Hope Avenue, Rochester, NY 14620, USA
and of Boydell & Brewer Limited
PO Box 9, Woodbridge, Suffolk IP12 3DF, UK
www.boydellandbrewer.com

ISBN-13: 978-1-64014-151-3

Library of Congress Cataloging-in-Publication Data

CIP data is available from the Library of Congress.

The publisher has no responsibility for the continued existence or accuracy of URLs for external or third-party internet websites referred to in this book, and does not guarantee that any content on such websites is, or will remain, accurate or appropriate

CONTENTS

Acknowledgments	vii
List of Abbreviations	xi
Introduction	1

Part I.
Origins and Early Development, 1949–1956

1	The Shadow of Weimar Political Violence in the Making of West Germany's BGS	17
2	Men of the First Hour: Veteran Soldiers and the Police Organization They Made	45
3	Who Wants to Be a Soldier? The BGS and West Germany's New Army	73

Part II.
Organizational Culture, 1956–1980

4	Recruitment and Rebuilding the BGS	99
5	Militarization and Training for War	123
6	Professional Ethics and Moral Training	150
7	The Debate over Combatant Status and Its Consequences	175

Part III.
Modernization: Becoming a Federal Police Agency, 1968–2005

8	Bonn's "Problem Child": The Struggle to Modernize the BGS	203
9	From Munich to Mogadishu: Fighting Terrorism at Home and Abroad	228
10	More than Guarding Borders: From BGS to Bundespolizei	255

Conclusion: Germany's Police: A Model for Democratic Policing? 285

Bibliography 293

Index 319

ACKNOWLEDGMENTS

I AM GRATEFUL TO the many people and institutions that made this book possible. First and foremost, I would like to Thank Bill Niven, Editor for the German History in Context series at Camden House, and Editorial Board members Stefan Berger, Atina Grossman, and Andrew I. Port for their support and the opportunity to include my book in this series. I also owe a huge debt of gratitude to Editorial Director Jim Walker for his encouragement and guidance through the publication process. Jim's expertise and knowledge truly made it a positive experience from beginning to end. I am very grateful for the comments of the anonymous readers and all the staff at Camden House for the time they took to read the manuscript and for their constructive criticism in helping me to strengthen its main arguments.

I also owe a great deal of thanks to Professor Frank Biess, my *Doktorvater* at the University of California, San Diego. Frank not only gave me an opportunity by taking a chance on an unconventional candidate who began graduate school while still working full-time as a Police Commander, but was also the first to suggest German policing as a potential research topic. His helpful insights, expertise on sources, encouragement, and friendship played a significant role in my development as a scholar and in the book that this revised manuscript became. I also thank UCSD Professors Rebecca Plant, Ulrike Strasser, Deborah Hertz, and Richard Biernacki for reading earlier versions of the manuscript and their advice on its further development. Professor Sagi Schaefer at Tel Aviv University read and commented on early chapter drafts and shared helpful insights from his work on the Inner-German border. I am also grateful to Professor Adam Seipp at Texas A&M University for first suggesting the Bundesgrenzschutz as an interesting German policing subject and for pointing me to a rich trove of archival sources in Germany.

Numerous archivists and librarians helped me over many years of research, including the employees and staff members at The German Federal Archives in Koblenz, Freiburg am Breisgau, and Ludwigsburg; The State Archives in Munich and North Rhine Westphalia; The Berlin State Library; The German Police University Library, Münster-Hiltrup; The US National Archives at College Park; The Special Collections Libraries at Amherst College, Princeton and Harvard Universities, and the Dwight D. Eisenhower and Harry S. Truman Presidential Libraries.

A special thanks to Cristina Meisner of the Harry Ransom Center at the University of Texas at Austin for her help in locating rare photographs from the David Douglas Duncan Life Magazine Collection, and also to Brian Kádár of the Federal Image Agency in Berlin for his help in securing the publication permissions for the cover image. I am also grateful to the inter-library loan personnel at both UCSD and California Lutheran University for their help in obtaining many rare, out-of-print, and foreign language sources.

My archival research was supported by a generous fellowship from the Fritz Thyssen Foundation and several UCSD History Department travel grants. I am especially thankful to Frau Doris Kock, librarian at the German Police University, for access to its excellent collection of secondary sources and for her gracious assistance in accommodating my use of the facilities during my stay at the University. Frau Kock also introduced me to Benjamin Fritsche, editor of the Federal Police employee magazine, *Kompakt*. Benjamin gave me digital access to thirty years of archived BGS magazines and obtained permission from the Federal Ministry of the Interior for me to use and quote from these sources. I cannot thank him enough for his efforts in saving me the time and expense that it would have taken to track these articles down at various libraries.

Studying German policing required me to step outside of my own law enforcement career and ultimately taught me more about the legacies of the profession I chose and its critical and at times problematic role in modern democracies. Indeed, during the writing of this book, policing dominated the headlines in the aftermath of many disturbing and violent incidents. The United States, Germany, and many other democracies are still trying to reimagine policing, while struggling to reconcile the consequences of violent and often unjustified uses of deadly force by their officers. Along these lines, I am grateful to my colleagues at the Simi Valley Police Department, where I spent thirty-four years serving the community before my retirement in 2022. Policing is a challenging profession even under the best of circumstances, but I was fortunate to work with and learn from some truly amazing officers over the years. My thinking about police militarization benefitted significantly from numerous conversations with my law enforcement colleagues and during public forums with members of the community in light of new calls for reform following the horrific murder of George Floyd.

While researching the book, I met and corresponded with numerous border police veterans and their family members. Their insights helped me find sources and understand German policing concepts less familiar to someone trained in US policing. I was particularly fortunate to meet three BGS veterans, who sadly passed away before seeing the final result of the book. Wolfgang Dorhmann, Richard Schumann, and legendary founder of GSG 9, Ulrich Wegener, took the time to meet with me and share memories, documents, and photographs. As president of the BGS Veterans Association, Wolfgang Dorhmann introduced me to many of his colleagues and gave me access to his own collection of organizational journals and articles. Ulrich Wegener pointed me to sources about the Munich Olympics and generously provided me with copies of his own published writings about the Mogadishu raid, which helped me to think about what was at stake for the Federal Republic during its struggle against terrorism. He was a consummate professional and generously offered to read earlier drafts of the terrorism chapter. Herr Schumann guided me on hikes along the rural footpaths of his former patrol routes near the city of Mödlareuth. Klaus and Dagmar Röder graciously opened their home to me during my stay in the Coburg region. I am also thankful to retired Federal Police Officer Josef Scheuring, who shared important memories about his experiences during the transition of the BGS into the Bundespolizei as well as his post-unification work integrating former East German police officers into the BGS. Josef graciously allowed me to quote from his book, *Den Menschen verpflichtet*. I also want to thank Frau Professorin Irmgard Müller and her family for sharing personal stories about their father, BGS Brigadier General Heinrich Müller, and for her permission to use photographs that she had donated to the Federal Military archive in Freiburg.

Finally, I am grateful for the love and support of family members on both sides of the Atlantic. My parents, Ralph and Helga Livingstone, instilled in me the love of reading and travelling as well as an innate curiosity about the world around us. The stories of my mother's childhood in Germany during the war and her emigration to the United States in 1962 sparked my interest in postwar Germany. I also want to thank my good friend and travel companion Stephen Bourque, professor emeritus, US Army School of Advanced Military Studies. I was an undergraduate at California State University, Northridge, when I first took Steve's historical seminar classes, and it was because of his encouragement that I decided to go on to graduate school. Steve graciously took time away from his own writing to read drafts of various chapters and provide constructive feedback. My aunt, Inge Dasch, and cousins Christina Toleikies, Sonja Obrist, and Christina Fries made me feel at home during many extended research trips in Germany. My wife, Stacie Galang, my daughter Breanne, and new grandchild, Baker, and in-laws Valentine and Josephine Galang encouraged me to keep pressing forward. I am certain the last thing Stacie, a full-time editor and news director, wanted to do after spending all day reading news copy was to come home and read my chapter drafts. Her sense about what makes a good story and her constructive feedback helped me to become a better writer in the process. I am fortunate to have such a great partner in life. Sadly, my father-in-law Valentine, an avid reader of history, who took a keen interest in the forthcoming book, passed away unexpectedly in 2023. He will be sorely missed and I know he would have loved to read the book that dominated so many of our family dinner conversations.

Ventura, California
July 2023

ABBREVIATIONS

APO	Außerparlamentarische Opposition (Extra-parliamentary Opposition)
BA-MA	Bundesarchiv Militärarchiv Freiburg (Federal Military Archive, Freiburg)
BArch-K	Bundesarchiv Koblenz (Federal Archive, Coblenz)
BArch-LW	Bundesarchiv Außenstelle Ludwigsburg (Federal Archives Branch, Ludwigsburg)
BePo	Bereitschaftspolizei (Riot Police)
BfV	Bundesverfassungschutz (Federal Office for the Protection of the Constitution)
BGS	Bundesgrenzschutz (Federal Border Guard)
BKA	Bundeskriminalamt (Federal Criminal Police Office)
BMI	Bundesministerium des Innern (Federal Ministry of the Interior)
BND	Bundesnachrichtendienst (Federal Intelligence Agency)
BP	Bayernpartei (Bavarian Party)
BPOL	Bundespolizei (Federal Police)
BT	Bundestag (Federal Parliament)
BVP	Bayerische Volkspartei (Bavarian Peoples Party)
CDU	Christlich Demokratische Union (Christian Democratic Party)
CIA	Central Intelligence Agency
CSU	Christlich-Soziale Union (Christian Social Party [Bavaria])
DGB	Deutsche Gewerkschaftsbund (German Confederation of Trade Unions)
EDC	European Defense Community
FAZ	*Frankfurter Allgemeine Zeitung*
FDJ	Freie Deutsche Jugend (Free German Youth [GDR])
FDP	Freie Demokratische Partei (Free Democratic Party)

FRG	Federal Republic of Germany
GdP	Gewerkschaft der deutschen Polizei (Union of German Police)
GDR	German Democratic Republic
GSE	Grenzschutzeinzeldienst (Border Police Individual Service)
GSG 9	Grenzschutzgruppe 9 (Border Protection Group 9)
HICOG	Allied High Commission for Germany
IOLP	International Federation of Police Leaders
KPD	Kommunistische Partei Deutschlands (Communist Party of Germany)
MFGA	Militärgeschichte Forschungsamt (Military History Research Office)
MfS	Ministry für Staatssicherheit (Ministry for State Security, Stasi [GDR])
NARA	National Archives and Records Administration (USA)
NATO	North Atlantic Treaty Organization
NHT	Naval Historical Team
NLA-HA	Niedersächsches Landesarchiv Hannover (State Archives of Lower Saxony, Hanover)
NVA	Nationale Volksarmee (National People's Army [GDR])
OrPo	Ordnungspolizei (Order Police)
ÖTV	Gewerkschaft Öffentliche Dienste, Transport und Verkehr (Union of Public Services, Transport, and Traffic Workers)
PGA	Personalgutachterausschuss (Personnel Advisory Committee)
PLFP	Popular Front for the Liberation of Palestine
POW	Prisoner of War
RAF	Rote Armee Fraktion (Red Army Faction)
RSHA	Reichssicherheitshauptamt (Reich Security Main Office)
SA	Sturmabteilung ([Nazi] Storm [Troopers] Division)
Schupo	Schutzpolizei (Protection Police)
SD	Sicherheitsdienst (Security Service)
SDS	Sozialistischer deutscher Studentenbund (Socialist German Students' Union)

SED	Sozialistische Einheitspartei (Socialist Unity Party [GDR])
SEK	Spezialeinsatzkommandos (Special Tactical Units)
SJD	Sozialistische Jugend Deutschlands, aka Die Falken (Socialist Youth of Germany; the Falcons)
SPD	Sozialdemokratische Partei Deutschlands (Social Democratic Party)
SRP	Sozialistische Reichspartei (Socialist Reich Party)
SS	Schutzstaffel ([Nazi] Protection Squads)
StArch-M	Staatsarchiv München (State Archives, Munich)
StB-Z	Staatsbibliothek zu Berlin (Berlin State Library)
SWAT	Special Weapons and Tactics
TNA	The National Archives (United Kingdom)
USPD	Unabhängige Sozialdemokratische Partei Deutschlands (Independent Social Democratic Party)
VdS	Verband deutscher Soldaten (Association of German Soldiers)
WASt	Wehrmachtauskunftstelle für Kriegerverluste und Kriegsgefangene (Wehrmacht Information Center for Casualties and Prisoners of War)
Zoll	Zollgrenzdienst (Federal Customs Service)

INTRODUCTION

On April 22, 1967, a platoon of heavily armed border police officers from West Germany's *Bundesgrenzschutz* (Federal Border Guard—BGS) arrived at Konrad Adenauer's home in the village of Rhöndorf on the Rhine. Three days earlier, the Federal Republic's ageing first chancellor had died in his sleep, and the men were there to escort his body in what would be the beloved old man's final journey to his former office at Bonn's Palais Schaumburg. The men, clad in military uniforms and steel helmets, looked more like members of Nazi Germany's Wehrmacht than law enforcement officers. As the bells of the local church tolled, nine officers solemnly emerged from Adenauer's home carrying his coffin on their shoulders. The crowd of spectators and reporters who gathered in the quiet neighborhood watched as the pallbearers carefully secured his flag-draped coffin to the open bed of an olive drab-colored BGS utility truck. A massive convoy of military trucks loaded with hundreds of rifle-wielding police officers escorted the makeshift hearse bearing Adenauer's remains. When the motorcade arrived in Bonn, the officers carried his coffin into the Palais Schaumburg's large cabinet room, where it was guarded by an "honor watch" consisting of the chief officers from each of six BGS regional command centers.[1]

All of these senior officers were veterans of the Nazi Wehrmacht and its security forces. Standing prominently at the head of Adenauer's coffin was BGS Brigadier General Otto Dippelhofer, a veteran SS and Field Gendarmerie officer who led police battalions on the Eastern Front. Next to Dippelhofer stood BGS Inspector Heinrich Müller, a veteran of Rommel's Africa Corps and an instructor at the Third Reich's War Academy. Behind them stood Brigadier Generals Willy Langkeit and Detlev von Platen. Langkeit was a tank officer who commanded the *Grossdeutschland* and *Kurmark* divisions on the Eastern Front; von Platen was a member of the Nazi General Staff and commanded Army Group Center in Russia. The Interior Ministry had planned to limit displays of militarism during the funeral services, preferring instead to emphasize the Federal Republic's place among the Western democracies that made up the postwar Transatlantic Alliance. Why then was Adenauer, a man many

---

1   For the details on Adenauer's funeral service see Nina Koshofer's 2010 WDR documentary film, "Adenauer's letzte Reise," available online at https://www.youtube.com/watch?v=yq9aoQJXGo4.

Figure I.1. BGS Inspector Heinrich Müller, left front, along with Brigadier Generals from each BGS command, stand watch over Adenauer's casket lying in state in the cabinet room at Palais Schaumburg, Bonn, April 22, 1967. Photo by Ludwig Wegermann, courtesy of the Presse- und Informationsamt der Bundesregierung, Bundesbildstelle, Photo no. 299412.

considered to be the father of West German democracy, guarded by men with such dubious connections to Germany's authoritarian past?[2]

This book is a social history of West Germany's *Bundesgrenzschutz*, a federal border police force that was established in 1951 to guard its frontiers, but which was armed, equipped, and trained to fight wars. The BGS had its own marine division, the *Seegrenzschutz*, as well as an aviation unit with modern military helicopters. Although there is a rich scholarship devoted to the sociocultural history of the Iron Curtain and the experiences of Germans on both sides of the demarcation line, far less is known about those who guarded West Germany's borders.[3] Given

---

2   For the Interior Ministry's funeral plan see "Schutz- und Sicherungsmassnahmen anlässlich des Staatsbegräbnisses für Dr. Konrad Adenauer 1967," BArch-K, B106/78698; the photo of the BGS Chief's "honor watch" is from Nachlass Müller, Heinrich (Brigadier General in BGS), Band 5, "Bilder aus der Zeit beim Bundesgrenzschutz," BA-MA, N 848/47; for Dippelhofer's SS and Police record see BArch-LW 409 AR 1657/64, Karte nos. 1 and 2, 10 AR 932/64; see BA-MA, PERS 6/13364 (Langkeit) and 6/302684 (von Platen).

3   See for example, Edith Sheffer, *Burned Bridge: How East and West Germans Made the Iron Curtain* (London: Oxford University Press, 2014); Sagi Schaefer,

that the BGS was one of the Federal Republic's first national law enforcement agencies and remained in service until 2005, its history provides an institutional perspective on Germany's democratization.[4] As the central argument of this book contends, the BGS was a peculiar internal security force in which the authoritarian traditions of militarized policing persisted long into the postwar era even though the Federal Republic had supposedly consigned these problematic legacies to the dustbin of 1945. In the BGS, the military duties of fighting enemy forces and counterinsurgency blended with those of a civilian law enforcement agency. On the one hand, it carried out typical border guarding duties such as checking passports and preventing illegal entries. On the other hand, however, its personnel looked, behaved, and were armed like soldiers. Besides their routine duties, border police officers, or *Grenzjäger* (border hunters) as they were known, took part in NATO military exercises and trained for guerilla warfare, and by 1965 the West German Bundestag legally designated them as military combatants in case of war with East German or Soviet forces.

Throughout its history, as this book argues, the BGS suffered from what can best be described as an internal identity crisis, because it was neither an army nor a police force, but a hybrid of the two. In this respect, it resembled other Western European paramilitary forces, such as the Italian Carabinieri, the French Gendarmerie, and the Spanish Civil Guard.[5] The BGS was like a time capsule of German militarism shaped by protracted institutional tensions between advocates for continuity and agents of change. My analysis shows how the organization and its personnel tried to adapt to West Germany's modernizing society but at times struggled to make what Konrad Jarausch has called the "incremental changes in the beliefs and behaviors that shape everyday life."[6] Despite its efforts to reform, the lure of militarized policing in the BGS remained a controversial aspect of its organizational culture and topic of public debate throughout its history. In this book I also question the notion of an ideal type of democratic policing that the Western Allies supposedly imparted to the Federal Republic or which developed, as some have argued, as the result of progressive internal learning processes grounded in the experience of total defeat. According to this interpretation, it was the bitter lessons of

---

States of Division: Borders and Boundary Formation in Cold War Rural Germany (London: Oxford University Press, 2014); Yuliya Komska, *The Icon Curtain: The Cold War's Quiet Border* (Chicago: University of Chicago Press, 2015).

4   The Federal Criminal Police (*Bundeskriminalamt* or BKA) was formed precisely one day before the BGS, on March 15, 1951.

5   See Clive Emsley, *Gendarmes and the State in Nineteenth Century Europe* (Oxford: Oxford University Press, 1999), 5.

6   Konrad Jarausch, *After Hitler: Recivilizing Germans, 1945–1995* (Oxford: Oxford University Press, 2006), vii, 40.

1945 that motivated West Germans to finally accept liberal democracy and fall in line with other Western nations. Thus while Konrad Jarausch has pointed to what he calls a "curious revival of Prussian military traditions under a proletarian banner" in East Germany's armed forces, in this book I argue that West Germany's BGS revived similar traditions under a democratic banner.[7]

German Policing during the Occupation, 1945–49

The BGS was precisely the type of police force the Allies intended to ban when they set out to demilitarize and democratize Germany after the war. When Allied armed forces entered Nazi Germany, they carried detailed plans and instructions to re-establish law and order.[8] In accordance with the Potsdam Agreement, all of Germany's police forces were to be demilitarized and purged of any personnel with ties to National Socialism. Law enforcement organizations were disarmed, decentralized, and placed under the joint command of Allied and state (*Länder*) officials in each occupation zone.[9] The reason for these strict measures was to prevent the police from becoming a force that might attempt to revive Nazism or undermine the occupation government. When the National Socialists assumed power in 1933, they centralized the police and dismissed many officers suspected of leftist tendencies or whose loyalty to the Third Reich was otherwise questionable. Henceforth, Germany's police institution became an instrument of National Socialism and its criminal policies. Between 1936 and 1939, all Nazi police forces were subordinated to SS Chief Heinrich Himmler's Reich Security Main Office (*Reichssicherheitshauptamt—RSHA*). Himmler's police battalions perpetrated the mass murder of Europe's Jews and enforced Nazi racial policies throughout the conquered territories.[10] Thus the Allies intended to

---

7   Konrad Jarausch, *After Hitler*, 40; see also Konrad Jarausch, "The Federal Republic at Sixty: Popular Myths, Actual Accomplishments and Competing Interpretations," *German Politics and Society 94*, 28, no. 1 (Spring 2010): 16–18.

8   The Public Safety Plan is outlined in Supreme Headquarters Allied Expeditionary Force, "Public Safety Manual of Procedures," Military Government of Germany, first edition, September 1944, Ike Skelton Combined Arms Research Library, Command and Staff College (Ft. Leavenworth, Kansas).

9   Jose Canoy, *The Discreet Charm of the Police State: The Landpolizei and the Transformation of Bavaria, 1945–1965* (Leiden: Brill, 2007), 68–71.

10 See for example, Michael Wildt, *An Uncompromising Generation: The Nazi Leadership of the Reich Security Main Office* (Madison: University of Wisconsin Press, 2009); Edward Westermann, *Hitler's Police Battalions: Enforcing Racial War in the East* (Lawrence: University Press of Kansas, 2010); Christopher

completely overhaul Germany's centralized police institution and prevent it from ever again becoming an instrument of militarism and war.

Long before the National Socialists came to power, however, policing in Germany was already linked to its armed forces. During the Wilhelmine and Weimar eras, most police officers were recruited from the ranks of veteran soldiers.[11] In peacetime, soldiers easily moved between the army and civilian law enforcement professions because of their common institutional ideals, discipline, and rank structure. Like the army, policing also provided the close-knit masculine camaraderie of life in the barracks, and the men attracted to these jobs were often politically conservative.[12] After the First World War, the Versailles Treaty limited the German army (*Reichswehr*) to 100,000 men, leaving thousands of veterans unemployed. Many former soldiers joined violent paramilitaries and free corps (*Freikorps*) units during the revolutionary uprisings that followed the collapse of the monarchy. After the postwar state disbanded these irregular units and the Versailles Treaty limited the *Reichswehr* to 100,000 men, many veterans found jobs in state and municipal police departments. Most of these men viewed the political left and especially communists as state enemies. Later, when the Weimar government collapsed and the Nazis took over, some police officers resigned or were forced out by the new regime—most, however, accepted National Socialism and remained on the job because it aligned well with their pre-existing political ideals.[13]

In 1945, the Allies found few experienced police officers who were not compromised in some way or another by their past service to the Nazi state. Nevertheless, the Four Powers (Britain, France, America, and the

---

Browning, *Ordinary Men: Reserve Police Battalion 101 and the Final Solution in Poland* (New York: Harper Perennial, 1998).

11 See Elaine Glovka Spencer, "Police-Military Relations in Prussia, 1848–1914," *Journal of Social History* 19, no. 2 (Winter, 1985): 305–17; Herbert Reinke, "Armed as if for War: The State, the Military and the Professionalization of the Prussian Police in Imperial Germany," in *Policing Western Europe: Politics, Professionalization, and Public Order, 1850–1940*, ed. Clive Emsley and Barbara Weinberger (Westport: Greenwood, 1991), 55–73, 68; Alf Lüdtke, *Police and State in Prussia, 1815–1850* (New York: Cambridge University Press, 1989), 140–45.

12 Ute Frevert, *A Nation in Barracks: Modern Germany, Military Conscription, and Civil Society* (New York: Berg, 2004), 201–5.

13 See for example, Christopher Clark, *Iron Kingdom: The Rise and Downfall of Prussia 1600–1947* (Cambridge, MA: Harvard University Press, 2006), 633; Mark Jones, *Founding Weimar: Violence and the German Revolution of 1918–1919* (Cambridge: Cambridge University Press, 2018); Dirk Schumann, *Political Violence in the Weimar Republic, 1918–1933* (New York: Berghahn Books, 2012); Robert Gerwarth and John Horne, eds., *War in Peace: Paramilitary Violence in Europe after the Great War* (Oxford: Oxford University Press, 2012).

Soviet Union) agreed, at least initially, to demilitarize civilian police forces and return them to the jurisdiction of municipal authorities. Establishing law and order was a primary objective for the Allies as Germany descended into chaos following the final collapse of Hitler's regime. At first, German police officers were paired with Allied soldiers in joint patrols. With the breakdown of authority in Germany's cities, displaced persons, petty criminals, and angry mobs often resisted or violently attacked the police. German officers were unarmed or had wooden batons to defend themselves. Partnering with Allied soldiers and military police officers at least gave them better odds when confronting violent criminals and helped to restore their legitimacy in the eyes of the public.[14]

As the Allies established greater administrative control over occupied Germany, they devoted more attention and resources towards rebuilding the police. German police departments in each zone conformed to the national policing models of the individual occupation authorities. In the British zone, for example, specialists from the London Metropolitan Police trained their German colleagues. In the US occupation zone, Captain William H. Parker, who in civilian life was a veteran Los Angeles Police Officer, helped rebuild the Frankfurt am Main and Munich police departments. Parker, who later became the LAPD's Chief of Police, is remembered most for his racist policies, the Watts Riots, and his authoritarian leadership style.[15] Although the Western occupation authorities tried to purge National Socialist personnel from the police, the results were mixed. The Soviets claimed to have taken a more comprehensive approach to denazification, but there was no perfect solution, and they faced many of the same dilemmas as officials in the West. The uneven results meant that there was a greater level of continuity in personnel and practices from older policing models in all of the occupation zones.[16]

A decisive split in the approach to policing between east and west took place during the first year of the occupation when the Soviets began militarizing the civilian forces in their zone. They did this by transferring jurisdiction over the police from municipal authorities to the centralized

---

14 Keith Lowe, *Savage Continent: Europe in the Aftermath of World War Two* (New York: St. Martin's, 2012), 102, 147; Richard Bessel, *Germany 1945: From War to Peace* (New York: Harper Perennial, 2009), 205.

15 For an analysis of Chief Parker's problematic legacies see Alisa Sarah Kramer, "William H. Parker and the Thin Blue Line: Politics, Public Relations and Policing in Postwar Los Angeles," PhD diss. (American University, 2007); see also O. W. Wilson, ed., *Parker on Police* (Springfield: Charles C. Thomas, 1957), x.

16 Stefan Noethen, "Polizei in der Besatzungszeit—Vorstellungen und Einflüsse der Alliierten," in *Die Polizei der Gesellschaft: Zur Soziologie der Inneren Sicherheit*, ed. Hans-Jürgen Lange (Wiesbaden: Springer, 2003), 78–88; Richard Bessel, *Germany 1945*, 193–99.

state interior ministers. In 1946, the Soviets established the paramilitary People's Police (*Volkspolizei*). The force directly supported East German communist officials and by extension the Soviet Military regime. Many of its personnel came from the working classes recently freed from Soviet captivity and began their new jobs without prior law enforcement experience. The force grew rapidly, and later became the basis for a new barracked riot police squad, the *Bereitschaftspolizei* (BePo). The BePo was armed with infantry weapons and its units eventually formed the first regiments of East Germany's army.[17]

Nevertheless, the change in Soviet policy towards the police did not cause an immediate reaction in the Western occupation zones. The Allies still feared that allowing militarized police forces in their zones might undermine the democratization process. Thus German law enforcement agencies in the West remained decentralized and under strict Allied control. Even the tensions caused by the 1948 Soviet blockade of Berlin were insufficient to nudge Western officials towards re-militarizing the police. At the peak of the Berlin crisis, for example, US Military Governor General Lucius Clay told CBS news correspondent Larry LeSueur that he would never condone militarizing the German police to defend Berlin.[18]

In the first months after Nazi Germany's collapse there were major outbreaks of violent crime, including rape, murder, and robbery, and property crime was endemic.[19] Petty theft, possession of stolen property and the illicit black-market trade in coffee, tobacco, butter, and other luxury goods represented the biggest problems in the West. German police officers also had to deal with suspects accused of stealing Allied property. Although acts of violence continued, trial records of cases adjudicated in the British and American courts show that violent crime remained relatively low in comparison to property crime.[20] To be sure, not every crime was reported, but the high number of property crimes was consistent with the economic hardships and food shortages many Germans faced during the early postwar period. According to the Allied High Commission (HICOG), the German police were adequately staffed to address these crimes. A report by HICOG's Security Branch noted that in the US zone (including the western sector of Berlin), there were 61,634 German police officers serving a population of approximately 19

17 Richard Bessel, "Policing in East German in the Wake of the Second World War," *Crime, History and Societies* 7, no. 2 (2003), 17.
18 Jean Edward Smith, ed., *The Papers of General Lucius G. Clay: Germany, 1945–1949, Vol. II* (Bloomington: Indiana University Press, 1974), 965.
19 Keith Lowe, *Savage Continent*, 98–100.
20 See Thomas J. Kehoe and James E. Kehoe, "Civilian Crime During the British and American Occupation of Western Germany, 1945–1946: Analyses of Military Government Court Records," *European Journal of Criminology* 19, no. 2 (November 15, 2019): 17.

million. The number was equivalent to a ratio of 2.2 policemen per 1,000 residents. Part of this total, or 19,709 police officers, served in specialized law enforcement units such as border, railway, customs, and marine police units.[21] By way of comparison, in 2016, the US Department of Justice reported that the average number of police officers per 1,000 residents in the United States was 2.4.[22] Thus by 1949, when the Federal Republic was established, there were more than enough police officers to maintain internal security.

A History Critical of West Germany's Success Narrative

This book is informed by and enters into conversation with a growing body of recent critical literature that engages with the problems of writing the Federal Republic's history as a "success story."[23] West Germany's postwar development was far more complicated when viewed outside the retroactive lens focused on the end result. Some of these studies have described its postwar transformation as a counterpoint to its twelve-year descent into National Socialism.[24] Different generations of historians on both sides of the Atlantic have employed variations on theoretical paradigms such as "Americanization," "Westernization," "liberalization," and more recently, "recivilization" to analyze the Federal Republic.[25] But the emergence of its strong economy and welfare state, its political alignment with the West, and its leading role in the Transatlantic Alliance emphasized by these interpretations tells an incomplete and often triumphalist story of its postwar evolution. Former Nazi elites inundated many of the

---

21 Press Release no. 279: Office of the US High Commissioner for Germany, "US Zone has 2.2 Policemen per 1,000 Population," National Archives and Records Administration, RG 466 Records of the US High Commissioner for Germany: US High Commissioner, John J. McCloy: Classified General Records, 1949–1952, Box 12.

22 Shelly Hyland and Elizabeth Davis, "Local Police Departments, 2016 Personnel," US Department of Justice, Office of Justice Programs, Bureau of Justice Statistics (October, 2019), 4–5.

23 For a comprehensive historiography of this approach see Frank Biess and Astrid M. Eckert, "Introduction: Why Do We Need New Narratives for the History of the Federal Republic," *Central European History* 52 (2019): 1–18.

24 Sonja Levsen and Cornelius Torp, *Wo liegt die Bundesrepublik?* (Göttingen, Vandenhoeck & Ruprecht, 2016), 14.

25 See, for example, Heinrich August Winkler, *Germany: The Long Road West*, vols. 1 & 2 (Oxford: Oxford University Press, 2006–2007); Anselm Doering-Manteuffel *Wie westlich sind die Deutschen? Amerikanisierung und Westernisierung im 20. Jahrhundert* (Göttingen: Vandenhoeck & Ruprecht, 1999); Konrad Jarausch, *After Hitler*.

Federal Republic's governmental institutions, and police forces like the BGS in particular. By the early 1950s, many police officers returned to and remained in the law enforcement profession with little or no scrutiny of their prior service to the Third Reich.[26]

By questioning the success narrative as a conceptual paradigm for explaining the Federal Republic's history, in this book I suggest an alternative interpretation that elicits a more complex and nuanced account of its emergence from dictatorship and war. Employing this approach, however, does not diminish the postwar accomplishments of the Federal Republic or claim that the persistence of militarized policing in the BGS suggests its democratization failed. Instead, I show how its postwar evolution followed a crooked, non-linear path highlighted by a protracted struggle between continuity and change evident in the institutional development of the BGS. Rather than focusing on the end result as a vanishing point or tracing a straight line from bad past to better future, my analysis concentrates on the contradictions as well as the twists and turns that marked its path to democracy. West Germany's BGS demonstrated that militarized policing had a longer history in prewar Germany that survived beyond the rupture of 1945. Moreover, militarization also inundated police forces in the Western democracies that occupied the Federal Republic. In this book, I use the terms "militarized" or "police militarization" to explain civilian law enforcement agencies that employ military equipment and tactics.[27] To be sure, the Nazis succeeded in taking over Germany's civilian police forces precisely because they were militarized long before they assumed power in 1933.

Police officers serving in Germany's first democracy, the Weimar Republic, formed the "coalitions of order" that historian Eric Weitz has argued were instrumental in the conservative government's use of violence against forces on the political left.[28] Thus, while Weimar's Interior Minister Carl Severing, a conservative Social Democrat, could promote his Prussian *Schutzpolizei* officers (*Schupos*) as the public's "friends and

---

26 There are several good studies that look at West Germany's state and municipal law enforcement agencies. A good starting point is Stefan Noethen, *Alte Kameraden und neue Kollegen: Polizei in Nordrhein-Westfalen, 1945–1963* (Essen: Klartext, 2003); See also Klaus Weinhauer, *Schutzpolizei in der Bundesrepublik: Zwischen Bürgerkrieg und innere Sicherheit; Die turbulenten sechziger Jahre* (Leiden: Brill, 2003); and Jose Canoy, *The Discreet Charm of the Police State*.

27 Hsi-Huey Liang, *The Berlin Police Force in the Weimar Republic* (Berkeley: University of California Press, 1970), 71–73; Peter B. Kraska, "Police Militarization 101," in Roger G. Dunham, Geoffrey P. Alpert, and Kyle D. McLean eds., *Critical Issues in Policing: Contemporary Readings* (Long Grove, IL: Waveland, 2021), 445–47.

28 Eric D. Weitz, *Creating German Communism, 1890–1990* (Princeton, NJ: Princeton University Press, 1996), 6.

helpers," these same men routinely used extreme violence as a means to squelch dissent.[29] Weimar Germany reflected the practices of fellow democratic states that also deployed veteran soldiers in militarized police forces to quell political violence and strikes. In England, for example, Sir Robert Peel's celebrated London Metropolitan Police Force (The Met)—supposedly an ideal model for democratic civilian policing everywhere—also promoted militarization. Despite its exceptional reputation, the majority of its chief commissioners were military veterans, and many of Peel's "Bobbies" served in England's colonial police forces before joining the Met. Moreover, France, Italy, Belgium, and the Netherlands all deployed colonial police forces the veterans of which returned home to join civilian departments where their colonial experiences shaped policing in the metropole.[30]

In this book, therefore, I question the concept of holding "Western" policing as an ideal without also acknowledging the West's own problematic record of militarization, racism, and violence. Police forces in the United States, Great Britain, and France did not always demonstrate positive examples of the demilitarized, liberal democratic principles they tried to implement in the Federal Republic. In Great Britain, London's Metropolitan Police Commissioner Joseph Simpson blamed the 1958 Notting Hill Race Riots on what he called a "concentration of colonial immigrants."[31] During the 1950s, US police departments routinely singled out and used excessive violence against African American and immigrant communities.[32] In France, Paris police chief Maurice Papon, a former Vichy police official who collaborated with the SS to deport and

29 Sara F. Hall, "Moving Images and the Policing of Political Action in the Early Weimar Period," *German Studies Review* 31, no. 2 (May 2008): 287; Jonathan Dunnage, "Policing Right-Wing Dictatorships: Some Preliminary Comparisons of Fascist Italy, Nazi Germany and Franco's Spain," *Crime, Histoire & Sociétés 10*, no. 1 (2006): 97.

30 Richard Bessel, "Policing, Professionalization and Politics in Weimar Germany" in *Policing Western Europe*, ed. Emsley and Weinberger, 187–88; David A. Campion, "Policing the Peelers: Parliament, the Public, and the Metropolitan Police, 1829–33" in *London Politics, 1760–1914*, ed. Matthew Cragoe and Anthony Taylor (London: Palgrave Macmillan, 2005), 52; Martin Thomas, *Violence and Colonial Order: Police, Workers and Protest in the European Colonial Empires, 1918–1940* (London: Cambridge University Press, 2012), 17–23; Danielle Beaujon, "Policing Colonial Migrants: The Brigade Nord-Africaine in Paris, 1923–44," *French Historical Studies* 42, no. 4 (October 2019): 656–57.

31 Sam Collings-Wells, "Policing the Windrush Generation: Police Brutality and Stop-and-Search Are Yet Another Legacy of Empire," *History Today* 69, no. 11 (November 2019):

32 Clarence Taylor, *Fight the Power: African Americans and the Long History of Police Brutality in New York City* (New York: New York University Press, 2019), 88.

murder the Jews of Bordeaux, perpetrated the murder of Algerian citizens protesting French colonial policies during the 1960s.[33] Thus police forces in all three Western occupation regimes suffered from the same organizational problems that they supposedly tried to root out of the Federal Republic's police culture.

Scope of the Book

In this book I explore the BGS from its foundation in 1951 through 2005 when it became Germany's federal police agency, the *Bundespolizei* (BPOL). My analysis follows the recent suggestion by Jennifer Allen to write across the caesura of 1989–1990 and "re-think the history of the Federal Republic" by avoiding what she calls the "narratives of ends: the final triumph of the Western political project or the end of a German *Sonderweg* (special path)."[34] West Germany established the BGS in response to Cold War tensions, but it remained in service fifteen years after the collapse of communism and the opening of Europe's borders. Thus it had a post-unification history even though the Iron Curtain no longer existed. The politics and tensions of the Inner-German border remained a powerful *raison d'être* for the BGS, but decolonization and the Federal Republic's place in a globalizing world also shaped the organization.[35] Its first deployment, for example, was not to the Iron Curtain, but along the Belgian "coffee border" to fight smuggling gangs near the city of Aachen. BGS officers also deployed abroad to the global south and beyond to guard the Federal Republic's embassies, Olympic teams and the offices and staff of its national airline, Lufthansa. Thus the wars of decolonization in the developing world fought by its allies the United States, France, and Great Britain also played a decisive role in the persistence of militarized policing in the BGS.[36]

In this book I employ an organizational structure that is both chronological and thematic. In part 1 I discuss the origins and early development of the BGS. In chapter 1 I analyze how legacies of Weimar political violence shaped approaches to internal security in the Federal Republic.

---

33 Jim House and Neil Macmaster, *Paris 1961: Algerians, State Terror, and Memory* (Oxford: Oxford University Press, 2006), 26–35.

34 Jennifer L. Allen, "Against the 1989–1990 Ending Myth," *Central European History* 52, no. 1 (2019): 138.

35 Ibid., 129–30.

36 See for example, Quinn Slobodian, *Foreign Front: Third World Politics in Sixties West Germany* (Durham, NC: Duke University Press, 2012); Timothy Scott Brown, *West Germany and the Global Sixties: The Antiauthoritarian Revolt, 1961–1978* (Cambridge: Cambridge University Press, 2013); Young-Sun Hong, *Cold War Germany, the Third World, and the Global Humanitarian Regime* (Cambridge: Cambridge University Press, 2015).

Adenauer's conservative government did not need another border security force, but it had no other means to legally justify the BGS—a force they created to militarily defend the state against the threat of internal Bolshevist enemies or to fight a German-German civil war. Chapter 2 shows how Wehrmacht veterans set the tone for its organizational culture for years to come. These men transported the legacies of Germany's authoritarian pasts and militarism into the BGS during its formative years. Chapter 3 investigates the debate over the government's decision to use border police officers as a personnel source for West Germany's new army, the Bundeswehr. The Wehrmacht veterans who first joined the BGS expected to transfer to the army once it was re-established, but the Ministry of Defense rejected many transfer candidates. The army's reformers, and General von Baudissin in particular, believed the BGS promoted anti-democratic attitudes and included reactionary officers who might revive Prussian militarism. The schism between the two forces led to a press scandal and competing visions over the role of policing in national defense.

Part 2 focuses on the organizational culture of the BGS and the internal identity crisis its personnel suffered because of its peculiar blending of policing and military duties. The emergence of a critical public sphere meant that the BGS had to deal with the press and develop a better approach to public relations amidst ongoing criticisms of its militarization. After thousands of its officers transferred to the army and became soldiers, the government still fought to retain the BGS because it lacked other independent means through which to monopolize the state's coercive forces of legitimate violence. Yet border police officers still thought of themselves as soldiers. Chapter 4 analyzes recruitment practices and reveals how the Interior Ministry struggled to rebuild the BGS by trying to make it more appealing to a younger generation that rejected militarism and war. My analysis shows how the Federal Republic re-defined the ideal postwar male and promoted BGS service as a means to reinforce conservative notions of masculinity in the aftermath of the war.[37] Recruiters used films and other innovative advertising methods to convince potential applicants that the BGS provided a path to a secure career and more profitable future. In chapter 5 I analyze training and education programs. Military themes and xenophobic tropes stereotyping eastern people as "wild" or part of "Asiatic hordes" persisted well into the 1970s despite efforts by some members of the Interior Ministry to root them

---

37 See for example, Joan Scott, "Gender: A Useful Category of Historical Analysis," *American Historical Review* 91, no. 5 (December 1986): 1053–75; see also Frank Biess, *Homecomings: Returning POWs and the Legacies of Defeat in Postwar Germany* (Princeton, NJ: Princeton: University Press, 2006), 12.

out. Senior officers trained recruits to deal with civil unrest by using the Wehrmacht's suppression of the 1944 Warsaw Uprising as a model.

Chapter 6 explores the professional ethics programs taught and managed by the border police chaplaincy (*Seelsorge*). Ethics provided a means through which the organization could re-emphasize conservatism and traditional gender roles by linking Christian morals and anti-communism with liberal democracy. The topics covered in these courses promoted state service as a manly and godly duty while also legitimizing democracy to the older veterans by reaffirming the value of their expertise in fighting communists.[38] The efforts of the chaplains to shape the morals of border police officers also reflected an attempt to counter the appeal of modern culture at a time of declining interest in traditional conservative values. Chapter 7 analyzes the government's controversial decision to designate border police officers to be military combatants. The legislation and debate that surrounded this decision evoked memories of German militarism and violence going back to the colonial period and both World Wars. It also showed how current events like the Vietnam War and decolonization influenced how its commanding officers imagined the organization's role. Thus despite the growing spirit of détente linked to Willy Brandt's *Ostpolitik* and hardened border defenses, BGS commanders still believed in the inevitability of fighting a civil war against East German forces.

Part 3 shows how the government attempted to preserve the BGS by aligning it with West Germany's state and municipal law enforcement agencies. As I argue in chapter 8, the BGS faced a legitimacy crisis as questions about its relevance surfaced during the emergency legislation debates and extra-parliamentary opposition crisis. The passage of the Emergency Acts brought the BGS new internal security duties that ultimately saved the organization from fading into the background or becoming obsolete, but it still struggled to overcome staffing shortages from its use to build the new army. Chapter 9 highlights the role of the BGS as a response to domestic and international terrorism by focusing on its use during the Munich Olympic Games and against the radical Red Army Faction (RAF). The chapter shows how in spite of its tactical training, jurisdictional tensions and personalities sidelined the BGS while government officials blundered the hostage rescue attempt with catastrophic consequences. In response to the brutal murder of Israeli athletes on German soil the Interior Ministry established a paramilitary counterterrorism unit, GSG 9, made up of BGS personnel. Chapter 10 explains how the BGS became reunified Germany's national police force, the *Bundespolizei*. The opening of Europe's borders, the end of the Cold War

---

38 Stefan Creuzberger and Dierk Hoffmann, eds., *"Geistige Gefahr" und "Immunisierung der Gesellschaft": Antikommunismus und politische Kultur in der frühen Bundesrepublik* (Berlin: Walter de Gruyter, 2014)

and the integration of the first women and East Germans into its ranks brought new organizational challenges. Despite improvements in training and increased professionalization, militarization and war remained enduring themes of its organizational culture until the Bundestag finally terminated combatant status for the BGS in 1994.

PART I

ORIGINS AND EARLY DEVELOPMENT, 1949–1956

CHAPTER ONE

THE SHADOW OF WEIMAR POLITICAL VIOLENCE IN THE MAKING OF WEST GERMANY'S BGS

BY ITS LEGAL DEFINITION, the *Bundesgrenzschutz* was a law enforcement agency. Its jurisdiction was restricted to a space within thirty kilometers of West Germany's frontiers, and its size was limited to 10,000 men. In reality, however, the Federal Republic's conservative government never intended to use the force they envisioned for border security. Instead, border security was a convenient justification that enabled Adenauer and his second Interior Minister, Robert Lehr, to establish a militarized civil guard they could deploy against West Germany's internal enemies. They believed and argued that the survival of the democratic state depended upon its ability to use decisive force. Adenauer, Lehr, and others in the Interior Ministry approached domestic security based on their experiences of political violence and revolutionary chaos during Germany's interwar years. Although grounded in the reality of their experiences, they also exaggerated these fears to convince the Allied High Commission that building a federal police force was urgent to the survival of the Bonn Republic. West Germany had neither an independent army nor a centralized police force. The government created the BGS to fill this void and in so doing, set the tone for its militarized organizational culture for decades to come.

Border Security: A Solution Searching for a Problem

When it was founded in 1949, West Germany lacked the monopolization over legitimate coercive violence that sociologist Max Weber has identified as fundamental to the modern state.[1] Allied armed forces provided for national defense and its state police agencies handled criminal

---

1   Paul Reitter and Chad Wellmon, *Charisma and Disenchantment: Max Weber: The Vocation Lectures* (New York: New York Review of Books: 2020), 46–47.

activity. The Allies intended to gradually transfer more autonomy to the new West German government, but they were reluctant to relinquish their controls over internal security and policing. Because of the crimes perpetrated by Nazi police forces during the war, the Allies believed the West Germans needed more time to accept and practice democracy before being given full control over civilian law enforcement. Against this backdrop, Chancellor Adenauer began seeking a security force he could use to defend the state against its internal political enemies. He complained to the Allies that his government was weak and in grave danger of being undermined or overthrown by communist revolutionaries. To be sure, he never invoked the threat from right-wing radicals in his descriptions of the revolutionary violence his nation allegedly faced. For Adenauer, the most pressing security challenge came from Bolshevism or "fifth-column" communist insurgents lying in wait to overthrow his government from within.

In late 1949, Adenauer tasked Federal Justice Minister Thomas Dehler to find a legal means that permitted the formation of an independent national police force.[2] Dehler was a member of the conservative Free Democratic Party (FDP) and a veteran of the First World War. During the interwar years he went to law school and got caught up in paramilitary politics when he joined the Black-Red-Gold (*Schwarz-Rote-Gold*) anti-fascist league. While studying law in Munich, he also joined and was active in an antisemitic student fraternity, but later came under suspicion of the Nazis for marrying a Jewish woman. During the Third Reich, his record of anti-fascism and mixed marriage prevented his participation in politics. After the war, the Americans appointed him to the position of District Administrator (*Landrat*) in Bamberg.[3]

After researching the federal police question, Dehler reported to Adenauer that he could not proceed without first amending the Basic Law (Constitution). The amendment process required a two-thirds majority vote that would not be possible with the current political distribution of the Bundestag. Policing remained a matter for the states unless the Allied High Commission ruled otherwise.[4] Adenauer knew he could not alter this arrangement because despite increasing tensions with the Soviets and East Germans, the High Commissioners still opposed centralized law enforcement in the Federal Republic. A few weeks before

2   Dr. Thomas Dehler, "Rechtsgutach über die Möglichkeit, eine Bundespolizei aufzustellen," November 28, 1949, BArch-K, B144/229.
3   Udo Wengst, *Thomas Dehler: 1897–1967: Eine politische Biographie* (Munich: R. Oldenbourg, 1997), 43, 69.
4   Minutes of Federal Cabinet Meeting, analysis by Federal Minister of Justice, Dr. Thomas Dehler, "Rechtsgutach über die Möglichkeit, eine Bundespolizei aufzustellen," November 28, 1949, BArch-K, B144/229.

Dehler submitted his report on the policing question, the US High Commissioner John J. McCloy told reporters that paramilitary or centralized police forces of any kind remained off-limits in West Germany.[5]

Dehler did not give up, however, and began looking for alternative legal solutions. In mid-January 1950, he wrote to State Secretary (*Staatssekretär*) Hans Ritter von Lex at the Interior Ministry asking for his assistance. Ritter von Lex was the highest-ranking civil servant and second in command at the Interior Ministry. He was also a veteran of the First World War and active in Bavarian politics during the interwar years. He later rose to a prominent position in the Nazi Interior Ministry where he willingly carried out many of Hitler's criminal policies.[6] In the letter, Dehler mentioned border security as a potential solution to the legal problems of building a federal police force. His suggestion was the first mention of border security as a possible justification for what later became the BGS. He referred Lex to Article 87 of the Basic Law, which outlined the government's legal obligation to regulate and monitor its frontiers. He explained that the Allied Military Government had already granted West Germany's Federal Council (*Bundesrat*) the authority to establish agencies for controlling cross-border passenger and freight traffic.[7] Dehler argued that "if there are no internal political reasons against it, the Federal Border Police should be set up by virtue of German sovereignty, i.e., by a federal law." He also told Lex that "the federal government must not surrender part of its sovereign power without need. Whatever it can create and achieve on its own [...] it must not leave the occupying powers to do."[8] Dehler's remarks revealed that the federal policing question not only concerned security, but was also connected to the politics of West German sovereignty and the symbolic legitimacy of Adenauer's government.

The problem with Dehler's interpretation of Article 87, however, was that West Germany and the Allies already had thousands of security personnel policing the state's frontiers. Since 1946, the Federal Republic

---

5   John J. McCloy quoted in "Reviving Germany: An Interview with John J. McCloy, US High Commissioner for Germany," *US News and World Report*, November 4, 1949, 26–30, John J. McCloy Papers, Amherst College, Box SP 1, Folder 30.

6   Dominik Rigoll, "From Denazification to Renazification? West German Government Officials after 1945," in Camilo Erlichman and Christopher Knowles, *Transforming Occupation in the Western Zones of Germany: Politics, Everyday Life and Social Interactions, 1945–55* (London: Bloomsbury Academic, 2018), 260.

7   Memorandum from Federal Minister of Justice, Thomas Dehler to State Secretary Ritter von Lex, Federal Interior Ministry Bonn, January 12, 1950, Subject: "Federal Border Police," BArch-K, B136/1927.

8   Memorandum from Dehler to Ritter von Lex, January 12, 1950, "Federal Border Police," BArch-K, B136/1927.

had its own independent customs service (*Zollgrenzdienst* or *Zoll*) in the British Occupation Zone. The British established the *Zoll*, but the West Germans took it over in 1947 and redesignated it the "Passport Control Service." In 1949, all three western occupation zones integrated their customs and passport control personnel into an agency called the "Combined Travel Board." By 1950, the Federal Ministry of Finance administered the *Zoll*. With a staff of 15,000 men, it was West Germany's primary agency for dealing with smuggling, passport control and illegal border crossings. Thus, the *Zoll* already fulfilled the function of border security and customs enforcement permitted under Article 87.[9]

Besides the *Zoll* the US Constabulary, a 30,000-man military customs force, patrolled West Germany's frontiers. The Constabulary and its personnel could access remote areas of the Inner-German border in trucks, tanks, and even on horseback if necessary. The United States also deployed specialized military police customs units to help deal with the lucrative black market and smuggling activities perpetrated by Allied personnel and displaced persons (DPs). Besides these mobile security forces, the individual federal states of Bavaria, Baden-Württemberg, and Hesse all had their own state border guarding agencies. Bavaria had the largest of these forces with some 2,000 personnel, and its government steadfastly refused to consider surrendering the sovereignty of its borders to a federal authority. At the time Adenauer began petitioning HICOG for a new federal police force, the Inner-German border already had sufficient West German and Allied personnel to handle a variety of security issues—it was one of the most heavily policed and secured frontiers in postwar Europe.[10] Thus border security was a solution seeking a problem.

The Legacies of Revolution and Weimar Political Violence

Adenauer's quest for an independent national police force was not based on any empirical need for more border security. In fact, he never invoked border security as a justification until he had exhausted all other options. The West German and Allied security and customs units were sufficient to

---

9 See "Vermerk zu dem Schreiben des Bundeskanzleramts (Verbindungsstelle zur Alliierten Hohen Kommission) vom 7 Feb. 1950 bezw. der Note des Allgemeines Ausschusses der Alliierten Hohen Kommission vom 3 Feb. 1950," BArch-K, B106/83869.

10 William E. Stacy, "US Army Border Operations in Germany, 1945–1983," Unclassified, Headquarters US Army, Europe, and 7th Army (Military History Office: 1984), available online at https://history.army.mil/documents/border ops/content.htm; Robert L. Gunnarsson Sr., *American Military Police in Europe, 1945–1991: Unit Histories* (Jefferson, NC: McFarland, 2011), 341–45.

deal with crimes perpetrated at the border. Instead, Adenauer's motivation to establish a federal police force came from his experiences of political violence as Mayor of Cologne in the aftermath of the First World War. He blamed the failure of Germany's first democracy on its government for what he later claimed was the "spineless abdication" of its public officials. Although an anti-Nazi to the core, as a conservative politician he still favored authoritarian or heavy-handed responses to security. From his perspective, the government needed a strong force to use violence against its enemies or it would inevitably suffer the same fate as the Weimar Republic. As Mayor of Cologne in 1918, he experienced the revolutionary upheavals that marked the collapse of Imperial Germany's monarchy first hand. He pled with the military governor of Cologne, General Günther von Kruge, to use his artillery troops to restore order against sailors who incited local crowds. He never hesitated or wavered in his support for this level of violence and criticized von Kruge for refusing his pleas to use the weapons and troops at his disposal to restore order.[11]

Adenauer's fears of disorder focused exclusively upon the forces of the political left. He believed Bolshevism was the greatest ideological and existential threat facing the newly formed Federal Republic. He never mentioned radical right-wing groups in his repeated demands to the Allies for more security. According to his biographer Hans-Peter Schwarz, for Adenauer "any power that caused chaos in Germany was preparing the way for Bolshevik revolution."[12] As chancellor, he was determined not to make the same mistakes as the "spineless" officials he blamed for Weimar's collapse. Although the Neo-Nazi Socialist Reich Party (SRP) gained increasing traction in West German politics, for his government it remained a low-priority threat behind communists and other groups associated with the political left.[13] To be fair, Adenauer's perceptions of strategic vulnerability from a Soviet invasion shaped his security concerns as chancellor. Although he could rely on the Western Alliance for external security, he wanted a paramilitary force he could use against the internal unrest he feared would undermine the new Bonn Republic and might encourage the Soviets to risk an attack. Yet while speaking with the French High Commissioner André Francois-Poncet, Adenauer never mentioned border security as a duty for the force he envisioned. Instead, he told Francois-Poncet that he intended to create

---

11 Hans-Peter Schwarz, *Konrad Adenauer: A German Politician and Statesman in a Period of War, Revolution and Reconstruction, Vol. 1: From the German Empire to the Federal Republic, 1876–1952* (Providence: Berghahn, 1995), 121–22, 223.
12 Ibid.
13 Norbert Frei, *Adenauer's Germany and the Nazi Past: The Politics of Amnesty and Integration* (New York: Columbia University Press, 2002), 253–54.

a paramilitary unit in "accordance with the provisions that applied to the police forces in the Weimar Republic." He referred here to the Weimar era militarized Prussian *Schutzpolizei* (protection police—Schupo), a civilian police force made up of veteran soldiers trained in infantry tactics and armed for combat.[14]

A good example of how these legacies continued to shape Adenauer's approach to internal security surfaced during his visceral reaction to a 1950 truck drivers' strike in Bonn. The disgruntled drivers, angry about recent gasoline price increases, blocked all traffic in the government quarter as a form of protest. The drivers rallied enough disruption to force the adjournment of the Bundestag. The democratic process itself came to a halt. The strike and its outcome confirmed Adenauer's fears of internal unrest and he used it to emphasize his government's weakness. While speaking to reporters in Bochum after the protest, he complained: "The Federal Government has no means of exerting power and no law enforcement agency. What the motorists can do today could be done tomorrow by the unemployed, the expellees, the communists, and finally by strikers … the Federal Republic and, with it, Western Europe would go down!"[15] In revealing the sources of his angst—"the unemployed, expellees, communists, and strikers"—Adenauer made no reference to dangers along West Germany's borders or radical right-wing groups. He used the truck driver's strike as a reason to push the Allied High Commission for authorization to establish a new police force.

Adenauer's second Interior Minister, Robert Lehr, a conservative politician later known as the "father of the BGS," also drew on his experiences of revolutionary violence in 1918 to form his approach to security in the postwar Federal Republic. Born into a Protestant family in Celle in 1883, he spent his childhood and teen years moving around Germany due to his father's military career. Medical issues kept him from pursuing military service, and while many of his friends joined the army, he went to law school.[16] In 1913 the City of Düsseldorf hired him as an assessor,

14 Document Nr. 117, September 2, 1950, "Bundeskanzler Adenauer an den Geschäftsführenden Vorsitzenden der Alliierten Hohen Kommission, François-Poncet," in Kosthorst and Feldkamp, *Akten zur auswärtigen Politik*, 336–37; Hsi-Huey Liang, *The Berlin Police*, 55.

15 Minutes of the HICOG Twelfth Meeting with the Federal Chancellor, February 16, 1950, NARA RG 466, Records of the US High Commission for Germany, John J. McCloy, General Classified Records, 1949–1952, 1950. Nos. 410–604, Box 9, Folder: Feb. 50 D(50)410 to D(50)455; Adenauer's speech at Bochum is recorded in the minutes of the HICOG meeting.

16 Brigitte Kaff, "Robert Lehr (1883–1956)," in *Christliche Demokraten gegen Hitler: Aus Verfolgung und Widerstand zur Union*, edited by Günter Buchstabe, Brigitte Kaff, and Hans-Otto Kleinmann, 337–43 (Freiburg im Breisgau: Herder, 2004), 337–43.

and soon thereafter he became the city's Chief of Police. As police chief he censored the press and surveilled radical leftists. In 1918, like many other cities in the region, Düsseldorf experienced the wave of political violence that followed the war. As an industrial center, the city became a regional hub for radical Social Democrats (USPD) and the Communist Spartacus League.[17]

On November 8, 1918, sailors from Cologne arrived at Düsseldorf's main train station and fanned out across the city disarming soldiers and occupying police stations. Like Adenauer in Cologne, Lehr first turned to the military for help. He sent an urgent letter to the Deputy Commander of the VII Army Corps stationed in Münster, asking for troops to restore order. Officials in Berlin denied his request on the grounds that sending the army to confront the sailors might lead to needless bloodshed.[18] He never hesitated to consider military force as an option to restore order— only the intervention of higher authorities in Berlin prevented him from doing so. Since he could not use the military, he negotiated a power-sharing agreement with representatives from the soldiers and workers councils instead. As part of the agreement, he formed an auxiliary police force to keep order in the city. The men selected as auxiliary police officers wore special armbands and he authorized them to use deadly force if necessary. Lehr posted signs around the city warning that anyone caught looting or robbing would be immediately shot.[19]

The negotiated settlement with the soldiers and workers councils eventually broke down, however, and Lehr's auxiliary police fired on the Spartacists demonstrating at the main train station. The violence claimed the lives of several protestors. The auxiliary police were unable to quell the rioters and Lehr fled the city. It took the intervention of government troops and heavily armed *Freikorps* units to finally restore order. Lehr returned to his work in city administration and was later elected Mayor in 1924.[20] Adenauer could not have chosen a more like-minded politician to take over his Interior Ministry. Yet in contrast to Adenauer, Lehr did not focus exclusively on security threats from the political left, even though communism remained a priority. He led a determined campaign to convince Adenauer that the government must take action against the growing influence of the SRP. To be sure, Lehr's efforts combined with warnings from HICOG and support from West Germany's state interior

---

17 Steven von Lipski, "Dokumentation zur Geschichte der Stadt Düsseldorf während der Revolution 1918–1919 (November 1918 bis März 1919)," Quellensammlung (Pädagogisches Institut der Landeshauptstadt Düsseldorf: June 1983), 57.
18 Ibid.
19 Ibid. 14.
20 Ibid.

ministers finally pushed Adenauer to act against the ambivalent attitude of many in his administration who ignored the growing threat. In 1952, the Federal Constitutional Court banned the SRP in spite of its recent popularity and local electoral successes.[21]

Internal Opposition and Competing Interpretations of Border Security

On February 18, 1950, a few weeks after the truck driver's strike in Bonn, State Secretary Ritter von Lex met with Federal Minister of Finance Fritz Schäffer about possibly using the *Zoll* as the nucleus for a new police force. Lex supported Dehler's suggestion of forming a national police force under the guise of border security. He thought he could coax Schäffer into giving the Interior Ministry control or jurisdiction over a portion of the *Zoll's* personnel that he could use to build the new force Adenauer envisioned.[22] Schäffer and Lex knew each other as members of Bavarian Peoples Party (BVP) during the interwar years. The US Military Government appointed Schäffer, a founding member of the Christian Social Union (CSU), to the post of Prime Minister in Bavaria. General Eisenhower later dismissed Schäffer because he appointed too many former Nazis to posts in his administration. Schäffer and Lex both reflected the problematic authoritarian continuities of former elite Nazi civil servants and officials that found a place in the Adenauer administration.[23]

Lex tried in vain to convince Schäffer to support his plan for incorporating part of the *Zoll* into the Interior Ministry, but Schäffer had his own agenda. He told Lex that the Allied reserved powers over security "could only be removed by a formal Allied regulation, since occupation law takes precedence over constitutional law."[24] After failing to convince Schäffer to go along with his plans, Lex wrote an urgent letter to Hans Egidi, head of Interior Ministry Division I (Constitution, Administration, and Security), asking for immediate clarification on Schäffer's claim that

---

21 Norbert Frei, *Adenauer's Germany*, 262–65.

22 "Vermerk über die Besprechung mit Bundesfinanzminister Schäffer am 18 Feb. 1950 wegen Fragen des Zoll u. Grenzschutzes," BArch-K, B106/83869.

23 Christoph Henzler, *Fritz Schäffer (1945–1967): Eine biographische Studie zum ersten bayerischen Nachskriegs-Ministerpräsidenten und ersten Finanzminister der Bundesrepublik Deutschland* (Munich: Hans-Seidel-Stiftung, 1997); Dominik Rigoll, "From Denazification to Renazification?, 261–62; Norbert Frei, *Adenauer's Germany*, xxi; Michael R Hayse, *Recasting West German Elites: Higher Civil Servants, Business Leaders, and Physicians in Hesse Between Nazism and Democracy, 1945–1955* (New York: Berghahn Books, 2003).

24 "Vermerk über die Besprechung mit Bundesfinanzminister Schäffer am 18 Feb. 1950," BArch-K, B106/83869.

"customs and border protection" is an exclusive economic activity of the Ministry of Finance.[25]

On February 24, 1950, Adenauer's assistant Herbert Blankenhorn raised the issue of border security during a regular meeting with HICOG's Central Committee. Deputy High Commissioner General George P. Hays rejected the suggestion that the Federal Republic required another border police force. Hays agreed to increase the *Zoll's* staffing, which is what Schäffer wanted all along, but would not permit the formation of a new federal border police force.[26] Nevertheless, Ritter von Lex tried once again to convince Schäffer to reconsider his opposition. Schäffer refused to budge and told Lex he preferred to discuss the matter directly with Adenauer. As a compromise, Lex suggested that perhaps a member of the Interior Ministry could be assigned as a liaison to the customs headquarters. Schäffer rejected this idea as well. He knew policing was a controversial topic in the Federal Republic and did not want Lex and others at the Interior Ministry to undermine his chances of getting the extra staffing he needed. Schäffer warned his old friend: "Reinforcing the Customs Border Service can only be realized under the justification of combating smuggling ... the more I am doing and talking about police and policing tasks, the more I endanger my own position."[27]

Ritter von Lex requested further legal clarification, so Hans Egidi turned to the Interior Ministry's Constitutional Division Chief (*Referatsleiter*) Dr. Arnold Köttgen. Köttgen, like many of his colleagues, had loyally served the Third Reich. During the 1920s he studied law in Jena under Professor Otto Kollreutter, an authoritarian critic of parliamentary democracy. Kollreutter promoted radical right-wing paramilitaries and joined both the *Stahlhelm* and the Nazi *Sturmabteilung*—SA. Köttgen shared his mentor's loathing of parliamentary democracy and dedicated his habilitation thesis on Germany's Civil Service to Kollreutter.[28] During the war, Köttgen served as the general police councillor at Auschwitz and in the Polish City of Katowice. The record of Nazi

---

25   Staatssekretär Hans Ritter von Lex to Abteilungsleiter I (Hans Egidi), 18 Feb. 1950, BArch-K, B106/83869.

26   Document Nr. 37, "Aufzeichnung des Ministerialdirigenten Blankenthorn," Geheim, February 25, 1950, in Daniel Kosthorst and Michael F. Feldkamp, eds., *Akten zur Auswärtigen Politik der Bundesrepublik Deutschland, 1949–1950* (Munich: Oldenbourg Wissenschaftsverlag, 2013), 94–96.

27   Letter from Fritz Schäffer to Hans Ritter von Lex, March 20, 1950, BArch-K, B136/1927; Letter exchange between Fritz Schäffer and Hans Ritter von Lex, March 7, 1950, BArch-K, B136/1927.

28   Carola Dietze, *Nachgeholtes Leben: Helmuth Plessner 1892–1895* (Göttingen: Wallstein, 2013), 427; Peter Badura, "Arnold Köttgen (1902–1967)," in *Staatsrechtslehrer des 20. Jahrhunderts*, edited by Michael Kilian, Heinrich Amadeus Wolff, and Peter Häberle (Boston: De Gruyter, 2018), 731.

atrocities in Poland is well documented, and Hitler's mobile killing squads (*Einsatzgruppen*) used the region around Katowice as a base for their operations.[29] When German armed forces invaded Poland in 1939, they burned Katowice's neo-gothic synagogue to the ground and massacred its entire Jewish population. Carola Dietze has argued that Köttgen was "demonstrably involved in the local planning of Germanization policies that included at least the deportation of Jews."[30] Despite his troubling record and Nazi service, Köttgen did not offer Egidi or Lex any suggestions outside of amending the Basic Law. Instead, he reminded them that per West Germany's Basic Law, the federal states still had authority over policing. He also emphasized that HICOG prohibited centralized policing, and thus any federal control over the police would require their express approval in addition to a constitutional amendment.[31]

Militarized Policing: A Solution to Rearmament

In spite of the efforts by Ritter von Lex and others at the Interior Ministry, no clear legal path existed for the Federal Republic to build a centralized police force. For Adenauer, however, a narrow window of hope emerged from secret discussions between members of the US Joint Chiefs of Staff, the State Department, and some members of HICOG's Public Safety Branch. Key figures in these organizations had been secretly discussing hypothetical ideas for militarizing West Germany's police forces as an interim step toward full rearmament.[32]

High Commissioner McCloy's Special Assistant, Colonel H. A. Gerhardt, his Deputy High Commissioner George P. Hays, and the State Department's Director of German Affairs, Colonel Henry A. Byroade, all considered various schemes for rearming West Germany through the police. It is important to note that these proposals remained theoretical and reflected the gradual Allied shift away from holding Germans accountable for their Nazi past and towards enlisting their support in defending Western Europe. Historians have mistakenly cited these secret

---

29 Mary Fulbrook, *A Small Town near Auschwitz: Ordinary Nazis and the Holocaust* (Oxford: Oxford University Press, 2012), 240–41.

30 Carola Dietze, *Nachgeholtes Leben*, 427.

31 See the note from Dr. Arnold Köttgen, "Einsatzmöglichkeiten eines Bundesschutz," September 8, 1950; Note from Köttgen an Dr. Hans Egidi, "Organisation eines Bundesverteidigung," September 10, 1950, BArch-K, B106/83869.

32 See NSC 71, Top Secret, "United States Policy towards Germany," June 8, 1950, Dwight D. Eisenhower Library, White House Office, National Security Council Staff: Papers 1948–61, Disaster File, Box 48.

discussions and theories as empirical evidence to argue that the Federal Republic intended to use the BGS as a clandestine effort to rearm. Hans-Peter Schwarz, for example, argued that Adenauer's federal police proposals were "... the core of a concealed rearmament." David Parma has suggested that the federal government likely intended for the BGS to become an army, but could not publicly say so for political reasons related to burdens of the Nazi past.[33] Indeed, Hays did secretly tell Adenauer's assistant Herbert Blankenhorn that the West German police might be useful as a "camouflaged" army.[34] Moreover, in 1949, the Allied High Commission circulated a top-secret paper written by a member of McCloy's staff that promoted the German police as a first step to rearmament. The analysis claimed that this approach would appease the French and Eastern Bloc countries who feared the prospects of a resurgent West Germany.[35] Although the clandestine army interpretation seems plausible given the fact that West Germany lacked armed forces, these plans and schemes never came to fruition. Moreover, this interpretation also fails to account for the larger body of evidence that shows Adenauer and his Interior Ministry focused on internal rather than external security as justification for establishing the new force.

The British High Commissioners also secretly discussed rearmament through a police or gendarmerie option. UK High Commissioner Brian Robertson and his successor Ivone Kirkpatrick spoke privately about this possibility with former General Gerhard Graf von Schwerin, who at the same time was engaged in secret discussions with other Wehrmacht veterans about a future West German army.[36] Robertson and his deputy, Sir Christopher Steele, recommended Schwerin as a security advisor to Adenauer. Based on these suggestions, the chancellor decided to appoint Schwerin to lead his proto ministry of defense, the Office for Homeland

---

33 Hans-Peter Schwarz, *Adenauer Vol. 1*, 524–25; David Parma, *Installation und Konsolidierung des Bundesgrenzschutzes 1949 bis 1972: Eine Untersuchung der Gesetzgebungsprozesse unter besonderer Betrachtung der inneradministrativen und politischen Vorgänge* (Wiesbaden: Springer Fachmedien, 2016), 256.

34 Document Nr. 94, July 17, 1950, "Aufzeichnung des Ministerialdirektors Blankenhorn," Geheim, in Kosthorst and Feldkamp, *Akten zur auswärtigen Politik*, 263–68.

35 Top Secret Position Paper, Lt. Colonel Edwards to Colonel H. A. Gerhardt, "Basic Considerations with Regards to Germany," June 13, 1949, p. 2, NARA RG 466, Records of the Office of the High Commissioner for Germany, Office of the Executive Director, Misc. Files Maintained by Col. H. A. Gerhardt, Boxes 11–12, Box 2.

36 See telegram, July 6, 1950, US Ambassador Lewis Douglas to Secretary of State Dean Acheson, FRUS, vol. IV, 1950, 695; Spencer Mawby, *Containing Germany: Britain and the Arming of the Federal Republic* (London: Macmillan, 1999), 27–32; Alaric Searle, *Wehrmacht Generals*, 52.

Service (*Zentrale für Heimatdienst*).[37] Schwerin advocated the establishment of motorized police forces as a foundation for a future army because he believed any overt action to rearm would provoke the Soviets into a war before the Federal Republic or the Allies had the manpower to respond. For Schwerin, federal policing was a temporary solution to rearmament as opposed to the internal security focus of Adenauer and his Interior Ministry.[38]

Still, in spite of his internal security goals, Adenauer exploited the opportunity created by these theoretical discussions. Nevertheless, he continued to advocate the force as an instrument for protecting the democratic state against internal communist revolutionaries. In April 1950 he formally requested HICOG's approval for a 25,000-man federal police force. In his request, he never mentioned defending the border or using the force as a first step in building a new army. Instead, he returned to familiar tropes that claimed West Germany's weak police forces faced the same predicament as their Weimar predecessors, who failed to quell civil unrest without assistance from the Reichswehr.[39] Again and again, Adenauer invoked the political violence and disorder of the Weimar Republic and his fear of Bolshevik revolution in the Federal Republic as the reason he needed a centralized internal security force.

It would not be fair to claim Adenauer constructed or invented his anxiety and fear of Bolshevism to justify the new force, but at times he embellished its potential to overthrow his government as a means to convince the Allies to give in to his demands. The violent Soviet occupation of Eastern Germany and the abuses perpetrated by its soldiers at the end of the Second World War played a role in stoking his fears. During the revolutionary upheavals of 1918 and later during the Weimar Republic, the Bolsheviks failed to establish a political state in Germany. The government's police and paramilitary forces fought violent street battles against

37 Bundesarchiv-Militärisch Archiv, Freiburg BA-MA, BW/3105: Personal Memorandum, May 25, 1950. Schwerin recalled this recommendation himself in this personal memorandum and claimed he was given the job after a one-hour interview with Adenauer; According to David Clay Large, it was the publisher of *Die Zeit*, Countess Marion Dönhoff, who originally suggested Schwerin to Robertson; see David Clay Large, *Germans to the Front*, 57; Roland Förster, "Innenpolitische Aspekte," 456.

38 Document Nr. 68, June 8, 1950, "Aufzeichnung des Beraters in des Sicherheitsfragen Graf von Schwerin," in *Akten zur auswärtigen Politik*, ed. Kosthorst and Feldkamp, 172.

39 Quoted from pp. 1–2, letter from Chancellor Adenauer to General Sir Brian Robertson, Chairman of the Council of the Allied High Command, April 28, 1950, The National Archives of the UK (TNA), Foreign Office Files FO 371/85324; he was referring here to the Bonn demonstration and also recent activities by the FDJ.

communist revolutionaries that tried, but failed to achieve their goal of overthrowing the Republic. In 1945, however, Soviet forces occupied Germany, setting off the migration of thousands of people to the west. The refugees brought with them stories of mass rapes and atrocities committed by the advancing Soviet armed forces in their drive to take Berlin. Thus, for Adenauer and other officials in his government, the Bolsheviks succeeded this time, at least partially, in realizing their enduring goal of establishing a German Communist state. East Germany became a stark, ever-present reminder for what might be in store for the Federal Republic if it did not have a force to put down Bolshevik insurrectionists.[40]

At the time Adenauer asked HICOG for a 25,000-man force, he relied on what later proved to be faulty intelligence reports that armed contingents of the People's Police and Free German Youth (*Freie Deutsche Jugend*—FDJ) planned armed May Day insurrections in Berlin.[41] The East Germans established the FDJ in 1946 as a means to promote nationalist ideals of education, career development, and civic engagement among its youth. Although the FDJ eventually grew into a politicized instrument of the East German Socialist Union Party (SED), in 1950 HICOG had allowed it to establish a chapter in West Berlin. The FDJ also caused social concerns for conservative West Germans because they believed its dynamic propaganda might appeal to West Germany's youth and thus seduce them with its leftist ideology in an effort to pave the way for a communist take-over.[42]

The rise in FDJ activity, however, did not convince HICOG that Adenauer needed a new security force and they denied his request. The High Commissioners preferred rearming West Germany in a measured, supervised approach instead of allowing Adenauer to build an independent militarized police force. Yet High Commissioner McCloy also wanted

---

40 Norman Naimark, *The Russians in Germany: A History of the Soviet Zone of Occupation, 1945–1949* (Cambridge: Belknap Press of Harvard University Press, 1995), 72–74.

41 Telegram from HICOG Director of Intelligence B. R. Schute to United States Command, Berlin, April 18, 1950, "Berlin Situation No. 14," NARA RG 466, Records for the US High Commissioner for Germany, John J. McCloy, Classified General Records, 1949–1950, 1950 Box 12, Folder: Apr. 50 D (50) 1168 to D (50) 1225; See also Frank Pace Jr., Secretary of the Army, "Top Secret Report to the National Security Council: May Day and Whitsuntide Youth Rallies in Berlin," April 28, 1950, Eisenhower Presidential Library, White House Office, National Security Council Staff: Papers, 1948–61, Disaster File, Box 48, Folder: Germany (4).

42 Alan McDougall, *Youth Politics in East Germany: The Free German Youth Movement, 1946–1968* (Oxford: Clarendon, 2004), 20; Mary Fulbrook, *Anatomy of a Dictatorship: Inside the GDR, 1949–1989* (New York: Oxford University Press, 1995), 131.

to find some way to appease Adenauer and keep him firmly aligned with the West. On May 12, 1950, he secretly proposed to his fellow High Commissioners that the Chancellor be allowed to build a small national police force. McCloy argued that it would be a good symbolic gesture to "uphold the prestige" of Adenauer's government.[43] With the London Foreign Ministers Conference fast approaching, McCloy thought it was a good time to act. He wanted to keep any decisions about West German security or policing secret in order to avoid giving any impression that the High Commissioners had tried to placate Adenauer or reward him for his repeated complaints.[44]

During the London Conference the Foreign Ministers quietly approved McCloy's suggestion, but asked that any force established by the Adenauer government be limited to no more than 5,000 men. Because the Foreign Ministers still feared the legacies of Nazi police abuses more than any risks of irritating Adenauer, McCloy suggested that the proposed force should be called a "Republican Guard" rather than a "federal police."[45] Although McCloy failed to explain in his correspondence how using the term "police" might be controversial, he did insist that the so-called Republican Guard be prohibited from having arrest powers or any jurisdiction over state police forces. Thus most likely he proceeded in this manner to avoid conflict with West Germany's states, which under the Basic Law still had legal authority over policing. In any case, McCloy intended that its main purpose remained purely symbolic. He warned his colleagues to keep the decision secret and directed that it be presented as an "Allied decision" so as not be construed as a "concession."[46]

When the London Foreign Ministers Conference ended, the Allies reaffirmed their commitment to defend West Germany against foreign invasion under Article 5 of the North Atlantic Treaty—again showing the Allied commitment to militarily defend Adenauer's government. Any Soviet or East German invasion of West Germany would trigger

---

43 See Memorandum from C. A. E. Shuckburgh, May 11, 1950: "Ministerial Talks United States/United Kingdom/France, Item No. 3: Germany," 1, TNA FO 371/85324.

44 Remarkably, the documents are still classified by the State Department, but portions existed in declassified format in McCloy's personal papers and in files at the Eisenhower Presidential Library (see below).

45 See "NSC 71, A Report to the National Security Council by the Secretary of Defense on United States Policy towards Germany, June 8, 1950," Dwight D. Eisenhower Presidential Library, White House Office, National Security Council Staff: Papers, 1948–1961, Disaster File, Box 48, Folder A: Germany.

46 Top Secret memorandum written on behalf of McCloy by his Assistant, Col. H. A. Gerhardt to the British and French Foreign Ministers, May 12, 1950, The John J. McCloy Papers, Amherst College, Box +HC5, Folder 79: HICOG Correspondence.

an immediate response, even though the Federal Republic had not yet been formally incorporated as a NATO member state.[47] Any concerns Adenauer had about a communist invasion should have been mollified by this security guarantee. Yet the Foreign Ministers said nothing about West Germany's internal security or how they might respond to defend the state against communist insurrections or agitation by the People's Police—the real motivation behind Adenauer's federal police proposals. Despite all the fuss and McCloy's clandestine scheming, his plans for a Republican Guard never materialized, because the Allied strategic outlook for Western European defense suddenly changed against the backdrop of events unfolding on the Korean Peninsula.

The Korean War: A Blueprint for Divided Germany?

The surprise invasion of South Korea by communist North Korean forces on June 25, 1950, sent shockwaves through the Transatlantic community. It was the first major armed conflict to test the resolve of the Western Alliance during the Cold War era. The war convinced the Allies of the urgency in rearming West Germany to defend Europe. Just two days after hostilities began, McCloy directed HICOG's Public Security Subcommittee to end its longstanding ban preventing members of Nazi Germany's Wehrmacht and paramilitary forces from serving in the police.[48] It was a sudden and complete reversal of policy. The Korean War erupted at a pivotal moment when McCarthyism and "red scares" besieged domestic politics in the United States and the Soviets had acquired nuclear weapons. The Truman Administration moved quickly to implement its policy of containing communism wherever it emerged. The war and its effect on the strategic situation in Europe gave Adenauer another opportunity to sound the alarm and renew his request for a federal police force.[49]

---

47 Article 5 remained in effect as long as Allied forces occupied the FRG, See FRUS, Vol. III, 1950, 1085.

48 Allied High Commission Public Safety Subcommittee Confidential Memorandum: "Employment in the German Police and Fire Services of Members of the German Armed Forces and Paramilitary Organizations," June 27, 1950, NARA RG 466 Records of the High Commissioner for Germany, Military Security Board: Military Division, Secret General Records, 1949–55, F-P, Box 2, Folder: German Police, Miscellaneous.

49 John Lewis Gaddis, *Strategies of Containment: A Critical Appraisal of American National Security Policy during the Cold War* (New York: Oxford University Press, 2005), 107–12; William I. Hitchcock, *The Age of Eisenhower: America and the World in the 1950s* (New York: Simon & Schuster, 2018), 152.

Although the Korean War increased Allied concerns over security in the Federal Republic, General Schwerin's plans for rearming through mobile police forces remained unpopular. US Secretary of State Dean Acheson argued against Schwerin's plans and explained that West Germany's state police already had the strength to deal with crime and maintain domestic security without "recreating dangers to democracy inherent in strong centralized German police forces." His assessment made sense. In their ongoing conversations, Deputy High Commissioner Hays told General Schwerin that he could in no way approve of his ideas for building armed forces through a militarized mobile police force.[50]

Adenauer grew impatient with the High Commission. He never missed a chance to publicly proclaim that the Allies should look no further than the communist actions in Korea to know what fate awaited divided Germany. In correspondence with his personal friend Dane Heineman he expressed his frustration that the Allies seemed intent on remaining "passive observers" to the dangers of communist revolution in the Federal Republic.[51] His comparisons of Korea and divided Germany reflected his ongoing and calculated effort to convince the High Commissioners to grant his requests for a federal police force. Nevertheless, policing the Federal Republic's borders still did not factor into either his public or private conversations regarding the purpose for the force he intended to create.

Adenauer's public statements comparing Korea and divided Germany soon gained the attention of the press and convinced many Germans that another war loomed on the horizon. The *New York Times* Reporter Jack Raymond observed that West Germans followed developments in Korea so closely that in many cities maps of the peninsula tracing the movement of armed forces appeared in public spaces and press kiosks.[52] Adenauer fueled this general sense of angst by promoting the idea that communist "gangs" and insurgents had spread internal dissent in South Korea making it a perfect "soft target" for a North Korean invasion. Without credible evidence, he alleged that an East German fifth column had already prepared the way for a similar communist invasion of the Federal Republic. He repeated his usual claim about the weaknesses of West Germany's state

---

50 Telegram from Secretary of State Dean Acheson to US High Commissioner McCloy, June 21, 1950 RG 466, Classified General Records 1949–1952, Box 11, Folder: TS(50)40-49, June 1950; for General Hays's statement, see BA-MA, BW 9/3105, meeting minutes, Schwerin, Hays, Poncet, Blankenthorn, Bonn, July 7, 1950, 2.

51 Letter from Konrad Adenauer to D. N. Heineman, November 15, 1950, Amherst College, John J. McCloy Papers, Box +HC5, Folder 93: HICOG Correspondence, Heineman, D. N. June 1949–January 1951.

52 David Clay Large, *Germans to the Front*, 66; Jack Raymond, "Germany Views the Border," *New York Times*, July 30, 1950, E5.

police and pointed to their recent failures to exert sufficient command presence to take streamers and banners away from FDJ protestors.[53]

General Schwerin contributed to Adenauer's outlook by suggesting he had credible intelligence of strong communist fifth-column forces already operating in the Federal Republic. He also reiterated that only a barracked federal police force could deal with an insurrection, should one break out. Schwerin told Adenauer that without militarized police to combat them, these fifth columnists might "paralyze the government by cutting off traffic routes, endangering supply and communications networks, and would attempt to usurp government power locally and regionally."[54] Adenauer and Schwerin greatly exaggerated the strategic comparisons of West Germany to South Korea, and frankly, most of what they claimed had no basis in fact. In prewar South Korea, the paranoid, corrupt President Syngman Rhee ruthlessly purged anyone he suspected of leftist sympathies. Whereas the Federal Republic dealt with FDJ protestors and occasional labor strikes, President Rhee turned prewar South Korea into a formidable police state. With the clandestine support of US intelligence agencies, Rhee's security forces imprisoned, tortured, and executed thousands of dissidents before the war broke out. During the 1946 Jeju Uprising, for example, Rhee's anti-communist purges killed 14,000 civilians.[55] Nothing comparable to this ever took place in the Federal Republic.

Besides General Schwerin, several other prominent Wehrmacht veterans got involved in the debate over the Federal Republic's security. Generals Adolf Heusinger, Hans Speidel, and Franz Halder all opposed Schwerin's plan to rearm through the police. Instead, these men and many of their colleagues wanted to build tank divisions and revive the old German General Staff system. At the same the time, Schwerin also secretly worked as a contact for the US Central Intelligence Agency (CIA) and forged close ties with its controversial director, Allen Dulles. Schwerin's clandestine intelligence activities soon brought him into conflict with the Federal Republic's own spymaster and future head of intelligence, Reinhard Gehlen. During the war, Gehlen served under General Franz Halder and thus favored his approach to rearmament. Schwerin tried to undermine Gehlen by telling Deputy High Commissioner Hays

---

53 Konrad Adenauer, *Memoirs 1945–1953, Vol. 1* (Chicago: Henry Regnery, 1966), 271–74.

54 Document Nr. 94, July 17, 1950, "Aufzeichnung des Ministerialdirektors Blankenhorn," in Kosthorst and Feldkamp, *Akten zur auswärtigen Politik*, 263.

55 Dong Choon Kim, "Forgotten War, Forgotten Massacres: The Korean War (1950–1953) as Licensed Mass Killings," *Journal of Genocide Research* 6, no. 4 (2004), 523–44.

that his intelligence organization was full of "leaks" and needed an "urgent cleansing."[56]

Many of the former Wehrmacht officers concerned with rearmament also joined the emerging postwar circles of veterans' associations that advocated the restoration of honor for Germany's soldiers.[57] These veterans claimed that the Wehrmacht fought honorably in spite of the war crimes committed by what they argued was only a small minority of its soldiers. Adenauer, always the strong advocate for the collective amnesia regarding the past and instead focusing on the future, even convinced US General Eisenhower to publicly endorse these tropes as a price for West German participation in rearmament. Extensive research, however, has debunked this narrative and empirically shown that the Wehrmacht also willingly perpetrated Hitler's war of annihilation. What scholars later called the myth of the Wehrmacht's "clean hands" came about as a direct result of these early rearmament debates.[58]

On August 16, 1950, Adenauer used the Korean War to revive his bid for a federal police force. He wrote another lengthy security memorandum to High Commissioner McCloy, this time requesting a 150,000-man federal police force to resist what he called a "Korean style" attack by the People's Police.[59] The People's Police had increased in size, but McCloy's staff reported that Adenauer had exaggerated its ability to carry out large-scale attacks. After meeting with Adenauer, McCloy told Dean Acheson that he too believed Adenauer had exaggerated the threats and suggested instead that he may only be trying to "strengthen his government by the creation of a federal police force and using the Korean incident as a gambit for this purpose." McCloy's assistant, Samuel Reber, also reported that Adenauer wrote the security memorandum in such a manner as to "stress the alarming nature of the current military situation."[60]

---

56 Document Nr. 97, July 22, 1950, "Besprechung mit dem amerikanischen stellvertretenden Hohen Kommissar Hays," in Kosthorst and Feldkamp, *Akten zur auswärtigen Politik*, 279; for Gehlen's role see Alaric Searle, "Internecine Secret Service Wars Revisited: The Intelligence Career of Count Gerhard von Schwerin, 1945–1956," *Militärgeschichtliche Zeitschrift* 71, no. 1 (2012): 25–55.

57 See Thomas Kühne, *The Rise and Fall of Comradeship: Hitler's Soldiers, Male Bonding and Mass Violence in the Twentieth Century* (Cambridge: Cambridge University Press, 2017), 229–30.

58 See for example, Hannes Heer and Klaus Naumann, eds., *War of Extermination: The German Military in World War II, 1941–1944* (New York: Berghahn, 2000); Wolfram Wette, *The Wehrmacht: History, Myth, Reality* (Cambridge, MA: Harvard University Press, 2006); Norbert Frei, *Adenauer's Germany*.

59 Adenauer, *Memoirs*, 274–75.

60 McCloy to Acheson July 14, 1950, FRUS Vol. IV, 1950, 696–97; Letter from Adenauer to John J. McCloy, August 29, 1950, NARA RG 466, Records of the Office of the High Commissioner for Germany, Office of the Executive

Adenauer's memorandum and open discussions with Wehrmacht veterans angered his first Interior Minister, Gustav Heinemann. Heinemann opposed rearmament and the federal police force Adenauer had been trying to create. Heinemann reflected the way many postwar Germans felt about militarism and war—count me out (*Ohne mich*). He once told Adenauer: "God knocked our weapons out of our hands twice: we shouldn't pick them up a third time."[61] He did not trust the Wehrmacht veterans Adenauer had consulted. When he learned about the exaggerated security memorandum he sent to the High Commission, he resigned. Adenauer refused to accept his resignation, however, and he reluctantly agreed to remain at his post until October 1950, when Robert Lehr took over.

Heinemann feared that Adenauer and the veteran soldiers he consulted might lead the Federal Republic down a regressive path towards the authoritarian form of government it had supposedly consigned to the past. His service in the Protestant Church brought him into close contact with the charismatic pastor and antiwar theologian, Martin Niemöller. Niemöller, an outspoken critic of rearmament, accused Adenauer of attempting to build a shadow army disguised as a police force. Niemöller also learned through press reports that General Schwerin wanted to secretly arm the German Labor Service Units (*Dienstgruppen*). These units included veteran soldiers that the Allies employed for a variety of construction and public service projects. Niemöller told Adenauer that if the Western Allies needed armed forces, they should supply them on their own, since West Germans had had enough of wars and militarism. Adenauer now found himself in a difficult position: West Germans might view Heinemann and Niemöller as champions of peace, while he and his government embraced militarism.[62]

Director, General Hay's Executive Files 1949–1951, Boxes 15–16, Box 2, folder: "Federal Chancellor Adenauer Intelligence Estimate, 1950"; Reber to McCloy, August 31, 1950.

61 Document Nr. 125, September 24, 1950, "Gespräch des Bundeskanzlers Adenauer mit dem amerikanischen Hohen Kommissar McCloy," in Kosthorst and Feldkamp, *Akten zur auswärtigen Politik*, 358–60.

62 Dr. Martin Niemöller to Chancellor Konrad Adenauer, October 4, 1950, Papers of John J. McCloy, Special Collections Library Amherst College, Box +HC5, Folder 184; General Schwerin, "Persönliche Aktennotiz" Bonn, May 25, 1950, BA-MA, BW 9/3105; Dominik Rigoll, "Kampf um die innere Sicherheit: Schutz des Staates oder Demokratie?" in *Hüter der Ordnung: Die Innenministerien in Bonn und Ost Berlin nach dem Nationalsozialismus*, ed. Frank Bösch and Andreas Wirsching (Göttingen: Wallstein, 2018), 476; Jon David K. Wyneken, "The Western Allies, German Churches, and the Emerging Cold War in Germany, 1948–1952," in, *Religion and the Cold War: A Global Perspective*, ed. Philip E. Muehlenbeck (Nashville: Vanderbilt University Press, 2012), 25.

McCloy sent Adenauer's security memorandum to the Allied foreign ministers for consideration during their upcoming rearmament conference in New York City. The war in Korea had advanced the timetable of rearmament, with the United States leading the effort. During the conference the foreign ministers agreed in principle to rearm West Germany, but only as part of a broad supranational European defense strategy. They considered and then rejected Adenauer's request for an independent federal police force. The three ministers decided, however, to reinforce West Germany's existing state police departments by an additional 30,000 men. The agreement specified that 10,000 of these men could be kept as a ready reserve for the federal government's use in case of a national emergency.[63] The government's use of this "readiness" force was to be determined in a separate agreement with the individual state interior ministers. The foreign ministers dealt a direct blow to Adenauer's federal police force, but they empowered West Germany's states to revive the militarized Weimar era Riot Police (*Bereitschaftspolizei*—BePo). The paramilitary BePo could deal with civil unrest and riots that exceeded the capabilities of regular state and municipal forces.[64]

Thus jurisdiction over policing remained with the federal states. Adenauer's government could not use these new forces unless one of the state interior ministers declared a national emergency as outlined in Article 91, Section 1 of the Basic Law. Article 91 Section 2, however, gave the federal government authority over all state police forces, subject to veto at any time by the Federal Council (*Bundesrat*), if it could show that one or more of its states could not handle the situation or became suddenly overwhelmed during a given emergency.[65] The Foreign Ministers also directed that during a declared state of emergency, any police officers subordinated to the federal government "would have no normal powers of arrest, and would not perform routine police duties, but would be trained and used solely for the preservation of public order."[66] Once the emergency ended, Article 91 Section 2 required that federal authority over civilian policing be immediately terminated. Emergency legislation remained a controversial topic in the Federal Republic's jurisprudence since Hitler used the emergency laws outlined in Article 48 of the Weimar

---

63 "Decision of the Foreign Ministers of the United States, the United Kingdom and France with Regards to Germany," Secret, New York, September 19, 1950, Document 37 (Final), FRUS 1950, Western Europe Vol. III, 1294–1295.

64 Erika Fairchild, *The German Police*, 24–25; Eugen Raible, *Geschichte der Polizei*, 125.

65 "Grundgesetz für die Bundesrepublik Deutschland," Bundeszentrale für politische Bildung (2006), 55.

66 Transcript of New York Foreign Ministers Meeting, September 19, 1950, "German Mobile Police Forces," NARA RG 466, General Hays Executive Files 1949–51, Boxes 15–16, Box 2—Tripartite Meeting, 1–2.

Constitution to rule by decree and destroy democracy from within.[67] The Allies and the framers of West Germany's Basic Law wanted better safeguards to prevent a strong executive from abusing the extensive powers granted during a state of emergency.

The Foreign Ministers upheld the rigid constitutional limits on policing in West Germany, but the return of the paramilitary BePo should have been more than sufficient to address the internal security concerns expressed in Adenauer's memorandum. The text of the Foreign Minister's agreement, for example, justified the decision to form the state BePo "in view of the communist threat to instigate and carry out sabotage, civil disorder and resistance," all of which Adenauer cited as justifications for the force he proposed.[68] The Foreign Ministers believed they were helping Adenauer, but the unintended consequence of their decision to reinforce the state police meant that his government still lacked an independent means to use force. The federal government had no choice but to rely on and deal with the state interior ministries for their internal security needs.

Adenauer may have been frustrated with the Foreign Ministers, but the abuses perpetrated by Nazi police forces still weighed heavily on Allied policies towards reestablishing the monopolization of legitimate coercive forces in the Federal Republic. Behind the scenes at the New York Conference, West Germany's Ambassador to the United States, Heinz Krekeler reported that French High Commissioner André François-Poncet "refused to touch" the policing issue.[69] Moreover, during the proceedings François-Poncet allegedly made sarcastic remarks that Adenauer exaggerated the danger from the East and "just wanted to force our hand."[70] The French in particular did not trust the Germans with armed forces, let alone an independent paramilitary police force that might be used to remilitarize the Federal Republic. For the French, rearmament was only possible through a supranational solution. François-Poncet also knew that veteran Wehrmacht officers secretly advised Adenauer, and he claimed they formed "a new military cabinet" in Bonn. His stance

---

67 Benjamin Carter Hett, *Burning the Reichstag: An Investigation into the Third Reich's Enduring Mystery* (Oxford: Oxford University Press, 2014); Germany's Basic Law available online: bundesregierung.de/breg-en/chancellor/basic-law-470510.

68 "Decision of the Foreign Ministers of the United States, the United Kingdom and France with Regards to Germany," Secret, New York, September 19, 1950, Document 37 (Final), FRUS 1950, Western Europe Vol. III, 1294–95.

69 Document Nr. 122, September 16, 1950, "Generalkonsul I. Klasse Krekeler, New York, an die Dienststelle für auswärtige Angelegenheiten," in Kosthorst and Feldkamp, *Akten zur auswärtigen Politik*, 348–49.

70 Ibid.

reflected a broader effort by France to contain German power and gain the upper hand in postwar continental Europe.[71]

Robert Lehr, Militant Democracy and West German Federalism

Adenauer's effort to form a federal police force did not end with the Foreign Minister's decision. As part of the agreement, the Foreign Ministers also amended the Occupation Statute to give West Germany more legislative authority and reduce the need for Allied legal review.[72] Because of this legislative change, Adenauer had more agency over domestic politics in the Federal Republic, and he used it to revive his bid for a federal police force. It was now up to his capable and trusted Interior Minister Robert Lehr to find a legal path forward. Lehr's biggest obstacle was not HICOG but West Germany's Social Democratic lawmakers and the state governments who wanted to limit Adenauer's executive power—Bavaria in particular. Although Adenauer claimed in his memoirs that he never intended to circumvent the amendment process, his actions in establishing the BGS suggested otherwise.[73] In November 1950, after the Foreign Ministers ruled against him, the Chancellor decided to unilaterally form an 1800-man paramilitary protection squad (*Begleitskommando*) to guard his offices in Bonn. He did this without consulting the North Rhine-Westphalian State Interior Minister who had jurisdiction over policing in Bonn. State police officers already handled these duties and Deputy High Commissioner Hays denied earlier requests for a Bonn protection squad. By forming his own elite guard unit, he tried to circumvent West Germany's lawmakers and quietly use it as the foundation for the federal police he had been trying to establish since 1949. He proceeded on the mantra that the ends justified the means and simply hoped he could pass it off without inviting closer scrutiny.[74]

---

71 William I. Hitchcock, *France Restored: Cold War Diplomacy and the Quest for Leadership in Europe, 1944–1954* (Chapel Hill: University of North Carolina Press), 133–35.

72 See John J. McCloy, "Report on Germany: September 21, 1949–July 31, 1952," *Office of the US High Commissioner for Germany* (Cologne: Greven & Bechtold, 1952), 13.

73 Adenauer, *Memoirs*, 291.

74 See Document Nr. 37, "Aufzeichnung des Ministerialdirigenten Blankenthorn," Geheim, February 25, 1950, in Kosthorst and Feldkamp, *Akten zur auswärtigen Politik der Bundesrepublik Deutschland*. Bundesminister des Innern Robert Lehr to Chancellor Konrad Adenauer, November 13, 1950, BArch-K, B136/1927.

Adenauer miscalculated the political resistance to his decision, however, after the SPD constitutional expert Walter Menzel learned about his executive protection squad.[75] Menzel's district (North Rhein Westphalia) included Bonn's government quarter and he had a great deal of experience in German policing. His exposure of Adenauer's security detail publicly embarrassed the chancellor, who at the urging of Interior Minister Lehr reluctantly disbanded it and transferred the responsibilities for securing his offices to the newly formed state BePo.[76] During the 1920s Menzel had been a magistrate in Potsdam and also served as a government assessor for the Essen Police. His father-in-law, the famous Weimar Interior Minister Carl Severing led the Prussian Schupo. In 1933 the Nazis dismissed Menzel from his government post, but he remained in Germany during the Third Reich, working as an attorney defending German citizens persecuted by the National Socialists. He favored centralized police forces, but opposed Adenauer's approach to security and remained wary of executive power.[77]

In principle, the SPD did not oppose the concept of a national police force but insisted that it be established by constitutional amendment. Menzel had even tried to establish a national police force in 1949 while serving as a framer of West Germany's Basic Law, but the Allies dismissed his proposal. He and his fellow constitutional framers worried that police chiefs in smaller decentralized departments might abuse their power.[78] Menzel and his colleagues believed it safer to invest police power in one central body because officers could be held accountable to a single authority and trained in the same manner. He believed Adenauer should be allowed to build a federal police force, but disagreed with what he called the "underhanded" manner in which the Chancellor was going about it.[79]

West Germany's state politicians presented another obstacle to centralized police forces because they rejected meddling in state affairs by the federal government. Bavaria, for example, refused ratification of the Basic Law in 1949 on the grounds that it did not give enough power to the federal states.[80] The Chairman of the Bavarian SPD, Wilhelm Hoegner,

75 Deutscher Bundestag (BT), 97. Sitzung, November 7, 1950, 3540.

76 Lehr to Adenauer, "Schutz- und Begleitskommando," November 13, 1950, BArch-K, B136/1927.

77 Otto Stolberg-Werinigerode, *New German Biography, vol. 17, Melander-Moller* (Berlin: Duncker & Humblot, 1994), 107–8.

78 For an overview of the SPD on policing see Karrin Hanshew, *Terror and Democracy in West Germany* (New York: Cambridge University Press, 2014), 41–46.

79 Deutscher Bundestag (BT), 97. Sitzung, November 7, 1950, 3540.

80 Erich Langenbacher and David P. Conradt, *The German Polity*, 11th edition (New York: Rowman & Littlefield, 2017), 308.

accused Adenauer and Lehr of exaggerating the east-west tensions to increase their own political power. Hoegner, a lawyer and long-serving member of the Bavarian Parliament, succeeded Fritz Schäffer as its prime minister after General Eisenhower dismissed him from his post. In the debate over federal policing, Hoegner took a firm stand against any policies he believed might undermine Bavarian autonomy.[81] In statements to the press earlier in the year, he invoked the Nazi past by warning against centralizing the police, which he saw as a "trend about to go back to where the misfortune of Germany had begun."[82]

The attempts by Adenauer and Interior Minister Robert Lehr to establish a national police force by avoiding the amendment process reflected their preference for a strong executive. They emphasized the sovereignty of executive power in matters of national security and promoted the state as a "militant democracy." Militant democracies are regimes in which the ends of protecting the state justify the means of limiting the civil liberties of their citizens in the process.[83] Adenauer and Lehr argued that the Federal Republic could not defend itself against its internal enemies unless its government had an instrument in which to monopolize the coercive forces of legitimate violence. Many of the officials who worked in the Interior Ministry promoted the authoritarian philosophies of political theorists like Carl Schmitt, Werner Weber, and others who championed executive power over parliamentary rule.[84] Schmitt's philosophies in particular reflected the authoritarian "Hobbesian" state and functioned on the premise that sovereignty is grounded in the necessity of leaders to make exceptions rather than rigidly adhere to a given rule of law.[85] Schmitt argued that "the sovereign is whoever decides what constitutes an exception." He also argued that parliament debated rules while "decision making and protection of state secrets belong to the executive."[86]

---

81 Jose Canoy, *The Discreet Charm of the Police State*, 63.
82 Quoted from Hoegner's interview in "Landtagprotest gegen Bundespolizei," *Süddeutsche Zeitung*, June 6, 1950.
83 See Carlo Invernizzi Accetti and Ian Zuckerman, "What's Wrong with Militant Democracy?" *Political Studies* 65 (2017): 183.
84 Jan-Werner Müller, *A Dangerous Mind: Carl Schmitt in Post-War European Thought* (New Haven, CT: Yale University Press, 2003), 64.
85 Patricia Springboard, "Hobbes and Schmitt on the Name and Nature of Leviathan Revisited," in *Thomas Hobbes and Carl Schmitt: The Politics of Order and Myth* (New York: Routledge, 2011), edited by John Tralau, 39–42.
86 Carl Schmitt, *The Crisis of Parliamentary Democracy* (Cambridge, MA: MIT Press, 1985), 43–45; Schmitt, a Catholic, had been publicly discredited for his support of the Nazis, but remained influential in postwar conservative-Catholic circles. See Tracy B. Strong, "Carl Schmitt and Thomas Hobbes: Myth and Politics," in *The Leviathan in the State Theory of Thomas Hobbes: Meaning and*

For his part, Weber criticized the Federal Republic's Basic Law because unlike the Weimar Constitution it de-emphasized executive power.[87]

Both Weber and Schmitt publicly questioned the Federal Republic's ability to defend itself during domestic emergencies. Although Schmitt's credibility suffered greatly because of his active support and defense of National Socialism, his philosophies re-emerged and gained popularity among the Federal Republic's conservative elite, many of whom held positions at the Interior Ministry or other government posts. Indeed, even though he was persona non grata in public, Schmitt often hosted former students and colleagues at his home and became an unofficial confidant to many conservatives during the postwar era. While there is no direct empirical evidence personally linking Adenauer to Schmitt or Weber, Hendrik Christoph-Müller has argued that their ideas remained popular among the conservative elite in Adenauer's governing circle during the 1950s.[88]

On November 7, 1950, Lehr introduced a bill in the Bundestag to create a federal border police in accordance with Article 87 of the Basic Law. He followed Justice Minister Dehler's earlier suggestions to use Article 87 because it required only a simple majority as opposed to the two-thirds vote required to amend the Basic Law, which Lehr knew never had a chance against the current political opposition. In the debate over the proposed law, SPD and Communist (KPD) deputies accused Lehr of purposely avoiding the amendment process. He pushed back and argued that the "amendment requires a two-thirds majority and the consent of the Bundesrat, and—let us not forget—the consent of the Allies. Informal inquiries have already shown that at the moment such consent is, in any case, unobtainable."[89] Menzel accused Lehr of exaggerating the communist threat and demanded that he and Adenauer "finally show their true colors." He advised Lehr to form a parliamentary advisory council so that others had a chance to weigh in on the federal policing question. From Menzel's perspective, the federal government appeared to be remilitarizing the police—a grave error that evoked legacies of National Socialism. He told Lehr: "We want to show those in the outside world, but also those here in Germany, that we do not intend to allow a remilitarization

---

Failure of a Political Symbol, ed. Carl Schmitt (Chicago: University of Chicago Press, 2008), vii–viii.

87 Werner Weber, *Weimarer Verfassung und Bonner Grundgesetz* (Göttingen: Fleischer, 1949), 6–10.

88 Hendrik Christoph-Müller, *West Germans against the West: Anti-Americanism in the Media and Public Opinion in the Federal Republic of Germany, 1949–1968* (New York: Palgrave-Macmillan, 2010), 89.

89 See Telegram: General Hays to Secretary Acheson, December 19, 1950, FRUS, Vol. IV, Central and Eastern Europe; The Soviet Union, 1950, 733; Deutsche BT, 97/Sitzung, 3544.

of the police. I want to stress that all of us—not go back in the direction we had gone after 1918. Also, the government should have an interest in preventing the image that they are trying to hide something."[90]

After Menzel's criticisms, the conservative parliamentary members came to Lehr's defense. Deputy Dr. Max Becker (FDP) claimed that communist fifth column agents already had a foothold in West Germany and could only be stopped by a federal police force.[91] Adolf von Thadden (DRP), a right-wing politician, veteran Wehrmacht Officer and Nazi Party member, ridiculed Menzel's suggestion of a parliamentary advisory council. He claimed there had already been "way too much talk and far too little being done."[92] The conservative politicians gave Lehr the political boost he needed. Menzel and his colleagues did not have enough votes to block the proposal to use Article 87.

Nevertheless, the spirited debate along with Lehr's willingness to negotiate the legal basis for the federal police force ended with a series of intraparty compromises that limited the size and jurisdiction of the BGS. Even though the SPD invoked the Nazi past and warned of the real danger in remilitarizing the police, the intraparty compromises reflected the increasing role of parliamentary democracy in checking Adenauer's executive power. The compromises held the BGS to 10,000 men and this figure could not be increased without parliamentary approval. The opposition also restricted its units and personnel to a thirty-kilometer radius of West Germany's frontiers.[93] Moreover, the intraparty negotiations also led to provisions that permitted each individual state to maintain their own border police unless they voluntarily agreed to relinquish these powers to the federal government.[94] Bavarian politicians welcomed this provision, but still opposed the measure because they wanted to retain control of their own borders. Finally, despite their longstanding opposition to centralized policing and repeated rejections of Adenauer's proposals, HICOG approved the new law.[95] Although the Allies still had control over security through the reserved powers guaranteed by the Occupation Statute, Cold War strategic concerns and the defense of Western Europe

90 Ibid., 3538, 3541, 3543.
91 97/Sitzung, 3552.
92 97/Sitzung, 3556; Daniel Koehler, *Right-Wing Terrorism in the 21st Century: The "National Socialist Underground" and the History of Terror from the Far Right in Germany* (London: Routledge, 2017), 72.
93 Ibid., 4512–4513.
94 Memorandum from Bundestag President Ehlers to Chancellor Konrad Adenauer announcing the terms of the BGS Law, February 15, 1951, BArch-K, B136/1927.
95 Top Secret memorandum from Robert Lehr to Allied High Commission, February 15, 1951, BArch-K, B136/1927; BT 118/Sitzung, 4516; General Hays to Secretary Acheson, December 19, 1950, FRUS Vol. IV, 1950, 735.

now eclipsed their fears of resurgent German militarism. The Allies did not want to embarrass and subsequently weaken Adenauer's government by intervening or overruling its legislative process. Thus on February 15, 1951, the Bundestag approved the second reading of the new law and the Federal Council ratified it on March 2, 1951. Only the Bavarian representative invoking federalist concerns abstained from the final vote.[96]

The BGS came into being at a time when the Federal Republic had gradually gone from a defeated and occupied enemy into an important ally and critical front in the emerging Cold War. By 1950 its expanding internal security infrastructure included the clandestine Gehlen intelligence service—later reorganized into the *Bundesnachrichtendienst* (BND, Federal Intelligence Agency), the Federal Office for the Protection of the Constitution (*Bundesverfassungschutz*-BfV), and the Federal Criminal Police Office (*Bundeskriminalamt*-BKA). 1950 also marked the official end of denazification, a process fraught with contradictory practices, uneven application and loathed by most Germans. In April 1951 the Bundestag also passed Article 131 of the Basic Law, which restored the pensions of many former civil servants and reinstated them in the positions they had held as of May 5, 1945. In addition to the general amnesty law of 1949, West Germany's lawmakers largely supported these legal reforms and this underscored their preference to emphasize their own victimhood over a more serious or introspective reckoning with the Nazi past.[97]

The end of denazification and passage of controversial amnesty legislation meant that many individuals compromised by their Nazi past returned to prominent positions in the Federal Republic. In addressing the Bundestag after the final reading of Article 131, Adenauer offered a stunning bookend to this policy of forgetting the past when he claimed: "The percentage of those who are truly guilty is so insignificant and so exceptionally small, that I would like to say in this context, that they do not tarnish the honor of the former German armed forces."[98]

Against all odds, Adenauer had shown great resilience in overcoming the political obstacles that hindered a nearly two-year effort to establish the BGS. He succeeded at a time when thousands of veteran police officers and soldiers became eligible for re-employment in the state's security forces. On April 18, 1951, the front-page headline of the *Frankfurter Allgemeine Zeitung* declared: "Wanted: Border Police Officers for the

---

96 Minutes of Deutsche BT, 118/Sitzung February 15, 1951.
97 Norbert Frei, *Adenauer's Germany and the Nazi Past*, 27–66; Robert Moeller, *War Stories: The Search for a Useable Past in the Federal Republic of Germany* (Berkeley: University of California Press, 2003).
98 Deutsche BT, 130 Sitzung, 5. April 1951, 4984.

Bundesgrenzschutz."[99] Veteran soldiers and police officers eagerly answered the call and more than 65,000 men applied—15,000 for its 650 commanding officer posts alone. Officials in the Interior Ministry had their police force, but now they faced the daunting prospect of screening, hiring, and training men for duties that had not yet been fully defined.[100]

[99] Staff, "Gesucht: Grenzschutzbeamte für den Bundesgrenzschutz!," *Frankfurter Allgemeine Zeitung*, April 18, 1951, 1.

[100] Falco Werkentin, *Die Restauration der deutschen Polizei: Innere Rüstung von 1945 bis zur Notstandsgesetzgebung* (Frankfurt am Main: Campus Verlag, 1984), 92.

CHAPTER TWO

MEN OF THE FIRST HOUR: VETERAN SOLDIERS AND THE POLICE ORGANIZATION THEY MADE

ON A COLD, DAMP April morning, BGS Major Kurt Andersen was staring through his field glasses scanning forest trails near the town of Simmerath on the German-Belgian border. Andersen was the commanding officer of "Operation Martha" codename for the deployment of BGS units against smugglers peddling coffee, butter, and stolen property through the Eifel Forest near Aachen. "Operation Martha," the first major deployment for the new BGS, must have revived a certain sense of familiarity for Andersen and the men under his command now back in the field carrying weapons less than six years after many of them had fought in the war. At fifty-four years of age, Andersen had extensive experience leading men in field operations. The Federal Republic represented the fourth German political regime to which he had sworn an oath of allegiance. In 1915, he enlisted in the Kaiser's army and fought with a machine-gun company. When Germany's armed forces surrendered in 1918, he joined the Iron Brigade, an ultra-nationalist *Freikorps* (free corps) paramilitary unit that continued to fight communist forces in the Baltic states.[1] In 1919, he became a member of the Prussian *Schutzpolizei* and served the Weimar Republic as a law enforcement officer in the cities of Elbing-Marienburg, Dortmund, and Düsseldorf. In 1935 he enlisted in the Nazi Wehrmacht and led a Luftwaffe anti-tank unit in combat on both the Eastern and Western Fronts. Captured by the British in 1945, he

---

1   On the *Freikorps* see Robert Gewarth, "Fighting the Red Beast: Counter-Revolutionary Violence in the Defeated States of Central Europe," in *War in Peace*, ed. Robert Gerwarth and John Horne, 57; Vejas Gabriel Liulevicius, *War Land on the Eastern Front: Culture, National Identity, and German Occupation in World War I* (London: Cambridge University Press, 2000), 228–29; Annemarie H. Sammartino, *The Impossible Border: Germany and the East, 1914–1922* (Ithaca, NY: Cornell University Press, 2010), 48–49.

spent three years as a POW at the maximum-security Island Farm Camp Number 11 outside Bridgend, South Wales before being repatriated to Germany in 1948.[2]

Major Andersen's notable service record was not exceptional. Known in organizational lore as "men of the first hour," he and his colleagues were the veteran soldiers and police officers who founded and led the BGS in 1951. The organization they made, however, was not the civilian law enforcement agency Adenauer, Lehr, and others at the Interior Ministry had promised the Bundestag. Instead, they created a militarized force steeped in the doctrines of counterinsurgency warfare and into which they imported their years of experience fighting Germany's wars.[3] Many of these men had recently fought in Wehrmacht and SS anti-partisan units or served at the front with militarized *Ordnungspolizei* (Order Police—OrPo) battalions. The personnel roster of officers and non-commissioned officers the Interior Ministry hired to lead the organization reads like a "who's who" of Germany's authoritarian past. Lieutenant Hans Stern, for example, had been a state police officer before he transferred into the SS, where he served until 1945, attaining the rank of Lieutenant Colonel. Franz Winterle, an instructor at the BGS school in Lübeck, also began as a state police officer and later joined the army fighting on the Eastern Front in Stalingrad. Before he joined the BGS and began teaching new recruits, Lieutenant Hans-Jürgen Pantenius taught at the Wehrmacht's Combat School for Street and Fortress Fighting and took part in the suppression of the Warsaw Uprising of 1944—a popular topic of his lectures in Lübeck. And the list goes on.[4]

In spite of the collective amnesia, the end of denazification, and the controversial amnesty laws that shaped 1950s West German society, the government still implemented what they considered at the time

---

2   For biographical details of Kurt Andersen see, "Personalunterlagen von Angehörigen der Reichswehr und Wehrmacht," BA-MA, PERS 6/1042: Generalmajor Kurt Andersen, geb. 2.10.1898; see also "Bundesgrenzschutz—Übernahme von Angehörigen in die Bundeswehr," Bd. 5, Liste A, Blatt 1, Generalmajor Kurt Andersen, BA-MA, BW1/5484.

3   For a discussion of how military veterans "import" militarization into civilian policing, see Julian Go, "The Imperial Origins of American Policing: Militarization and Imperial Feedback in the Early 20th Century," *American Journal of Sociology* 125, no. 5 (March 2020): 1193–1254.

4   For the service records for these individuals, see, "Bundesgrenzschutz—Übernahme von Angehörigen in die Bundeswehr," Bd. 5, BA-MA, BW1/5484; see also Oberleutnant i. BGS Pantenius, "Einführung zum Vortrag: Der Aufstand in Warschau 1944," anlässlich der Planuntersuchung "Strassenkampf" am 25.11.1965, BArch-K, B106/83898.

to be a rigorous scrutiny of new applicants.[5] West Germany's Office of Constitutional Protection (BfV) evaluated every candidate for suitability, and all those considered for employment had to provide a clean record from their local police department. Once they had passed the initial screening, they also had to produce letters of reference from at least two citizens deemed to be "influential in public life." Nevertheless, most of these men had previously obtained similar letters, known as *Persilscheine*—literally "clean tickets"—during the denazification process. The BfV also employed former Nazi elites, and the extent to which they probed into a candidate's past is debatable, since many of those doing the probing also had problematic service records.[6]

Although some members of the early BGS tried to temper its military ethos, their efforts existed in constant tension with the authoritarian impulse reflected by a majority of its commanding officers. For many West Germans and their Allies, it was disconcerting to see armed men back in the similar uniforms, steel helmets, and barracks of the Wehrmacht. Yet for the founding "men of the first hour" the BGS represented more than just a job with a chance to earn a living. Instead, it provided them with a means to restore their dignity in the aftermath of the lost war. They could take pride in the fact that the state once again called upon and trusted them to bear arms in its defense. Their wartime experiences as soldiers and police officers militarized the BGS and set the tone for its organizational culture for years to come.

New Beginnings or More of the Same?

On March 16, 1951, with the approval of the Allied High Commission, the law establishing the BGS took effect. Although the Allied High Commission had given the Federal Republic more autonomy over its internal affairs, the Occupation Statute, reserved powers, and contractual agreements over its use of police forces remained in effect. The June 1951 contractual agreements in the police field explicitly prohibited the "revival of the para-militarization in the police forces." The Allies

---

5   On the amnesty legislation see the seminal study by Norbert Frei, *Adenauer's Germany*; on the challenges of de-Nazification see Dominik Rigoll, *Staatsschutz in Westdeutschland: Von der Entnazifizierung zur Extremistenabwehr* (Göttingen: Wallstein Verlag, 2013), 36–52.

6   Persil was a German washing detergent; Sabrina Nowack, *Sicherheitsrisiko NS-Belastung: Personalüberprüfungen im Bundesnachrichtendienst in den 1960er Jahren* (Berlin: Ch. Links, 2016), 31; See also Constantin Goschler and Michael Wala, *Keine neue Gestapo: Das Bundesamt für Verfassungsschutz und die NS-Vergangenheit* (Hamburg: Rowohlt, 2015).

believed these agreements curtailed these practices because the Federal Republic had to obtain specific approval for any BGS training or armaments of a military character.[7]

In spite of the contractual agreements, however, the Allied attempt to enforce them in the police field had mixed results. Their concerns with Soviet expansionism and their strategic goal to enlist West Germany as a partner in European defense took precedence over criticizing the BGS for its military uniforms and equipment. Moreover, Britain and the United States remained largely indifferent towards the BGS, and both nations quietly supported the idea of militarizing the civilian police as part of a preliminary rearmament. As long as they needed the Federal Republic to help defend Europe, they did little to scrutinize its civilian police forces. Besides, neither the United States nor Great Britain offered great examples of the demilitarized policing models they envisioned for postwar Germany. In the US, military veterans influenced by their own participation in counterinsurgency operations ran many of its police departments, and they incorporated these experiences to police immigrant and African American communities. Great Britain had a long legacy of paramilitary colonial policing reflected in the policing of its immigrant communities at home and the suppression of Irish independence. The French also had a poor record of policing and a legacy of violence towards immigrant communities, but remained ambivalent towards the BGS because they saw it as another German ruse to build a clandestine army.[8] The French High Commissioner, André François-Poncet, complained that members of the BGS guarding Adenauer's offices looked more like members of the Nazi Wehrmacht than police officers. He called the BGS a "Black Reichswehr"

---

7   See Allied High Commission for Germany General Committee, "Contractual Arrangements in the Police Field," GEN/P(51)18, June 15, 1951, NARA RG 466, Records of the Office of the High Commission for Germany, Office of the Executive Director, General Hays Executive Files 1949–1951, Box 1.

8   See for example, Stuart Schrader, *Badges without Borders: How Global Counterinsurgency Transformed American Policing* (Oakland: University of California Press, 2019), 216–18; Willard Oliver, *August Vollmer: the Father of American Policing* (Durham, NC: Carolina Academic Press, 2017); Caroline Elkins has recently argued that the use of police and security forces by Great Britain amounted to what she calls "legalized lawlessness"; see Caroline Elkins, *Legacy of Violence: A History of the British Empire* (New York: Knopf, 2022); on France see Connor Woodman, "The Imperial Boomerang: How France Used Colonial Methods to Massacre Algerians in Paris," Verso Books (June 18, 2020) available online at https://www.versobooks.com/blogs/news/4418-the-imperial-boomerang-how-france-used-colonial-methods-to-massacre-algerians-in-paris; see also Jim House and Neil Macmaster, *Paris 1961: Algerians, State Terror, and Memory* (Oxford: Oxford University Press, 2006).

invoking the secret rearmament campaign conducted by German army officers during the 1920s.[9]

Interior Minister Lehr had his federal police force, but now had to equip, train, and house the men selected to fill the 10,000 available positions. His immediate concern was finding a suitable leader who could be trusted to ensure that the BGS would be ready for action by July. Lehr and Adenauer had already been seeking veteran military officers for the new post and thus from the very beginning created an organization that blended the role of soldiers with police officers. On August 25, 1950, Adenauer hosted a reception at the Chancellery for Wehrmacht officers. Despite the fact that neither the BGS nor the state riot police had yet been legally established, he promised those in attendance an end to the defamation of their character, and their eligibility for employment as federal police officers. General Anton Grasser attended the reception and reflected precisely the type of leader Lehr sought to lead the BGS.[10] A decorated soldier with an extensive history of both military and police experience, Grasser fought in many of the major battles on the Western Front during the First World War. When the war ended, he briefly served as a staff officer in the Reichswehr and then joined the police in the state of Baden-Württemberg, where he served in the cities of Mannheim, Freiburg im Breisgau, and Heidelberg. He transferred from the police into the Wehrmacht during the Third Reich and led Nazi troops in combat against Soviet forces on the Eastern Front.[11]

Adenauer's former Chief of the Central Office for Homeland Defense, General Schwerin, recommended Grasser as a possible chief of the BGS. Schwerin described Grasser to Adenauer as a "jovial and democratically oriented" soldier.[12] Grasser's captured military personnel file, however, tells a much different story. In a series of performance evaluations, his superiors commented on his commitment to National Socialism. According to these evaluations, Grasser was "tried and tested

---

9 André François Poncet, *Les rapports mensuels d'André François-Poncet: Haut-Commissaire français en Allemagne, 1949–1955: Les débuts des la république fédérale d'Allemagne / puliés et annotés par Hans Manfred Bock*, Vol II (Paris: Imprimerie Nationale, 1996), 906; see also "Adenauer Sentries Early with Old German Helmets," Special to the New York Times, *New York Times*, June 4, 1952, 3.

10 Adenauer's reception is referred to in Aktennotiz Zentrale für Heimatdienst, "Rekrutierung ehemaliger Wehrmachtsangehöriger im Polizei," Planung für die Bundespolizei, BA-MA, BW 9/3106.

11 See Grasser, Anton, born November 3, 1891, "Personalakte," BA-MA, PERS 6/299743.

12 "Rekrutierung ehemaliger Wehrmachtsangehöriger im Polizei," BA-MA, BW 9/3106.

in the hardest of battles … ruthless with the enemy, and holds deep National Socialist convictions in which he educates his subordinates." Another evaluator called him "a good National Socialist."[13] After the war, he also joined the Gehlen Organization, West Germany's clandestine proto-intelligence agency. In the Gehlen Organization he helped to establish and train West German "civil war" defense forces that in case of an invasion would fight the Soviets in a guerilla war.[14] On November 11, 1950, the Interior Ministry gave him command of the BePo. In 1951, Interior Minister Lehr and State Secretary Ritter von Lex transferred him from the BePo to lead the BGS. Thus a career soldier and loyal National Socialist who planned clandestine guerila war operations took over the Federal Republic's first postwar national police force.

On May 28, 1951, Grasser organized a staff of 1800 veteran Wehrmacht officers recruited to set up the first BGS training program at Lübeck-St. Hubertus.[15] These men were supposed to be the core of a new, democratic national police force. They designed the curriculum and trained the instructors responsible for preparing the first recruits to go into service. Grasser explained to this formation staff that the BGS was a "new institution which, in terms of education and training, deliberately does not follow previous models, but tries to build up an organization that is most closely connected with the people in new ways."[16] Yet if the BGS was really supposed to be a departure from the past as Grasser proclaimed, why were all the men he chose to establish the new force veteran soldiers with combat experience? Moreover, despite the federal government's repeated claims that the BGS had a law enforcement role, the Interior Ministry failed to choose any civilian police veterans to help build the new organization because, as Lehr later argued, they were too old. The Interior Ministry appointed Ludwig Dierske, a fifty-two-year-old Prussian Schupo veteran as director of the BGS and Riot Police, but

---

13 General Schörmer, Oberkommando Heeresgruppe Nord, "Beurteilung zum General der Infanterie Anton Grasser," NARA, German Army Officer 201 Files, 1900–1945, Box 237.

14 See Dominik Rigoll, "Kampf um die innere Sicherheit," 481; Agilolf Keßelring, *Die Organisation Gehlen und die Neuformierung des Militärs in der Bundesrepublik* (Berlin: Ch. Links, 2017), 237, 244–45.

15 See commemorative brochure, "1951–1971: 20 Jahre Bundesgrenzschutz" (Bad Godesberg: Marketing Volker Stoltz, 1971), 22, BArch-K, B106/93290; Regierungsdirigent Walter Bargatzky, "Notiz für die Unterredung des Herrn Bundesministers Dr. Lehr mit dem Herrn Bundeskanzler, 19. Mai 1951: Aufbau Grenzschutz," Nachlass von Lex, Hans Ritter, N 244/23.

16 Anton Grasser, "Ausbildung der Grenzschutz-Abteilungen für die Zeit bis zum 1.10.1951," June 20, 1951, BArch-K, B106/15076.

even he had been a soldier during both World Wars.[17] Moreover, if old age really did factor into the decision to reject many police veterans, then Grasser and most of his colleagues also should have been disqualified. In fact, only seven percent of the BGS officer corps consisted of former police officers, while the rest consisted of veteran soldiers or former police officers who had combat experience with the armed forces.[18]

In truth, neither the Interior Ministry nor the men they selected to lead the BGS had any intention of abandoning militarized policing. Rather, they deliberately chose men who had combat experience and were familiar with weapons and infantry tactics, because they wanted officers who could use violence against communist forces that might attempt to foment revolution and civil war. Lehr and State Secretary von Lex certainly had options when it came to recruiting and selecting personnel. 15,000 men applied for the 600 officer-level positions and strikingly, another 50,000 men requested applications for the 9,000 regular *Grenzjäger* (border hunters) posts.[19] Yet neither Lehr nor Lex objected when Grasser chose men, who like himself, had fighting experience. Their pressing concern focused on getting the first recruits trained before the beginning of the third World Youth Festival scheduled for early August. Adenauer and his Interior Ministry worried about intelligence reports that claimed the FDJ planned to created mass disturbances during the festival in Berlin and all along the "green" or Inner-German border. The Federal Cabinet had already banned the FDJ as a subversive organization that threatened West Germany's free democratic order.[20]

On June 22, 1951, the organizational staff completed their foundational training and the men turned out for their first formal inspection on the parade grounds of the former Wehrmacht Pionier-Kaserne in Lübeck-St. Lorencz. Robert Lehr, Ritter von Lex, and several other government officials conducted the inspection. The ceremonies had all the pomp of a military parade to include the first playing of the German National Anthem—the *Deutschland Lied*—since the end of the war and before its revision to include only the third verse.[21] To an observer, it

17 Dierske fought in the First World War and served in the Luftwaffe during the Second World War; for Dierske's service record, see BA-MA, PERS 6/141778.

18 Headquarters European Command Intelligence Division, "Intelligence Summary no. 127" (December 19, 1951), Section C-6, US Army Heritage and Education Center, Carlisle Barracks, Pennsylvania; see also "Menzels Angriff auf Lehr: Sind die Grenzpolizisten Soldaten?" *FAZ*, October 23, 1951, 3.

19 Falco Werkentin, *Die Restauration der deutschen Polizei*, 92.

20 See telegram 762A.00/6-2761: Deputy High Commissioner Hays to Department of State, June 27, 1951, FRUS Vol. 3, 1951, 1776–1778.

21 The problematic phrase of the first verse associated with Nazi Germany was *Deutschland Deutschland über alles* (Germany Germany above all)—by 1952

would have appeared that the ghosts of Nazi Germany's Wehrmacht had risen from defeat and returned to their former barracks. For many candidates, the BGS provided a chance to relive the lives they had known as soldiers prior to 1945. Ulrich Freytag, a member of this first cohort, said he joined the BGS because he wanted to be a professional soldier and believed it reflected the closest thing to an army at the time. Freytag said the new troops "were practically put into the uniforms that the Wehrmacht had taken off in 1945. Not police, but military ranks with the corresponding rank insignia were introduced. The trainers were mostly seasoned Wehrmacht officers and non-commissioned officers."[22]

The Interior Ministry organized the BGS into three area command centers: North in Hannover, West in Lübeck, and South in Stadtsteinach, each led by a high-ranking military veteran. Herbert Giese, a Luftwaffe Major General and Reichswehr officer with combat experience in both world wars, commanded BGS-North; Johannes Bruhn, the commander of BGS-West, fought in both world wars and rose to the rank of Major General in the Wehrmacht. He served with the Baltic Freikorps and in 1920 transferred into Weimar Germany's state police forces. Anton Grasser, in addition to his duties as the Chief Inspector, also commanded BGS-South.[23]

Although Interior Minister Lehr answered directly to the Chancellor and the Bundestag, authority over the BGS was exercised through the office of his second in command, State Secretary Ritter von Lex. Under Lex, Hans Egidi, Director of Division VI—Public Safety, had authority over three separate federal law enforcement agencies—the BGS, the BKA, and the BfV. Egidi also served as a soldier in the First World War and worked as a civil servant in the Third Reich's Interior Ministry. After the war, he helped to found the East German branch of the Christian Democratic Party (CDU), but later fled to the Federal Republic because of a political conflict with the Soviet occupation authorities. Former Interior Minister Gustav Heinemann hired him to lead the Public Safety

---

only the third verse was sung at official functions; see Toby Thacker, *Music after Hitler* (Burlington, VT: Ashgate, 2007), 170–71.

22 Ulrich Freytag, "Warum ich Soldat wurde!" *Internationales Magazin für Sicherheit*, no. 3 (2006), 58; see also PHK Schulz, "Die Grenzschutzschule—eine "Bestandsaufnahme," *Zeitschrift des Bundesgrenzschutzes* 4, no. 5 (May 5, 1977): 4.

23 See Bruhn, Johannes, Major General, "Personal Records of Members of the Wehrmacht and Reichswehr," BA-MA, PERS 6/1138; Giese, Herbert, Major General, "Bundesgrenzschutz: Übernahme von Angehörigen in die Bundeswehr," Band 5 (1954–57), List A, Page 2, BA-MA, BW 1/5484.

Branch, and he also became involved with the Gehlen Organization after the war.[24]

By far, the veteran Wehrmacht General Gerhard Matzky had been one of the most influential leaders with direct operational control and significant influence over the early BGS. As Director of Subdivision VI B—Deployment and Training, he replaced Grasser as Chief on July 1, 1951. Grasser remained in command of BGS-South. Like his colleagues, Matzky had deep connections to Germany's authoritarian past. Born in 1894 in the Brandenburg fortress city of Küstrin on the Oder River, he enlisted in the Prussian Infantry in 1912 at the age of eighteen. He fought with Infantry Regiment 63 and suffered multiple wounds in combat on both the Eastern and Western Fronts during the First World War. In 1919, he joined *Grenzschutz Ost* (Eastern Border Guard) a Freikorps paramilitary unit engaged in the fighting against Bolshevist forces along the disputed Silesian borderlands. In 1920 the Reichswehr absorbed *Grenzschutz Ost*, and Matzky rose to the rank of Lieutenant Colonel on its General Staff. Captured German documents reveal that he took part in the Reichswehr's clandestine rearmament operations during the late 1920s and authored secret orders on behalf of then Minister of Defense Wilhelm Groener.[25]

In 1935 the National Socialist government disbanded the Reichswehr and transferred its personnel to the Wehrmacht. By then Matzky, already a career military officer and full Colonel, held a prominent post on the Nazi General Staff in Berlin. Between 1938 and 1940, he lived in Tokyo as Germany's military attaché to Japan. He returned to Berlin in 1940, was promoted to the rank of Major General, and spent the remaining war years leading troops in battle. The Soviets captured him in 1945 during heavy fighting in East Prussia, but he managed to escape to the West, where he surrendered to Allied forces. He remained in custody as a POW until 1948. During the 1950s, Matzky also joined the Association of

---

24 Egidi was arrested and released by the Soviets, but fled after he learned they were planning to re-arrest him: see Andreas Hilger, Milke Schmeitzner, and Ute Schmidt, eds., *Sowjetische Militärtribunale Band 2: Die Verurteilung deutscher Zivilisten 1945–1955* (Cologne: Böhlau, 2003), 377; Thomas Wolf, *Die Entstehung des BND: Aufbau, Finanzierung, Kontrolle* (Berlin: Ch. Links, 2018), 194–95.

25 For Matzky's personnel file, see BA-MA, PERS 6/302472; on his role in 1920s secret rearmament program, see "Notiz aus dem Vortrag bei Herrn Amtschef vom 8/7/1929: Vorbereitung der vorhandenen schwarzen Maschinenbestände für spätere Verwendung," in the Political Intelligence Department of the Foreign Office, "German Secret Rearmament: 1924–33," World War II Occupation Papers, Box 80A, Folder 8, Political Intelligence Department, German, US Army Heritage and Education Center, Carlisle Barracks, Pennsylvania.

Figure 2.1. General Gerhard Matzky, far left, future leader of the BGS, during a 1941 military advisory conference with Adolf Hitler; also pictured are General Wilhelm Keitel, Finnish General Harald Oehquvist, and Nazi Foreign Minister Joachim von Ribbentrop. Courtesy of the United States Holocaust Memorial Museum, Photo no. 50990.

German Soldiers (*Verband deutscher Soldaten*—VdS) and later became its president from 1965 to 1978.[26]

While the first members of the organizational staff completed their foundational training, the Interior Ministry separately established a marine component of the BGS, the *Seegrenzschutz*. The new seagoing force functioned like a naval flotilla patrolling West Germany's rivers and coastal regions.[27] Like their land-based colleagues, members of the Seegrenzschutz came exclusively from the ranks of veteran Nazi personnel, in their case from the navy. Most of the naval veterans assigned to the new force had also been employed by the British in postwar minesweeping operations. These former sailors attracted the attention of the

26 Gerhard Matzky, "Korrespondence 1951–1983," BA-MA, N 181/6 Bd. 2; on the VdS see James M. Diehl, *The Thanks of the Fatherland: German Veterans after the Second World War* (Chapel Hill: University of North Carolina Press, 1993), 210; Thomas Kühne, *The Rise and Fall of Comradeship*, 230.

27 Robert Lehr, "Aufgaben des Seegrenzschutz," N 244/23, Nachlass Robert Lehr.

Allies while working on postwar operational histories for the US Naval Historical Team (NHT). The United States Office of Naval Intelligence established the NHT in 1949 to evaluate Germany's naval performance during the war. Based on NHT recommendations, the Interior Ministry selected former U-Boat Captain Fritz Poske to organize, train, and lead the *Seegrenzschutz*. Poske was a U-Boat ace who sank 78,123 tons of Allied shipping during the war and later piloted Hitler's private yacht the "Aviso Grille." Poske and his staff built up a marine force of 500 men organized into three flotillas with eighteen boats. In 1956, the Ministry of Defense took over the *Seegrenzschutz* with all of its personnel and boats to build the new West German Navy, the *Bundesmarine*. In 1964, the BGS reestablished its own marine unit to patrol the Federal Republic's coastal waters and inland rivers.[28]

We Wanted Police but You Gave Us Soldiers!

The rapid build-up of the BGS with its military structure and personnel upset leading members of West Germany's SPD. The federal government and the men they had chosen to lead the new force focused on fighting communists rather than enforcing laws. After learning of the parade ceremonies in Lübeck and the veteran Wehrmacht officers leading the BGS, SPD leader Kurt Schumacher accused Robert Lehr of trying to remilitarize the Federal Republic. Schumacher, a disabled combat veteran of the Great War and an outspoken critic of National Socialism, spent the war years in concentration camps.[29] It was the blending of military with policing duties in the BGS that worried Schumacher. He and other lawmakers feared that the veteran Wehrmacht officers in charge of it would try to use it as a clandestine army. Schumacher called the BGS command staff "military surrogates" and complained that the appointment of Gerhard Matzky to lead the force was a "Wilhelmine military gimmick." He told reporters that "what started out as a police force should not end up as a military force."[30]

On July 19, 1951, Schumacher, Lex, and Lehr met in Bonn to discuss their differences. During the meeting, Lehr and Ritter von Lex

---

28 Fritz Poske, *Der Seegrenzschutz, 1951–1956: Erinnerung, Bericht, Dokumentation* (Munich: Bernard & Graefe, 1982), 30; see also Bundesministers des Innern, "1951–1971: 20-Jahre Bundesgrenzschutz," 34.

29 Tony Judt, *Postwar: A History of Europe since 1945* (New York: Penguin, 2005), 268; Adam Seipp, "A Reasonable Yes: The Social Democrats and West German Rearmament, 1945–56," in James S. Corum, *Rearming Germany* (Leiden: Brill, 2022), 55.

30 Staff, "Schumacher: Die Bedingung fehlt noch: Oppositionsführer gegen militärische Stellvertreter," *FAZ*, July 14, 1951, 1.

denied that they had secretly planned to remilitarize the Federal Republic. The BGS, they argued, was a police force modeled after the paramilitary Italian Carabinieri and Japanese mobile police forces. Lehr's comparison did not satisfy Schumacher, however, since both the Japanese and Italian models he described were the same type of militarized counterinsurgency forces that West Germany's postwar lawmakers wanted to avoid.[31] Lehr claimed the BGS stood to defend the liberal-democratic order of the Federal Republic and could only be deployed domestically "against large revolutionary actions such as mass union strikes."[32] This is precisely what worried the SPD, however, since the Nazis had effectively used paramilitary police forces like the SA and SS as instruments of terror to crush their political opponents. During the Third Reich, the Nazis banned the SPD and violently targeted its members and imprisoned others without cause in concentration camps.[33]

Gerhard Matzky also defended his force and argued that he could "Categorically state that all the rumors which indicate the border police is a precursor to a new German Wehrmacht are politically motivated and incorrect. Every civilized country in the world has one serving police force for internal security. The BGS is nothing else, its main task is to defend the borders."[34] Yet West Germany already had more than one agency watching its borders. Moreover, privately, Matzky expressed the exact opposite point of view, telling his good friend retired General Heinz Guderian that "At the BGS we have always taken the straight path that our soldierly feelings dictate to us, and we do not intend to deviate from it, even if here and there tendentious criticism is leveled at it."[35]

Despite the Interior Ministry's descriptions of the BGS as a police force, its activities fit more in line with the "soldierly" ethos Matzky described to Guderian. Evidence of this surfaced in July and August 1951, when the federal government sent the BGS to counter the FDJ at the Inner-German border in the weeks leading up to the Third World Youth Festival in East Berlin. As a propaganda stunt, the festival's antimilitarist theme aimed to show off the German Democratic Republic (GDR) as the more peaceful of the two postwar states. Most of the FDJ

31 David H. Bayley, *Patterns of Policing: A Comparative International Analysis* (New Brunswick, NJ: Rutgers University Press, 1985), 238; Thomas French, *National Police Reserve: The Origins of Japan's Self Defense Forces* (Leiden: Brill, 2014), 125.
32 Staff, "Der BGS als Bundespolizei: Innenminister erklärt keine geheime Remilitarisierung. Bericht von unseren Korrespondenten," *FAZ*, July 20, 1951, 3.
33 Donna Harsch, *German Social Democracy and the Rise of Nazism* (Chapel Hill: University of North Carolina Press, 1993), 228–29.
34 Staff, "Unmilitaristisches BGS," *FAZ*, August 4, 1951, 3.
35 Private Letter from Gerhard Matzky to Heinz Guderian, June 9, 1954, Correspondence of Gerhard Matzky, BA-MA, N 181/6, Bd. 6, G thru H.

Figure 2.2. BGS members preparing for field exercises, 1954. David Douglas Duncan Life Magazine Collection, University of Texas at Austin, Harry Ransom Center

activities took place in Berlin, but its members also planned mass crossings along the unsecured Inner-German border. From the perspective of the Interior Ministry's Security Branch, the People's Police and Soviets planned to send FDJ "guides" to escort West German teens to the festivities in Berlin. Intelligence estimates claimed that anywhere from 10 to 20,000 youth might storm the border.[36]

To a certain extent, West German responses towards the FDJ reflected what sociologists have identified as a moral panic. In this case, the panic underscored the government's fears that communist agitators might corrupt or even worse, turn West German teens against the state. In his classic study the sociologist Stanley Cohen defined a moral panic as a case in which a "condition, episode, person or group of persons emerges to become defined as a threat to societal values and interests" to the extent that "moral barricades are manned by editors, bishops, politicians and other right-thinking people." The FDJ with its campaign against rearmament precisely fit the type of organization that West German conservatives saw as a threat to their societal values. Building on the work of Cohen, Kenneth Thompson argued that "no age group is

---

36 See Durchschlag für Bundesgrenzschutz: Bundesministerium des Inneren, Geheim: "Grenzübergang bei den Weltjugendfestspielen," June 20, 1951, BArch-K, B 106/15179.

more associated with risk in the public imagination than that of youth."[37] Some officials believed that FDJ operatives undermined the Federal Republic's sovereignty by attempting to lure West German teens across the border. Thus the government sent the BGS as both a physical and moral barricade aimed to defend its conservative social order. Adenauer frequently employed the metaphor of barriers or dams against the physical and ideological threat of communism. In a 1951 letter to Allied High Commissioner John J. McCloy, for example, Adenauer explained that "Russia has been pursuing an imperialist policy of conquest for hundreds of years" and "that it is necessary to erect a permanent dam against Soviet Russia, otherwise it will dominate all of Europe."[38]

General Matzky sent 13 border police *Hundertschaften* (100-man companies) to confront the FDJ activists. In addition to the BGS, the Bavarian Border Police, the BfV, the US Army Constabulary, the *Zoll* and state police forces also took part. The West German press described the operation as an elaborate game of "cat and mouse," but border police officers deployed to the border had pistols, rifles, and submachineguns. By sending the BGS, the government introduced a militarized response to what essentially amounted to a youth protest action. Matzky, however, issued explicit orders that the use of weapons should be avoided at all costs unless in an emergency situation or for self-defense. As the leader of the organization, his behavior and the example he set carried significant weight. The outcome of the operation depended upon it. In this case, his tone and words of caution promoted a culture of restraint for those under his command and this stood in contrast to the lawmakers and critics who worried that sending former soldiers to deal with teens might lead to dangerous consequences.[39] Still, the deployment of 1300 heavily armed men trained for combat in armored vehicles seemed like an overreaction, since these duties could have been handled more appropriately by existing customs and state police forces. More likely, such a response reflected the new government's deep fears of communism combined with the Interior Ministry's desire to prove or justify a need for the force.

During the operation, BGS units intercepted and detained hundreds of teens crossing into and out of the Federal Republic in public trains,

---

37 Stanley Cohen, *Folk Devils and Moral Panics: The Creation of the Mods and Rockers*, 3rd (New York: Routledge, 2002), 1; Kenneth Thompson, *Moral Panics* (New York: Routledge, 1998), 43–44.

38 Konrad Adenauer to High Commissioner John J. McCloy, no. 44, June 7, 1951 in Konrad Adenauer and Hans-Peter Mensing, *Briefe, 1951–1953* (Berlin: Siedler, 1987), 64–70.

39 See "An der heißen grünen Grenze: Kinder in der Frontlinie des kalten Krieges, *Der Stern* 4, August 1, 1951, 4–5; telegram from Matzky to GSK-West, "Maßnahmen aus Anlaß der Weltjugendfestspiele in Berlin," July 19, 1951, BArch-K, B 106/15179.

buses, and on foot. The majority of the teens detained came from World Youth Festival events and ultimately got sent back home. The BGS interrogated anyone suspected of membership in the FDJ and sent them back across the border into East Germany. Hundreds of West German teenagers got caught attempting to cross the border, but the Interior Ministry estimated another 30 to 40 percent eluded the BGS.[40] While border police officers found no direct evidence of involvement by armed members of the People's Police, they did seize large amounts of communist propaganda material in the form of leaflets and other FDJ literature. Although the activities took place without any major acts of violence or injury, the press criticized the BGS for the use of what they called "military style tactics" to round up the teenagers and sarcastically referred to the new force as "Adenauer's private army."[41]

Further evidence that the BGS did not carry out the policing duties it had been supposedly established to enforce was reflected by the Interior Ministry's efforts to transfer its responsibility for passport control—one of the fundamental legal justifications for its creation. After the war and during the military occupation, a confusing array of federal, state, and local agencies screened passports in West Germany. In Bavaria, for example, its independent state border police handled this task, while the Hanseatic Marine Police handled screening in Hamburg, Bremen, and Bremerhaven. In other regions, the *Zoll* checked passports. In some cases, cross-border travelers had to present their documents to both state and federal officers. Municipal police forces also screened passengers arriving at some West German airports and train stations. Yet with the passage of the first BGS law in 1951, these duties supposedly became its sole responsibility. Instead of consolidating the function under the BGS, however, the Interior Ministry looked for alternatives that would not affect its staffing levels. The effort to transfer these duties to a separate agency as outlined in a series of secret memorandums underscores how typical border policing duties became a secondary concern or nuisance for those who led the BGS.[42]

State Secretary Ritter von Lex, who pleaded in 1950 with Finance Minister Fritz Schäffer to help him justify a new federal police force under the pretext of enhancing border security (see chapter 1), now attempted to find a way to shirk these duties. Lex and members of his staff Fritz Schuchardt, Walter Bargatzky, and Hans Egidi discussed forming a separate Federal Passport Control Office in order that the duties of checking

40 "Illegale Grenzgänger nach Ost-Berlin," *FAZ*, July 3, 1951, 2.
41 See for example, "Polizeitruppe oder neue Wehrmacht," *Franken Morgen Post*, August 25, 1951, BArch-K, B 106/15179.
42 Passkontrolldirektion Koblenz, December 19, 1955, "Geschichte des Bundespaßkontrolldienstes," BArch-K, B 273/33.

passports could be separated from the BGS. The Bavarians, however, rejected this plan. According to Bargatzky, the BGS was supposed to deal with "mass" crossings like those of the FDJ and argued "it would therefore be important to split up the BGS as little as possible by patrol or other duties."[43] By "other duties" he meant passport screening. Karl Riedl, head of the Bavarian Border Guard, accused the Interior Ministry of violating the Basic Law and threatened to bring the matter before the Federal Republic's Constitutional Court. Bavaria's politicians rejected any policies that might undermine their autonomy in West Germany's federalist system. Riedl also worried that the Federal Government might try to disband his state police force and absorb its personnel into the BGS.[44]

On September 19, 1951, State Secretary von Lex decided to go ahead and form a separate Federal Passport Control Office within the BGS, but only for the major border crossings into West Germany. With this approach, he left the Bavarian Border Police intact and thus avoided a constitutional conflict. The new Federal Passport Office only had jurisdiction at six major crossings—Flensburg, Idar-Oberstein, Braunschweig, Kehl, Konstanz, and Hamburg.[45] Thus instead of ensuring the BGS carried out the policing role for which it was created, the Interior Ministry transferred these duties to other state and federal agencies. The policy allowed border police officers to remain in barracks ready to respond and put down a communist uprising or an attack by the East German People's Police. It reinforced the complaint by critics that the Interior Ministry intended to use the force for military rather than law enforcement duties.

While the Interior Ministry dealt with its passport control dilemma, the behavior and misconduct of some border police officers brought negative publicity. On September 3, 1951, a group of seven officers based at the Sigfried Barracks in Braunschweig spent the afternoon and early evening drinking in the local canteen. According to press reports, the men got drunk after consuming several cases of beer and numerous bottles of schnapps. At some point during the evening, they began singing the Nazi Horst Wessel Song.[46] One of the men also proclaimed his devotion

---

43   Memorandum from Freiherr von Wolff to Ministerialrat Fritz Schuchardt: 1215 C—346 III/51, April 5, 1951, pp. 2–3, BArch-K, B 273/30.

44   Ministerialrat Fritz Schuchardt, "Gründe für die Einrichtung einer unabhängigen Passkontrollstelle im Gebiet der Bundesrepublik Deutschland," 5. April 1951, BArch-K, B 273/30.

45   Memorandum from Staatssekretär Ritter von Lex to Bundes- und Landesbehörden, Betreff: Bundespasskontrolldienst, 6215 A—2486 I/51, September 19, 1951, BArch-K, B 273/30.

46   Horst Wessel was an SA leader who was murdered by a Communist in 1930. He became a martyr for the Nazi cause—he wrote the song "Raise the Flag," which after his murder was sung along with the national anthem and was popularly known as the Horst Wessel-Lied (song); see Daniel Siemens, *The*

to the neo-Nazi SRP. Local residents overheard the singing and drunken behavior and promptly reported it to the office of the public prosecutor. Soon reporters from the local newspaper learned of the incident and ran it as a headline on the front page of the morning edition. Similar cases of drunken behavior and the singing of Nazi songs by BGS members took place at barracks in Bonn and Brunswick. The Interior Ministry launched an immediate investigation into these embarrassing episodes and disciplined all the men involved.[47] Although the behavior followed bouts of heavy drinking, in each case the drunken revelry involved singing National Socialist anthems.

In October 1951 Adenauer caused another stir when he replaced the regular Nordrhein-Westfalen police officers assigned to guard his Chancellery with a special BGS watch battalion. Bundestag Deputy Walter Menzel had already criticized Adenauer for trying to create a paramilitary palace guard in 1950 (see chapter 1). This time the complaint came from Heinrich von Brentano (CDU), a Bundestag deputy from his own party. Brentano had been a member of the Nazi Party, but believed Adenauer's use of BGS units to guard his offices went too far. He believed the Chancellor handed the SPD a political wedge to use against conservatives in the Bundestag. Brentano complained about the uniforms and Wehrmacht steel helmets worn by members of the watch battalion, which he compared to a "Prussian praetorian guard." He told Lehr that stationing the militarized BGS at the Palais Schaumburg looked ridiculous and requested that he reassign these security duties to the regular state police who, according to Brentano, had always done a good job protecting the Chancellor's offices.[48] Brentano's suggestion did not reach the Chancellor before Menzel and the State Interior Minister of Nordrhein-Westfalen, Dr. Adolf Flecken, publicly accused Adenauer of circumventing the law.[49]

As Brentano warned, the SPD politicized the situation and began sarcastically referring to the BGS as "Die Lehrmacht." Yet neither Lehr nor Adenauer made any attempt to follow von Brentano's suggestions. In a later article about Adenauer's watch battalion that appeared in the BGS professional journal *Die Parole*, the author reported: "A few weeks ago,

---

Making of a Nazi Hero: The Murder and Myth of Horst Wessel (London: I. B. Tauris, 2009).

47 "Bundesgrenzschutz: Ein Kasten Bier," *Der Spiegel* 5, no.37, 13–14.

48 Letter from Dr. Heinrich von Brentano to Lehr, October 12, 1951, BArch-K, B 136/1929, Fiche no. 3, slides 74–75.

49 Kleine Anfrage Nr. 67 des Abgeordneten Dr. Menzel (SPD), Betreffend: Ablösung der Polizeibeamten von der Bewachung des Bundeskanzleramtes, Drucksache Nr. 67, Landtag Nordrhein-Westfalen—2. Wahlperiode—Band 3, BArch-K, B 136/1929; Letter from Adolf Flecken to Konrad Adenauer, October 15, 1951, BArch-K, B 136/1929 Fiche 1, slide 78.

the police posts that had previously guarded the gates were replaced by a larger number of border hunters, strengthening what had previously been weak security measures."[50] This followed Adenauer's repeated claims that state police forces were too weak. Flecken, however, disagreed, and Menzel demanded that Lehr and Adenauer be publicly censured. According to Menzel, Adenauer violated the Basic Law by stationing BGS forces in West Germany's interior, far from the borders that they were supposed to be patrolling. Moreover, Flecken reminded Lehr that Article 73 of the Basic Law made policing an exclusive duty of the Federal Republic's states. Lehr countered that since the BGS was motorized, it made no difference where they were stationed because they could rapidly move to problem areas along the frontiers as needed. He also claimed that the measure was only a temporary solution until the duties could be taken over by the state riot police. Yet neither Lehr nor any of his successors at the Interior Ministry ever followed through with this claim and the matter fell by the wayside.[51]

With the drunken behavior in Braunschweig and other cities, parades in Lübeck, and controversy over Adenauer's watch battalion, the SPD had seen enough. On October 10, 1951, Interior Minister Lehr appeared before the Bundestag to address their concerns. Walter Menzel accused Lehr of militarizing what was supposed to be a police force and proclaimed:

> Article 87 allowed for the establishment of border control authorities to handle passport control, but what have you made of it? A barracked police force! And now, as far as passport control is concerned, nobody in the federal government cares! What would members of the parliamentary council say today if they knew that your definition of border protection meant ten thousand or more quartered troops? I think they would have preferred to derail the entire constitution and thus the ongoing integration of the three western zones instead of accepting it. Why do we have a constitution, and what would be the gain from the disposal of National Socialism, when in

---

50 Inge Randolf, "Wachablösung im Palais Schaumburg," *Die Parole* 2, no. 1 (January 1, 1952): 7.

51 Kleine Anfrage Nr. 67 des Abgeordneten Dr. Menzel (SPD), Betreffend: Ablösung der Polizeibeamten von der Bewachung des Bundeskanzleramtes, Drucksache Nr. 67, Landtag Nordrhein-Westfalen—2. Wahlperiode—Band 3, BArch-K, B 136/1929 Fiche no. 3, Slide 78; for Lehr's temporary solution claim see his confidential notes, "Notizen für eine Pressekonferenz des Herrn Staatssekretärs I über die Angriffe des Abgeordneten Dr. Menzel gegen den Bundesgrenzschutz," N 244/23, Nachlaß, Lehr, Robert.

the presence of alleged necessities the constitution can be pushed aside at any time?[52]

Lehr acknowledged the embarrassing incidents in Braunschweig and Bonn, but denied they reflected deeper patterns of misconduct or clandestine right-wing behavior by the majority of his officers. He reminded the deputies of the recent performance by the BGS in dealing with the FDJ. He claimed that he disciplined all of those involved in what he called "drunken affairs" and demoted their commanding officers. He reassured the Bundestag that he would "emphatically eliminate these personnel so long as there must be trust in the relationship between you [Bundestag Deputies] and me."[53]

Although Menzel had no problem publicly criticizing Lehr, he did not push too far, because he feared conservatives might accuse the SPD of pro-communist sympathies. As Michael Hughes has argued, "Anti-communism, often presented as anti-totalitarianism, was a particularly powerful force in West German politics." And, Eric Weitz has suggested that Adenauer, "… was able throughout the 1950s to depict the social democrats as the party that would open the gates for the communists."[54] Thus SPD delegates tried at all costs to avoid falling into political traps in which conservatives might accuse them of being sympathetic towards communism. To avoid this accusation, Menzel wrote an open letter to the BGS that the editors of *Die Parole* published in their January 1952 edition.[55] He reminded readers that he and other members of his party called for a centralized national police force during the framing of the Federal Republic's Basic Law, which the Allied authorities rejected. He explained that he never intended to disparage the BGS or its personnel and would "continue to advocate strong and impeccable border protection" for the Federal Republic.[56]

---

52 Deutsche Bundestag, 166 Sitzung, October 10, 1951, 6783–6784.
53 Deutsche Bundestag, 166 Sitzung, 6787–6788.
54 Michael L. Hughes, *Embracing Democracy in Modern Germany: Political Citizenship and Participation, 1871–2000* (London: Bloomsbury Academic, 2021), 91; Eric D. Weitz, "The Ever Present Other: Communism in the Making of West Germany," in *The Miracle Years: A Cultural History of West Germany, 1949–1968*, ed. Hanna Schissler (Princeton, NJ: Princeton University Press, 2001), 220; see also Patrick Major, *The Death of the KPD: Communism and Anti-Communism in West Germany, 1945–1956* (Oxford: Clarendon, 1998), 44.
55 Menzel, Walter, "Dr. Menzel (SPD) schreibt an Die Parole," *Die Parole* 2, no. 1 (January 1, 1952): 18
56 Ibid.

Operation Martha: Fighting West Germany's Coffee Wars

In spite of repeated attempts by Lehr, Adenauer, and other officials to describe the BGS as a law enforcement agency, the actions and behavior of its personnel consistently reflected military themes. Border police officers acted like soldiers and the organization they served remained at its core a quasi-military rather than a police force. Evidence of this emerged when the Interior Ministry sent it to reinforce the *Zoll* during its campaign against coffee smuggling on West Germany's Belgian-Dutch frontier. Under the codename "Operation Martha," the Interior Ministry sent two BGS divisions from Lübeck under the command of Major Kurt Andersen to help interdict the notorious "Rabatzer" smuggling bands. Orders instructed the BGS to "paralyze" smuggling in the region during the busy period leading up to the Christmas holiday. Overall authority for the operation, however, remained with the *Zoll*.[57]

The smugglers had been using the rural frontier trails and paths to sneak Belgian coffee and other luxury goods to West Germans, who could thus obtain them tax free. The Ministry of Finance estimated that black marketeering in the region cost the Federal Republic about 400 million DM in lost tax revenue per year.[58] The smugglers had won the respect and admiration of their German customers for delivering the goods that they desired but could not otherwise afford. The towns and villages in the Eifel Forest region near Aachen still suffered from the widespread damage caused by the heavy fighting on Germany's western front during the war's final months. Even the priests at St. Hubertus Church in Nideggen assisted the smugglers because they filled their coffers with the funds to rebuild their badly damaged church, later referred to by the nickname

---

57 The name "Martha" was used because the staging area was located at Camp Martha in the Wahnerheide Forest; see Interior Minister Lehr to Major Andersen, Grenzschutz-Kommando West, "Unternehmen Martha," October 12, 1951; Lehr to Andersen, "Verlegung auf den Truppe Übungsplatz Wahnerheide, Übungslager Martha," October 15, 1951, BArch-K, B 106/15183; The root of the name "Rabatzer" is not certain. In German "Rabatzer" translates as "Discounter." According to an article in *Der Spiegel*, the name was allegedly linked to a Polish displaced person called "Rabatz" who like the Dickensian character "Fagin" corrupted children by teaching them to become criminals—in this case, by organizing them into smuggling columns. See "Rabatz-Bande: Marianne an der Grenze," *Der Spiegel* 38, September 18, 1951, 26.

58 Grenzschutz-Kommando West an den Bundesministerium des Innern, "Einsatz von Einheiten des BGS zur Bekämpfung von Schmugglerbanden im Raum von Marienberg—Aachen—Losheim—Trier," BArch-K, B 106/15183.

"Saint Mocha."[59] People in the Eifel took advantage of the lucrative black-market trade. Customs officials not only had to contend with smugglers, but also with the local residents who supported and concealed them. Black marketeering thrived in this region to such an extent that the press began calling the German-Belgian frontier the "Coffee Border."

By 1951 the high demand for Belgian coffee produced what could best be described as a "coffee war." The trade in illicit coffee even crossed into popular culture and featured as the subject of West German filmmaker Robert A. Stemmle's 1951 crime noir film, *Die sündige Grenze* (Sinful/Illegal Border).[60] The film highlighted how smugglers enticed children and teens to act as coffee runners because they were fast on their feet, they could be easily hidden and the *Zoll* officials were reluctant to search them. Thus the government perceived the smugglers like the FDJ—as a moral threat to West German society. Not only did the gangs violate the Federal Republic's sovereignty and undermine its economy, but they also corrupted young West Germans by enlisting them to help commit their crimes. When the magazine *Der Spiegel* interviewed Stemmle about his film, he emphasized that his depiction of the fight against the smugglers "should be understood as a social indictment" of postwar West German society, because the border residents allowed their weaknesses for goods to corrupt their own children by turning them into criminals.[61] Stemmle's point reflected the widespread unease among West Germans about juvenile delinquency linked to the social consequences of the lost war with its fatherless families, rising divorce rates, and poverty. The film also contained a moral lesson or warning in its main character, Marianne Mertens, portrayed as a decent working-class girl easily seduced by the Rabatzer gang leader. Her desire for nice clothing ultimately ruined Marianne's future, because she compromised her values in exchange for luxury goods and material well-being.[62]

Major Kurt Andersen took command of all BGS forces sent to the region and established his headquarters near the city of Aachen. Designated as *Einsatzstab Andersen* (Task Force Andersen), the two divisions travelled like an army to their staging area in large convoys that included mobile field kitchens and telecommunications trucks. The top-secret operational plan sent by Matzky to Andersen read more like

59 Harald Jähner, *Aftermath: Life in the Fallout of the Third Reich, 1945–1955* (New York: Knopf, 2022), 179.
60 Angelica Fenner, *Race Under Reconstruction in German Cinema: Robert Stemmle's Toxi* (Toronto: University of Toronto Press, 2011), 44.
61 "Rabatz-Bande: Marianne an der Grenze," *Der Spiegel* 38, Sept. 8, 1951, 26.
62 "Rabatz-Bande," 26; see also Edward Ross Dickinson, *The Politics of German Child Welfare from the Empire to the Federal Republic* (Cambridge, MA: Harvard University Press, 1996), 250.

a military order of battle than a law enforcement operation to interdict smuggling and property crimes. Andersen and a small staff travelled to Aachen in civilian clothes and in unmarked vehicles ahead of the main force to preserve complete secrecy.[63] The men assigned to Operation Martha deployed to their assignments with rifles, pistols, and machine guns. To the BGS, the Rabatzer, whom they called "bandits," resembled partisans being hidden by the local population who could only be caught if the border hunters set ambushes. Moreover, Andersen ordered his men assigned to approach conditions in the operational area in the same way they had handled security in "partisan areas" during the war. Using similar language, Major Andersen described the coffee border to reporters as "a magnet for all sorts of riffraff and professional criminals who want to recklessly and brutally make money."[64]

The comparison of smugglers to partisans contradicted orders issued by other authorities with jurisdiction over the operational area. The Federal Finance Minister, for example, gave explicit orders that to avoid border incidents, the BGS "should in no case be deployed at a distance of less than two kilometers from a 'safety zone' established at a depth of three kilometers from the current customs border."[65] In any case, the *Zoll* still had jurisdiction when enforcing customs laws, and they did not want the militarized BGS to cause any incidents that might jeopardize their cooperative relationships with their colleagues on the Dutch-Belgian side of the border. Major Andersen's command staff also issued specific rules of engagement that covered the circumstances in which a border police officer could use force. Like Matzky's orders concerning the use of weapons against members of the FDJ, the orders for dealing with smugglers emphasized restraint. The orders explained that smugglers rarely perpetrated violent acts. Unless otherwise authorized, only those on duty and engaged in patrol activities carried weapons. Commanders emphasized safety and discouraged careless or negligent handling of weapons.

---

63 Memorandum from Matzky to Andersen, VI B 2—Nr. 686/51, Streng Geheim, "Unternehmen Martha," October 12, 1951, BArch-K, B 106/15183; Einsatzstab Andersen, Br. B. Nr. 696/51, "Marschbefehl für dem Marsch aus dem Rastraum Hangelar in den Einsatzraum am 1. Januar 1952," December 30, 1951, BArch-K, B 106/15183.

64 Grenzschutz-Kommando West an den Bundesministerium des Innern, "Einsatz von Einheiten des BGS zur Bekämpfung von Schmugglerbanden im Raum von Marienberg—Aachen—Losheim—Trier," BArch-K, B 106/15183; "Jäger jagen Schmüggler: Einsatz an der Kaffee Grenze," *Die Parole* 2, no. 1 (January 1, 1952): 5; "Nylons, Schokalade, Zigaretten: Den Illegalen saust der Frak," *Die Parole* 2, no. 2 (February 1, 1952): 4.

65 Bundesminister der Finanzen an die Oberfinanzdirektionen Köln und Koblenz, "Unternehmen Martha zur Schmuggelbekämpfung: Besprechung am October 31, 1951 in Aachen," III 0 3055-22/51, BArch-K, B 106/15183.

Moreover, the guiding principle for the use of force dictated that it was, "better for a smuggler with coffee to escape than for an innocent person to be hurt."[66] Here again, the internal struggle between continuity and change exposed the inherent contradictions and problems that overshadowed militarized policing. Thus on the one hand Major Andersen could tell his officers in the field to treat smugglers and those that harbored them like partisans, while on the other hand, officials at the Interior and Finance Ministries preached restraint. How was a young border police officer supposed to interpret these divergent attitudes? This is precisely the problem that occurs when blending what should be law enforcement duties with military operational tactics.

In a short time Andersen's units, with their advantages in manpower and equipment, began disrupting the smugglers to an extent they had never experienced when dealing with the *Zoll*. In the first fourteen days of the deployment, the BGS arrested 245 smugglers and seized 4600 kilos of coffee. They also collected tea, cocoa, chocolate, and cigarettes along with twelve vehicles, seven bicycles, and 90,000 Deutsche Marks. Andersen proudly told reporters that the "paralysis of smuggling is noticeable, and the hunters—a little proud and also a bit disappointed at the same time complain that now there is nothing more going on. Initially, not a day passed without large seizures, but now the devilish smugglers have adjusted and become more cautious."[67] By the end of November, the BGS added a further 719 arrests, 5,802 kilos of coffee, and 14,405 cartons of cigarettes. The lists of items confiscated by Andersen's men varied from the basics needed for everyday life such as butter, women's nylon stockings, men's razors, and detergent, to expensive jewelry, cash, vehicles, and even horses. By far, the lists of arrested persons consisted mainly of local residents, but they also included foreign nationals, displaced persons, and Allied personnel.[68]

Before long, border residents began feeling the pressure of the BGS operation as the flow of items they depended on began to slow. On November 9, 1951, the Interior Minister of Nordrhein-Westfalen Dr. Adolf Flecken lodged a formal complaint against the BGS on behalf of the residents of Ruhrberg, a small border village in the district of Monschau. According to the complaint, in the early morning hours of November 3, the BGS roused the villagers from their beds and forced them from their homes in order to accommodate 80 border police officers. Flecken

---

66 Führungsstab West: Unternehmen Martha, "Einsatzanweisung für das Unternehmen Martha II," December 20, 195, BArch-K, B 106/15183.
67 "Jäger jagen Schmüggler," *Die Parole 2*, no. 5 (May 1, 1952).
68 Einsatzstab Andersen to the Interior Minister, Memo Nr. 403/51, "Erfolgsübersicht 'Unternehmen Martha' für die Zeit vom 3.–30. November, 1951," BArch-K, B 106/15183.

explained that the population had already suffered many hardships during the war, but had never been expelled from their homes and forced out into the cold.[69] Lehr immediately ordered an investigation. In summary, no evidence could be found to substantiate the allegations as conveyed in Flecken's complaint. Ruhrberg's Mayor Johann Meder explained that residents might have been disturbed by the BGS trucks arriving in the village, but he denied that anyone had been forced from their home. Meder said that he found accommodations for the men over a period of several days in local barns, homes, and businesses. In all likelihood, some of the residents resented the presence of the BGS because of their effectiveness against the smugglers and thus embellished the story of the men displacing them from their homes.[70]

In another incident, a resident from Aachen complained that a joint *Zoll*-BGS patrol illegally detained his wife, roughed her up and slapped her in the face resulting in injuries. The man wrote about the incident in a letter to the editor published by the local newspaper.[71] He claimed that his wife had been returning home from a visit to her sister and decided to buy a kilogram of coffee when the patrol stopped her. The woman admitted to having the coffee and gave it to the officials. The members of the patrol believed she might still be concealing coffee and attempted to escort her to a nearby inn for a strip-search. When she refused to go along, the officers forcibly pushed her to the ground and punched her in the face causing visible injuries. In his letter, the man stated: "My wife offered only passive resistance … she is not a smuggler but has been employed in the same position in the textile industry for a good salary for many years. We are not criminals here in Aachen, so such methods are inappropriate."[72]

Major Andersen ordered his staff to investigate the man's claims and reported the results to the Interior Ministry.[73] The investigation, however, focused exclusively on the statement provided by the lone BGS member of the patrol, Peter B. He claimed that he and the others believed that the woman still had concealed coffee and attempted to escort her

69 Letter from Dr. Adolf Flecken to Interior Minister Dr. Robert Lehr, "Schmuggelbekämpfungsaktion im Grenzgebiet," November 9, 1951, BArch-K, B 106/15183.

70 Investigative Report from BGS-West to Einsatzstab Andersen (Aachen), "Unterbringung Ruhrberg," November 16, 1951; Letter from Burgermeister Meder to BGS-West, November 16, 1951, BArch-K, B 106/15183.

71 Caspar Knorr, "Faustschläge ins Gesicht: Zollübergriffe gegenüber einer Frau!" *Aachener Volkszeitung*, Leser an die AVZ (February 5, 1952).

72 Ibid.

73 Einsatzstab Andersen an den Bundesministerium des Innern, Br. B Nr. 388/52, "Zeitungsausschnitt der Aachener Volkszeitung vom Feb. 5, 1952: Ohne Vorgang," February 5, 1952, BArch-K, B 106/15183.

to a location where a female attendant could perform a strip search. He said that the woman resisted by grabbing onto a fence and fell to the ground after one of the *Zoll* officers tried to pry her hand free. Once on the ground, the woman began screaming. The officer told interrogators that when the *Zoll* officer tried to use what he described as a "police hold" to get her off of the ground, she bit his hand and he slapped her in the face. Without speaking to the woman or the *Zoll* officers, the investigator accepted Peter B's version of the events and reported to Andersen that the BGS had no responsibility for the woman's injuries. Andersen's staff put very little effort into the case and did not take the man's claims seriously, as evidenced by Andersen reporting the results to the Interior Ministry on the same day that the article first appeared. Thus, instead of doing a thorough investigation, the officer in charge accepted the narrative of events as given by Peter B. and dropped the matter.[74]

One of the more embarrassing incidents involving the use of firearms by the BGS also took place despite the Interior Ministry's emphasis on the need to exercise caution and restraint. On the evening of November 7, 1951, for example, a member of a BGS patrol near the Walheim train station fired on a Belgian government vehicle.[75] The officer had observed an Opel Kapitän sedan approaching the checkpoint that he later claimed fit the description of a similar vehicle known to be used by smugglers. When the vehicle slowed and then proceeded past the patrol, one of the officers fired two shots from his pistol at the Opel's rear tires. The sedan continued on its way and the occupants did not discover they had been fired upon until the tires went flat several miles away from the checkpoint. The vehicle displayed the Belgian flag and license plates. Moreover, colleagues of the officer who fired the shots waved it through the checkpoint because they recognized it as an official vehicle.[76] The officer later claimed to be blinded by the Opel's headlights and thus unable to see the vehicle clearly. Andersen's staff blamed the incident on poor weather and the Opel's "dirty license plates" without questioning how the officer's colleagues could clearly identify it and wave it through. Perhaps the interrogators should have asked the more obvious question of why the officer fired at a vehicle that he could not apparently even see.[77]

---

74 Einsatzstab Andersen an den Bundesministerium des Innern, Br. B Nr. 388/52.

75 Zollassistent Friedrich Breuer, "Bericht: 7. November 1951 gegen 19.15 Uhr beschossenen Personenkraftwagen," November 15, 1951, BArch-K, B 106/15183.

76 Leutnant Lippert an den Grenzschutz—Ausbildungs-Abteilung West IV, "Stellungnahme," November 15, 1951, BArch-K, B 106/15183.

77 Einsatzstab Andersen an Frontier Inspection Service von Mr. Stuart D.A.D. in Aachen, Rote Kaserne, November 15, 1951, "Beschuß eines belgischen Militärfahrzeuges am 7. November 1951 in Walheim," BArch-K, B 106/15183.

In another embarrassing incident, a BGS sergeant accidentally shot a citizen in the foot during a drunken brawl at a local bar in the village of Schmidthof.[78] The problems began when a sergeant and seven of his subordinates went into the bar for a night of drinking. The uniformed men went out for a night of drinking while still armed with their service pistols, in direct violation of their orders, which stated: "When off-duty, firearms and batons may not be carried either visibly or concealed."[79] The sergeant had run into a disabled veteran with whom he had served during the war. While the two men talked in a hallway, a drunken *Zoll* officer in civilian clothes accidentally knocked the disabled veteran to the ground and a fight broke out with some of the civilians in the bar later identified as smugglers. Everyone involved in the incident was intoxicated. During the brawl, one of the young border police officers drew his pistol to defend his sergeant and fired two warning shots into a wall. The sergeant, recognizing the danger of the situation, tried to forcibly disarm the officer, who still had his finger on the trigger. As the men wrestled for control of the pistol, it fired again, striking the foot of a patron in the bar.[80]

The Schmidthof incident differed from the others in that it was investigated by the State Police in Aachen rather than by Andersen's staff.[81] The investigating officer, Sergeant Vollmer of the Aachen State Criminal Police, recommended that two of the civilians, whom he identified as "thugs" and "smugglers," should be charged criminally for assaulting the uniformed BGS personnel. Vollmer sent his report to Major Andersen but did not recommend charging any BGS personnel for shooting the citizen in the foot.[82] In his report to the Interior Minister, Andersen explained that the sergeant and his subordinates violated BGS rules of conduct and his own standing orders for Operation Martha. The violations included staying out after curfew, carrying firearms while off-duty, consuming alcohol in excess, and disorderly conduct. Andersen recommended dismissal for all of the men involved because they had grossly violated their sworn

---

78 Einsatzstab Andersen an Bundesministerium des Innern, "Zwischenfall zwischen BGS-Angehörigen und Zivilpersonen in Schmidthof," December 10, 1951, BArch-K, B 106/15183.

79 Führungsstab West: Unternehmen Martha, "Einsatzanweisung für das Unternehmen Martha II," December 20, 1951, BArch-K, B 106/15183.

80 Abschrift, Chef der Polizei Milkereit, Die Polizeibehörde des Regierungsbezirk Aachen, K-3370/51, an Bundesgrenzschutzleitung in Raum Aachen Herrn Oberst Andersen, December 5, 1951, BArch-K, B 106/15183.

81 Kriminal Polizei Obermeister Vollmer, Die Polizeibehörde des Regierungsbezirk Aachen, Bericht Abschrift: "Zwischenfall zwischen BGS-Angehörigen und Zivilpersonen in Schmidthof," December 10, 1951, BArch-K, B 106/15183.

82 Ibid.

duty to uphold the law and existing service regulations, and above all, damaged the public reputation of the BGS through their poor behavior.[83]

In spite of these incidents, however, Operation Martha proved to be so successful that the Interior Ministry extended it until Easter, 1952. Major Höffner assumed overall command when Andersen promoted to colonel and transferred to a new assignment.[84] The operation continued until April 15, 1952. In his after-action report, Höffner claimed that there had been no major incidents involving conflicts between his border police officers and the local population. He also spoke of the operation in military terms, reporting to the Interior Ministry that among the border hunters engaged in the fight against smuggling, "the front spirit came to life again." The use of the term "front spirit" obviously worried the report's reviewer, because he underlined it and marked it with a large question mark in red ink. In the following paragraph, Höffner also reported that he had dismissed a sergeant for singing Nazi songs.

In a few sentences, Höffner's after-action report captured the contradictions of an organization that was shaped by the experiences of the founding "men of the first hour." Yet it also evoked the underlying theme of an organization suffering from an identity crisis caught as it was in a protracted struggle between continuity and change. Thus Höffner could speak in positive terms about a "front spirit" among his men while also reporting the dismissal of a non-commissioned officer for singing Nazi songs. Matzky could speak of the BGS not deviating from the path of its "soldiery feelings" while preaching restraint in its use of firearms against the FDJ. Finally, Andersen could instruct his subordinates to use their experiences with partisans in the war as a model for security in the fight against smugglers while the Interior Ministry issued orders against using deadly force against black marketeers.

When Andersen relinquished command to Höffner, Lehr praised him for his leadership, commenting that his units arrested 1,581 smugglers, seized 36 luxury vehicles, 300 pounds of coffee, and significant amounts of tobacco, jewelry, and other contraband totaling more than 655,884 DM.[85] Both Lehr and Adenauer celebrated the achievements of the BGS and had already begun seeking a way to increase its strength by an

---

83 Einsatzstab Andersen an Bundesminister des Innern, I-Br. B. Nr. 423/51, "Zwischenfall zwischen Grenzschutzangehörigen und Zivilpersonen in Schmidthof Krs. Aachen," December 5, 1951, BArch-K, B 106/15183.

84 Hans Egidi—Bundesministerium des Innern an GSK Nord, GSK West, Einsatzstab Andersen, "Verlängerung des Einsatzunternehmens Martha und Durchführung der Ablösung," BArch-K, B 106/15183; Einsatzstab Aachen, Br. B. Nr. 905/52, "Befehl über den Vormarsch," 9. April 1952, BArch-K, B 106/15183.

85 Robert Lehr an Einsatzstab Andersen, 17. Januar 1952, BArch-K, B136/1929, Fiche Nr. 1, Slide Nr. 110.

additional 10,000 men. The biggest obstacles standing in their way, however, continued to be resistance by the SPD to militarized policing and the high costs of doubling the size of the current force. Yet Allied plans to rearm West Germany created new opportunities for Adenauer and Lehr to exploit in their campaign to add a further 10,000 men to the BGS.

CHAPTER THREE

WHO WANTS TO BE A SOLDIER? THE BGS AND WEST GERMANY'S NEW ARMY

On November 20, 1951, while BGS units fought the coffee wars, Adenauer travelled to Paris to sign a draft of the European Defense Community (EDC) Treaty. French Premier René Pleven and the architect of the Schuman Coal and Steel Plan, Jean Monnet, outlined the terms of the new treaty. If ratified, the EDC would have given the Federal Republic its first chance to have armed forces since the end of the war, but only as part of a larger supranational European army. Rearming under a French plan, however, proved unpopular among West Germany's veteran soldiers, who had recently proposed their own plan calling for twenty-five divisions led by German officers.[1] But for Adenauer, establishing a new army in any form was a chance to gain more sovereignty. The day he initialed the draft of the proposed treaty, he confided in his memoirs that: "On this day the Federal Government was beginning to speak with its own authority in association with the Western World."[2]

These proceedings should have had no immediate effect on border policing. Article 11 of the treaty exempted the police forces of signatory nations from its terms. But now that the rearmament of West Germany appeared inevitable, members of the BGS believed the government would call upon them to staff the new army. Since the majority of its personnel and their leaders had come from the Wehrmacht, it seemed like the logical next step. Some of the men claimed that the government had promised to make them soldiers once the new army was formed. For Interior Minister Robert Lehr and his successor Gerhard Schröder, the creation of German armed forces caused an existential crisis. What did the future hold for the BGS now that West Germany had a new army?

1 David Clay Large, *Germans to the Front*, 93; "Himmeroder Denkschrift," October 9, 1950, BA-MA, BW 9/3119.
2 David Clay Large, *Germans to the Front*, 112; see also Michael Geyer, "Cold War Angst: The Case of West-German Opposition to Rearmament and Nuclear Weapons," in *The Miracle Years*, ed. Hanna Schissler, 376–408.

Although members of the BGS assumed they would be instrumental in founding the army, military veterans in Adenauer's proto-defense ministry, the Blank Office (*Amt Blank*) had other ideas. These veteran officers intended to build an army free of the burdens and traditions of the recent past. Many of those in the Blank Office considered the BGS to be a force of reactionaries that might reject the new beginning they had envisioned.[3] This narrative, however, had no real basis in fact, but emerged as a consequence of organizational competition for limited resources and philosophical differences among veteran Wehrmacht officers. To be sure, the Interior Ministry worked to preserve and expand the BGS regardless of how it figured in the construction of the new army. Besides, they argued that the Federal Republic still needed an independent national force below the threshold of NATO to fight communist insurgents and maintain internal security. The debate over the future of the BGS contributed to the ongoing identity crisis its personnel suffered as a result of the Federal Republic's decision to blend policing and military duties into one force. Yet in spite of the opportunity to finally settle the matter and limit the BGS to enforcing laws rather than fighting wars, the Interior Ministry chose to maintain the status quo and keep it as peculiar hybrid between a police and military force.

The EDC and Expansion of the BGS

On January 19, 1952, Lehr wrote to Adenauer's State Secretary, Otto Lenz, outlining his plans to expand the BGS. In the letter, he explained to Lenz that the force in its present strength could not deal with the "growing threat to internal security due to an influx of agents, propaganda material, and acts of sabotage."[4] Presumably, he meant the FDJ activities associated with the World Youth Festival in August, 1951. Lehr's request reflected his ongoing fear of civil war erupting on the border or a revolutionary insurgency emerging from within the Federal Republic. He made no mention in his letter that the increase had anything to do with meeting the staffing levels of a future German Army. Adenauer approved the plans and by January 26, 1952, State Secretary Karl Gumbel presented a draft of the proposed increase to the Federal Cabinet. During his presentation, Gumbel emphasized the lack of funds in the budget to cover the increase and suggested that the costs might be covered as part of the EDC since guarding the border was considered a function of national defense. In fact, Lehr had also made this argument

---

3   Detlef Bald, *Militär und Gesellschaft, 1945–1990: Die Bundeswehr der Bonner Republik* (Baden Baden: Nomos, 1994), 34.
4   Secret memorandum from Robert Lehr to Staatsekretär Otto Lenz, January 19, 1952, BArch-K, B 136/1929, Fiche 3, Slides 106–9.

in his original request claiming that the Allies had to consider "the important role this police unit plays in the protection of the Eastern border." Gumbel also told the cabinet members that the BGS "is expected to remain the only power factor, which is immediately and always available to the federal government."[5]

At the time, SPD lawmakers rejected any notion that the BGS be expanded beyond its present staffing levels. Social Democrats began to make progress in regional elections and in the state of Hesse gained an overwhelming 38.5 percent of the popular vote against the 17.5 percent won by Adenauer's CDU.[6] Cold War Politics also played a role in the debate, as the SPD and Adenauer disagreed over the manner in which to rearm the Federal Republic. Besides the EDC negotiations, Adenauer also engaged in talks with representatives from the United States, Great Britain, and France over the terms of the German Treaty—an agreement with the three powers to formally end the occupation. The SPD, however, preferred to renew four-power talks as outlined by the infamous 1952 "Stalin Note," which offered Soviet support for German reunification, economic freedom and the withdrawal of all occupation forces from German soil in exchange for a guarantee of neutrality. Adenauer signed the German Treaty on May 26, 1952, and the EDC—a prerequisite of the German Treaty—on May 27. SPD leader Kurt Schumacher immediately condemned Adenauer calling his signing of the two treaties a "clumsy triumph of the Allied-clerical coalition over the German people."[7] Thus, from the perspective of his critics, Adenauer had chosen alignment with the West over reunification.

Although Lehr faced an uphill battle to convince West Germany's lawmakers to back the proposed increase, Adenauer's preliminary acceptance of the EDC and German treaties had immediate consequences for residents living near the Inner-German Border. The treaties, which the Soviets and East Germans called "war treaties" signaled that in spite of their recent attempts to renew four power talks, the Federal Republic had clearly chosen alignment with the West. Almost immediately, the East German Ministry for State Security (MfS) ordered the plowing of a 10-meter-wide strip backed by a 500-meter security zone along the Inner-German border. They erected barbed wire barriers and placed the

5   Robert Lehr to Staatssekretär Otto Lenz, January 19, 1952; Vermerk für die Kabinettssitzung, "Personalvermehrung beim Bundesgrenzschutz," January 26, 1952, BArch-K, B 136/1929, Fiche 3, Slide 110.
6   "Socialists Win in Hesse Poll; Oppose Arming of Germany: Political Foes of Adenauer's Bonn Policy for European Defense Action Score Strongly in Frankfurt—Reds Lag," *New York Times*, May 5, 1952, 1.
7   "German Socialist Attacks Accords: Schumacher Says His People Will Bear Most of Burden—Adenauer Faces New Rifts," *New York Times*, June 3, 1952, 7; Adenauer, Memoirs, 415.

entire zone under the command of the People's Police. At the beginning of June, they implemented "Action Vermin"—the expulsion and forced resettlement of border residents deemed to be politically unreliable. Thousands of people suffered during this sudden hardening of the border and many of them fled to the West.[8] Adenauer called the expulsions "atrocities" and this confirmed for both himself and Lehr that the BGS had to be expanded in order to counter what they saw as growing aggression from the GDR and its militarized People's Police.[9]

In spite of Action Vermin, however, the majority of SPD representatives still opposed the increase, claiming that the government used it as an excuse to remilitarize the Federal Republic. Press reports complained about the military uniforms and steel helmets worn by members of the BGS which, "invoked memories of the military police and occupying forces."[10] Director of Public Security, Hans Egidi, used Action Vermin to justify the proposed increase and argued that the current force of approximately 9,000 men could not effectively patrol all of West Germany's frontiers. Bundestag member Friedrich Maier (SPD) suggested that the Interior Ministry already had the extra personnel if it were to replace the two companies guarding Adenauer's offices with state police forces.[11] Bavaria's political parties also opposed the increase, since they saw it as another trick by the federal government to supplant their own state police forces. Lehr knew that without the Bavarian parties he lacked the votes to achieve the simple majority needed for the increase. He complained to Adenauer that the Bavarians had "overstated the emphasis on federalism while ignoring the vital questions of the larger aspects of strengthening the power of our federal state."[12]

In the meantime, Bundestag member Richard Jaeger of Bavaria's Christian Social Party (CSU) wrote to Adenauer and reminded him that during a recent private conversation, the Chancellor had promised to reduce the BGS back to 10,000 men after the EDC went into effect. Jaeger told Adenauer that his CSU colleagues would be more supportive

---

8   Edith Sheffer, *Burned Bridge*, 112–16; Inge Bennewitz and Rainer Potratz, *Zwangsaussiedlungen an der innerdeutschen Grenze: Analysen und Dokumente* (Berlin: Ch. Links, 2012).

9   Letter Nr. 226: Adenauer to André François-Poncet and Sir Ivone Kirkpatrick Allied High Commission, Wahnerheide, in *Adenauer Rhöndorfer Ausgabe*, ed.Konrad Adenauer and Hans Peter Mensing, 240–41.

10   "Warum Feldgrau?" *FAZ* September 30, 1952, 2.

11   For Maier and Egidi's comments see "Protokoll 48. Sitzung des Ausschusses für Angelegenheiten der inneren Verwaltung am Mittwoch, 9/10/1952," BArch-K, B 136/1929 Fiche Nr. 3, Slide Nr. 134; see also "Stärkerer Grenzschutz: Wiederholte Forderungen von Egidis," *FAZ*, September 4, 1952), 3.

12   Letter from Lehr to Adenauer, October 24, 1952, BArch-K, B 136/1929, Fiche Nr. 3, Slide Nr. 137.

of the expansion if he could confirm his promise in writing. Jaeger also told him that constitutionally, the states had jurisdiction over policing and asked that he sign an agreement guaranteeing the independence of Bavaria's state police.[13] Adenauer took the matter directly to the head of the CSU, Franz Josef Strauss. He reassured Strauss that the federal government had no intention of disrupting the Bavarian State Police or supplanting their oversight of its borders. Adenauer also linked the proposed expansion to the EDC by telling Strauss that "the strength of the BGS will again be reset to 10,000 men after the creation of a new [army] ... and should begin no later than one year after entry into force of the EDC."[14]

So, based on Adenauer's correspondence with Strauss, it might be argued that the proposed expansion corresponded to the establishment of the new army. Yet further evidence shows that his promise to reduce the force was solely a means that justified the ends. Neither Adenauer nor Lehr ever intended to follow through with the promise to reduce the size of the BGS. In fact, a year before he wrote to Strauss, Adenauer requested that Bundestag President Hermann Ehlers (SPD) add the increase to the agenda and never mentioned the EDC or any plans to reduce the BGS back to 10,000 men.[15] In fact, Adenauer and Lehr discussed increasing and maintaining its strength to at least 50,000 men regardless of the outcome of the EDC. Lehr confirmed this figure to United Press International Bonn Correspondent Rüdiger von Wechmar during a 1953 interview. He never mentioned the EDC or Adenauer's promised reduction to von Wechmar. Instead, he focused his answers regarding the need for BGS forces to fight potential communist fifth column agents that he alleged had been infiltrating the Federal Republic in large numbers. Lehr told von Wechmar that "There is no unrest in the Federal Republic which is not connected with the situation on the border ... in internal disturbances ... the police can only master the situation quickly if the frontier is closed effectively."[16]

---

13 Letter from Jaeger to Adenauer, November 25, 1952, BArch-K, B 126/10837, Bd. 1, 1951–1955.
14 Letter from Adenauer to Franz Josef Strauss, February 4, 1953, BArch-K, B 136/1929, Fiche Nr. 3, Slide Nr. 184.
15 Letter from Adenauer to Hermann Ehlers, "Erhöhung der Gesamtstärke des Bundesgrenzschutzes," April 16, 1952, BArch-K, B 136/1929, Fiche Nr. 3, Slide Nr. 114.
16 Rüdiger von Wechmar, "Increase in the Strength of Frontier Guard Necessary for the Protection of the Frontier Population and as a Safeguard against Communist Infiltration," *United Press International* (1953), translated interview copy in British Foreign Office files, TNA FO/371/104140.

The Collapse of the EDC

On the same day Adenauer wrote his letter to Strauss promising the reduction, the center-right *Freie Democratische Partei* (FDP) introduced a bill proposing an increase of the BGS to 20,000 men. Lehr's arch nemesis, Walter Menzel (SPD), repeated his familiar objections to militarized policing. He also tried to turn Bavarian lawmakers against Lehr by describing the expansion as a blatant effort by the government to take control of their borders and police forces.[17] Although the bill survived its first reading by a slim margin of 44 votes, it still lacked enough support to become legally binding. The SPD in conjunction with some members of the Bavarian Party (BP) succeeded in stalling it. But for French members of HICOG, the vote came too close for comfort and they called an emergency meeting of the General Committee on February 6. Armand Bérard, the Assistant High Commissioner for France, reported to the United States that any increase in the BGS would be "catastrophic" to the EDC.[18] Jean Sauvagnargues, a member of the French Delegation in London, took the matter directly to Under Secretary Frank Roberts in the UK Foreign Office and accused the West Germans of building clandestine armed forces in direct violation of the rules outlined by the EDC.[19]

Adenauer, frustrated by the French opposition to his plans, appealed directly to the new US High Commissioner James Conant for help. Adenauer's ally and close friend McCloy left his post as High Commissioner in August 1952. Conant did not share the same congenial working relationship that his predecessor had forged with Adenauer. In fact, Adenauer often went around Conant and found more empathy from President Eisenhower's Secretary of State John Foster Dulles.[20] In his appeal to Conant, Adenauer claimed that "experience gained in

---

17 Deutscher Bundestag, 249 Sitzung, Bonn, Mittwoch, 4. Februar 1953, 11895–11904.

18 Telegram from Acting US High Commissioner Samuel Reber to US State Department, February 7, 1953, FRUS Vol. II, 1952–1954, 400–403.

19 "Reports of Talks with Jean Sauvagnargues of the French Delegation on the Subject of the Proposal to Double the Number of Frontier Police, February 20, 1953, The National Archives (TNA) FO 371/104138, "The Arming of the BGS, 1953: Papers 1–14."

20 McCloy had recommended Conant, an academic and former president of Harvard University, as his replacement because of his ability to speak German fluently. See the letter from John J. McCloy to Konrad Adenauer, January 22, 1953, Amherst College, Papers of John J. McCloy, Correspondence and Administrative Documents, Box GY1, Folder Nr. 1: Adenauer, Konrad; for Adenauer's relationship to Conant, see Memorandum from Secretary of State John Foster Dulles to President Eisenhower, April 2, 1955, Dwight D. Eisenhower Presidential Library, Eisenhower, Dwight D.: Papers as President, 1953–1961 (Ann Whitman File), Dulles-Herter Series, Box 5, Folder: Dulles, John Foster, April 1955 (2).

the past thirty years has made it clear to the German security agencies that communist terrorist activities excel through particular violence and obduracy." He also invoked Weimar Germany and told Conant that "communist insurrections in the former Reich could only be quelled by the police forces with serious losses and after the use of heavy arms." He provided Conant with a list of weapons he needed for the BGS that included armored vehicles equipped with 3.7 cm armor-piercing guns, medium range mortars, fast patrol boats, and aircraft. In an attachment to Adenauer's request, Lehr justified the need for mortars to deal with "house to house or gang fighting as well as the firing at hidden targets, which due to communist tactics will have to be resorted to on a large scale."[21] The letter should have been a clear indication to anyone reading it that Adenauer and Lehr clearly intended to use the BGS for combat rather than enforcing customs and border security regulations.

Unfortunately for Adenauer and Lehr, at that time André François-Poncet of France held the chair of the High Commission. François-Poncet reminded them that "mobile police forces should not be transferred into organizations of a paramilitary nature." Adenauer called François-Poncet's comments about the BGS "unthinkable." Furthermore, Adenauer claimed that he was "all the more surprised by the attitude hitherto adopted by the High Commission on this important matter, and ... disconcerted at the resistance and numerous objections which have been voiced on the Allied side against the modest requests of the federal government."[22]

The Council of the Allied High Commission met on March 23 to discuss the expansion and armament of the BGS. Of course, François-Poncet argued against it calling it a "shameless tactic" by Adenauer and Lehr to try and gain power by using the EDC as a ploy to fund the increase. François-Poncet saw through all the hyperbole of Lehr's justifications. He supported the Federal Republic, but his overriding concern focused on keeping Adenauer quiet about mortars and armor-piercing weapons in order to prevent him from undermining French support for the EDC. He warned Adenauer that his French colleagues already considered the BGS to be a clandestine army that might prove "disastrous" to EDC ratification. Thus he denied Adenauer's requests.[23] US High Commissioner

21 Letter from Adenauer to Conant, February 21, 1953, TNA FO 371/104139, "The Arming of the BGS 1953: Papers 15–29."

22 André François-Poncet to Konrad Adenauer, March 2, 1953 and Konrad Adenauer to André François-Poncet, March 19, 1953, TNA FO 371/104139, "Arming of the BGS 1953: Papers 15–29."

23 Letter from US High Commissioner Conant to Adenauer, May 15, 1953, "Armament of the Federal Frontier Police and Länder Mobile Police," 3, TNA FO 371/104139; Letter from UK High Commissioner Jack Ward to Sir W. D. Allen, Foreign Office, London, April 10, 1953, TNA FO 371/104139, "Arming of the BGS 1953," Papers 15–29.

Conant agreed and confided in his diary that "a totalitarian government will always hang over this nation [Germany] as a threat for years to come. Minister Lehr's proposal to arm the border police is not a good omen. A border police well-armed of 60,000 men would be used in a putsch."[24]

Adenauer and Lehr had few options left. They failed to gain enough support from West Germany's lawmakers, and the Allies remained ambivalent. With Adenauer's conservative ally McCloy out of the picture, he found it much harder to overcome French resistance. Although the British secretly supported the increase, they worried that any unilateral moves by Adenauer might undermine any hope of France ratifying the EDC. UK Deputy High Commissioner Jack Ward reported to his superiors at the Foreign Office that it would be "inopportune" if the West Germans decided to increase the force before the EDC went into effect.[25]

Events developing outside of West Germany, however, worked in Adenauer's favor. On June 16, 1953, a construction strike in East Berlin erupted into a larger uprising against the entire communist government.[26] Rioting began in many of East Germany's largest cities and also spread to its smaller regions. The People's Police failed to contain the riots and restore order without the help of Soviet armed forces. The number of protestors killed and injured is still debated, but by far the most serious casualties occurred when Soviet tanks fired on the crowds.[27] To restore order, the Soviets executed protestors, and with them many of their own soldiers who refused to fire on the crowds. Recently declassified documents claim the Soviets killed 40 people and wounded 450; they also arrested a further 6,521 people.[28] The uprisings gave Adenauer an excellent opportunity to renew his call for expanding the BGS. On June 19, 1953, while the violence in East Berlin still raged out of control, Lehr's proposed expansion came before the Bundestag for a vote on its second reading. This time, however, the Bavarian CSU, probably

---

24 James Bryant Conant, "James Bryant Conant's Journal: Germany, 1953," p. J-4, Conant Papers Harvard: Box 139—Germany (Courtesy of Harvard University Archives).

25 UK High Commissioner Jack Ward to Sir W. D. Allen, Foreign Office, London, April 10, 1953, TNA FO 371/104139.

26 Christian Ostermann, ed., *Uprising in East Germany, 1953: The Cold War, The German Question, and the First Major Upheaval Behind the Iron Curtain* (New York: Central European University Press, 2001), 3–22.

27 Ibid., 166.

28 Report from Vasilii Sokolovskii, Vladimir Semyonov, and Pavel Yudin "On the Events of 17–19 June 1953 in Berlin and the GDR and Certain Conclusions from These Events," June 24, 1953, reprinted in full and translated from the Russian in Christoph Ostermann, *Uprising in East Germany, 1953*, 283–84.

influenced by Adenauer's promise to reduce the force, backed the proposal and it passed by a majority of 228 to 147 votes.[29]

The damage to the EDC after the Bundestag had passed the proposal took effect almost immediately. France demanded that HICOG intervene to prevent the expansion from going forward, but Lehr had already been secretly adding personnel to the BGS all along. With Adenauer facing difficult elections in the coming fall, neither Britain nor the United States wanted to weaken his government by blocking the legislation. Sir Patrick Hancock of the British Foreign Office met with State Secretary Ritter von Lex, who admitted that the Interior Ministry had already secretly increased the force. Hancock argued that "since the German defence contribution seemed to be a long way ahead, it would be just as well to augment the Bundesgrenzschutz."[30] Likewise, US Secretary of State John Foster Dulles wrote to his embassy in London that "delays in ratification of the EDC by other nations, especially France, have only reemphasized the need from the German standpoint to take some security measures themselves ... we feel annulling this legislation might undermine the prestige of the Adenauer government and have an unfavorable effect in the coming elections."[31] During a meeting of President Eisenhower's National Security Council, CIA Director Allen Dulles urged the president to support the [BGS] expansion as a "matter of urgency."[32]

Not everyone agreed with this hands-off approach. Great Britain's Undersecretary, Sir Christopher F. A. Warner, for example, added the following handwritten note to a telegram about the increase from UK High Commissioner Ivone Kirkpatrick: "Like [French Prime Minister] M. Bidault, I do not feel at all enthusiastic about this. It bears a terrible resemblance to the para-military forces with which we used to be familiar before the war and which were structurally, if I remember rightly, indistinguishable from the German armed forces."[33]

In spite of the Allied concerns over Adenauer's chances for reelection, on September 6, 1953, he won decisively in both the popular vote and in

---

29 Deutsche Bundestag, 274 Sitzung, 13609.
30 Letter from Sir Patrick F. Hancock to Foreign Office, June 20, 1953, Proposed Strength of the Bundesgrenzschutz, "Arming of the BGS Papers 15–29," TNA FO 372/104139.
31 Cable from Secretary of State John Foster Dulles to US Embassy London, June 23, 1953, FRUS, 1952–1954, Germany and Austria, vol. VII, p. 476.
32 Minutes of Discussion at the 150th Meeting of the National Security Council on June 18, 1953, June 19, 1953, reprinted in its entirety in Christian Ostermann, *Uprising in East Germany, 1953*, 229.
33 Telegram from UK High Commissioner Ivone Kirkpatrick to the Foreign Office, Subject: The Bundesgrenzschutz, July 25, 1953, "Arming of the BGS 1953," Papers 30 to the End, TNA FO 371/104140.

the number of Bundestag seats gained for the CDU.[34] The election also marked a new beginning for the Interior Ministry as Gerhard Schröder (CDU) replaced Robert Lehr, who had to retire for health reasons. Schröder, a former Nazi Party member and combat veteran, continued to promote the Interior Ministry's conservative-authoritarian policies. Adenauer, empowered by his reelection, led the Federal Republic into a new era of economic prosperity. In December, *Time* magazine named him its "Man of the Year." West Germany's export industry grew into one of the strongest in Europe and 1953 marked the beginning of the postwar *Wirtschaftswunder* (economic miracle).[35] The death of Joseph Stalin in March and an armistice in Korea also produced a short period of détente in Cold War European politics. For Adenauer and Schröder, national security and fear of attack from the east remained a top priority.[36] When press reports surfaced in late 1953 that West Germany had budgeted for the additional 10,000 officers in fiscal year 1954/55, Armand Bérard again warned his Allied colleagues that expanding the militarized BGS might prevent French lawmakers from ratifying the EDC.[37]

Adenauer's hubris in moving ahead with the expansion came on the back of his triumph in the federal elections and added to the growing list of tensions in postwar Franco-German relations that undermined the EDC. Yet historians have largely ignored the effect of expanding the BGS as a factor in the list of grievances French parliamentarians cited as justification to abandon the EDC. Against this backdrop, Franco-German relations also suffered from the unresolved question over political control of the disputed Saar region and what André François-Poncet described as a latent Francophobia among West Germans who suspected the Foreign Legion as a "white slave trade in which France would engage Germany for the purpose of the war in Indochina."[38] Moreover, the fall of Dien Bien Phu in 1954 signaled the collapse of French Indochina and along with it the conservative French government of Joseph Laniel. Thus, despite

---

34 See Statistisches Bundesamt, *Statistik der Bundesrepublik Deutschland, Band 100: Die Wahl zum 2. Deutschen Bundestag am 6. September 1953*, Heft 1: Allgemeine Wahlergebnisse nach Ländern und Wahlkreisen (Stuttgart: Kohlhammer, 1991); Clifton Daniel, "Adenauer Wins Decisively; Bonn Tie to the West Endorsed in Rout of 'Neutral' Parties, *New York Times*, September 7, 1953, 1.

35 Hans-Peter Schwarz, *Konrad Adenauer Vol. 2*, 35.

36 Mark Kramer, "International Politics in the Early Post-Stalin Era: A Lost Opportunity, a Turning Point, or More of the Same?" in *The Cold War after Stalin's Death: A Missed Opportunity for Peace?* ed. Klaus Larres and Kenneth Osgood, xvii (Lanham: Rowan & Littlefield, 2006).

37 Confidential memorandum from UK Deputy High Commissioner Jack Ward to the Foreign Office, January 25, 1954, TNA FO 371/109719.

38 Andre François Poncet, *Les rapports mensuels d'André François Poncet, Haut-Commissaire français en Allemagne 1949–1955, Vol II*, 904.

repeated warnings by moderate French politicians, the National Assembly voted against ratifying the EDC by a margin of 319 to 264.[39]

The Conflict between Tradition and Reform

The failure of the EDC came as a sudden shock for Adenauer. When news of the French National Assembly's decision reached him at his Black Forest retreat near Bühlerhöhe, his Press Secretary Felix von Eckardt recalled that he had never seen the Chancellor so dismayed.[40] But the collapse of the EDC only proved to be a temporary setback. Once Adenauer acknowledged the futility of saving the treaty, he began negotiating with the Allied Powers to create armed forces under the framework of the North Atlantic Treaty Organization (NATO). Less than a month after the EDC collapsed, Allied delegates met at the Nine-Power Conference in London and tentatively agreed to incorporate West Germany into NATO.[41] At the time the EDC collapsed, the BGS had already reached a strength of 17,500 men and represented the largest resource available to rapidly build up German armed forces. Most border police officers assumed the federal government would give them the first posts in the new army, a belief their command staff encouraged. Many veteran soldiers admitted that they only joined the border police because they had no other options without an army. Even *Life Magazine* promoted the BGS as a "Nucleus of a German Army" in an article focused on emphasizing recent accomplishments by the Federal Republic.[42]

Unfortunately for those expecting a quick transfer, the solution proved to be more complicated. For the veteran army officers at the Ministry of Defense, the collapse of the EDC undermined plans they had been developing in the Blank Office since the early 1950s. To these men, the BGS represented the old, Prussian traditions of Germany's military past with its emphasis on rigid discipline, hard training, and absolute obedience to orders from above. Most, but certainly not all, of the military planners in the Blank Office wanted a complete break with this past and argued against using the BGS. Adenauer's first military adviser, General Gerhard von Schwerin, favored rearming with mobile police forces, but Blank's inner circle rejected this approach (See chapter 1). The veteran Wehrmacht General Staff Officer, Colonel Johann von Kielmansegg, rejected suggestions for a wholesale transfer of BGS divisions into the

---

39   Tony Judt, *Postwar*, 245.
40   Felix von Eckardt, *Ein unordentliches Leben: Lebenserinnerungen* (Düsseldorf: Econ-Verlag, 1967), 301.
41   David Clay Large, *Germans to the Front*, 217–23.
42   Staff, "Nucleus of a German Army: EDC's Death Turns Spotlight on a Surprising New Military Look," *Life*, September 13, 1954, 42–43.

new armed forces. Kielmansegg helped produce the 1950 Himmerod Memorandum, a secret protocol outlining the West German vision for rearmament.[43] He and his colleagues wanted to form an army with candidates they could train in the spirit of democracy rather than with veterans already tainted by years of service in the old army. As early as 1951, Kielmansegg told Blank that "the border guards must not, not even in thought, be set up as a cadre for a German contingent or with the intention of transferring them later."[44]

Kielmansegg's colleague in the Blank Office, Colonel Wolf von Baudissin, shared his misgivings about the BGS. Baudissin spent many years during the war in Allied POW camps, where he first began to develop the intellectual basis for what became his philosophy of *Innere Führung* (internal leadership), a concept he later championed as the basis for the ideological foundation of the Bundeswehr.[45] *Innere Führung* functioned like an internal conscience or moral compass so that a soldier, as an individual, took responsibility for his actions. The philosophy aimed to replace the rigid notion of blind obedience to orders that many German soldiers and their officers had invoked to excuse criminal behavior during the war. Thus soldiers in the new army were expected to refuse immoral or criminal orders or face the consequences. At the same time, Baudissin promoted an idea, first introduced by the influential SPD military adviser Friederich Beermann, that soldiers should be "citizens in uniform."[46] Beermann, a veteran soldier and member of the SPD's conservative wing, supported a measured approach to rearmament.[47] The "citizens in uniform" model Baudissin advocated along with *Innere Führung* sought to break the barriers between the army and the population. Baudissin believed soldiers should be integrated as participants into the civic society they served. He warned Beermann that using the BGS as the basis for

---

43 Detlef Bald, *Militär und Gesellschaft*, 18.
44 Günther Kießling, *Staatsbürger und General* (Düsseldorf: Verlag Blazek & Bergmann, 2000), 132.
45 Wolf Graf Baudissin, "Innere Führung: EVG und Inneres Gefüge," in *Von Himmerod bis Andernach: Dokumente zur Entstehungsgeschichte der Bundeswehr* (Führungsstab der Streitkräfte: 1985), ed. Bundesministerium der Verteidigung, 181–83; Wolf Graf Baudissin, *Soldat für den Frieden: Entwürfe für eine zeitgemäße Bundeswehr* (Munich: Piper, 1969), 117–19.
46 John Zimmermann, *Ulrich de Maiziére: General der Bonner Republik, 1912 bis 2006* (Munich: Oldenbourg, 2012), 187.
47 Donald Abenheim, *Reforging the Iron Cross: The Search for Tradition in the West German Armed Forces* (Princeton, NJ: Princeton University Press, 1988), 123–24; for the SPD role in rearmament see also David Clay Large, *Germans to the Front*, 192–93.

rebuilding armed forces "would be a deathblow" for any chance of the constructive reforms he was planning.[48]

The commanding officers of the BGS criticized the Ministry of Defense for questioning their commitment to democracy. After all, they argued, border police officers had been the only line of defense against communist infiltration over the past five years, during which they had proven their absolute loyalty to the democratic state. Some border police officers claimed that former Interior Minister Lehr and General Adolf Heusinger, a member of the Blank Office, promised them they would become soldiers in the future.[49] To be sure, there is no empirical evidence to support this claim, but it is quite possible that the hypothetical plans discussed among senior members of both ministries might have led some men to believe this. Members of the Blank Office and those leading the BGS served together in the Wehrmacht and maintained postwar friendships despite the organizational tensions. Generals Hans Speidel and Adolf Heusinger, for example, maintained close relations with BGS Chief Gerhard Matzky. Speidel had been a lead negotiator for West German interests in the EDC. In 1952 he requested that Matzky and his assistant, Colonel Kurt Spitzer, participate in the European Defense Interim Committee negotiations in Paris relating to military and police cooperation.[50] If the BGS was to have no future military role, why would Speidel involve Matzky in these critical negotiations when the French already expressed misgivings about the BGS?

Heusinger and Speidel remained ambivalent, however, when it came to their dealings with Matzky and the future of the BGS. In 1952, Matzky published an article in *Die Parole* calling for the creation of a "doctrine of duties" that he compared to the "obligations of the German soldier" established by General Hans von Seeckt's Reichswehr in the 1920s. He also took aim at reformers in the Blank Office warning his readers to be "sober and skeptical of highfalutin' words and reject inappropriate pathos."[51] His praise of Seeckt, who many saw as the archetypal example of the anti-democratic ethos in German civil-military relations during the

---

48 Friedrich Beermann, "Stellungnahme zu dem Brief des Grafen Schwerin, bzgl. des BGS vom December 12, 1954," BA-MA, N 597/30.

49 David Parma, *Installation und Konsolidierung des Bundesgrenzschutzes*, 285–87.

50 Walter Bargatzky to Leiter der deutschen Delegation bei der Konferenz für die Organisation einer europäischen Verteidigungsgemeinschaft, Bonn, August 29, 1952, "Verhandlungen des Interimsausschusses der EVG," copied to Gerhard Matzky, BA-MA, N 181/10, Bd. 7, 1952–1983.

51 Gerhard Matzky, "Kriegsartikel oder Pflichtenlehre? Vom Inspekteur des BGS a.D. Matzky," *Die Parole* 2, no. 2 (February 1952): 2.

1920s, fit the stereotypes of that earlier time that members of the Blank Office saw in the BGS.[52]

Matzky further complicated matters when on July 13, 1954, he delivered a lecture to the Bundestag's Committee for European Security.[53] Many of the points he made in his comments reinforced the Prussian traditions Blank's men, and Baudissin in particular, wanted to jettison. During the lecture, for example, he spoke about the need for discipline to overcome "softness" in the postwar generation of young men who looked with disdain upon military service.[54] On the place of drill in the BGS, he quoted the British military historian, Basil Lidell Hart, who said "Drill, rightly understood, is inseparable from the organization of human activity ... repeating a movement over and over again until it becomes habit."[55] Matzky also explained that West Germany's youth could not be "brought up to form a real community and be prepared for operational tasks without a certain degree of toughness." Finally, he took a direct swipe at Baudissin when he said "looking at the countless speeches and writings of our most recent reformers dealing with the future citizen in uniform, I do not hesitate to admire the idealism, at times bordering on romanticism, with which they try to achieve their goal."[56]

Matzky's lecture placed him squarely among the military traditionalists, which according to historian Donald Abenheim viewed Baudissin as "little more than a charlatan, ignorant of the face of battle, who tendentiously denied his own aristocratic values and background to capitalize on the spirit of the times."[57] But it is also important to contextualize Matzky's comments with the duties expected of border police officers. He argued "hardness" in training prepared young men for the stress of cold nights on the border, confrontations with smugglers, difficult terrain, and performance in natural disasters. Tough training, he claimed, made border police veterans into the ideal candidates for the new army. He sent a personal copy of his lecture to Heusinger in an apparent attempt to gain an ally for the BGS in the Blank Office. In a note accompanying

---

52   Recent research has challenged Seeckt's reputation as anti-democratic, but he still reflected the conservative-authoritarian Prussian traditions that those in the Blank Office wanted to avoid; see Karen Schaefer, *German Military and the Weimar Republic: General Hans von Seeckt, General Erich Ludendorff and the Rise of Hitler* (Haverton, PA: Pen & Sword, 2020), 26–27.

53   Gerhard Matzky, "Vortrag vor dem Ausschuss für Fragen der europäischen Sicherheit am 13. Juli 1954," BA-MA, N 245/42, Nachlaß Generaloberst Hans-Georg Reinhardt.

54   Ibid., 3.

55   Ibid., 8.

56   Gerhard Matzky, "Vortrag vor dem Ausschuss für Fragen der europäischen Sicherheit," 20.

57   Donald Abenheim, *Reforging the Iron Cross*, 100.

the lecture Matzky wrote: "I hope to be able to assume that you share the misgivings raised in my presentation about the possible hasty nature of the future army build-up as well as my views on the value of experience in the field of training and education, which apparently gets too little attention these days."[58] Heusinger remained non-committal, however, and thanked Matzky in his brief response telling him only that he read his remarks "with great interest."[59] Matzky's attitude towards the Blank Office is also evident in a letter he wrote to his former Wehrmacht colleague General Bernhard von Loßberg, whose son had recently completed BGS training. Loßberg complimented Matzky on the military preparedness and quality of the BGS, which he compared to "our old Reichswehr." Matzky thanked Lohsberg and told him that the men in the Blank Office were viewing rearmament through "rose-colored spectacles" if they thought they could proceed without the BGS.[60]

Matzky turned next to his other personal connection in the Blank Office, General Hans Speidel. On October 29, 1954, he wrote a lengthy letter to Speidel gently criticizing him for not following through on a promise Speidel had allegedly made to discuss the use of the BGS. He told Speidel that by April 1, 1955, the BGS would have more than 19,000 trained men that could "compete in every respect with the infantry of our former Reichswehr."[61] He suggested that the BGS might also be used as a militarized gendarmerie of the type set up by "Hitler's Wehrmacht in the form of the so-called army posts" in order to "counter major military raids from the East in order to win a few hours or to localize minor attacks."[62] He concluded by telling Speidel that without the BGS he could "hardly imagine a real task for such a Federal Police in the foreseeable future." This was a frank admission coming from the head of an organization that the Interior Ministry and Matzky himself had gone to great lengths defending as nothing more than a police force. Like Heusinger, Speidel remained ambivalent to Matzky's ideas and responded with short congenial letters apologizing for being too busy attending to his duties in Paris.[63]

Heusinger expressed his real attitude towards the BGS in a secret planning document for the build-up of the West German Army that he wrote just three months after telling Matzky that he read over his ideas

---

58 Gerhard Matzky to Adolf Heusinger, July 17, 1954, BA-MA, N 181/6 Bd. 3, G-H, 1952–1983.

59 Ibid.

60 Correspondence between Gerhard Matzky and General (ret.) Lohsberg, August 15–18, 1954, BA-MA, N 181/6 Bd. 3, G-H, 1952–1983.

61 Gerhard Matzky to Hans Speidel, October 29, 1954, BA-MA, N 181/10 Bd. 7, S, 1952–1983.

62 Ibid.

63 Ibid.

with great interest.⁶⁴ In the document, Heusinger argued that policing and military duties should never be mixed, and without providing names he blamed the commanding officers of the BGS for training their men like soldiers. He concluded that bringing border police officers into the army would "likely jeopardize our ideas about the internal structure of the armed forces."⁶⁵ For his part, Speidel had never been an open advocate of rearming through mobile police forces. In a January 1950 memorandum (*Denkschrift*), Speidel evaluated the option of establishing barracked police forces modeled after the East German People's Police, but warned against it because it would jeopardize the "internal structure" they intended to achieve with a new army.⁶⁶

Yet in spite of all their philosophical differences over tradition and reform in the debate over the new army, not much separated members of the Defense and Interior Ministries on their visions of the future German soldier. Even Baudissin admitted as much when he accepted an invitation from BGS Colonel Heinrich Müller to take part in the professional ethics seminar in 1955 at the Protestant Social Academy in Friedewald. Müller lectured on the officer's position in the social fabric of democracy, to which Baudissin followed up with his own lecture on the same topic in direct response to Müller.⁶⁷ As he began, Baudissin thanked the members of the BGS for inviting him to take part and told the audience that "I will openly admit to you that, based on various statements, including those in writing, I had certain fears that there were contradictions in our opinions, and I am glad that's not the case. There are many things that connect us … above all, we have a common task."⁶⁸ The lectures revealed only

---

64 Document 27, "Bundesgrenzschutz und Aufbau westdeutscher Streitkräfte: Der Beauftragte des Bundeskanzlers für die mit der Vermehrung der Alliierten Truppen zusammenhängenden Fragen (Amt Blank), II/1. Schreiben, Bonn, November, 4, 1954, Geheim," reprinted in *Dokumente zur deutschen Militärgeschichte 1945–1990: Bundesrepublik und DDR im Ost-West-Konflikt*, ed. Christoph Nübel (Berlin: Ch. Links, 2019), 167–69.

65 Document 27, "Bundesgrenzschutz und Aufbau westdeutscher Streitkräfte," in Christoph Nübel, *Dokumente zur deutschen Militärgeschichte*, 167–69.

66 Document 12, Hermann Foertsch, Adolf Heusinger, Hans Speidel, Denkschrift, January 5, 1950, "Politische, soziale und organisatorische Fragen der Verteidigung in der Bundesrepublik," reprinted in Christoph Nübel, *Dokumente zur deutschen Militärgeschichte*, 104–12.

67 BGS Colonel Heinrich Müller, "Die Stellung des Offiziers im Sozialgefüge der Demokratie," gehalten am 9. Dezember 1955 an der Evangelischen Sozialakademie Friedewald vor Offizieren des Bundesgrenzschutzes," BArch-K, B 106/20765.

68 Wolf Graf von Baudissin, "Auszug aus einem Vortrag des Grafen von Baudissin, Bundesministerium für Verteidigung, gedacht als Antwort auf den Vortrag, den Oberst i. BGS Müller anlässlich einer Tagung von Gs-Offizieren an der

Figure 3.1. Future BGS Inspector Heinrich Müller as a young officer in Rommel's Africa Corps, ca. 1942. BA-MA, N 848/42, courtesy of Dr. Irmgard Müller.

subtle differences between how each man envisioned the future role of military officers and mainly focused on the idea put forth by Müller that democracy depended upon the role of what he called a "class of elites." According to Müller, these elites formed "a group of chosen individuals linked by a common ideal ... bound by a shared social responsibility ... willing to translate their knowledge and intellectual decisions into political action."[69] Baudissin disagreed with Müller's idea of military officers as elites. Instead Baudissin argued:"We should never claim this label for ourselves, but always behave in a way that makes others look at us for it ... there is only one ethos, which is also binding for the soldier: the civil!"[70]

Social Considerations and Their Consequences

On February 27, 1955, the Bundestag ratified the Paris Treaties, paving the way for West Germany's incorporation into NATO. Despite all the tensions between the Interior and Defense Ministries, on November 4, 1955, the Federal Defense Council decided to use the BGS as a nucleus for new armed forces. In the end, it proved to be the only viable solution to rapidly meet NATO troop levels. On November 7, 1955, representatives from the Interior and Defense Ministries met to begin the preliminary discussions on how to manage the transfer process.[71] Almost immediately both sides struggled over differences in how best to carry out the process and over what to do with those who remained in the BGS. Representatives from the Interior Ministry argued that border police officers should be taken into the army in closed or whole units since they had trained together. Gerhard Matzky suggested that at least 15,000 border police officers would volunteer, giving the army enough for three 5,000-man divisions. The Defense Ministry, however, wanted individuals with specialized training in artillery and aviation as opposed to keeping units together. Moreover, they also wanted the right to reject any border police candidate they deemed unsuitable whether due to age, lack of army experience, or problematic service records.[72]

Representatives from both ministries met again on November 17, 1955, but still struggled to resolve their fundamental differences. They did, however, establish three sub-commissions with representatives from both

---

Evangelischen Sozialakademie in Friedwald am 9. Dezember 1955, gehalten hat," BA-MA, N 848/30, Bd. 1.
  69   Müller, "Die Stellung des Offiziers," 9.
  70   Baudissin, "Antwort auf den Vortrag, den Oberst i. BGS Müller," 4.
  71   Abteilungsleiter III, November 8, 1955, "Vertraulicher Vermerk über Staatssekretär-Besprechung über Bundesgrenzschutz von November 7, 1955," BA-MA, BW 1/17960, 1.
  72   Ibid.

ministries to help facilitate the transfer process. A Selection Commission decided who would be transferred, an Administrative Commission dealt with equipment and accommodations, and the Personnel Commission handled all issues relating to rank, pay, and benefits. A major point of contention involved the role of the Personnel Advisory Committee (PGA). The PGA consisted of an independent board of civilians and retired veterans not seeking a new commission, established by the Bundestag on July 23, 1955, to screen all applicants for officer positions from the rank of colonel and above.[73] The Ministry of Defense insisted that all BGS officers had to be screened by the PGA. At the same time, Dr. Josef Rust at the Defense Ministry argued that subjecting any former member of the Blank Office to such a screening would be "intolerable."[74] For the Interior Ministry, this amounted to a blatant double standard. The BGS, they argued, had already proven its democratic reliability and should not have to face further scrutiny.

Border police officers also complained about what they perceived as discrimination against members of their organization. They pushed back against the narrative that they were anti-democratic fostered by the press and some members of the SPD. The majority of the SPD wanted the BGS disbanded now that a new army had been established, and they renewed their criticisms of the Interior Ministry for allegedly blurring the lines between policing and the military. SPD representatives called for the immediate reassignment of any border police officers not taken into the army to the state riot police.[75] An anonymous author in the BGS employee magazine *Der Grenzjäger* argued, "Now that the decision to use the BGS as a cadre for the new army has been made, voices suddenly rose accusing the BGS of outdated militaristic education and training procedures. One went so far as to refer to the proposed takeover of the BGS by the armed forces as undesirable because its inner structure would not correspond to that of the future armed forces, making any new [democratic] reforms useless."[76] Moreover, the author blamed the SPD for fostering the majority of this criticism, arguing they had ignored that "the unconditional and blind slavish obedience that Hitler had built up

---

73 Hans Ehlert, Christian Greiner, Georg Meyer, and Bruno Thoß, *Anfänge westdeutscher Sicherheitspolitik 1945–1956, Band 3, Die NATO-Option* (Munich: R. Oldenbourg, 1993), 1022–23.

74 "Vermerk über den Übergang des Bundesgrenzschutzes in die Streitkräfte fand am 15. November im BMI eine weitere Staatssekretärbesprechung statt," VIII/2/200/55, Geheim, Bonn, November 17, 1955, BA-MA, BW 1/17960.

75 Press Release, SPD Presse Dienst, February 1, 1956, BArch-K, B 136/1928, Fiche No. 1, Slides 87–88.

76 Anonymous author, "Unrichtige und ungerechte Kritik am Bundesgrenzschutz," *Der Grenzjäger* 1 (January 1956): 21.

in the German Wehrmacht [was] not only rejected by the BGS but [had] already been successfully overcome."[77]

The president of the BGS Employees' Association, Friedrich von Stülpnagel, complained to the SPD parliamentary coalition on behalf of his members calling the accusations questioning their democratic character "unconscionable."[78] He argued that all border police officers had already undergone rigorous screening and proven their loyalty to the democratic state by guarding the "Iron Curtain" for the past five years. Moreover, he suggested that most, if not all, of these men had endured at least one denazification hearing. Stülpnagel called it "absurd to now demand that another standard be applied in evaluating the men who had been solely responsible for upholding and guaranteeing the free democratic order of the Federal Republic."[79] In a letter to PGA Chairman Dr. Wilhelm Rombach, Stülpnagel pleaded with him to speak out against the humiliation of subjecting high-ranking BGS officers to another examination of their characters. He told Rombach: "Border police officers have already embraced the principles of the citizen in uniform, both individually and in the internal structure of the organization." Stülpnagel argued they had distinguished themselves by fostering a positive working relationship with the democratic West German state.[80]

The debate about whether border police leaders should be subjected to evaluation by the PGA was one of many significant issues facing West German lawmakers as they worked to revise the BGS law of 1951. Those responsible for establishing new legal guidelines also had to outline new duties for the BGS now that external defense appeared to be an exclusive responsibility for the army. And the new law also had to address many of the concerns expressed by police officers about rank, pay, and benefits if they chose to become soldiers. While some of these issues had already been discussed in secret, they remained largely unresolved when Adenauer wrote to the presidents of the Bundestag political parties requesting they add the new law to the agenda for early February 1956.[81] The draft revised the original BGS law passed on 16 March 1951. Representatives from the chancellor's office and Ministries of the Interior, Defense, Justice, and Finance worked collaboratively to produce the revised draft

77 Ibid.
78 Open letter from Friedrich von Stülpnagel to the SPD *Bundestagsfraktion*, December 13, 1955, BArch-K, B 136/1928, Fiche No. 2, Slides 61–63.
79 Ibid.
80 Letter from Friedrich von Stülpnagel to PGA member Dr. Wilhelm Rombach, December 29, 1955, BArch-K, B 136/1928, Fiche No. 2, Slides 59–60.
81 These preliminary meetings took place in November 1955 between representatives of the Interior and Defense Ministries. See BA-MA, BW1/17960; Letter from Adenauer to Presidents of the German Bundestag, January 25, 1956, BArch-K, B 136/1927, Fiche No. 3, Slide No. 90.

on November 22, 1955.[82] Building the new army and how to go about transferring members of the BGS who wanted to join fell to the Federal Minster of Defense. The Federal Council reviewed and approved the draft on November 30, 1955. The decision of the council directed the Minister of Defense to work closely with the Interior Minister to build three infantry divisions out of various border police forces with priority given, if possible, to transfering whole units instead of individual personnel.[83]

The proposed law changed the status of border police officers who transferred to the army from civil servants to that of career soldiers or soldiers for fixed terms (*Soldaten auf Zeit*). This change of status took effect one month after the new law was passed. Border police officers assigned to the Passport Control Service were exempt. Members of the BGS were to be brought into the armed forces at a rank equivalent to that which they already held at the time of their transfer. In cases where there was no equivalent military rank, the Ministry of Defense assigned a rank that closely matched their existing responsibilities. Thus a lieutenant in the border police would begin service in the army as a lieutenant, while a police commander, a rank that had no military equivalent, would be automatically brought in as a brigadier general.[84] The law also gave individual officers the option to stay in the BGS, but they had to express this desire in writing within thirty days after the law took effect. Finally, to the dismay of the BGS Employee Association, the law mandated that any senior border police candidate at the rank of colonel or above who chose transfer to the army had to face evaluation by the PGA, which had the sole right to dismiss anyone it deemed unfit for service in the new army.[85]

As border police officers and their union representatives began to analyze the effect of the new law on their organization, many of them complained that it favored candidates who chose to transfer to the army by offering better pay and benefits. A sergeant in the army, for example, was paid slightly more than a sergeant who elected to remain in the border police. Higher pay provided one incentive for more men to leave their current police careers. The BGS Association took these grievances to the Bundestag and demanded they intervene to resolve the disparities prior to the adoption of the law. To address these legitimate concerns, the

82 Letter and draft of second *Bundesgrenzschutz* law from Staatssekretär Ritter von Lex to Hans Globke, November 22, 1955, BArch-K, B 136/1004, Fiche No. 1, Slide No. 24.

83 Kabinettsbeschluss: Vorbereitung der Ausführung des zweiten Gesetzes über den Bundesgrenzschutz, BArch-K, B 136/1004, Fiche No. 1, Slide No. 35.

84 Anlage zum zweiten Gesetz über den Bundesgrenzschutz, BArch-K, B 136/1004, Fiche No. 1, Slide No. 27.

85 Draft of Second Bundesgrenzschutz law, BArch-K, B 136/1004, Fiche No. 1, Slide No. 24.

Bundestag decided to revise the Civil Service Remuneration Act of 1927 by equalizing the salaries of soldiers and border police officers holding the same ranks.[86] In the meantime, the Interior Ministry offered the men who chose to stay in the BGS a supplementary allowance that temporarily raised their salaries to match those of soldiers with equivalent ranks. As an added incentive, the officers could count the supplementary allowances towards the final compensation of their pensions.[87] The efforts by the BGS Association and the Interior Ministry on behalf of its members reflected the larger role played by social benefits in one's decision whether to remain a police officer or join the new army.

Nevertheless, the future prospects and long-term survival of the BGS remained in flux as Gerhard Schröder's Interior Ministry tried to decide what to do with organization in the aftermath of its use to build the army. Soon, this uncertainty proved to be a serious morale issue. Many of those who chose to remain police officers wondered if the organization they had dutifully served for many years would be disbanded. Hence many younger police officers thought the army might be their best option for stable employment.[88] The decline in morale motivated Schröder to write an open letter calling for unity within its ranks. He assured the officers that he would work tirelessly to preserve the organization, but told its command staff that he relied upon them "to preserve the trust of subordinates and achieve the maximum cohesion in each respective unit."[89]

After the revised Border Police Act passed its first reading in the Bundestag, West Germany's politicians and government experts began working in committees to resolve various points of the new law before

---

86 The details of these changes were published in the Bundesgrenzschutz Association's journal; See Friedrich von Stülpnagel, "Rückblick und Ausschau: Die Entwicklung unseres-Berufes Vertrauen in die Zukunft zweites Gesetz über den Bundesgrenzschutz," *Der Grenzjäger* 1 (January, 1956): 3–6; Dr. Brill, "Unsere Berufsorganisation: Jetzt und in Zukunft—Wirkungen des Tätigkeits-Wechsels auf den BGS-Verband," *Der Grenzjäger* 1 (January 1956): 5–6.

87 See Deutscher Bundestag, Drucksache 2306, "Schriftlicher Bericht: Des Ausschusses für Beamtenrecht (9. Ausschusses) über den Entwurf eines Gesetzes zur Angleichung der Dienstbezüge von Vollzugsbeamten des Bundesgrenzschutzes an die Besoldung der Freiwilligen in den Streitkräften (Besoldungsangleichungsgesetz für den Bundesgrenzschutz)," 13. April 1956.

88 Matthias Molt, "Von der Wehrmacht zur Bundeswehr: Personelle Kontinuität und Diskontinuität beim Aufbau der deutschen Streitkräfte, 1955–1966," PhD diss. (University of Heidelberg, 2007), 342.

89 Letter BMI Gerhard Schröder to BGS Commanders, August 11, 1954, reprinted in Heinz Brill, *Bogislaw von Bonin im Spannungsfeld zwischen Wiederbewaffnung—Westintegration—Wiedervereinigung: Ein Beitrag zur Entstehungsgeschichte der Bundeswehr, 1952–1955, Band II, Dokumente und Materialien* (Baden Baden: Nomost Verlagsgesellschaft, 1987), 198.

holding the final vote. As with other debates over national security, federalism played a significant role. For Schröder's Interior Ministry and those choosing to remain in the BGS, preserving and rebuilding the organization remained the highest priority. Parliamentary resolutions 1881 and 2306 codified the rights of equal pay and benefits guaranteed under the Civil Service Act, aligning the salaries of border police officers with those of soldiers of the same rank.[90] Many of West Germany's Social Democratic politicians, however, wanted to disband the BGS and return policing to the jurisdiction of the federal states. SPD deputies and their supporters proposed resolution 607 calling for the complete dissolution of the BGS and the reassignment of its remaining officers to the state police.[91] Schröder, like his predecessor Robert Lehr, took a hard stand against any suggestion of giving up or disbanding the federal government's only source of police power. He urged the representatives to reject resolution 607 at all costs because it would leave West Germany's borders unguarded. He proclaimed: "I was shocked when I saw this motion from the socialist group, which overlooks one of the most important security instruments that the federal government has at its disposal to deal with the currently most important security questions and that they would suggest that an instrument this essential to our national security should be unceremoniously destroyed here."[92]

During Schröder's address, Wilhelm Mellies (SPD) interrupted him and claimed it was not the socialists who "doomed" the BGS, but rather the federal government's decision to use them as a cadre for the army. Schröder reiterated that the government still needed the BGS as an instrument to enforce West Germany's "national interests." He reminded the representatives that the army would always be a "NATO-bound" military force and thus could not be used by the Federal Republic for its own internal security needs.[93] As the debate ended, Vice President Schmid called for a vote on resolution 607. To Schröder's great relief, the resolution failed, ensuring, at least for the time being, the survival of the BGS.[94] Yet those who elected to remain border police officers still faced uncertain futures. Although the Interior Ministry decided to rebuild the

---

90 See Drucksachen 1881 and 2306, Deutscher Bundestag 2. Wahlperiode 1953, "Schriftlicher Bericht des Ausschusses für Beamtenrecht (9. Ausschuß) über den Entwurf eines Gesetzes zur Angleichung der Dienstbezüge von Vollzugsbeamten des Bundesgrenzschutzes an die Besoldung der Freiwilligen in den Streitkräften (Besoldungsangleichungsgesetz für den Bundesgrenzschutz)," 1–5.

91 See Umdruck Numbers 602 and 607, "Entschließungsantrag der Fraktion der SPD zur dritten Beratung des Entwurfs eines zweiten Gesetzes über den Bundesgrenzschutz," BT 145 Sitzung, Anlage 7, 7690.

92 Ibid., 7658.
93 Ibid., 7660.
94 Ibid.

force, nagging questions about its security role remained now that the Federal Republic had a new armed force—the Bundeswehr. Rather than using the opportunity to reform the organization into a traditional law enforcement agency, however, Schröder and his colleagues opted for the status quo. Thus for the time being, members of the BGS remained caught between their duty to enforce laws and the expectation that they also fight wars.

PART II

ORGANIZATIONAL CULTURE, 1956–1980

CHAPTER FOUR

RECRUITMENT AND REBUILDING THE BGS

Although the number of border police officers who transferred to the army never reached the levels predicted by Gerhard Matzky, the strength of the BGS plummeted. More than 9,572 border police officers transferred to the army, leaving a total of 7,042. Besides the obvious shortage in manpower, the army requisitioned the majority of BGS equipment and took over its best barracks, leaving entire units to billet in local hostels or temporary accommodations. It was questionable whether the BGS would ever recover. Interior Minister Schröder tried desperately to reassure his personnel and their commanding officers that the organization could expect a secure future. He wrote to Konrad Adenauer and implored him to publicly recognize the BGS as a way to boost the men's faltering morale.[1] Adenauer did his part, and in an open letter to the organization, thanked its staff for their loyal service, but also reassured them that the nation still needed them. The chancellor affirmed that "even those who remain in the BGS will have to fulfill an important duty, which although it might be in other fields, cannot be considered less significant to the duties of the military ... the living spirit in the BGS and their future work in the service of the Fatherland will continue up to the day in which a reunified Germany will thank you."[2]

Nevertheless, serious questions about the future of the organization remained. What purpose did a militarized police force serve now that the Federal Republic had an army? How would the Interior Ministry reach a new generation of young men and convince them to join an organization like the BGS? To be sure, recruitment had never been a significant challenge for the Interior Ministry, since there had always been more applicants than available positions. Yet the birth of West Germany's economic miracle and the declining postwar unemployment figures meant that the BGS now had to compete for candidates with the army in addition to the

---

1   Letter from BMI Schröder to Chancellor Adenauer, May 23, 1956, BArch-K, B136/1927, Fiche No. 3, Slide No. 251.
2   Erlass des Herrn Bundeskanzlers an den Bundesgrenzschutz, 23. Mai 1956, BArch-K, B136/1927, Fiche No. 3, Slide No. 250.

other career opportunities available for young men in both the public and private sectors. Since it faced many challenges and steep costs to rebuild the organization, why did the Federal Republic keep the BGS rather than transfer its duties to state security agencies? The extent of the recruitment and rebuilding program shows that neither the Interior Ministry nor the federal government wanted to surrender its only source of executive police power. With the armed forces under NATO, they justified the need to retain the BGS as a force to fight small wars, insurgents, or border incursions by the communist People's Police before they erupted into larger conflicts.

The BGS as a Multipurpose Border Militia

In the months after the EDC collapsed, secret discussions between the SPD military advisor Friedrich Beermann (SPD), BGS Colonel Kurt Spitzer, and others revealed that despite the formation of a new army, they planned, at all costs, to retain and rebuild the BGS. Rather than finally remaking the force into a police agency, those in command increased its militarization and renewed its focus on fighting wars. They argued that the BGS should become a border militia force to fight communist insurgents and "bandits" who might attack the Federal Republic using guerilla war tactics. For these men, the greater threat to West Germany was not a Soviet invasion but rather a conventional attack by the People's Police. Spitzer, who had joined the new army, developed an alternative plan for defending West Germany while working as Gerhard Matzky's chief of staff in the BGS. Spitzer's plan "Sword and Shield" tried to propose solutions that avoided nuclear destruction if NATO and Soviet forces clashed in West Germany.[3] According to Spitzer, the state had to defend itself regardless of how NATO used its armed forces and thus his use of the term "shield" was at the core of his thinking about border police units and their importance to national defense. He called for stationary border police forces to be kept numerically strong in order to fight from fixed positions and "protect gaps in the territory of the Federal Republic."[4]

In Spitzer's plan, border police units would be armed with conventional armor-piercing weapons and housed in nuclear-proof shelters. Besides anti-tank defense, he suggested the BGS could protect the civilian population near the Iron Curtain. Police officers would direct civilians to pre-designated shelters. More importantly, Spitzer emphasized that the BGS would be vital in countering the large number of communist

---

3 Not to be confused with the NATO doctrine of the same name—shield being the conventional forces and sword the nuclear weapons.
4 Heinz Brill, *Dokumente und Materialien*, 177.

partisans he believed already operated in West Germany.[5] Spitzer's plan, however theoretical, reflected the government's real fears that relying on NATO's atomic "sword" meant nuclear annihilation for the Federal Republic. Thus disbanding the BGS to rely exclusively on NATO was unthinkable—or as Spitzer concluded, "To liberate mass graves makes little sense!"[6]

Beermann agreed with Spitzer and in a lengthy memorandum discussing the possibilities of what to do with the BGS going forward, he argued that "incorporating the BGS into the NATO forces would be a mistake." Moreover, he suggested that the government had to stop thinking about the BGS as either a police or military force when from his perspective, the Inner-German border with its potential for civil war had always necessitated what he defined as a, "multipurpose organization ... which allows for a scope ranging from purely police to fully military operations." Like Spitzer, Beermann did not want to leave the defense of West Germany entirely to NATO forces. He argued that the BGS could deal with counterinsurgency operations or what he called "bandit fighting" (Bandenbekämpfung). According to Beermann, "when fighting bandits, especially paramilitary bandits, these tend to work with sharp reprisals against the civilian population, particularly when the bandits appear in civilian clothing." Thus he argued that the BGS should be returned to its authorized strength of 20,000 men as soon as possible and armed with heavy weapons such as 8cm canons, grenade launchers, heavy mortars, self-propelled guns, and 20 mm heavy machine-guns.

From Beermann's perspective, the overall objective of the BGS should be to keep border conflicts localized, because there would be a risk of war once NATO forces arrived. He recommended that the BGS be developed into "a border militia as they existed on the borders of the Weimar Republic in Pomerania and East Prussia." By invoking security operations during the Weimar Republic, Beermann favored the ideas that Adenauer and Schröder's predecessor Robert Lehr first conceived of for the BGS as a Weimar Style paramilitary fighting force (see chapter 1). In his study of border guarding during the Weimar Era, Jun Nakata has argued that military historians ignored the role played by border guard associations in national defense.[7] In fact, the head of the BGS employee association, Friedrich von Stülpnagel's favorite uncle, Joachim, was one of the main advocates of using private border guards as a secret arm of the Reichswehr, a concept that placed him in direct conflict with its chief,

5   Ibid., 179.
6   Ibid., 187.
7   Jun Nakata, *Der Grenz- und Landesschutz in der Weimarer Republik, 1918 bis 1933: Die geheime Aufrüstung und die deutsche Gesellschaft* (Freiburg im Breisgau: Rombach, 2002), 6.

General Hans von Seeckt, who opposed mixing policing with military matters.[8] It is rather unsurprising, then, that similar ideas resonated among these particular men at a time when Germany again faced strict limitations on its postwar armed forces.

Initial Challenges to a Rapid Reconstruction

Considering the alternative national defense plans and the federal government's fear of communist insurrection, there was no question that the BGS had to be rebuilt. Many of the organization's veteran commanders, including Gerhard Matzky, chose to transfer to the army. Although Ludwig Dierske temporarily took over for Matzky, Brigadier General Kurt Andersen soon replaced him. Andersen epitomized everything the reformers in the Ministry of Defense loathed about the BGS—he had the reputation of an uncompromising soldier who was still grounded in Prussian traditions of obedience. Prior to his promotion to chief, Andersen led the BGS school at Lübeck-St. Hubertus. Even Beermann, a strong advocate of rebuilding the BGS, did not care too much for him. On a visit to the school at Lübeck in 1955, Beermann described Andersen as a "typical East Prussian who gives me the impression of a very commiserative type, a man who knows exactly what he wants, and whose subordinates, I am convinced, know only submission."[9] Andersen's age and record of service with Baltic Freikorps units in 1918 caught the attention of the PGA when they considered him for the new army. Nevertheless, Andersen did not wait to be formally rejected by the PGA and instead voluntarily chose the option to remain in the BGS.[10]

On June 28, 1956 the Interior Ministry established a special formation staff (*Aufstellungsstab*) to manage the reconstruction of the BGS. Under the leadership of ministerial director Walter Bargatzky, the formation staff consisted of various experienced leaders from each command group who were tasked with reorganizing what remained of the force.[11]

   8   Ibid., 191; Friedrich von Stülpnagel claimed Joachim was his favorite uncle in a 1955 biographical story on his family by the magazine *Der Spiegel*; See "Bundesgrenzschutz: Stülpnagel, der silberne Igel, *Der Spiegel*, 9. Jahrgang, 45, February 11, 1955, 14–26, 16.
   9   Dr. Fritz Beermann, "Bericht: über den Besuch bei dem Bundesgrenzschutz," March 1–5, 1955, 4, BA-MA, N 597/30.
   10   Dr. Rombach an den Bundesminister für Verteidigung, Eilt Sehr!, "Der Vorstand vom Personalgutachterausschuss für die Streitkräfte Betrifft: Übernahme von Offizieren des Bundesgrenzschutzes in die Bundeswehr," 5 Juni 1956, BA-MA, BW 1/5483.
   11   Letter from Ministerialdirigent in the Bundesministerium des Innern Dr. Mosheim to all Border Police Commands, "Aufstellungsstäbe für die GS-Einheiten (Neu)," BArch-K, B106/93367; Memorandum from Ministerialdirektor Walter

With this framework in place, Andersen believed it was only a matter of time before his force was returned to its pre-army strength of 20,000 men. Yet before the command staff intensified its recruitment efforts, they first had to reorganize their remaining units. This proved to be complicated, because the army had taken so much of their equipment and occupied their barracks. Because a number of non-commissioned officers (NCOs) and officer candidates had elected to remain in the border police, Bargatzky believed he had enough men to staff the junior officer positions lost to the army. Most of these men had prior military experience.[12]

Equipment shortages caused Bargatzky and his staff larger problems, especially the deficits in weapons, vehicles, and telecommunications components.[13] He repeatedly criticized the Ministry of Defense for taking this vital equipment, arguing that it greatly weakened West Germany's national security.[14] By joint agreement, the army absorbed the entire equipment stores of what could supply six full border police battalions. There were plans to re-supply these units, but in the interim the Interior Ministry had to requisition all of the equipment from its training facilities at the Federal Police Academy in Lübeck.[15] Thus training programs suffered temporary setbacks so that field units could continue their daily operations at the inner-German border. Bargatzky also complained about the housing shortage caused by the loss of barracks. The higher quality accommodations that remained went to married police officers with families, while single men were housed in temporary barracks or billeted in hostels close to the border zones they patrolled.[16]

After working through the logistics of the transfer, Bargatzky and his staff recognized the true scope of the personnel shortage. Border activity reports beginning in July 1956 began sounding the alarm as the persons and traffic crossing the borders dramatically increased while staffing declined. The "European Bridge" checkpoint between Kehl and Strasbourg, for example, reported in excess of 2,000,000 persons coming

---

Bargatzky to all Border Police Commands, June 26, 1956, "Organisation des wieder aufzufüllenden BGS," BArch-K, B106/93367.

12   Schnellbrief: Walter Bargatzky, Bundesministerium des Innern an Bundesgrenzschutz Kommandos, 18 Juli 1956, "Organisation des BGS," 6, BArch-K, B106/93367; Memorandum from Dr. Mosheim, Bundesministerium des Innern Referat VI C 2, June 13, 1956, "Wiederauffüllung des Bundesgrenzschutzes; hier: Bildung von Aufstellungsstäben," BArch-K, B106/93367.

13   Ibid.

14   Memorandum from Ministerialdirektor Walter Bargatzky to the Bundesministerium für Verteidigung, March 29, 1956, "Überführung des Bundesgrenzschutzes in die Bundeswehr," BA-MA, BW1-313099.

15   Schnellbrief: Walter Bargatzky, "Organisation des BGS," 6, BArch-K, B106/93367.

16   Ibid.

and going during the height of the summer vacation season.[17] The number of travelers through Kehl was typical of most West German border stations during 1956, all of which complained of inadequate staffing due to the loss of so many officers to the army.[18] The commander of the Braunschweig checkpoint complained to his superiors, remarking: "It is a puzzle to me how I am expected to fulfill the duties of my post with these reductions! I can only hope that my complaints might be valuable for those who keep insisting on disposing of our organization!"[19] Traffic levels also overwhelmed the Konstanz checkpoint on the Bodensee. Its commander reported: "With the progressive motorization of the Federal Republic, there is already greater traffic at my post, which on some days, especially on weekends and holidays, has reached levels previously unseen."[20] To make matters worse, during the fall of 1956 the uprising in Hungary caused a massive refugee crisis as thousands fled the violent Soviet crackdown. At Kehl, for example, officers reported that 7,150 Hungarian refugees crossed the European Bridge from West Germany into France during the last quarter of 1956.[21] The BGS desperately needed recruits to keep up with its most basic duties.

West Germany's new generation of young men expressed little interest in border policing as a career, and this hampered staffing levels even before so many personnel transferred to the army. Border Command North, for example, reported that its applicant pool had declined to the extent that it would be unable to fill anticipated vacancies during the calendar year 1954. Application quotas that once exceeded 700 per month in 1953 decreased to less than 200 at the beginning of 1954.[22] By March 1957, certain members of the Interior Ministry feared the BGS might never recover its full strength. In a confidential inter-office memorandum,

17 Passkontrollamt Kehl: Tätigkeitsbericht für die Monate Juli–September 1956, 6. Oktober 1956, BArch-K, B273/18.

18 The individual border checkpoints filed their activity reports quarterly with the central Passkontrolldirektion in Koblenz; The checkpoints were located at Kehl, Konstanz, Braunschweig, Lorrach, Flensburg, Emden, Kleve, Aachen, Idar-Oberstein, Hamburg, and Saarbrücken, which opened in 1957 after the Saar once again became part of West Germany. See border activity reports under Bundespolizeidirektion/Grenzschutzdirektion, BArch-K, B273.

19 Passkontrollamt Braunschweig: Tätigkeitsbericht für die Monate Juli–September 1956, 10. Oktober 1956, pp. 8–9, BArch-K, B273/18.

20 Passkontrollamt Konstanz: Tätigkeitsbericht für die Monate April–June 1956, July 9, 1956, BArch-K, B273/18.

21 Passkontrollamt Kehl: Tätigkeitsbericht für die Monate Oktober–Januar 1957, January 8, 1957, BArch-K, B273/18.

22 Memorandum from Grenzschutzkommando-Nord an den Bundesminister des Innern, June 14, 1954, "Werbung für den Bundesgrenzschutz," BArch-K, B106/14024.

the CDU legal expert Eberhard Döge told Hanns Küffner, of the Press and Informations Office: "The reconstruction of the BGS is difficult, almost hopeless. The vacancies from the Bundeswehr are hardly replenished."[23] Küffner complained that recruitment efforts failed to take hold because of competition over funds for advertising with the army. Moreover, border police recruiters had to compete for personnel with state and municipal police forces. Young men had a wide variety of traditional civil service professions to choose from, including positions in the national postal service and West Germany's national railway. As the immediate effects of losing over 9,000 men to the army settled in, the BGS faced a personnel shortage that necessitated a swift and particularly innovative approach to recruitment.

Border Policing and Conceptions of a New Postwar Masculinity

Since the Interior Ministry could not count on an endless supply of veteran soldiers to fill its vacant positions, new recruitment methods also had to reconcile with the new ways postwar society defined masculinity. Recent groundbreaking work by historians of the West German army has shown that postwar military masculinity was shaped to a greater extent by "civilian norms" rather than the "traditional military values" of the first generation of BGS applicants.[24] Other than being a solider, policing offered the Federal Republic's male citizens one of the strongest public roles available to them in postwar society. According to the sociologist Matthew McCormack, "police work is largely performed by men, requires physical attributes such as strength and stature, and is associated with a cluster of masculine qualities such as authority, decisiveness and courage."[25] Before the army was created, border police officers were the first armed defenders of the new democratic state. Their duty to guard the nation's frontiers was different from the "community-care" duties of men serving in municipal and state police forces.[26]

---

23 Confidential memorandum from Staatssekretär Kuffner to Bundesministerium des Innern, March 5, 1957, BArch-K, B145/3423.

24 See Friederike Brühöfener, "Defining the West German Soldier: Military, Masculinity and Society in West Germany, 1945–1989," PhD diss. (University of North Carolina at Chapel Hill, 2014), iii.

25 Matthew McCormack, "A Species of Civil Soldier: Masculinity, Policing and the Military in 1780s England," in *A History of Police and Masculinities, 1700–2010*, ed. David G. Barrie and Susan Broomhall (London: Routledge, 2012), 56.

26 Rainer Prätorius, "Polizei in der Kommune," in *Die Polizei der Gesellschaft*, ed. Hans-Jürgen Lange, 308.

The protection of the democratic West German state itself was to a large extent bound up in the identities of these first BGS officers.[27] In other words, as James Sheehan has suggested: "Men in uniform personified the virtues on which the state's existence depended."[28] When the BGS was created in 1951, hyper-masculine themes were present in all aspects of the organization. It replicated the images and traditions of the Wehrmacht in everything, from its uniforms and equipment to its rank structure. Men who served in lower or line-level positions were not referred to as police officers (*Schutzmann or Polizist*) like their counterparts in municipal and state forces, but rather held the more masculine title of *Grenzjäger* (border hunters). Its first institutional journal, *Der Grenzjäger*, reflected many of these masculine themes. Scholars have shown that police journals and magazines are sites for a distinct "cult of masculinity."[29] The same is true for border police journals. This "cult of masculinity" was based on the notion that police officers must be tough, courageous, and aggressive. These journals also promoted traditional gender roles and marriage as normative or ideal behaviors for police officers.[30]

The institutional regulation of marriage in the BGS revealed insights on masculinity and the importance of changing gender roles in the postwar era. Members of the BGS were prohibited from marrying until the age of twenty-seven and in exceptional cases could do so at twenty-five or with the express permission of a superior officer.[31] The ban was problematic, because it gave the organization influence over the men's private lives and contradicted the basic freedom of choice afforded to their fellow citizens and civil servants. The restriction was codified in the Federal Police Act of 1953 and did not apply to civil servants who served in other branches of the government.[32] The Interior Ministry justified the marriage prohibition based on an understanding that "the nature of a police force, which must be ready at all times, results in the need for a certain

---

27 Matthew McCormack argues this was also true in the self-conception of eighteenth-century British police forces, which faced an internal threat to the democratic state as a result of violent riots; see Matthew McCormack, "A Species of Civil Soldier," 57.

28 James J. Sheehan, *Where Have All the Soldiers Gone? The Transformation of Europe* (Boston: Mariner, 2009), 6–7.

29 See P. A .J. Waddington, *Policing Citizens: Authority and Rights* (London: Routledge, 1999), 99.

30 Ibid.

31 "Was muss der Bewerber vom Bundesgrenzschutz wissen?" recruitment brochure/leaflet, BArch-K, B106/16992.

32 Ludwig Dierske, *Der Bundesgrenzschutz*, 112.

restriction on the fundamental rights of officers."[33] Police officers who violated these rules faced discipline. Besides the need for "readiness" in the BGS, the Interior Ministry also tried to regulate the type of women its personnel chose for wives. Similar thinking influenced the Ministry of Defense, which debated a marriage ban in the army. The Ministry of Defense, however, decided against implementing a marriage ban, because it contradicted the "citizen in uniform" ideal and it might lead to more children born out of wedlock.[34]

Evidence of how the BGS defined "suitable" women matched ideals envisioned in the army and was also reflected in organizational literature. A confidential report filed by an observer of the border police barracks at Braunschweig and Detelsdorf, for example, claimed that local women found the men of the BGS very desirable.[35] The report sheds light on expectations the organization had for its police officers and the women they chose as companions. According to the observer:

> In general, the young men are morally healthy and they do not read pornographic magazines. And even though naked pictures in one's locker are not forbidden, it is more common for the men to have photographs of their girlfriends on their nightstands. The men have consistently only been dating ordinary girls: most want to marry soon, which shows a strong desire for the bonding of home life. The strict requirement that one must be twenty-seven years of age to marry is viewed as overly harsh. There are no other marriage restrictions, and a supervisor's approval is not necessary, although they are expected to act in an advisory capacity for the young men in their care. STDs have not yet made an appearance.[36]

The report underscored the paternal role of superior officers in shaping the personal lives of their subordinates. According to historian Friederike Brühöfener, there was a desire among young soldiers for "domesticity" in the aftermath of the Second World War.[37] The observer quoted above defines this domesticity in the BGS as "a strong desire for the bonding of home life." Other historians have suggested there was a wider campaign on the part of state authorities to "define normative gender roles" as an

---

33 "Was muss der Bewerber vom Bundesgrenzschutz wissen?" recruitment brochure/leaflet, BArch-K, B106/16992.
34 For an excellent analysis of the debate over marriage in the Bundeswehr, see Friederike Brühöfener, "Defining the West German Soldier," 128–37.
35 "Bericht über den Besuch der Grenzschutzkommandos Braunschweig und Detelsdorf, vom 26.6—1.3.52," BA-MA, BW1/15792.
36 Ibid.
37 Friederike Brühöfener, "Defining the West German Soldier," 130.

approach to "reconfigure and revalidate Germanness."[38] The observations of the men living in barracks at Braunschweig and Detelsdorf reflected these ideals.

Evidence for "suitable" or ideal women and normative gender roles can be found in the advertisements, photographs, and artwork of organizational journals. Many of these ads depicted young men riding motorcycles or men and women together in convertible sports cars taking advantage of leisure time. Leisure activities were intended to show readers that while they were expected to defend the state, they were still permitted to have a normal civilian life. A photograph in a 1953 edition of *Die Parole*, for example, shows a young woman dressed for carnival (*Fasching*) winking at the reader. Below the photograph is a caption telling readers that carnival is a time for "charming adventures ... in which the border hunters should also be on guard because other boundaries have shifted too!"[39] The cover of a 1952 edition of *Die Parole* depicts a uniformed border police officer with his wife on his lap; both are holding flutes of champagne with a caption that reads: *Prosit Neujahr*! (Cheers New Year!). Inside, there is a full-page photograph of a woman wearing a revealing blouse and smiling at the reader with the caption "*Charmantes Mädchen, Charmantes Blüschen*" (charming girl, charming blouse). The caption further instructs border police officers to hold the photo horizontally and close one eye to find "undreamt of perspectives." Women are encouraged to take the photo to a department store, buy a similar blouse and then send the bill to their husbands, who will pay any price to see their wives in similar clothing.[40] The point here is to show that by buying the same blouse, women had a role in preventing their husbands from the temptations of a promiscuous sexual relationship outside of their marriage. Moreover, adultery was a punishable "service offense" for border policemen in the same way that it was for soldiers.[41]

These ads reinforced the socially acceptable roles expected of men and women in postwar West Germany. On the one hand, border officers are tempted with sexualized images of women. On the other hand,

---

38   Uta G. Poiger, "Rock 'n' Roll, Female Sexuality, and the Cold War Battle over German Identities," *Journal of Modern History* 68, no. 3 (1996): 579; See also Frank Biess, *Homecomings*, 87–91; Dagmar Herzog, "Pleasure, Sex, and Politics Belong Together: Post-Holocaust Memory and the Sexual Revolution in West Germany," *Critical Inquiry* 24, no. 2 (1998): 418; Robert Moeller, *Protecting Motherhood: Women and the Family in the Politics of Postwar West Germany* (Berkeley: University of California Press, 1993), 2.

39   *Die Parole* 2, no. 2 (February 1952): 22.

40   *Die Parole* 1. no. 1 (January 1952): 22.

41   See "Ein interessanter Bericht des Bundesrechnungshofes: Der Bundesrechnungshof über den Grenzschutz," *Der Grenzjäger* 5, no. 7 (July 1955): 8; See also Friederike Brühöfener, "Defining the West German Soldier," 202.

however, sexual boundaries were clearly identified. The advertisement for carnival, for example, implied that border policemen should guard against temptations to engage in irresponsible sexual behavior during a holiday when normal limits might be temporarily set aside. There was an element of risk or danger in succumbing to the temptations of carnival. Instead, these images emphasized marriage as the ideal. This is also reflected in the full-page cover photo of the husband and wife toasting the New Year, both of which are prominently displaying their wedding bands. During the Adenauer era, topics in these journals show how men were expected and indeed encouraged to promote heterosexuality without falling prey to promiscuity, while a healthy marriage to a "suitable" woman was revered as the ideal.

Beginning in the 1960s and extending into the 1970s editions of these journals, there was a greater effort to show readers that while they were expected to guard against communist enemies, they could and should also enjoy civilian activities and leisure time. In many of the editions, full-page ads encouraged border policemen to take vacations while featuring profiles of West Germany's popular destination cities. Of course, to promote idealized relationships, many of these ads included romantic or sexualized images of female fashion models. The objective was to promote the idea that you could join the BGS and still live a normal civilian life. The back cover of the July 1959 edition of *Die Parole*, for example, featured a young woman clad in a revealing bathing suit under the title: "Die Parole Wishes You a Joyful Vacation."[42] The September 1962 edition featured a café in Bad Kissingen with border policemen in civilian attire enjoying ice cream with their fashionably dressed female companions. The advertisement promoted the new barracks built in the region and states: "In Bad Kissingen, border policemen soon make friends—not just because of the beautiful girls in the Kurgarten-Café. See our report about the new barracks in Oerlenbach."[43] Additional full-page back covers went even further in promoting leisure time. The September 1961 edition included a photo of a young woman on a beach in Greece and prompted border policemen to submit photos from their own vacations for a contest.[44] The June 1961 edition featured a woman on the beach using her hand to draw a heart in the sand under the title: "When the sun is shining, being alone is only half bad!"[45]

The examples cited above are a representative sampling of the evolving definition of a new postwar masculinity that was an ideal shared by

---

42   *Die Parole*, 9, no. 7 (July 15, 1959): back cover.
43   *Die Parole* 12, no. 9 (September 15, 1962): back cover.
44   *Die Parole* 11, no. 9 (September 15, 1961): back cover.
45   *Die Parole* 11, no. 6 (June 15, 1961): back cover.

recruiters in the BGS and the army alike.[46] Border police recruiters competed with the army from the same pool of potential applicants. The Ministry of Defense decision against a marriage ban in the army made it more difficult for border police recruiters to attract candidates who instead opted to become soldiers so they could marry at a younger age. The Interior Ministry argued against lifting the marriage ban because border police officers lived in barracks and it was impossible for them to live with their wives if they were married.[47] The BGS Employees' Association called these claims ridiculous—married soldiers also lived in barracks and their wives lived nearby. The Association, however, suggested the government should provide subsidized housing for married border police officers because it was not ideal for families to live apart.[48] The Association also pointed out that many young recruits chose the Bundeswehr because they allowed marriage, which made the effort to rebuild border police units all the more problematic. Since a significant aspect of this ideal or new postwar masculinity was, as the ads above show, the expectation that soldiers and border police officers were civilians in addition to their duties as state servants, banning marriage in the BGS was problematic if its goal was to appeal to a new generation of young men. Thus the Border Police Association listed the elimination of the marriage ban as their signature wish following the creation of the army.[49] Nevertheless, revision of the Federal Police Act was mired in lengthy legal debates in the Bundestag until July 19, 1960 when the marriage ban was finally eliminated.[50]

What Friederike Brühöfener emphasized was the ideal type of man sought after for the new army—"men who would simultaneously be restrained, full-fledged soldiers, free men and good state citizens"—was the same objective for border police recruiters.[51] While this ideal type evolved, the traditionalists in the BGS resisted these definitions to the same extent as they were contested by certain elements in the armed forces.[52] What these tensions reflected, however, was the ongoing or protracted process of democratization. As the definitions of postwar masculinity changed and newer generations of men came of age, BGS

46 Friederike Brühöfener, "Defining the West German Soldier."
47 See "In treuer Kameradschaft weiter voran! Unsere Aufgaben im neuen Jahr," *Der Grenzjäger*, Jahrgang 7, no.1 (January 1957): 4.
48 Ibid.
49 See "Offene Personalwünsche: Eheschließung," *Der Grenzjäger*, Jahrgang 6, no. 9 (September 1956): 7.
50 Ludwig Dierske, *Der Bundesgrenzschutz: Geschichtliche Darstellung seiner Aufgabe und Entwicklung von der Aufstellung bis zum 31. März 1963* (Munich: Walhalla & Praetoria, 1967), 115.
51 Friederike Brühöfener, "Defining the West German Soldier," 121.
52 Ibid.; see also the discussion in chapter 3—Expansion in the use of the BGS to staff the Bundeswehr and the controversies with the PGA.

recruiters had to adapt their methods if they hoped to overcome personnel shortages.

Cinema and the Use of Film in Recruiting

Reaching the new generation and appealing to the evolving masculinity of West Germany's young men required innovation and experimentation. Nowhere was this more apparent than in the Interior Ministry's use of film to advertise careers in the BGS. There is already a significant body of work on postwar cinema and film, but much less emphasis on its use as a recruiting tool.[53] West Germans went to the movies in record numbers during the Adenauer era and films were a reliable medium in which to reach the widest possible audience. According to Heide Fehrenbach, "film attendance figures soared between 1945 and 1956, during which time box-office sales jumped from 150 to over 817 million tickets."[54] And while the people going to cinemas ranged in age and social status, the majority of those consistently attending were young men fascinated by westerns, detective stories, and adventure films. To be sure, this age cohort—eighteen to thirty years old—was within the ideal range targeted by BGS recruiters.[55] Border Command North ran a newspaper advertisement in 1955, for example, that specifically requested applicants between the ages of eighteen and twenty-two years of age who were in good health and free of criminal convictions.[56]

The first recruiting film was a twenty-four-minute documentary called *Zum Schutz der Heimat* (To Protect the Homeland). The Interior Ministry contracted with the Munich firm *Deutsche Industrie und Auftragsfilm* (German Industry and Film Commission (DIA) to oversee its production. The screenplay was written, adapted, and directed by "K. Richter" and Fritz Andelfinger.[57] Andelfinger had a lengthy career

---

53 See for example, John Davidson and Sabine Hake, *Framing the Fifties: Cinema in a Divided Germany* (New York: Berghahn, 2007); Detlef Kannapin, *Dialektik der Bilder: Der Nationalsozialismus im deutschen Film: Ein Ost-West-Vergleich* (Berlin: Karl Dietz, 2005); Anja Horbrügger, *Aufbruch zur Kontinuität: Kontinuität im Aufbruch: Geschlechterkonstruktionen im west- und ostdeutschen Nachkriegsfilm von 1945 bis 1952* (Marburg: Schüren, 2007).

54 Heide Fehrenbach, *Cinema in Democratizing Germany: Reconstructing National Identity after Hitler* (Chapel Hill: University of North Carolina Press, 1995), 118.

55 Ibid., 165.

56 "Der Bundesgrenzschutz," *Hannoverische Allgemeine Zeitung*, October 15, 1955, 10, BArch-K, B106/14024.

57 "Zum Schutz der Heimat," Inhaltsangabe, von Dr. K. Richter und Fritz Andelfinger, BArch-K, B106/14024—K. Richter's full name and background are unknown.

producing, directing, and writing German films, including a number of Nazi propaganda films. He had also written and directed films in the *Heimat* (homeland) genre during the Third Reich and postwar eras, including *Heimatland* (1939) and *Heimat, die uns blieb* (Home that Remained for Us—1949).[58] Film historians have shown that *Heimat* was a popular genre in 1950s West German cinema because it offered those still suffering the consequences of war and defeat an idealistic or de-politicized way of imagining a new national identity. The concept of *Heimat*, however, came to represent much more than just an idyllic homeland. The framing of home and hearth in these films provided an ideal basis for which the postwar Federal Republic envisioned its reconstruction.[59] Moreover, while the *Heimat* was something to defend at all costs, it was certainly not a masculine construct, like the notion of a "fatherland," which might be invoked to justify an offensive war.[60] Thus to protect or defend the homeland, as suggested in Andelfinger's script, was an approach that reflected West Germany's new postwar democratic national identity and the BGS as its guardian.

Andelfinger's experience making propaganda films for the Nazis, while morally problematic proved to be useful in the production of a persuasive recruiting film like *Zum Schutz der Heimat*. A close analysis of Andelfinger's annotated script and the film it yielded sheds light on how West Germany's postwar national identity was reshaped during the 1950s and the importance of border policing in protecting it.[61] The film opens with the narrator emphasizing the date of Germany's surrender—8 May 1945—while an image of the rubble and destruction of Germany's cities is slowly panned across the screen. The viewer's attention is next diverted to the Potsdam Conference and its role in dividing Germany. Images of

58 Rolf Giessen, *Nazi Propaganda Films: A History and Filmography* (Jefferson, North Carolina: McFarland, 2003), 186; Eric Rentschler, *The Ministry of Illusion: Nazi Cinema and its Afterlife* (Cambridge: Harvard University Press, 1996), 349; For a complete filmography of Fritz Andelfinger see Deutsches Filmportal, online, http://www.filmportal.de.
59 Heide Fehrenbach, 151; Elizabeth Boa and Rachel Palfreyman, *Heimat, A German Dream: Regional Loyalties and National Identity in German Culture 1890–1990* (New York: Oxford University Press, 2000), 2–4.
60 Heide Fehrenbach, 151; see also Celia Applegate, *A Nation of Provincials: The German Idea of Heimat* (Berkeley: University of California Press, 1990); Alon Confino, *Germany as a Culture of Remembrance: Promises and Limits of Writing History* (Chapel Hill: University of North Carolina Press, 2006)
61 "Zum Schutz der Heimat," Kommentar und Sprechertext, BArch-K, B106/14024; Letter from Bundesministerium des Innern Referat VI B 1 an Referate VI C 2, 3, 4, and 5, July 11, 1956, "Bundesgrenzschutzfilm," BArch-K, B106/14024; The final version of the film is also available online at https://www.youtube.com/watch?v=dgNTyz2T7J8.

villages, railways, and highways severed by Germany's postwar east-west division were set against the narrator's description of fragmented families and the refugee crisis created by those attempting to flee the Soviet Occupation zone. The first part of the film emphasized the danger to the West German free and democratic way of life posed by the Soviets and East Germans, who were seemingly ready to strike across the rural border at any moment.

At key points in the script, Andelfinger suggested imagery to accompany the narration. When the narrator described the Soviet Zone, for example, Andelfinger's notes suggested adding images that showed "Soviet marchers with banners; women and children at shooting practice, and an armed workers militia marching."[62] The focus on images of women and children perpetrating violent action was a deliberately gendered construct aimed to show the otherness of eastern society.[63] According to Uta Poiger, images of armed women evoked total war during the Third Reich and were used to show what might happen if West German men failed to protect their families. Photos of militarized East German women were also a regular feature in *Die Parole* magazine articles.[64] The film's narrator described in detail how the People's Police increased their strength to 60,000 men with 30,000 assigned to the inter-German border. Andelfinger's marginal notes recommended adding images of armed People's Police and border guards marching and patrolling the rural borders. The threat posed by the communist enemy as depicted in these images was set against the backdrop of refugees fleeing the militant east for a better life in a new homeland (*Neue Heimat*).[65] At the beginning of the film, Andelfinger succeeded in creating a persuasive argument that a distinct and powerful communist enemy was lying in wait to destroy the West German democratic way of life. His latent message was also reflected in press reports about the new film. Writing for the *Norddeutsche Zeitung*, Werner Neumann compared Andelfinger's film to a similar recruitment film produced by East Germany for its People's

62 Marginal notes in "Zum Schutz der Heimat," Kommentar und Sprechertext, 2, BArch-K, B106/14024.

63 For a good analysis of how gender is used to frame otherness, see Ulrike Zitzlsperger, ed., *Gender, Agency and Violence: European Perspectives from Early Modern Times to the Present Day* (Newcastle upon Tyne: Cambridge Scholars, 2013), ix–x.

64 Uta Poiger, *Jazz, Rock and Rebels*, 73–74; see for example Ullrich Rühmland, "Stalinstadt—eine erste Stadt auf deutschem Boden ohne Kirche," *Die Parole* 9, no. 7 (July 15, 1959): 7–9.

65 Marginal notes in "Zum Schutz der Heimat," Kommentar und Sprechertext, 2, BArch-K, B106/14024.

Police—"Wir tragen Gewehre" (We Carry Guns).[66] Neumann suggested that the title of the East German film alone, "expressed with all clarity that the Soviet Zone border police threatened the Federal Republic while the title protecting the homeland reflects an apt title for the BGS film." Neumann's point of view shows how postwar West Germans distanced themselves from militarism while also propagating their own self-image as the pacifists on the other side of the Iron Curtain.[67]

Once he had set the stage reflecting an existential danger to West Germany from the east, Andelfinger switched the viewer's attention to the heroes of the story—the men of the BGS. In one particular scene, a young man sitting in a border police recruitment center asked the senior officer, "and what will become of me after seven years of service?" The officer answered that the young man will receive important training that he could use for future professions along with excellent opportunities for further education and promotion. The intent of this scene was to show that border police service was part of civil society, since it was relevant to civilian career training. After 1945 the values of civilian life such as a stable job, health care, and a secure pension were more enticing to recruits than the promise of life in the barracks. This theme reflected what historian James Sheehan has argued was the replacement of the military or "garrison" state by a civilian state following more than thirty years of war.[68] The young man, known in the film as border hunter Carstens, and two of his colleagues, Brettschneider and Wagner, were followed through a course of action-oriented training at the border police school in Lübeck-St Hubertus. The film sequence demonstrated for potential recruits that joining the border police required physical stamina and athleticism, but also provided an outlet for the expression of masculine interests such as shooting, cross country skiing, fencing, and judo training. As the training came to a conclusion, Carstens led his colleagues in a mock field exercise where they encountered a group of enemy saboteurs crossing the inner-German border. Carstens and his patrol group detained and searched the saboteurs before calling on a mobile unit to transport the detainees to a secure police facility. Having successfully completed their field-exercises, Carstens and his colleagues graduated from their basic training in Lübeck by swearing and oath of loyalty to West Germany's Basic Law.

The film followed Carstens, Brettschneider, and Wagner as each goes on to different assignments. Here the objective of the film was twofold. On the one hand, the producers wanted to demonstrate through

---

66 Werner Neumann, "Schutz der Heimat—Wir tragen Gewehre," *Norddeutsche Zeitung*, November 11, 1956.
67 Ibid.
68 James J. Sheehan, *Where Have All the Soldiers Gone?* 172–73.

individual examples that the opportunities for young men who joined the BGS were useful beyond their seven-year service commitments. Yet on the other hand, they also wanted to emphasize a particular democratic national identity juxtaposed against imagery and descriptions of the east as wild, dangerous, and foreign. Thus the implication for those watching the film was that policing offered an opportunity for a noble profession defending a decent, democratic way of life, while also providing useable skills for civilian careers. Border Hunter Carstens, for example, was rapidly promoted to non-commissioned officer and assigned to patrol the Iron Curtain, where according to the film's narrator "he learns for himself about the division of Germany that has been forced upon us by a foreign power ... Carstens and his comrades never forget that millions of Germans in the east live each day placing their hopes in the Federal Republic."[69] Andelfinger's objective was to emphasize West Germany as the true, peaceful German nation while those in the east were held captive by totalitarian communism. The script annotations recommended a panning shot of the inter-German border's death strip and a sequence of marching communist border guards to accompany the narrator's comments. The death strip, or *Todesstreifen*, was a name West Germans used to refer to the border protective zones between fortifications where East German guards were authorized to shoot anyone caught within them.[70]

But Carstens' leadership skills were also helpful if he chose to transfer into a banking career or decided to work for the Federal Postal Service. Brettschneider, on the other hand, demonstrated an aptitude for working with his hands and took advantage of vocational schools offered by the BGS in vehicle repair and maintenance. Wagner received telecommunications training and attended a variety of technical and engineering schools. The men were shown applying these learned skills in a variety of action sequences such as patrolling the border, helping victims of natural disasters, rebuilding damaged bridges, and repairing vehicles in the motor pool. As the film concluded, the narrator addressed his comments directly to potential recruits. The overall message conveyed that border police service was certainly challenging, but also fulfilled one's duty to serve the nation and prepared men for a variety of potential civilian careers. The narrator's closing remarks reflected the importance West Germany's government ascribed to the BGS: "The BGS is the most important police security instrument of the federal government. It is intended to reduce border incidents by police methods without using the military, and is called to protect the democratic constitution of

---

69 Ibid., 6.
70 Gordon L. Rottman, *The Berlin Wall and the Intra-German Border, 1961–89* (Oxford: Osprey, 2008), 24.

Germany, now and after reunification."[71] Here again, emphasizing the non-military themes shows how the film's intent depicted West Germany as a defensive civilian state.

The Interior Ministry immediately distributed the first copies of *Zum Schutz der Heimat* to the headquarters of Border Command North, Middle, and South to use at local schools and in recruitment centers. These were 16-millimeter copies that could be easily projected with portable equipment.[72] Initially, there were only nine copies made of the narrow 16-millimeter film, but an order was placed in October 1956 with the editing firm Hadeko in Neuss for an additional forty-four copies. Of these copies, the Interior Ministry sent fourteen to various BGS offices for use in local communities, while sending the remaining thirty copies to West Germany's national cinema for distribution and screening in public movie theaters.[73] The success of *Zum Schutz der Heimat* was difficult to assess, but the Interior Ministry reported that in combination with other more traditional recruitment methods—posters, newspaper ads, etc.—there was a noticeable rise in application and information requests from young men interested in joining. By November 1956 there were 6,365 new inquiries or application requests recorded. Southern Command reported the highest number with 2,540 requests, while Middle and North reported 1,667 and 2,158 respectively.[74] The success of the film encouraged the Interior Ministry to seek ways of increasing its distribution. While reaching moviegoers in West Germany's larger cities was easy, this was not the case for rural communities and villages, a promising source for additional recruits.

To address this dilemma, the Interior Ministry contracted with the Remagen firm Mobilwerbung GmbH (mobile advertising).[75] Mobilwerbung used specialized vehicles capable of showing movies at outdoor venues and reaching out to numerous smaller communities on a single day. The company's strategy involved local advertising in the weeks before the film vehicle was scheduled to arrive at a particular village or town. On the day of the event, representatives arrived at the location approximately one hour beforehand and used a public address system to announce the film for those who might have missed the advertisements. After the 26-minute film was screened, representatives from

71 Ibid., 10.
72 Memorandum from Dr. Kolbe, Bundesministerium des Innern, Referat VI B 1 an BGS Abteilungsleiter VI A, B, und C, November 12, 1956, "Werbemassnahmen für den BGS," BArch-K, B106/14024.
73 Ibid.
74 Ibid.
75 Letter from Herr Pohlmann, Mobilwerbung, to Bundesministerium des Inneren Regierungsrat Attenberger, 25 September 1958, "Einsatz von Werbomobilen im Rahmen der Werbung für den Bundesgrenzschutz," BArch-K, B106/16991.

Mobilwerbung handed out informational brochures and applications to potential recruits.[76] Using *Mobilwerbung* was not cheap. A typical four-week vehicle rental cost 4,900 DM. To be effective, however, the firm recommended a minimum of six vehicles operating simultaneously, which they estimated would cost roughly 49,000 DM.[77] According to the firm's chief, Herr Pohlmann, "The Werbomobil was created for outdoor events in rural areas of fewer than 3,000 inhabitants, where our experience has shown that visitor numbers are considerably higher, since an outdoor venue does not require a viewer to enter a building or restaurant."[78] In spite of these high costs, the Interior Ministry was encouraged by the success of the film to use any medium available to access the widest possible audience, and hence, the best chance to increase applicants.

At the end of 1960, however, the Interior Ministry had begun to address the public image of the BGS by revising and updating the film *Zum Schutz der Heimat*, which Interior Ministry representative Siegfried Fröhlich complained was outdated. He argued that existing copies of the film were wearing out and failed to accurately represent organizational changes since its production in 1956. He wanted a new film created that was based on the content of the first one, but focused more on a documentary style with action sequences.[79] The Interior Ministry chose the award-winning documentary filmmaker Carl Erras to make the new film, which was called *Für Frieden in Freiheit* (For Peace in Freedom). Erras was a graphic artist who had abandoned his work because of psychological trauma he suffered as a soldier in the Second World War. After his recovery he briefly returned to freelance painting before beginning a career making short documentary films for the Munich firm DIA-Film.[80] Production for the film began at Deggendorf in November 1960. Erras planned the film around 400 scenes, with the intent of depicting a typical day in the life of a border policeman. It took five days to complete the actual filming before the final cut was edited into a 33-minute short to be shown in theaters throughout West Germany. Erras explained to

76 Ibid.
77 Ibid.
78 Ibid.
79 Fröhlich to Referate VI, B2, B3, and B4, "Produktion eines neue BGS Werbung Film," April 8, 1960, BArch-K, B106/14024; See also "Niederschrift: Über die Dienstbesprechung mit den Leitern der Abteilung II der Grenzschutzkommandos am 3. Februar 1960 im Bundesministerium des Innern über Werbemassnahmen für die Wiederauffüllung des Bundesgrenzschutzes," BArch-K, B106/14024.

80 Inter Nationes, *Films of the Federal Republic of Germany: Volume I—Documentary Films* (Press and Information Office of the Federal Government: 1986), 155.

reporters on hand for the filming in Deggendorf that it was "intended to stimulate interest in the Bundesgrenzschutz."[81]

Für Frieden und Freiheit emphasized many of the same themes in *Zum Schutz der Heimat* by depicting action sequences that reflected masculine themes of strength, toughness, and heroism.[82] But the film also reflected the new masculine themes of the postwar era—men who could be tough, but also intelligent, career driven, and above all, a participant in civilian life. Border police officers were shown piloting helicopters to rescue stranded mountaineers, scanning the rural border, driving light tanks and armored vehicles, patrolling the Elbe River in high-speed boats, and frightening away members of the People's Police without having to fire their weapons.[83] Besides these action sequences, the film also featured intimate views of what daily life was like in a typical BGS barracks. Here the career-driven professional man took center stage. Officers were shown attending classes where the instructor quizzed them on democracy and various articles in the Basic Law. The officers were also followed into mess halls, where they were treated to three substantial meals a day. Throughout the film, Erras had a reporter approach various officers and ask them specific questions about the career prospects, training, and education provided during their service. The effect of these interviews provided the viewer with a sense of realism missing from the first film, which only focused on three individuals. As the day in the film concluded, border police officers were shown enjoying their free time in a variety of activities that included reading, playing pinball machines, and bowling. The narrator explained that the men were also free to dress in civilian attire and leave the barracks if they chose.[84] This was an attempt to show one of the advantages BGS men had over soldiers, who usually had to remain in their barracks unless granted official leave. But it was also aimed to show recruits that the new West German man could use force to defend the homeland while remaining an active participant in civil society.

Reaching the Ideal BGS Candidates

Besides film and cinema, the Interior Ministry used many different advertising methods in its campaign to rebuild and ultimately save the BGS. A border-police board game and commemorative stamp series, for example, were created as pedagogical instruments to market the force to teenage

---

81 Sergeant Günther Rossner, "In Deggendorf wurde gefilmt," *Die Parole* 10, no.. 11 (November 15, 1960): 7.
82 See *Für Frieden in Freiheit*, available for viewing at https://www.youtube.com/watch?v=A55fYsZhvxQ.
83 Ibid.
84 Ibid.

boys.[85] The Interior Ministry hired the firm Kinderdruckereien, Spiele und Stempelwaren-Fabrik to produce these games after its owner, Georg Reulein, made a successful bid based upon his company's experience producing similar games for the Wehrmacht during the Second World War.[86] The central objective of these recruitment tactics, as had been the case with the film *Zum Schutz der Heimat*, was to educate the West German public, but especially prospective recruits, about the necessity of the organization and its career opportunities. If the public embraced a positive image of the BGS and their role in maintaining West Germany's national security, then Interior Ministry officials believed they might be in a stronger position to fend off calls from critics of the force that it should be disbanded.

Creative methods like films and board games were helpful in reaching potential recruits, but border police leaders still relied heavily on traditional advertising, such as brochures, posters, and newspaper ads. Beginning in 1956 the Interior Ministry generated over 200,000 recruitment brochures and leaflets for nationwide distribution in schools, post offices, career centers, and BGS facilities. In addition to the brochures, more than 100,000 large-format color posters were produced advertising border policing as a masculine or adventuresome career defending the free world, and the west in particular, against communist enslavement.[87] These posters depicted border policemen driving motorcycles and off-road vehicles and standing guard over West Germany's rural borders. In one particular poster created in the heroic-realism style, a tall border police officer with tough, chiseled facial features stands with a slung rifle looking through binoculars towards the east, which appears in the print as a sinister and surrealistic no-man's land. The appearance of a guard tower in the image invoked the comparison of East Germany to a communist concentration camp (See fig. 4.1). Heroic realism was an artistic style favored by fascists and communists to depict the strength of soldiers and workers; it was popular during the twentieth century.[88] By 1960, the Interior Ministry was spending 600,000 DM per year on magazine

---

85 Letter from Georg Reulein, Kinderdruckereien-, Spiele- und Stempelwaren-Fabrik Fürth, to Bundesministerium des Innern, October 7, 1957, BArch-K, B106/16991.

86 Ibid.

87 Dr. Kölbe, "Werbemassnahmen für den BGS," BArch-K, B106/14024.

88 The fascist heroic-realism style is clearly evident in this recruitment poster, which might indicate that the unknown artist also produced such posters during the Nazi era; For a discussion of this style, see Christian Weikop, *New Expressions on Brücke Expressionism: Bridging History* (Burlington, VT: Ashgate, 2011), 204; See examples of these posters and ads produced by various firms for the Bundesministerium des Innern, in particular the heroic-realism style poster signed by an unknown artist, BArch-K, B106/16992.

and newspaper ads alone and planned to increase this figure to 800,000 DM during the next fiscal year.[89]

Young men who wrote to the BGS requesting information received a variety of informational literature, which explained in detail and photographs what they could expect from a border policing career. While fun and adventure remained popular enticements, the value of the career for civilian life remained more important. One of the more popular color brochures, "*Ein Weg in Ihre Zukunft*" (A path into your future), for example, was an illustrated twelve-page leaflet promoting the benefits candidates could expect during their careers. The first page depicted two uniformed policemen enjoying leisure time, while one of the officers played an accordion. Above this photograph, under the heading "What It Offers," the following information appeared: "Varied service as a federal officer in comradely circles, while at the same time earning unlimited tenure as a civil servant for life (*Beamter auf Lebenszeit*) in both federal or state service if you do not prefer the free labor market." Below this description, under the heading "what it requires" was an explanation that candidates must have a positive attitude toward the state and reflect what the "Transatlantic aviator Charles Lindbergh says about modern man: It's his character that counts!"[90]

The Interior Ministry also sent interested applicants a more detailed explanatory leaflet titled: "*Was muss der Bewerber vom Bundesgrenzschutz wissen?*" (What must the applicant/candidate know about the Federal Border Police?)[91] The objective was to emphasize the organization's value to the democratic state while distancing it from the elite forces of Germany's past such as the SS and Nazi Germany's security police units. The leaflet described the founding of the BGS as a response to the Korean War. It was presented as the only means available for the national government to protect the free democratic order of the Federal Republic from the threat of Soviet and East German forces. The candidate was told the BGS reflected the "good character and traditions of the German soldier, but without including anything outdated, tainted, or that which was incompatible with the principles of the new democratic state."[92] Here again, the intent was to draw a distinct line between the good, democratic forces and those used in the past to undermine the state. While the brochure pointed out the need for recruits to endure "hard

---

89 Memorandum from Regierungsdirektor Dr. Fröhlich, Bundesministerium des Innern, an Grenzschutzkommando Nord, Süd, Mitte, Küste, "Kommandeurbesprechung am 12., 13. November 1959," January 16, 1960, B 106/16991.

90 "Bundesgrenzschutz: Ein Weg in Ihre Zukunft," recruitment brochure copy, BArch-K, B106/16992.

91 "Was muss der Bewerber vom Bundesgrenzschutz wissen?" recruitment brochure/leaflet, BArch-K, B106/16992.

92 Ibid.

Figure 4.1. Recruitment poster depicting the East as a totalitarian no-man's land announces: "The BGS hires young men between 18 and 22 as civil servants." BArch-K, B 106/16992.

and physically demanding training," for example, it also emphasized that the intent was to foster "a healthy esprit de corps rather than a dark elite unit." The prospective applicant was also assured that the organization would never be disbanded, because they were the only reliable instrument of national defense, since the "deployment of the Bundeswehr in the zonal border or even within the federal territory must be avoided at all costs."[93] This reinforced the objective of West Germany's leaders that the BGS was a counterinsurgency force that might de-escalate a larger conflict with the Soviets.[94]

Unfortunately for the Interior Ministry, despite all the money and efforts devoted to recruitment, the BGS never came close to reaching its pre-army personnel levels. The border activity reports reflected that the organization was overwhelmed and unable to efficiently handle its most fundamental duty of securing the national borders unless adequate staffing could be restored. But recruitment efforts did not fail because of tough hiring practices or from a lack of innovative advertising methods. They failed largely because West Germany's postwar economy was particularly strong during the 1950s and 1960s, when unemployment levels had dropped to record lows. Even though border policing provided young men with excellent benefits and training, they could afford to be selective when considering career options during the years of the economic miracle. The lack of interest in the organization was also driven by the new ideals of non-military masculinity that emerged in the postwar era. In the beginning, the organization had more applicants than positions, but this trend soon came to an end after the government had established a new army. In spite of the Interior Ministry's efforts to promote border policing as an adventurous career, a new generation of West German men preferred to work in civilian professions. Thus on January 13, 1969, the Bundestag amended West Germany's basic conscription law, giving the federal government the ability to fill its border police vacancies from those young men already eligible for compulsory national service. The amendment also applied to West Germany's state police forces and effectively ended the competition for personnel between the BGS, state police forces, and the army.[95]

---

93 Ibid.
94 Bruno Thoß, *NATO-Strategie und nationale Verteidigungsplanung: Planung und Aufbau der Bundeswehr unter den Bedingungen einer massiven atomaren Vergeltungsstrategie 1952 bis 1960*, Sicherheitspolitik und Streitkräfte der Bundesrepublik Deutschland, Herausgegeben vom Militärgeschichtlichen Forschungsamt Band 1 (Munich: R. Oldenbourg, 2006), 249–52.
95 For the conscription amendment see "Sechstes Gesetz zur Änderung des Wehrpflichtgesetzes vom 13. Januar 1969," *Bundesgesetzblatt* Nr. 4, January 17, 1969, 41.

CHAPTER FIVE

MILITARIZATION AND TRAINING FOR WAR

LIFE MAGAZINE RAN A SPECIAL ISSUE in 1954 titled "Germany: A Giant Awakened," which included a cover photo of the iconic Neuschwanstein castle in Bavaria.[1] Inside, an article and a series of pictures by legendary twentieth-century photojournalist David Douglas Duncan highlighted a BGS company rounding up "bandits" during a training exercise. In one of the photos, border police officers wearing camouflage with machine guns at the ready have a group of civilians lined up against a wall.[2] The pictures had all the appearances of and indeed evoked the antipartisan operations of Nazi Germany's military security forces. Images and actions have meaning. Yet if the date and captions were removed, one could easily confuse these images of the BGS with similar photos of Nazi counterinsurgency operations on the Eastern Front.

Did it really matter that border police officers were trained to carry out military-style assaults? After all, what harm could there be in preparing its men for the possibility that they might face invading East German or Soviet armed forces at the Inner-German border? The point is not to say that West Germany became an illiberal regime because it trained its border police officers like soldiers, but rather to highlight the ways in which proceeding in this manner stood in contrast to its democratic ideals and postwar commitment to demilitarization. The government also undermined its credibility by claiming one thing in public while doing precisely the opposite in practice, giving the impression to many observers that it had formed an army disguised as a police force. If the BGS really was a law enforcement agency and nothing else, as the Interior Ministry often proclaimed, then it should have left fighting wars to the Bundeswehr or NATO. The sociologist George E. Berkley has argued that "nothing is

1   *Life* Special Edition: "Germany: A Giant Reawakened," *Life* 36, no. 1 May 10, 1954, cover.
2   David Douglas Duncan, "On Edge of Iron Curtain with Border Guard: Small Patrol Force is all the once Mighty Nation has left," *Life* 36, no. 1, May 10, 1954, 36–39.

more vital to the creation of a democratic policeman than education."[3] Although the BGS never fought the hypothetical wars they spent years training for, why risk the negative consequences of police militarization that proved so disastrous to Germany's first experiment with democracy? Training is thus a useful category of analysis because it lays bare the organizational tensions between continuity and change—between those who recognized a need to move away from past models and proponents of maintaining the status quo. At its heart, training shows us how the government envisioned the duties of the force even if in practice it never had the opportunity to deploy it in this manner.

Advocates of the status quo emphasized the need to prepare the men for war on the grounds that the BGS remained the only instrument of coercive force available to the West German government since NATO controlled the Bundeswehr. To be sure, militarized training not only continued after West Germany had an army, but it intensified, because members of the armed forces, conservative politicians, and key officials within the organization still treated the force like a border militia rather than a police agency. Thus many of its commanding officers held onto ideas about the need to prepare their personnel for counterinsurgency warfare. From this standpoint, training plans revived problematic themes rooted in Germany's authoritarian past, even though the BGS never had occasion to utilize these tactics in practice. The militarized approach to training contradicted the efforts of some officials at the Interior Ministry, and also within the upper echelons of the organization, who tried to emphasize the need for more training in law and police sciences.

The Problems of Training Police Officers to Fight Wars

The largest influence on BGS training, at least for the first twenty years of its existence, still came from its continuities with the military traditions of Germany's armed forces. To begin with, the Interior Ministry selected men with leadership experience from the Wehrmacht for key command and training posts. Even before the organization's founding, there was a deliberate effort by West Germany's conservative government to recruit combat veterans for its highest posts. In a 1950 top-secret memorandum, for example, Adenauer's staff requested that the Allied High Commission transfer all military personnel records from the Wehrmacht Information Office (WASt) in Berlin to Koblenz.[4] The memorandum also called for an end to the Allied ban against military

3   George E. Berkley, *The Democratic Policeman* (Boston: Beacon, 1974), 74.
4   Top-secret memorandum to General Hays, September 2, 1950, NARA RG 466: Records of the Office of the High Commissioner for Germany, Office of

and even SS veterans from serving in the police and suggested they "would doubtless be of great value for the morale of units to be newly formed."[5] Battle-tested veterans like Anton Grasser, Kurt Andersen, and Gerhard Matzky, to name just a few, were precisely the type of men that the Interior Ministry was looking for.[6]

At forty-four years of age, Colonel Heinrich Müller was one of several experienced Wehrmacht veterans with law enforcement backgrounds selected to train the first BGS recruits. Although never a member of the Nazi Party, his service record was typical of men from his professional cohort, which reflected continuities from Germany's past and strong ties between policing and the army. He began his police career in 1926 with the Prussian *Schutzpolizei*. Between 1931 and 1935 he worked with the Riot Police in Essen and as a Lieutenant Colonel with the barracked *Landespolizei* (state police) in Düsseldorf. In 1935, he was transferred with all *Landespolizei* forces into the Wehrmacht. During the Second World War he fought with a machine-gun company and served on the staff of the 15th Panzer Division attached to Field Marshal Erwin Rommel's Africa Corps. He also taught at the Prussian War Academy (*Kriegsakademie*). Müller fought in the Battle of El Alamein and also in Italy, where he earned numerous combat medals, including the infantry and tank assault badges, both classes of the Iron Cross, and the German Cross in Gold. In 1945 American armed forces captured him and held him in POW camps until 1946.[7] He joined the BGS in 1951 and worked in a variety of assignments, including on the training staff in Lübeck-St. Hubertus. In June 1956 the Ministry of Defense informed him that he qualified for transfer to the new army with the rank of Colonel. Müller promptly declined the offer, however, and chose instead to continue his career in the BGS. An insightful thinker grounded in the humanities, he exemplified the contradictions of an organization struggling to balance the forces of continuity with change. Well respected by his subordinates and superiors, he was perhaps one of the most influential organizational leaders of the BGS during the 1950s and 60s, rising to the rank of Inspector in 1963.[8]

---

the Executive Director, General Hay's Executive Files 1949–51, Folder: "Emergency Planning for Federal Republic," Boxes 15–16.

5   Ibid.

6   Letter from *Staatssekretär* Ritter von Lex to *Ministerialdirektor* Hans Globke, June 21, 1951, BArch-K, B 136/1929, Fiche Nr. 3, Slides 39–46.

7   For biographical details see "Brigade general im BGS Müller," *Die Parole* 4 (April 15, 1963): 3; for Müller's POW discharge papers and military/police service record see BA-MA, N 828/24.

8   Letter to Colonel Müller from Walter Bargatzky, June 5, 1956, and declaration of Colonel Müller declining transfer to the army, June 27, 1956, BA-MA, N 828/24.

126 ♦ MILITARIZATION AND TRAINING FOR WAR

Figure 5.1. Future BGS Inspector Heinrich Müller on horseback as a young lieutenant in the Nazi Army, ca. 1937. BA-MA, N 848/42, courtesy of Dr. Irmgard Müller.

In December 1951 Müller complained to Interior Minister Lehr about the first officer candidates chosen for leadership posts in the BGS. According to Müller, although the men came from every branch of the National Socialist armed forces, including the army, navy, air force, and *Waffen SS*, most lacked the basic skills to lead troops in battle.[9] The reason for this deficit, he argued, could be explained by the fact that many of them were conscripted as teenagers at the end of the war and sent to the front with limited training.[10] As an experienced combat veteran, he complained that most candidates were unfamiliar with the standard German MG-42 (*Machinegewehr*—machine-gun model 42). Nicknamed "Hitler's buzzsaw" by Allied soldiers, the MG-42 fired a devastating 1200 rounds per minute and was not suitable for law enforcement use.[11] Müller's concern over his men's proper use of this weapon had nothing to do with police work and everything to do with fighting wars. The MG-42 was a weapon designed for the explicit purpose of mass killing and thus had

9   Memorandum from Heinrich Müller to Interior Minister Robert Lehr, December 6, 1951, "*Zusammensetzung und Ausbildungsstand des 1. Lehrgangs*," BArch-K, B106/15083.
10   Ben H. Shepherd, *Hitler's Soldiers: The German Army in the Third Reich* (New Haven, CT: Yale University Press, 2016), 498.
11   Chris McNab, *The MG 34 and 42 Machine-Guns* (Oxford: Osprey, 2012), 62.

Figure 5.2. BGS light machine-gun crew during field training exercises, 1954. David Douglas Duncan Life Magazine Collection, University of Texas at Austin, Harry Ransom Center.

no use compatible with civilian policing. Müller and his colleagues were more concerned with preparing border police officers to fight and attack rather than teaching them to handle traditional law enforcement duties. Thus military topics and training still had a higher priority than courses in law, legal aspects of evidence, or civics.

Training BGS personnel to fight wars undermined West Germany's postwar commitment to demilitarize its civilian police forces. The duties of law enforcement officers and soldiers are distinct—the police enforce laws and keep the peace, soldiers fight wars. Mixing or blending these roles confuses those charged with carrying out these duties. Police officers trained to act and behave like warriors often treat civilians like enemy combatants—precisely the opposite effect of how democracies are supposed to police their citizens. Moreover, Brigadier General Anton Grasser told the first cohort of instructors at Lübeck-St. Hubertus, which included Heinrich Müller, that: "The *Bundesgrenzschutz* is a new institution that consciously does not follow former models in education and training, but seeks to build up an organization that is closest to the people, taking into account the experiences of the past."[12] Presumably, Grasser meant the need to abandon models of authoritarian policing that trained officers like

12 "Ausbildung der Grenzschutz-Abteilung für die Zeit bis zum 1.10.1951," Bundesministerium des Innern, BGS Inspektor, Bonn, June 20, 1951, BArch-K, B106/15076.

soldiers. Yet behind the closed doors of the training academy, continuities with the militarized policing traditions of Germany's past still eclipsed the ideal of forging new paths as emphasized by Grasser. Nevertheless, reemploying combat veterans in a civilian police force like the BGS might also be interpreted as part of a deliberate effort by the state to integrate them into roles that supported rather than undermined the democratic state. Indeed, it was difficult to find candidates for the BGS who did not serve in Nazi Germany's armed forces. Thus, as Bert-Oliver Manig has suggested, rehabilitating veteran soldiers by reintegrating them into the police, even though it came with risks, might have functioned as a "medium of their transition to democracy."[13]

Still, with 65,000 applicants to choose from in 1951, 15,000 of whom applied for leadership posts, it seems unlikely that the Interior Ministry only had combat veterans to choose from as the founding members of the force.[14] Thus militarized policing shaped the organizational culture of the BGS, even though it existed in tension with policies that advocated reform. In the written guidelines for officer candidate training, for example, BGS Brigadier General Otto Dippelhofer, a lawyer, former Nazi Party member and SS veteran, tried to distinguish the duties of police and soldiers. He emphasized that army tacticians taught their men to seek out and "annihilate the enemy," while police officers restored order, peace, and security.[15] According to Dippelhofer "the officer in the BGS must therefore be trained to assess not only the tactical situation but also the legal situation. If he wants to fully pursue his profession and always act according to the principles of sound police science, he must respect and have knowledge of the law in order to apply it legally and proportionally."[16] For Dippelhofer, the ideal officer candidate led by example and established his credibility by working his way through the hardships of the lower ranks. The perfect man, he argued, must have strong intellectual traits without being arrogant. Dippelhofer made it clear, however, that leaders had to be pragmatic "doers" rather than exclusively focused on the theoretical aspects of criminal, administrative, and constitutional law. Yet he still argued that legal and police science topics took secondary roles to the pragmatism of training men to fight and work through tactical problems.[17]

---

13 Bert-Oliver Manig, *Die Politik der Ehre: Die Rehabilitierung der Berufssoldaten in der frühen Bundesrepublik* (Göttingen: Wallstein Verlag, 2004), 8–9; James J. Sheehan, *Where Have All the Soldiers Gone?* 178–79.

14 Falco Werkentin, *Die Restauration*, 92.

15 Dr. Otto Dippelhofer, "Gedanken über eine künftige Offiziersausbildung im Bundesgrenzschutz," July 23, 1951, BArch-K, B106/15076.

16 Ibid.

17 Ibid.

Dippelhofer's statements reflected the tensions and contradictions inherent in the training programs of the BGS. On the one hand, his thinking about training appears to be progressive. His comments on law and civics coincided with his education and experience in law and public policy. Yet at the same time, his experience as a veteran SS officer in the police battalions must have shaped his views about the pragmatism and primacy of tactics in BGS training. How was it that a man with Dippelhofer's service record could be allowed back into the police service and how can we reconcile what appears to be his progressive comments about training? To be sure, he reflected the countless other veterans reintegrated into the police during the Adenauer era.[18] Some of these men falsified or were deliberately vague about their service records, to avoid accounting for criminal activities either they or their units perpetrated during the war. But the politics of rearmament and anti-communism played a significant role here too, since the Western Allies needed German support as a bulwark against the Soviets in the Cold War. As Norbert Frei and many other historians have shown, however, the Adenauer government was not interested in the wholesale prosecution of war criminals and discouraged a more comprehensive reckoning with the Nazi past. Despite the moral burdens of the Nazi past, West Germans preferred to focus on the future rather than the past during the immediate postwar years—better to bind men like Dippelhofer to the institutions of the state rather than probing too deeply into what he did during the war.[19]

Competing Training Philosophies of an Organization in Flux

While the first officer candidates began training in June 1951, instruction for the new border police recruits did not commence until October.[20] At the time, the curriculum for basic training was limited to providing the recruits with the most rudimentary skills in weapons-handling and tactics. The Interior Ministry's main objective in the weeks and months after the first BGS law went into effect was to get the force established and deployed as fast as possible. Whenever practical, men with military experience were organized into ready-reserve units that could be deployed to

---

18 See Jens Scholten, "Offiziere: Im Geiste unbesiegt," in *Hitlers Eliten nach 1945*, ed. Norbert Frei, 117–20 (Frankfurt am Main: Campus Verlag, 2012).

19 Norbert Frei, *Adenauer's Germany and the Nazi Past*, 56; See also Wolfram Wette, The *Wehrmacht*, 236–38; Klaus Naumann, "The Unblemished Wehrmacht: The Social History of a Myth," in *War of Extermination*, ed. Hannes Heer and Klaus Naumann, 417–29.

20 "Ausbildung der Grenzschutz-Abteilung für die Zeit bis zum 1.10.1951," BArch-K, B106/15076.

deal with any sudden emergencies, as was the case with the FDJ during the Third World Youth Festival.[21] For the new recruit entering basic training, the *Hundertschaftsführer* (company leader) was considered the most important figure in his life.[22] The recruits were taught to fear and respect the paternalistic officer who represented his main supervisor, teacher, and disciplinarian. The men assigned to this critical training position were hard on the new recruits and meted out severe punishment for minor infractions that took the form of public humiliation or strenuous physical exercise.

The military historian Richard Holmes has argued that "there is a direct link between the harshness of basic training and the cohesiveness of the group which emerges from it." Yet while the concepts of discipline and obedience were often linked to the harshness of Prussian militarism, and Nazi Germany's Wehrmacht in particular, border police drill instructors argued that these techniques were beneficial for training men to work together as a team rather than as individuals.[23] But as the legal scholar Rosa Brooks has argued "When police recruits are belittled by their instructors and ordered to refrain from responses other than 'yes sir!,' they may learn stoicism—but they may also learn that mocking and bellowing orders at those with less power are acceptable actions."[24] The opponents and critics of the BGS, such as those in the state police trade unions (*Gewerkschaft der deutschen Polizei*—GdP and *Gewerkschaft Öffentliche Dienste, Transport und Verkehr*—ÖTV) cited the militaristic training as evidence that the BGS was a backwards or anti-democratic organization.[25] But these criticisms were also politically motivated by the fear among state police unions that their members might be supplanted by federal police officers. Moreover, the state police agencies these unions represented were also inundated with former soldiers who trained their recruits like soldiers and housed them in barracks.[26]

The guidelines for the first BGS training classes tried, at least on paper, to minimize the warrior spirit in training. According to the instructions on discipline, for example, the guidelines stated that "no force can

21 Ibid.
22 Ibid.
23 See Richard Holmes, *Firing Line* (London: Jonathan Cape, 1985), 47; for Prussian Militarism see Christopher Clark, *Iron Kingdom*, xv. Clark argues that after the Second World War, Prussia became "synonymous with everything repellent in German history: militarism, conquest, arrogance, and illiberality."
24 Rosa Brooks, "Stop training police like they're joining the military," *The Atlantic*, June 10, 2020.
25 See for example, "Bürgerkriegsübung im Bundesgrenzschutz," *ÖTV-Press, Zentralorgan der Gewerkschaft Öffentliche Dienste, Transport und Verkehr*, 8 Jahrgang, Nr. 21 (November 1, 1956).
26 Klaus Weinhauer, *Schutzpolizei in der Bundesrepublik*, 168–73.

exist without discipline ... discipline is not based on fear of punishment, but rather springs from the knowledge of each individual, that the complex task of border protection can only be met by a willing submission of the individual to the whole."[27] Discipline as described here fit better with the concept of teamwork rather than the traditional Prussian idea of blind obedience to a higher authority. The rebuke of Prussian ideals in this manner was bound up with the burdens of the Nazi past and the postwar claims that blind obedience to orders laid the groundwork for the perpetration of war crimes. First of all, the idea that the Wehrmacht promoted Prussian disciplinary tradition is somewhat misleading, because it ignores the racial-ideological framing of martial law under the Third Reich that Omer Bartov described as "perverted discipline."[28] Thus rejecting notions of discipline based on blind obedience only reinforced false postwar narratives that soldiers committed war crimes because they had no other choice but to follow criminal orders or face harsh penalties—a claim that scholars of Nazi atrocities have largely refuted.[29]

Even a conservative veteran soldier like Colonel Heinrich Müller cautioned against disciplinary practices of older training models. His credibility among junior and senior officers lent meaning to what he said, thus giving him a unique opportunity to influence their further development. He made this clear in a lecture about authority and obedience he presented to border police officers at the Protestant Academy in Kurhessen-Waldeck.[30] Imposing any form of blind obedience within the ranks, he insisted, was anathema to what border police leaders were trying to achieve through discipline. He emphasized that there would always be a need to punish those who broke the rules, but discipline had more value when used as positive reinforcement. Of course, the giving and following of basic orders was always an essential facet of leadership, but Müller suggested those leaders who reflected fairness in their approach to discipline had a greater chance of winning the respect of their subordinates. Citing the German novelist Walter Flex, he explained: "Whoever has the heart

---

27 "Ausbildung der Grenzschutz-Abteilung für die Zeit bis zum 1.10.1951," BArch-K, B106/15076.

28 Omer Bartov, *Hitler's Army: Soldiers, Nazis, and War in the Third Reich* (New York: Oxford University Press, 1992), 7.

29 See for example, Christopher Browning, *Ordinary Men*; Sven Felix Kellerhoff, "Hatten SS-Mitglieder damals wirklich "keine Wahl?" *Die Welt*, July 15, 2015.

30 Colonel i. BGS Heinrich Müller, "Autorität und Gehorsam im BGS: Vortrag gehalten am 5.5.1955 im Rahmen der Tagung für Angehörige des Bundesgrenzschutz Kommando Mitte bei der Evangelischen Akademie von Kurhessen-Waldeck in Hofgeismar," BArch-K, B106/20765.

of his people also has discipline."[31] Müller's use of the Walter Flex quote epitomized the contradictions at the heart of BGS training, caught as it was between a militarized past and demands for a more democratic present. Flex, a conservative nationalist and member of dueling fraternities, wrote the pro-war novel *Wanderer zwischen beiden Welten*. Favored by the Nazis for romanticizing the war experience, he died in the First World War and reflected what George L. Mosse has called the "cult of the fallen soldier."[32] At the same time, Müller's use of Flex might be interpreted as part of a postwar cultural shift in patriarchal authority that took hold in 1950s and 1960s West Germany. As cultural historian Till van Rahden has suggested, although the "hierarchical conception of authority based on tradition and the spirit of order and obedience still prevailed ... it began to give way to an idea of authority based on trust embedded in egalitarian social relationships."[33] Rigid discipline and punishment for minor offenses remained, but now took the form of patriarchal authority based on a model of the firm yet "gentle" father figure.

The framing of discipline to reject blind obedience is still prevalent in the concepts of teamwork and professionalism emphasized by most modern democratic police training programs, even though teaching officers to be warriors rather than civil servants remains a significant problem.[34] Critics of the BGS, however, suggested the problem of militarized training might be addressed by using civilians rather than soldiers as instructors. In their study of police training, sociologists Greener and Fish found that "training by the military is more likely to be oriented towards elimination of an enemy threat, which can lead to disconnection

---

31 Ibid; Robert Wohl, *The Generation of 1914* (Cambridge, MA: Harvard University Press, 1979), 48; see also Lars Koch, *Der erste Weltkrieg als Medium der Gegenmoderne: Zu Werken von Walter Flex und Ernst Jünger* (Würzburg: Könighausen & Neumann, 2006), 117.

32 George L. Mosse, *Fallen Soldiers: Reshaping the Memory of the World Wars* (Oxford: Oxford University Press, 1991); K. Eckhard Kuhn-Osius, "Germany's Lessons from the Lost 'Great War': Pacifist Andreas Latzko and Bellicist Walter Flex," *Peace Research* 42, no. 1 (2010): 34.

33 Till van Rahden, "Fatherhood, Rechristianization, and the Quest for Democracy in Postwar West Germany," in Dirk Schumann ed., *Raising Citizens in the Century of the Child: The United States and German Central Europe in Comparative Perspective* (New York: Berghahn Books, 2010), 145.

34 See M. Berlin, "An Overview of Police Training in the United States, Historical Development, Current Trends and Critical Issues: The Evidence," in *International Perspectives on Police Education and Training*, ed. Peter Stanislas (New York: Routledge, 2014), 37; Radley Balko, *Rise of the Warrior Cop: The Militarization of America's Police Forces* (New York: Public Affairs, 2013).

between the police force and the community it is supposed to serve."[35] Despite their public comments and writings to the contrary, leaders such as Otto Dippelhofer and Heinrich Müller still favored military training in the BGS.[36] Memories of Weimar-era policing and its ambivalence, or, in certain cases, complicity with the radical right in undermining the democratic state, produced long-term skepticism of militarized policing as promoted in the BGS.

In spite of efforts by some of the instructors at Lübeck-St. Hubertus to devote more course hours to law enforcement practices, military tactical exercises still took priority. The Border Police psychologist, Dr. Leonhard von Renthe-Fink, supervised the curriculum development committee (*Referat* I C 5) and was keenly aware of the difficulties in demilitarizing BGS training. During the Third Reich, Dr. Renthe-Fink, a veteran Wehrmacht psychologist, led its "Inspectorate for Aptitude Testing." Like many psychologists of his generation, he found steady work and a chance to test his theories in the armed forces. For the BGS, he observed and reported on the effects and quality of the training and instruction provided to its personnel.[37] He noted that there was an obvious lack of training on the role and duties typical of a civilian police force, or for that matter on any topics related to the study of civics or law.

Renthe-Fink observed that topics such as ethics, political ideology, and professionalism were completely ignored in comparison with more popular military themes. He recognized that the training programs needed to be aligned with the duties expected of civilian law enforcement officers, but complained that "there was a particular open disdain by the training staff for any police-related topics."[38] At least outwardly, what he saw contradicted the intent to separate policing and soldiering as stressed by Dippelhofer in his public comments and writings. Yet having a psychologist oversee and critique BGS training programs was an innovative first step in correcting this problem. It demonstrated that at least some officials at the Interior Ministry were interested in improving the overall quality of the training programs in spite of the strong influence veteran

---

35 B. K. Greener and W. J. Fish, *Internal Security and Statebuilding: Aligning Agencies and Functions* (New York: Routledge, 2015), 161.

36 See Dr. Otto Dippelhofer, "Gedanken über eine künftige Offiziersausbildung im Bundesgrenzschutz," July 23, 1951, BArch-K, B106/15076.

37 Memorandum, Dr. Renthe-Fink zu Bundesministerium des Innern, "Schulung von Offizieren und Unterführern," July 23, 1951, BArch-K, B106/15076; for Renthe-Fink's work in the Wehrmacht, see Ulfried Geuter, *The Professionalization of Psychology in Nazi Germany* (Cambridge: Cambridge University Press, 1992), 37.

38 Memorandum, Dr. Renthe-Fink zu Bundesministerium des Innern, "Schulung von Offizieren und Unterführern," July 23, 1951, BArch-K, B106/15076.

soldiers still had over the organization. There were, however, no short-term solutions to cutting the ties that bound policing and the army in postwar West Germany.[39]

Dr. Renthe-Fink's analysis, however, identified several problem areas and helped lay the foundation for the improvement of education and training that later took hold during the 1970s. He emphasized that the men who were expected to fill leadership positions, and the sergeants in particular, needed much more training. Moreover, he argued that during the forthcoming training cycle, police science, civics, political-ideological training, professional ethics, and psychology should be given greater priority. To accomplish this, he suggested adapting the training plans to match those already in use by the state police schools. He pointed out that the state police course plans recently developed by the Interior Ministry under the supervision of Director Ludwig Dierske would be a good starting point. Dr. Renthe-Fink also recommended that the Interior Ministry hire instructors who were civilian academics, lawyers, or veteran police officers who specialized in legal studies rather than soldiers with combat experience. The challenge was to take these important theoretical topics and present them in such a manner that they were interesting, practical, and useable by border police officers.[40]

Dr. Renthe-Fink's analysis also pointed to a complete lack of education in subjects relating to political ideology.[41] He used the East German People's Police and its political training as a hypothetical model for how this could be accomplished in the BGS. He cited intelligence reports from the Bundesministerium für Gesamtdeutsche Fragen (Federal Ministry for Intra-German Relations), which reported that People's Police recruits and their commanding officers spent up to forty hours per week studying political topics, such as Marxism, Leninism, and the history of the German Revolution. While he was quick to dismiss the Marxist subject matter as "pure propaganda," he suggested that there were two primary learning points that West Germany's border police officers could adopt for their own training.[42] First, he believed it was critical to understand the worldview of their eastern enemies. Second, he argued that "while the west has no closed ideology like Marxism, more could and should be done to consolidate our own worldview and, more importantly, to develop the critical thinking and reasoning skills of our officers."[43]

39   Ibid.
40   Ibid.
41   Memorandum, Dr. Renthe-Fink zu Bundesministerium des Innern, "Schulung von Offizieren und Unterführern," July 23, 1951, BArch-K, B106/15076.
42   Ibid.
43   Ibid.

War Games and Legacies of "Bandit Fighting" in BGS Training

In spite of the efforts of Dr. Renthe-Fink, little changed in the overall training and education programs of the BGS. He was twenty years ahead of his time, and training remained grounded in the spirit and traditions brought to the organization by the veteran soldiers who led it. In spite of Renthe-Fink's recommendations, a memorandum addressed to all border police commanders for training during the winter quarter of 1955 emphasized the following points:

> All units must be trained to fight at night and in the forest ... in order to fully master all types of combat under these conditions by April 1, 1956. Within this framework and beyond, everyone must be accustomed to always behaving like a hunter in order to be able to cope with the demands of modern guerrilla warfare, as is particularly required in the case of sustained resistance and bandit fighting. Stalking exercises in Indian style, training in hand-to-hand combat ... and use of cunning and deception is of particular importance.[44]

The objectives, as stated above, had little to do with enforcing laws, checking passports, or, for that matter, dealing with smuggling and black-market crime. If the objective of training was to shape the men's responses in actual situations, then the use of terms like hunting, stalking, guerilla warfare, and hand-to-hand combat could not be any more explicit—these are not typical duties for police officers in a democracy. Such duties fly in the face of the express intention of the founders of the Federal Republic to avoid repeating the sins of Nazi Germany and in particular its militarization of the civilian police.

Nevertheless, SPD military advisor, Friedrich Beermann, and other key elites in West Germany embraced the ideas of people like Gerhard Matzky, BGS Colonel Kurt Spitzer, and Colonel Bogislaw von Bonin, who suggested in one form or another that the BGS should be expanded and converted into a border militia (see chapter 3).[45] Beermann went so far as to suggest that border police officers should be armed and trained with anti-tank weapons, mortars, and other military-grade weapons.

---

44 Der Bundesminister des Innern an GSK Süd, Mitte, Nord, Küste, "Weisungen für die Ausbildung im Winterhalbjahr 1955," 63 200-1 c—183/55, November 3, 1955, BArch-K, B 106/15078.

45 Dr. Friedrich Beermann, "Aktennotiz über ein Gespräch mit Oberst Spitzer vom Bundesgrenzschutz," November 2, 1955, 1–3; Dr. Friedrich Beermann, "Stellungnahme zu dem Brief des Grafen Schwerin bezgl. des Bundesgrenzschutzes vom 22. Dezember 1954," 7–8, BA-MA, N 597/30.

Beermann praised Spitzer's alternative plan, "Sword and Shield," from which he adopted these suggestions.[46] The most controversial proposal to use the BGS in this manner came from von Bonin, whose plan, according to historian Heinz Brill, "required a high-quality professional and temporary army geared to direct border security ... with armament focused on anti-tank defense ... to put a stop to any surprise actions by the opposite side of the Eastern border."[47]

After the Federal Republic had established a new army and decided to rebuild the BGS, there was no better opportunity or time in which to refocus its training and make it into the law enforcement agency it was supposed to be. Yet by 1957 even the Defense Ministry, which under its former Minister Theodor Blank rejected militarizing the police as a first step in rearmament, proposed infantry training in the BGS. In a top-secret memorandum to his staff, Blank's successor Franz Josef Strauss (CSU), who likened the BGS to, "a kind of Reichswehr," suggested its personnel be trained as an army reserve.[48] Strauss recommended that training the BGS to surveil the border, its main *raison d'être*, must be postponed and replaced with infantry training. He wanted to bring the force up to the same level as an army infantry battalion. Strauss even suggested that "the civil servant-oriented thinking of border fighters should give way to the purely military-soldier thinking of the fighter."[49]

The Interior Ministry and commanders in the BGS were of the same mind as the Ministry of Defense when it came to training. Four years after the army was founded, Kurt Andersen, former head of the BGS school in Lübeck-St. Hubertus took over as head of the organization when Matzky transferred to the army. In 1963, the Interior Ministry established the Office of BGS Inspector within the Public Security Branch and Andersen thus became the first commanding officer to officially achieve this designation.[50] He promoted a training doctrine that favored infantry weapons and combat tactics. His focus for training year 1959/60, for example, was to ensure that in the event of an enemy attack, all border police officers were prepared "to delay enemy advances in mobile warfare while largely

---

46 Kurt Spitzer, "Der Spitzer-Plan Schwert und Schild: Gedanken zum Aufbau der Verteidigung der Bundesrepublik Deutschland in Rahmen und in Ergänzung der NATO-Verteidigung (1955/56)," reprinted in Heinz Brill, *Dokumente und Materialien*, 172–87.

47 Heinz Brill, *Bogislaw von Bonin: Opposition gegen Adenauers Sicherheitspolitik: Eine Dokumentation* (Hamburg: Verlag Neue Politik, 1976).

48 Bundesminister für Verteidigung to FÜStab Heer Ausbildung, streng geheim, November 8, 1957, "Bundesgrenzschutz Besprechung October 29, 1957," BA-MA, BH 1/596; Franz Josef Strauss, *Die Erinnerung*, 286.

49 Ibid.

50 Bundesministerium des Innern, 33.

preserving the fighting strength of one's own troops."[51] The reference to police officers as "troops" and the lengthy focus on infantry weapons like mortars and anti-tank munitions had no real relevance to civilian policing. As a veteran of the Iron Brigade Freikorps and its brutal 1919 campaign in Germany's eastern borderlands, he wanted men who were prepared to fight communists rather than enforce laws. Andersen complained that law enforcement should not be the main focus of coursework, since in his opinion "thoroughness comes before versatility." He also requested that "for the purpose of comparison, as a suggestion for the designing of the lessons and for the study of the instructing officers, I support equipping the BGS officers' school with regulations of the army."[52]

Nowhere were these concepts and training more apparent than in the regular participation of BGS forces in military exercises. During these operations, border police officers used infantry tactics and weapons to attack and fight imaginary communist insurgents at the Inner-German border and in West Germany's interior. The BGS implemented and proctored some of these training exercises, but NATO also included border police officers in larger war games. Even though Dippelhofer claimed border police officers did not train to "annihilate" enemy forces, this is precisely what they trained for during the exercises. Border police officers deployed rifle-launched ENERGA anti-tank projectiles against mock soviet armor attacks. The ENERGA is a high-explosive hollow charge munition capable of penetrating the armor of a tank, and like many of the other weapons in the BGS arsenal, it had no valid use for a civilian law enforcement agency.[53]

The first of many such training exercises took place on May 28, 1952. The BGS held this exercise to highlight its weaknesses in order to justify the proposed increase from 10,000 to 20,000 men. Although many Social Democrats, the state police unions, and the Allied powers knew this was the motive for the exercise, they were nevertheless alarmed when BGS units deployed infantry weapons and military tactics. The Interior Ministry invited members of the Allied armed forces to observe the exercise—a simulated attack on the Federal Republic by a force of communist agitators who crossed the Inner-German border. The BGS reconnoitered the area where the crossing took place to locate and arrest the agitators. The Interior Ministry called the training a success, but Allied observers

---

51 BGS Inspector Kurt Andersen to all BGS commands, April 22, 1959, "Weisungen für die Ausbildung im BGS 1959/60," 4, BArch-K, B 106/15079.

52 Letter from BGS Inspekteur Kurt Andersen to Interior Minister Gerhard Schröder, "Erfahrungsbericht über den 9. OA-Lehrgang von July 29, 1958," April 29, 1959, BArch-K, B 106/15085, Bd. 10, 3.

53 See Bob Cashner, *The FN FAL Battle Rifle* (Oxford: Bloomsbury, 2013), 32.

Figure 5.3. BGS officer training in the use of the ENERGA anti-tank rifle grenade. Author's private collection.

reported that the capture of enemy forces by BGS units was "accomplished by the considerable firing of rifles and machine guns to an extent which did not seem necessary in a police action such as this was supposed to represent."[54]

On March 6, 1953, and again on April 4, 1954, BGS-North held consecutive exercises under the codename "Operation Blue"—a simulated national emergency caused by a mock uprising in the Ruhr between combat leagues of radical leftist and right-wing gangs. In the scenario, which mimicked the 1920 Ruhr uprising, the combat leagues called for national strikes, attacked government offices, and paralyzed all vehicle and railway traffic into and out of the Ruhr.[55] As in previous exercises, the BGS used military tactics and weapons, including machine

---

54 Memorandum to the Military Security Board: "Bundesgrenzschutz Exercise May 28, 1952," NARA RG 466 US High Commission for Germany: Industrial Division (US Element), Correspondence and Other Records Relating to the Regulation of German Industrial Companies, 1949–1955: "Bundesgrenzschutz thru Stahlbau Rheinhausen," Box 8.

55 For the Ruhr Uprising see Detlev Peukert, *The Weimar Republic: The Crisis of Classical Modernity* (New York: Hill & Wang, 1989), 69; Geheimes Planspiel, Grenzschutzkommando Nord, "Lage Blau: Spielbestimmungen Anlagen," NLA Nds. 220 Acc. 2009/015 Nr. 25.

guns and mortars. The scenario described the agitators on both the political left and the political right as "fanatical fighters" disguised in civilian clothing so as to blend in with local populations. In the after-action report for "Operation Blue" and similar exercises in Amberg, Gerhard Matzky and Commander of BGS-South Hans Höffner complained that the BGS suffered from a lack of heavy weapons and needed additional infantry training.[56]

One of the larger military training exercises codenamed "Operation Danube," took place in Bavaria from November 24–26, 1954. For the state police unions and critics of the BGS, it proved to be another glaring example of how the organization trained for war rather than law enforcement. The scenario simulated a cross-border attack by 90,000 communist partisans and took place in a region encompassing 55 by 40 square miles, north of the Danube River. As with previous exercises, the Interior Ministry invited Allied observers. British representatives from the High Commissioner's Office reported that "As expected, [the exercise] seems to have been completely military in form." At the end, General Matzky (inspector of the BGS) publicly expressed that "the BGS was no match for the [People's Police] and to make them so, at least 60,000 men with armor-piercing weapons were necessary."[57]

Matzky's desire for armor-piercing ammunition caused an immediate backlash with the SPD and French politicians, who at the time still debated the fate of the EDC. Ambassador François-Poncet lodged a protest with Chancellor Adenauer and the SPD expressed "astonishment that it was really an appropriate task for the border police to stop a first attack ... and pointed out this could not be the duty of the BGS under the law." Despite the Interior Ministry's efforts to minimize Matzky's statements by claiming they were taken out of context and even after support from the editorial staff of the center-right *Frankfurter Allgemeine Zeitung*, the damage was done.[58] Staff from the UK High Commission in Bonn who witnessed the exercise noted that the BGS completely "annihilated attacking [communist] parachute units."[59] UK High Commissioner Sir Hoyer Millar reported to Deputy Prime Minister Anthony Eden that

---

56 Memorandum from Oberfinanzdirektion Hannover to Bundesminister der Finanzen Dr. Grill, O 3048-34-Z 121, April 14, 1954, 2; Dr. Fürholzer, Oberfinanzdirektion Nürnberg to Bundesminister der Finanzen Dr. Grill, O 3048-19/Z 2, Vertraulich! May 11, 1954, 2, NLA NDS. 220 ACC. 2009/015 NR. 25.

57 E. J. W. Barnes, UK High Commission to P. F. Hancock Foreign Office Western Branch, December 4, 1954, 108/8/85/54, TNA FO 371/109719.

58 Bonn: "Erstaunen über Matzky—französische Vorstellungen in Bonn," *FAZ*, December 2, 1954, 1; see also "Matzky falsch verstanden," *FAZ* (December 3, 1954), 3; see OpEd, "befremden?" *FAZ* (December 8, 1954), 2.

59 J. R. Hall U.K. High Commission to H. W. Evans Foreign Office Western Branch, November 25, 1954, 108/8/81/54, TNA FO 371/109719.

Figure 5.4. Undated image: Heinrich Müller and Gerhard Matzky consult with unknown BGS officer during simulated war games; BGS Brigadier General Kurt Andersen is standing in the background. BA-MA N 848/25, courtesy of Dr. Irmgard Müller.

Hans Egidi, the civilian head of the Interior Ministry's Public Security Branch accompanied General Schwerin during the exercise—a clear sign that the state blended policing with the military. According to Hoyer Millar, Egidi praised the "offensive spirit" of the BGS and Schwerin claimed that "Even the former Wehrmacht could not have bettered the performance of the BGS."[60]

One might argue, however, that military training and exercises were an obvious consequence of the fact that, at the time, the government expected most border police officers to transfer to the army. To be sure, many of these exercises took place in the years before the Federal Republic had an army. Yet if this were the case, then why did the organization continue to promote infantry training after the new army was established and those who wanted to be soldiers had already transferred out? In fact, participation by the BGS in war games increased in the years after West Germany formed the Bundeswehr. Instead of using the separation of the two forces as an opportunity to introduce more law enforcement training, the Interior Ministry just treated the BGS as another, albeit smaller, armed force.

In 1962, for example, the BGS participated in a joint Allied military training exercise with members of the 10th US Special Forces Group that had nothing whatsoever to do with policing. The objective of the exercise, codenamed "Operation South Bavaria" (*Übung Südbayern*), was to train border police officers to fight "bandit groups" and learn how to resist "hard interrogation" measures if captured.[61] BGS Lieutenant Colonel Franz Sleik, another decorated combat veteran of the Wehrmacht who found a home in the BGS, commanded all the border police units.[62] According to Sleik's after-action report, his men learned how to interrogate prisoners and also learned the art of what he called "subversive bandit fighting (*Bandenbekämpfung*) and the art of destroying important objects in order to achieve one's goals, with strong security." He organized his men into "hunting commandos" (*Jagdkommandos*), which he used to "encircle and destroy the bandits."[63] The terms *Jagdkommando* and *Bandenbekämpfung* along with the tactics of encircling bandits—*Grossunternehmen* (large-scale operation) came straight from Nazi anti-partisan warfare doctrine. During the Third Reich, Nazi counterinsurgency forces, units that many future BGS officers served

60 UK High Commissioner Sir Hoyer Millar to Deputy Prime Minister Anthony Eden, December 23, 1954, 108/8/95/54, TNA FO 371/109719.
61 Grenzschutzabteilung I/1, Lieutenant Colonel Franz Sleik, Nr. 114/64, VS-Nur für den Dienstgebrauch, to Grenzschutzkommando Süd, München, June 11, 1964, "Übungsüdbayern Erfahrungsbericht," BArch-K, B 106/83904.
62 See military service record of Wehrmacht Captain Franz Sleik, BA-MA, PERS 6/66969.
63 Ibid.

Figure 5.5. BGS officers rounding up bandits during field exercises, 1954. David Douglas Duncan Life Magazine Collection, University of Texas at Austin, Harry Ransom Center.

with during the war, murdered civilians under the euphemistic rubric of *Bandenbekämpfung*.[64]

At the conclusion of Operation South Bavaria, 20 BGS officers complained that they had been brutalized by personnel from the US Special Forces. The officers had volunteered to act in the role of guerilla fighters and the US soldiers captured them during the operation. According to the men, the US soldiers forced them into cramped interrogation cells, stripped them naked, covered them in hoods, used aggressive German Shepherds to frighten them and otherwise subjected them to what Sleik described as the US Army's new "Controlled Harshness Measures." Sleik said his men exaggerated their grievances and claimed that they "were not prepared for the harshness of this treatment and were surprised by it."[65] The men endured loud noises and could not hold up after the soldiers splashed them with water. Sleik and his superiors in the BGS command disregarded the complaints and instead reported to the Interior Ministry that although "this type of training is alien to the BGS, it prepares them for real missions."[66] Here again, the reference to "real missions"

64 Omer Bartov, *Hitler's Army*, 83; Ben Shepherd, *Hitler's Soldiers*, 290.
65 Sleik, "Übungsüdbayern Erfahrungsbericht," BArch-K, B 106/83904, anlage.
66 Ibid.

Figure 5.6. BGS personnel conducting an amphibious assault during field exercises, 1954. David Douglas Duncan Life Magazine Collection, University of Texas at Austin, Harry Ransom Center.

highlights that these men were training to fight wars, since police officers would not be expected to endure capture and torture as part of their routine duties.

At the time, the Interior Ministry did nothing to follow-up on these allegations and considered the matter closed with Sleik's after-action report. The incident came to light years later in the early 1970s, however, as part of a series of complaints lodged against the BGS by the chairman of the state police union, Werner Kuhlmann (see chapter 9). Operations Danube and South-Bavaria were not exceptional. To be sure, despite repeated claims by the Interior Ministry that it was a police force, the manner in which BGS officers trained reveals how the government intended to use them. Border police officers never stopped training with Allied armed forces and also participated in the NATO joint training operations including ABLE ARCHER (1983), as well as the FALLEX and REFORGER exercises of the 1960s through the 1990s.[67] The US and NATO armed forces stationed in the Federal Republic during the

---

67 For an overview of the REFORGER and ABLE ARCHER exercises see the contributions in Dieter Krüger and Volker Bausch, eds., *Fulda Gap: Battlefield of the Cold War Alliances* (New York: Lexington, 2018); for FALLEX exercises see Ingo Trauschweizer, *The Cold War US Army: Building Deterrence for Limited War* (Lawrence: University Press of Kansas, 2008), 171.

Cold War thus included the BGS as an integral part of their strategic and operational planning. For the West Germans, however, the BGS remained a counterinsurgency force they could rely on, independent of NATO, to fight and stop communist incursions before they spread into a wider conflict.[68]

Competing Perspectives on Legal Training in the BGS

The recommendations by Dr. Renthe-Fink, although insufficient to bring militarized training to a halt, did have some influence on the addition of more police training in the BGS. The Interior Ministry implemented his suggestion to bring in civilian experts and academics to teach police sciences and law, but only for those men at the rank of sergeant and above. There was also an internal effort for reform that came from personnel within the organization itself. BGS Lieutenant Colonel Georg Mangelsdorf complained during a professional ethics course in 1958 that "instruction in police law, police employment and legal theory was very limited." Mangelsdorf also pointed out that "although it is constantly being emphasized that the BGS is a police force, the relevant police subjects are treated very negligently in training."[69] He attributed this to that fact that most candidates for the BGS came from the Wehrmacht and suggested that it would be better to have veteran police officers as instructors to address what he saw as an organizational shortcoming.

Mangelsdorf did not reflect the attitudes of his colleagues and superiors however, most of whom dismissed complaints and argued criminal law and police training should be restricted to those in leadership positions. In response to Mangelsdorf, the Public Security Branch pointed out that officer candidates received 825 hours of training of which 363 hours were devoted to policing topics while an additional 264 hours focused on law. Commanding officers attended two 16-day legal instruction courses during every half-year training cycle.[70] The Interior Ministry also rejected Mangelsdorf's suggestion that veteran state police officers be brought back as instructors in police science and criminal law citing their inability to understand the duties of the BGS as a special police force. Moreover, according to the Interior Ministry "the views of the

---

68 Friedrich Beermann, "Bericht über den Besuch bei dem Bundesgrenzschutz," March 1–5, 1955, BA-MA, N 597/30.

69 Abteilungsleiter VI to Herrn Referenten VI C 2, "Ausbildung des BGS," September 11, 1958, BArch-K, B 106/15079.

70 Memorandum from Referat VI C 2,—62 200—1 C/58—October 20, 1958, "Ausbildung des Bundesgrenzschutzes; Unterricht in Polizeiverwendung, Polizeirecht und Rechtslehre," BArch-K, B 106/15079.

federal states on the content of policing theories differ to a considerable extent ... and took the view that fighting armed bandits was not a police task." The memorandum concluded that the focus of the first two years of training should remain on the mastery of weapons. Thus police work and legal studies continued to make up less than half of the total training time for new recruits.[71]

In November 1958 the West German press began asking questions about the type of training the BGS was conducting. A Public Security Branch interoffice memorandum referred to a story that appeared in the October 11, 1958 edition of the *Stuttgarter Zeitung* and also similar inquiries that emerged from articles in *Die Zeit* and the *Frankfurter Rundschau*.[72] The press also questioned the leader of the ÖTV whether or not the BGS trained its personnel in criminal law and police sciences. The journal *ÖTV-Presse* ran a story in January 1959 that reported recent increases in legal training for border police officers, but it lacked specific details about the courses.[73] Since the ÖTV represented many BGS officers at the time, the Interior Ministry instructed Director Ludwig Dierske to prepare a detailed response outlining the curriculum for education and legal training. In his letter to the ÖTV, Dierske listed all the course hours devoted to criminal law and police sciences with a percentage of the course hours next to each of the categories he highlighted.[74]

The veteran soldiers and officers who led the BGS did not like the pressure from West Germany's press. While the majority of personnel in the Interior Ministry's public security branch, Chief Kurt Andersen, the training staff at Lübeck-St Hubertus, and even the Ministry of Defense promoted military training, the emergence of a critical press in postwar West Germany could no longer be ignored. Yet rather than making substantive changes, Andersen and his staff implemented what could at best be described as a façade meant to appease their critics. Thus the 1959/60 training plan included some additional legal and police science instruction.[75] Andersen complained that BGS personnel showed minimal interest in these legal topics unless they were presented in a "simple and pragmatic way." He believed legal training was a lower priority than ensuring his men had tactical competency. He argued that "legal training in the operational units is to be geared towards practice and must always

71 Ibid.
72 Referat VI B 1 to Referenten VI C, 351 B 344/58, November 5, 1958, "Rechtsunterricht im Bundesgrenzschutz," BArch-K, B 106/15079.
73 Ludwig Dierske in BMI to Referenten VI C 2, January 9, 1959, BArch-K, B 106/15079.
74 Ludwig Dierske, Privatdienstschreiben, to Herr Holtz, ÖTV-Presse, January 10, 1959, BArch-K, B 106/15079.
75 Kurt Andersen to all BGS Commands, "Rechtsausbildung im Ausbildungsjahr 1959/60," May 30, 1959, BArch-K, B 106/15079.

keep an eye on the goal of operational readiness ... on the legal assessment of a tactical situation."[76] He added eight hours of legal instruction per month, time permitting, just for the men in leadership positions. For police officers below the rank of sergeant, he limited it to two hours of legal coursework per quarter.[77]

Although the addition of more legal training in any form was better than nothing, not everyone found it to be useful and some rejected it altogether. Heinrich Müller, now in command of BGS-North, wrote to Dierske with a list of grievances about the new legal training.[78] According to Müller, it was a complete failure because it was taught by lawyers and from his perspective, had no relevance to the actual tactical duties performed by the BGS. The instructors, he asserted, offered examples of crimes that were much too theoretical and demanded from the "border hunters the same skills as a qualified lawyer who has at least ten semesters of study."[79] The solution, as he saw it, was to keep the training simple since "for us it is only essential that there is a legal basis for our actions ... [the men] therefore must be taught to quickly identify the most serious criminal offense so there will be no doubt about what means of coercion we can use." In other words, his main concern was the legal basis for the use of force and coercion rather than teaching officers the basics of enforcing criminal laws in a democracy. He concluded that legal training could and should be reduced to teaching the men when to intervene and when to use their firearms.[80]

In March 1961 the BGS celebrated its ten-year anniversary and its Chief, Brigadier General Kurt Andersen, announced his retirement. The government bestowed upon him its highest award, the Grand Cross (*Großes Verdienstkreuz*), becoming the fourth German political regime to award him a medal for serving the state.[81] Although Interior Minister Schröder could have replaced Andersen, a tough combat veteran of both world wars, with someone more inclined to promote the principles of modern civilian policing, instead, he promoted the aging Brigadier General Alfred Samlowski, another combat veteran. At sixty-two, his long service career mirrored many of his colleagues who like him were part of the founding "men of the first hour." He fought as a soldier in the First World War, served in the Prussian *Schutzpolizei* in the interwar years and

76 Ibid.
77 Ibid.
78 Heinrich Müller to Ludwig Dierske, March 26, 1959, BArch-K, B 106/15079.
79 Ibid.
80 Ibid.
81 "General Andersen in Ruhestand," *Der Grenzjäger* 4 (April 1961): 6.

then in the Wehrmacht during the Third Reich.[82] Samlowski reflected continuity rather than change and replicated the status quo when it came to training.

On April 1, 1961, the Interior Ministry in conjunction with the Border Protection Directorate in Koblenz renamed the Federal Passport Control Service (BPKD), established in 1951 as a separate division within the BGS (see chapter 2), as the Border Police Individual Service (Grenzschutzeinzeldienst—GSE).[83] GSE officers carried out more typical law enforcement duties including passport screening, searches of individuals and vehicles, seizure of contraband, and the arrest of wanted fugitives. Although the GSE remained part of the BGS, it only had 971 officers to cover more than 6,000 kilometers of the Federal Republic's land and sea borders. In 1961 West Germany had border checkpoints in 91 airports, 88 seaports, and at 471 highway crossings. Between 1952 and 1965, the number of persons entering through these crossings increased from 45 million per year to 273 million—arrests went up from 1,686 to 14,300.[84] With fewer than 1,000 officers, there was no way for the GSE to staff these offices or handle the increasing workload without support from the state police and federal customs officers (*Zoll*). Even though the BGS suffered from its own staffing shortages due to the transfer of half its personnel to the army, it still fielded 12,000 men in 1961. Since the federal government created the BGS to guard West Germany's borders by preventing illegal entries, why did the Interior Ministry assign fewer than 1,000 men to these critical checkpoints? In truth, the Interior Ministry's deliberate refusal to devote more law enforcement training and adequate staffing to these checkpoints shows convincingly that they intended the BGS to secure the border through military means rather than by a more conventional policing approach.

Warfare in the Global South and Its Effect on BGS Training

Samlowski's brief two-year tenure was marked by rising tensions in both domestic and international relations. By the early 1960s, the US increased its intervention in Vietnam, using its West German bases to support

82 "Der neue Inspekteur des Bundesgrenzschutzes," *Der Grenzjäger* 5 (May 1961): 8.
83 Der Leiter der Grenzschutzdirektion Freiherr von Linden to Ministerialdirigent Dr. Schultheis, "Die Paßnachschau als Mittel zur Sicherung der Bundesrepublik" 15 Jahre Grenzschutzeinzeldienst," November 2, 1965, BArch-K, B 273/33.
84 Manfred Milcher, *Der Bundesgrenzschutz: Ein Bildband* (Cologne: Markus, 1966), 80.

its military advisory operations there. Divided Berlin continued to be a source of conflict between the Soviet Union and the United States. After the failed summit between Kennedy and Soviet Premier Nikita Khrushchev in Vienna in 1961, Kennedy declared "So long as the communists insist that they are preparing to end by themselves unilaterally our rights in West Berlin and our commitments to its people, we must be prepared to defend those rights and those commitments."[85] On August 12, 1961, the Soviets began construction on the Berlin Wall, cutting off its citizens who were leaving by the millions to the West. Just as the East German hardening of the Inner-German border during Action Vermin had done in 1952, the surprise construction of the Berlin Wall confirmed for West Germans and the BGS in particular the real prospects for war with the East.[86] Then, in October of 1962, the world came to the brink of nuclear war after the Soviets began installing missiles in Cuba and the United States responded by implementing a naval blockade. The Cuban Missile Crisis raised the alert status of the BGS to its highest level since the Berlin uprisings of 1953. The Interior Ministry cancelled all training, planned vacations, and leave and recalled the entire command staff to their posts.[87]

These global Cold War crises kept BGS commanders and their subordinates focused on preparing to fight communists rather than enforcing laws. Under the circumstances, Samlowski had no intention of changing the way his men trained and he made no effort to do so during his brief tenure. When he retired in March of 1963, Schröder chose the head of BGS-north, Heinrich Müller, to replace him. Samlowski described Müller to Schröder as "an officer of high intelligence ... polite and correct, fits in, strong sense of camaraderie although idiosyncratic."[88] Müller, a leader widely known among his peers as a critical thinker and an intellectual, previously taught courses at the BGS school in Lübeck-St. Hubertus and at the Protestant Academy's quarterly professional ethics seminars. During his time as an instructor at the Nazi War Academy, he developed a strong interest in Germany's military history—a regular topic of his lectures at BGS training seminars. Müller may have been an intellectual or "idiosyncratic" as Samlowski thought, but without a doubt he shared

---

85 President John F. Kennedy, "Radio and Television Report to the American People on the Berlin Crisis," July 25, 1961, online, jfklibrary.org, Berlin Crisis Speeches.

86 Petra Goedde, *The Politics of Peace: A Global Cold War History* (Oxford: Oxford University Press, 2019), 119.

87 Interior Ministry Public Security Branch, Referat VI C 2 to all BGS-Kommandos, "Maßnahmen anläßlich Blockade Kuba," October 26, 1962, BArch-K, B 106/15178.

88 Alfred Samlowski, "Großer Beurteilungsbogen über Brigadegeneral Heinrich Müller," December 17, 1962, BA-MA, N 848/24.

the conservative-authoritarian mindset of his predecessors and this, more than anything else, shaped his approach to training. Enforcing laws for entering and leaving West Germany was a matter for the GSE as far as he was concerned.

By all accounts, Müller's prewar career in the police forces of the Weimar Republic should have set him up as an agent of organizational change. He was the youngest to assume the role as chief and had not started out as a soldier in the First World War like his predecessors. Nevertheless, Müller's combat experience as a Wehrmacht officer proved to be more influential than his police career when it came to training border police officers. As he assumed command of the BGS, civil wars and insurgencies associated with decolonization in the developing world shaped his emphasis on training his officers to fight subversive or guerilla wars. Even though security measures at the Inner-German border in the 1960s were formidable and the organizational need for more law enforcement training remained, Müller and his command staff still imagined and planned for communist insurgencies or the outbreak of civil war in divided Germany. During his tenure, the Bundestag passed legislation that recognized border police officers as military combatants, codifying their duty to fight enemy invaders with military means (see chapter 7). Warfare in the global south had now come home to West Germany.

CHAPTER SIX

PROFESSIONAL ETHICS AND MORAL TRAINING

THE INTRODUCTION IN THE 1955 edition of *Text and Reading Book for Political and Civics Education in the Federal Border Police*, states: "The foundations of human morality and thus also of the state-political education are founded in the West on the Christian religion and its cultivation by the Christian Churches."[1] On the face of it, the strong emphasis of religion in a textbook intended to teach police officers about politics and civics seems unusual. The police in democratic states are supposed to be impartial and apolitical when enforcing the law. With no official state church, West Germany's Basic Law and Federal Constitutional Court promoted religious neutrality. Yet the Federal Republic's stance on religion did not adhere to the same strict separation of church and state found in American constitutional jurisprudence. According to the legal scholar Donald Kommers, "Because it provides for peoples spiritual needs, the church is crucially important to the life of the state and society."[2]

Whereas combat veterans trained border police officers like soldiers, teaching them to use infantry weapons and preparing them to fight wars, Protestant and Catholic chaplains tried to instill moral behaviors they thought would arm the men for policing a democracy. They did this through the medium of professional ethics courses, first during basic training and then in a series of ongoing seminars where attendance was mandatory. To be sure, this approach revived a Weimar-era practice, where the churches administered pastoral care and ethics training to Germany's state police forces.[3] Although the National Socialists banned this practice during the 1930s, Germany's Christian churches and

1   Otto Breiting and Kurt M. Hoffmann, *Lehr- und Lesebuch für die politische Bildung und staatsbürgerliche Erziehung im Bundesgrenzschutz* (Braunschweig: Gersbach & Sohn, 1955), 6, 16.
2   Donald P. Kommers, "West German Constitutionalism and Church-State Relations," *German Politics & Society* 19 (Spring 1990): 7.
3   Ulrike Wagener, "Berufsethische Bildung für staatliche Sicherheitskräfte: Das Beispiel Polizei," in *Charakter—Haltung—Habitus: Persönlichkeit und*

their clergy came with their own moral baggage from the Third Reich. Historians have shown that both the Protestant and Catholic churches supported National Socialism, even though the state persecuted some of its members for speaking out against its racist policies. During the postwar period, many of the Wehrmacht's chaplains returned to their pastoral work, and several of them later joined the BGS. Omer Bartov and Phyllis Mack have argued that the postwar clergy behaved as if it was "their self-proclaimed task to restore the moral order in German society."[4] This is precisely what BGS chaplains attempted to accomplish through professional ethics, and it allowed them to obfuscate the role of their institutions in the perpetration of Nazi crimes. Although anti-Semitism disappeared from their teachings, anti-communism, another anchor of National Socialist ideology with its racist tropes of other and Eastern cultures in particular, did not.

The thematic residual from the Nazi past, however, did not overshadow all of the curriculum, and like other contradictory aspects of BGS organizational culture, negative legacies coexisted with efforts to emphasize moral behaviors and the ethical principles of democratic policing. As Pastor Dieter Beese, an ethics lecturer at Germany's National Police Leadership Academy in Münster-Hiltrup, suggested, "The ethos of the police profession is an indicator of the political and moral culture of an entire society."[5] In the BGS, however, this ethos reflected a brand of Christian conservatism that did not always square with societal trends, or for that matter, the personal lives of its own officers. The BGS ethos reflected the political and moral culture of its elite command staff and senior membership rather than of the young men it sought to retain or West German society as a whole.

Thus the professional ethics curriculum sometimes reflected broader social trends in the Federal Republic, and its conservative-authoritarian shifts in particular. Yet at other times, the BGS appeared out of touch and existed in tension with mainstream society as a whole—like the metaphor of a time capsule of 1950s conservatism. West Germany's youth culture made conservatives uneasy because both young men and young women

---

Verantwortung in der Bundeswehr, ed. Angelika Dörfler-Dierken and Christian Göbel (Wiesbaden: Springer, 2022), 10.

4 Deacon Fritz Ulbrich was one of many Wehrmacht chaplains whose biographical details were recalled in BGS literature: see Graf, "GS-Dekan i.R. Ulbrich feierte 80. Geburtstag," *Zeitschrift des Bundesgrenzschutzes* 12 (December 1989): 45; Omer Bartov and Phyllis Mack, eds., *In God's Name: Genocide and Religion in the Twentieth Century* (New York: Berghahn, 2001), 6.

5 Dieter Beese, "Polizei Berufsethik," in *Berufsethik—Glaube—Seelsorge: Evangelische Seelsorge im Bundesgrenzschutz Polizei des Bundes; Festschrift für Rolf Sauerzapf*, ed. Joachim Heubach and Klaus-Dieter Stephan, 31 (Leipzig: Evangelische Verlagsanstalt, 1997).

embraced new technologies, new music, and the thriving postwar culture of consumption.[6] Protestants and Catholics alike worried that modern culture, with its fatherless families and open promiscuity, threatened the moral foundation of the new democratic state. To counter these trends, BGS chaplains used professional ethics to re-emphasize the importance of the Christian family and linked it to the long-term success of West Germany's democracy. Like their Weimar counterparts, the Federal Republic's clergy believed that a moral and spiritual crisis plagued postwar society.[7] Gender also played a significant role. In the early postwar decades, the chaplains emphasized patriarchal masculinity in an attempt to restore prewar family relations. But the increasing agency of women as a result of Germany's total collapse in 1945 made the previous notions of masculinity untenable. A new form of civic-manliness replaced the pre-1945 cult of the soldier. Chaplains taught border police officers they could be civil servants, loyal family men and defenders of the new democratic state all at the same time.[8] Moreover, in the later postwar decades, the ethics courses incorporated not only the men but also their wives.

Professional Ethics: New Beginnings, Continuities and Problematic Legacies

The historian Shelley Baranowski has argued that "the churches, virtually the only institutions left intact at the defeat, played a leading role in the rehabilitation of conservatism."[9] During the war, however, very few of those who held high church offices ever spoke out against Hitler's criminal policies. Hundreds of Catholic and Protestant clergymen served as military chaplains, and historians have shown they had direct knowledge of, and in many cases were even complicit in the crimes perpetrated by Nazi armed forces. Edward Luttwak, for example, has argued we should not overestimate that "there were ordained chaplains with the Wehrmacht on every front, including the Eastern Front where all the rules of war

---

6   Mark Edward Ruff, *The Wayward Flock: Catholic Youth in Postwar West Germany, 1945–1965* (Chapel Hill: University of North Carolina Press, 2005), 4–6.

7   See Till van Rahden, "Fatherhood, Rechristianization, and the Quest for Democracy," 142; see also Eric D. Weitz, *Weimar Germany: Promise and Tragedy* (Princeton, NJ: Princeton University Press, 2007), 323–24.

8   See for example Uta G. Poiger, "A New, Western Hero? Reconstructing German Masculinity in the 1950s," in *The Miracle Years*, ed. Hannah Schissler, 412–27; Friederike Brühöfener, "Defining the West German Soldier."

9   Shelley Baranowski, *The Confessing Church, Conservative Elites, and the Nazi State*, Texts and Studies in Religion 28 (Lewiston: Edwin Mellen, 1986), 111.

were simply abrogated to unleash mass cruelties not seen in centuries."[10] Both churches found common ground with the National Socialist campaign against Bolshevism and its use in the anti-Semitic framing of Jews as the enemy of the German people. Many of the men who became chaplains in the BGS served with the Wehrmacht in the Soviet Union. It is difficult to trace the individual records, but a significant number of them had been military chaplains. Pastor Anton Wirtz, for example, served as division chaplain in the Second Infantry Division, which later became the 12th Panzer Division. He accompanied the Wehrmacht during its invasions of Poland, France, and the Soviet Union. After the bitter fighting in Kurland, he surrendered with the rest of his division to the Soviets on May 8, 1945. He joined the BGS in 1953 and retired in 1975 as its Catholic Dean. His retirement announcement said that during the war "he tried to give support and Christian consolation to countless soldiers, especially in their hour of death." Yet, as Ben Shepherd has argued about divisional chaplains on the Eastern Front, besides administering last rights they "often set to work trying to ameliorate the guilt soldiers may have felt."[11]

From the very beginning, the Inerior Ministry followed the Weimar-era practice of integrating professional ethics into the basic training curriculum for all border police officers. Later, as the organization grew, chaplains from both the BGS Evangelical and Catholic *Seelsorge* (pastoral care) taught professional ethics on a monthly basis in every unit. In 1951, however, only one Catholic priest and one Protestant pastor handled all spiritual care duties for the border police.[12] The subject matter or objective of ethics training remained consistent despite subtle confessional differences between the two churches. In some cases, Catholic

---

10 Lauren Faulkner Rossi, *Wehrmacht Priests: Catholicism and the Nazi War of Annihilation* (Cambridge, MA: Harvard University Press, 2015), 65; Edward Luttwak, "Franco-German Reconciliation: The Overlooked Role of the Moral Rearmament Movement," in *Religion: The Missing Dimension of Statecraft*, ed. Douglas Johnston and Cynthia Sampson, 44. (New York: Oxford University Press, 1994).
11 Pastor Helmut Oberle, "35 Jahre Truppenseelsorger: Der katholische GS-Dekan Wirtz tritt in den Ruhestand," *Zeitschrift des Bundesgrenzschutzes* 1 (January 1975): 37–38; Ben H. Shepherd, *Hitler's Soldiers*, 143.
12 Dekan Breuer, "Sind die ethischen Grundsätze tief genug verankert?" *Die Parole* 11, Sonderausgabe: *10 Jahre Bundesgrenzschutz* (May 28, 1961), 6; The Catholic priest Reinhold Friedrichs was arrested by the Gestapo during the war and was held in concentration camps at Sachsenhausen and Dachau. See Wolfgang Hinz, "Geschichtliche Entwicklung der Polizeiseelsorge," in *Handbuch Polizeiseelsorge*, ed. Kurt Grützner, Wolfgang Gröger, Claudia Kiehn, and Werner Schiewek, 54 (Göttingen: Vandenhoeck & Ruprecht, 2012).

and Evangelical chaplains taught together with senior members of the command staff.[13]

By 1965, the Interior Ministry formalized pastoral care and professional ethics instruction through an agreement that guaranteed a permanent role for both churches in the organization. It stated "Border guard chaplains are to be given the opportunity to comment on fundamental questions relating to the education, care and mental attitude of the police officers in the BGS."[14] The agreement required its commanding officers to support the chaplains in their work, and each member of the organization received one hour of instruction every fourteen days. The men could also discuss religious issues and attend church services during their regular working hours. The agreement designated a BGS Dean for each denomination. The Dean answered to his church administration through a designated Commissioner for Pastoral Care who acted on behalf of the ecclesiastical authorities. The Dean also reported directly to the Interior Minister, supervised all chaplains, and developed the professional ethics curriculum. Nine chaplains from each denomination and a number of part-time pastors and local church officials carried out these duties. The agreement also stipulated: "The professional ethics education of law enforcement officers in the federal border police, which is part of the overall education, is based on the principles of Christian living."[15] Besides the pastors, some of the senior members of the command staff also taught professional ethics or served as guest lecturers at the seminars.

The coursework and the men who taught it, however, often promoted problematic themes rooted in Germany's authoritarian past. On the one hand, the instructors tried to provide their students with a comprehensive morality-based education that included a series of regular lectures, detailed assigned readings, and discussion groups. The chaplains encouraged the men to think critically about the complex ethical issues they might encounter in both their professional and personal lives. After all, police officers had the responsibility to make life and death decisions. Lectures and discussions attempted to square Christian teachings about the right to kill and also on the morality of using nuclear weapons, but only in the context of self-defense.[16] On the other hand, however, at times the training evoked ethno-chauvinistic tropes about the superiority

---

13 See for example, Grenzschutzkommando Nord an den Bundesminister des Innern, betreffend: "Erfahrungsbericht über Arbeitstagungen für berufsethische Erziehung der Grenzschutzbeamten bei den evangelischen und katholischen Akademien," February 14, 1955, BArch-K, B106/20766.

14 Bundesministerium des Innern, "Vereinbarung über die katholische und evangelische Seelsorge im Bundesgrenzschutz," March 8, 1965, BArch-K, B 106/363158.

15 Ibid.

16 See course plans and lecture transcripts in BArch-K, B106/20765, 20766.

of the Occident (Christian West). The instructors frequently demonized Bolshevism in particular. They targeted Eastern or "Asiatic" culture as inherently Bolshevist and claimed it was the greatest existential threat to the Christian West. The men who taught ethics routinely employed the same ideological rhetoric and stereotypical labels used by the Nazis to justify their annihilationist war against the Soviets. In her study of the Wehrmacht's Catholic chaplaincy, Lauren Rossi estimated that around 17,000 priests served in a variety of military roles during the war. Thus continuities in the xenophobic framing of Bolshevism from the war on the Eastern Front fused well with 1950s anti-communism.[17]

Defending the Christian West

Christianity functioned as the main philosophical basis for teaching police officers how to behave ethically, but also to instill in them a traditional conservative worldview that rejected communism and Americanized culture. A 1954 lecture given by the popular BGS Colonel Heinrich Müller entitled, "Christian Beliefs and the Troops," sheds light on the broad, conservative re-Christianization effort in West Germany.[18] Müller, well-read in the humanities and known for his intellectualism, suggested that the purpose of professional ethics was to ensure that the men guarding West Germany's borders promoted a Christian conservative worldview. Christianity thus became the main foil to prevent the men from abusing their power or succumbing to the temptations of modern life. He argued that "the Westerner cannot disconnect from the embrace of Christianity unless he denies his Western existence [and] cannot be a Westerner without being a Christian at the same time."[19] Given the rising Cold War

17 See Lauren Faulkner Rossi, *Wehrmacht Priests*, 1. For a broader study of military pastoral care in the Wehrmacht, see Dagmar Pöpping, "Die Wehrmachtseelsorge im Zweiten Weltkrieg: Rolle und Selbstverständnis von Kriegs- und Wehrmachtpfarren im Ostkrieg, 1941–1945," in *Zerstrittene "Volksgemeinschaft": Glaube, Konfession und Religion im Nationalsozialismus*, ed. Manfred Gailus and Armin Nolzen (Göttingen: Vandenhoeck & Ruprecht, 2011); Martin Röw, *Militärseelsorge unter dem Hakenkreuz: Die katholische Feldpastoral 1939–1945* (Paderborn: Ferdinand Schöningh, 2014), 72–78.

18 Transcript: Colonel Heinrich Müller, "Christlicher Glaube und Truppe" (Vortrag gehalten am 3.9.54 auf der Tagung für Angehörige des BGS/GSK Mitte an der evangelischen Akademie von Kurhessen-Waldeck in Hofgeismar), September 6, 1954, BArch-K, B106/20765; see, for example, Mark Edward Ruff, "Catholic Elites, Gender, and Unintended Consequences in the 1950s: Toward a Reinterpretation of the Role of Conservatives in the Federal Republic," in, eds., *Conflict, Catastrophe, and Continuity: Essays on Modern German History*, ed. Frank Biess, Mark Roseman, and Hanna Schissler (New York: Berghahn, 2007).

19 Ibid.

political tensions, his ideas resonated with colleagues and subordinates. Müller's perspective came from his close reading of Oswald Spengler's *Decline of the West*. He praised the book and recommended that "it should be read by every officer because it remains such a superior historical overview with profound implications in all fields."[20] He also promoted the writings of Spanish philosopher José Ortega y Gasset, who warned against the rule of the masses and argued that democracies needed an aristocratic "elite" to lead them.[21] His preference for the writings of Spengler and Ortega y Gasset shows how conservative-authoritarian philosophies shaped his intellectualism.

Müller wanted his students to understand that they were not only guarding West Germany's physical frontiers but, more importantly, also its cultural borders. He told his audience that they were in the middle of a huge German battle between East and West that threatend to crush them, and that in the midst of this struggle they had been given a special position as guardians of a cultural border and were ultimately responsible for defending their Western heritage."[22] His concerns about the East-West struggle tied directly into the Interior Ministry's justification of the BGS as a "police buffer," the objective of which, he suggested, was to prevent a nuclear conflagration by resolving border incidents before they involved NATO forces. He encouraged his students to adopt a moral code or set of behaviors that struck "a path between the dull flatness of the Asian steppes and the cold objectivity of the American skyscrapers."[23]

In the closed, private sphere of the BGS, however, Müller's lectures also reflected xenophobic themes grounded in Western anti-communism. His experiences with labor strikes and KPD activity as a police officer in Essen during the late 1920s must have played a formative role in his attitude. In one lecture he suggested that the greatest ideological and physical threat to the Federal Republic emanated from what he called the "Asiatic far east." Russia, he explained, still lived with the memory and influences of thirteenth-century Mongol invaders and thrived "on the myth of Genghis Khan." He argued that the BGS needed Christianity as a means to shield the West against a new modern threat coming from the Asian steppes. His descriptions of the East revived the xenophobic

---

20 Memorandum from Heinrich Müller to Interior Minister Robert Lehr, Lübeck, March 28, 1952, BArch-K, B106/15076.

21 Heinrich Müller expressed his support for Ortega y Gasset's ideas in his 1955 lecture: "Autorität und Gehorsam im BGS," BArch-K, B106/20765; José Ortega y Gasset, *The Revolt of the Masses* (New York: W. W. Norton, 1993); See also Andrew Dobson, *An Introduction to the Politics and Philosophy of José Ortega y Gasset* (New York: Cambridge University Press, 1989), 75.

22 Transcript: Colonel Heinrich Müller, "Christlicher Glaube und Truppe," BArch-K, B106/20765.

23 Ibid.

stereotypes of Nazi propaganda, which included similar narratives.[24] It is difficult to evaluate the effects of ideas like this on the men. A post-lecture report by BGS Pastor Ulbrich reported only that productive student debates followed Müller's lecture, thereby affirming their commitment to the "Christian profession."[25]

The reemergence of these themes reflected one way in which West Germans reframed legacies of the Nazi past into useable narratives for the present. Anti-communism shaped Germany's conservative milieu long before the Second World War and became a central feature of Bonn's postwar political identity.[26] For the veteran soldiers employed by the BGS in particular, the war against Bolshevism did not end in 1945. They believed that modern Bolshevik hordes, in the form of the Red Army, planned to conquer the rest of Germany and with it, Christian Europe as well. Their experiences on the Eastern Front and time in Soviet captivity played a formative role in these narratives. The Soviet atrocities in Berlin (1945) and their suppression of popular uprisings in East Berlin (1953) and later at Budapest (1956) and Prague (1968) also reinforced these primal fears.[27]

To understand the prevalence of xenophobic perceptions of the East in the BGS, it is also important to analyze them within the context of their transnational manifestations. This does not mean, however, that we should excuse the troubling return of these tropes, because they also formed the basis for Nazi Germany's anti-Semitic claims linking Jews with Bolshevism. But we can also find them in the older, endemic traditions of anti-communism propagated by the West.[28] For Christian conservatives like Müller and his colleagues, "Godless" communism threatened

---

24   Aristotle A. Kallis, *Nazi Propaganda and the Second World War* (New York: Palgrave Macmillan, 2005), 66; Vejas Gabriel Liulevicius, *The German Myth of the East: 1800 to the Present* (Oxford: Oxford University Press, 2009), 226–27.

25   Pastor Ulbrich, Evangelische Seelsorge im Grenzschutzkommando Mitte, "Erfahrungsbericht über berufsethische Lehrgänge auf den evangelischen Akademien Hofgeismar und Friedewald für den Bereich des GSK Mitte," February 14, 1955, BArch-K, B106/20766; Graf, "GS-Dekan i.R. Ulbrich feierte 80. Geburtstag," *Zeitschrift des Bundesgrenzschutzes* 12 (December 1989): 45.

26   Stefan Creuzberger and Dierk Hoffmann, *Geistige Gefahr und Immunisierung der Gesellschaft: Antikommunismus und politische Kultur in der frühen Bundesrepublik* (Munich: Oldenbourg Verlag, 2014), 2.

27   Troy R. E. Paddock, *Creating the Russian Peril: Education, the Public Sphere, and National Identity in Imperial Germany, 1890–1914* (New York: Camden House, 2010), 230; see also Vejas Gabriel Liulevicius, *The German Myth of the East*, 98–102; and Norman Naimark, *The Russians in Germany*.

28   Ariane Knüsel, *Framing China: Media Images and Political Debates in Britain, the USA and Switzerland, 1900–1950* (Surrey, UK: Ashgate, 2012), 127–32.

the entire human race now that the Soviets had nuclear weapons. Thus his statements embodied similar rhetoric grounded in the "red scares" that shaped Western democracies from the late nineteenth century on. In the United States, for example, popular culture and government policies promulgated "yellow peril" narratives and fear of overthrow by "Asiatic" hordes. A 1929 novel by Floyd Gibbons, *The Red Napoleon*, tells the story of a fictional warlord from the Asian Steppes, Karakhan of Kazan, who attacks Russia and eventually the United States. Similar narratives appeared in the Buck Rogers adventure novels, where a Mongolian tribe known as the Han took over America and subjugated its white race. The themes reemerged during the Cold War in the popular science fiction novels of Robert Heinlein. In Heinlein's *The Day after Tomorrow*, America is overrun by "yellow masses" that he refers to as Pan-Asian Mongolians.[29]

Between the 1920s and 1970s many police departments in larger American cities deployed "red squads" to surveil anyone suspected of leftist or Bolshevist activities.[30] California's Governor Earl Warren, who later went on to become the Chief Justice of the US Supreme Court known for his landmark liberal constitutional rulings, also expressed xenophobic framings of communism. As Governor, Warren passed legislation that required "loyalty oaths" from public employees and argued that the state "needed protection from almost certain sabotage on the part of fanatical communists among us who, while enjoying the liberties of this country glorify in their disturbed minds the slavery of Soviet Russia."[31] The famous American aviator Charles Lindbergh, described Persians, Moors and Mongols as "Asiatic hordes"—an existential threat to Western culture.[32] British politicians also deployed racist language when describing communists. In his book *The World Crisis: The Aftermath*, Winston Churchill described Russia as "plague bearing ... a Russia of armed hordes not only smiting with bayonet and with cannon, but accompanied and preceded by swarms of typhus-bearing vermin." In a 1920 article he wrote for the *Evening News* he referred to communism

---

29 David Seed, "Constructing America's Enemies: The Invasions of the USA," *Yearbook of English Studies* 37, no. 2 (2007), 68–74.

30 See Frank J. Donner, *Protectors of Privilege: Red Squads and Police Repression in Urban America* (Berkeley: University of California Press, 1990).

31 M. J. Heale, "Red Scare Politics: California's Campaign against Un-American Activities, 1940–1970," *Journal of American Studies* 20, no. 1 (April 1986): 24.

32 Robert A Rosenbaum, *Waking to Danger: Americans and Nazi Germany, 1933–1941* (Oxford: Praeger, 2010), 182; see also Wayne S. Cole, *Charles A Lindbergh and the Battle against American Intervention in World War Two* (New York: Harcourt, 1974), 78.

as "The poison peril from the East" and asked his readers "Shall the red flood of Bolshevism swamp all Europe?"[33]

During another lecture, Müller's interpretation of Russian history focused on what he defined as the Christian or "Holy Russia" and its subjugation by the Bolsheviks. He argued for a difference between a European or "Holy Russia" and the "biological threat" posed by China's rapid population growth, which pushed Russia to start seeking territory in the West.[34] Thus he described Bolshevism as an "Asiatic" phenomenon forced upon Christian Russia. The imperial Cossack forces led by Generals Deniken, Yudenich, Kolchak, and Wrangel, he declared, "heroically" stood up against the millions of people from Asia only to be "bled to death in the fight for the honor of the Russian people and in loyalty to Holy Russia." While the West stood in silence "the last Cossacks perished miserably in the mines of the Urals."[35]

Müller based his analysis on the interpretation of the historian Michael Prawdin, who he called an "excellent expert on Russia."[36] Prawdin, a pseudonym for the Russian exile Michael Charol, lived in Germany and wrote histories of Genghis Khan and the Mongol invasions. Prawdin described the Mongols as "Terrible fellows ... short in the legs but with excessively long bodies, broad in the chest and dark of visage ... they drank blood."[37] Adolf Hitler and Chief of the SS, Heinrich Himmler, admired Prawdin's books so much that Himmler commissioned a special two-volume edition and issued a copy to every leader in the SS.[38] Hitler and Himmler both revered and feared the reputation of Genghis Khan. On the one hand, he impressed them with his fearsome reputation and prowess on the battlefield. On the other hand, however, they considered the Mongol race to be degenerate and sought to annihilate it. During the war, Nazi forces targeted Turkomans, Mongols, and other Eastern peoples they labeled "Asiatic" for elimination. Historian Richard Breitman has shown that for Hitler and Himmler "The Bolsheviks were

---

33 Winston Churchill, *The World Crisis: The Aftermath* (London: Thornton Butterworth, 1929), 262–63; *Evening News* articles reprinted in *The Collected Essays of Sir Winston Churchill*, vol. 1, ed. Winston Churchill and Michael Wolff (London: Library of Imperial History, 1976), 235.

34 Heinrich Müller, "Ich Dien' im BGS: Vortrag von Oberst i. BGS Müller, gehalten am July 7, 1955 im Rahmen einer Arbeitstagung für katholische Angehörige des Bundesgrenzschutzes Kommando Mitte im Bonifatiushaus Fulda," BA-MA, N 858/31.

35 Heinrich Müller, "Ich Dien' im BGS," BA-MA, N 848/31.

36 Ibid.

37 Michael Prawdin, *The Mongol Empire: Its Rise and Legacy*, 4th printing (New Brunswick: Transaction, 2009), 17.

38 Richard Breitman, "Hitler and Genghis Khan," *Journal of Contemporary History* 25, no. 2/3 (May–June 1990): 337–38.

merely the latest [Asiatic] ruling class over an age-old racial enemy ... and Hitler perceived a continuing threat from the potential successors of Genghis Khan."[39] Thus, Müller's xenophobic descriptions of the East not only reflected the broader conservative trends in Cold War Western anticommunism, but evoked continuities in racialized thinking informed by the same sources used by Nazi propagandists. Aristotle Kallis has argued that for National Socialists, Bolsheviks were "Asiatic, racially inferior and decidedly anti-European," which is precisely how Müller described them in his postwar lectures.[40]

Müller's interpretation of the East also corresponded to similar expressions found in organizational literature. Articles in BGS journals and magazines show how these racist stereotypes resonated among some of the border police officers. In a letter to the editor of the journal *Der Grenzjäger*, for example, an officer argued that he should be allowed to wear his original Nazi combat medals. He justified this by claiming that Nazi Germany had already been "fulfilling a European mission by fighting the Bolshevists, which should be recognized by the western world since it is now also engaged in the struggle against the advance of Bolshevism."[41] The BGS journal *Die Parole* also promoted xenophobic stereotypes. In a six-part article by BGS Major Günther Reischle entitled "The Defense of the West," he warned of cultural dangers from the Asian steppes.[42] He claimed that the survival of the Christian West depended exclusively upon the superior quality of its men and their leaders. The historians Axel Schildt and Arnold Sywottek have argued that this "Conservative rhetoric of a *christliches Abendland* not only helped establish the Federal Republic as a bulwark against the Soviet Union, it also hindered the development of liberal, democratic attitudes."[43] For the leading members of the Interior Ministry and their subordinates who commanded the BGS, defending the Christian West influenced its organizational identity.

In 1956, *Die Parole* published a lengthy article entitled: "What Does the West Have to Defend?"—an assessment of the professional ethics curriculum from a recent workshop held at the Protestant Academy in

---

39 Ibid., 343.
40 Kallis, *Nazi Propaganda and the Second World War*, 77.
41 Sergeant R., BGS Süd III, "Orden?" *Der Grenzjäger* 3 (April 1953): 7.
42 Major Reischle, "Die Verteidigung des Abendlandes: Die Abwehrkämpfe Europas gegen Angriffe auf seine Freiheit," *Die Parole* 5, no. 3 (March 15, 1955): 20.
43 Axel Schildt and Arnold Sywottek, "Reconstruction and Modernization: West German Social History during the 1950s," in *West Germany under Construction: Politics, Society, and Culture in the Adenauer Era*, ed. Robert Moeller, 437 (Ann Arbor: University of Michigan Press, 1997).

Hofgeismar.[44] During the workshop Pastor Werner Jentsch and BGS Colonel Kurt Voigt lectured on the "possibilities and limits of a defense of the Christian Heritage." Jentsch and Voigt identified "Mohammedanism and Hinduism ... religions that incorporated all colored peoples of Asia and parts of Africa (not controlled by Bolsheviks)," as mortal enemies of the West.[45] Jentsch, a veteran Wehrmacht chaplain, taught ethics into the early 1980s.

Along with the articles, the organizational journals also featured xenophobic cartoons. The caricatures of Asians exemplified certain aspects of Edward Said's Orientalism theories. Said argued, for example, that Orientalism invoked what he described as a "fourth dogma" that the "Orient is at bottom something either to be feared (the Yellow Peril, the Mongol hordes, the brown dominions) or to be controlled."[46] The August 1963 edition of *Die Parole* included a cartoon sketch of a bucktoothed Genghis Khan and another Mongol invader on horseback following a sign pointing to Moscow—the caption of which read: "Departure of the Golden Horde for the ideological conquest of Moscow."[47] The November 1968 edition included a cartoon called "The Guide" that depicted Chinese Premier Mao Zedong sitting on the gun-barrel of a tank being driven by Soviet leader Leonid Brezhnev and East German President Walter Ulbricht, both with overemphasized slanted eyes.[48] Additional cartoons included one titled "up or down" that showed Mao's head rising from a lake labeled "Congo" and another titled: "Damn Jostling" with a rabid Mao and a slant-eyed Nikita Khrushchev boarding a train marked "Afro-Asia Express."[49] Cartoons like this and the identification of non-Christian religions as enemies of the state, reflected conservative fears of communist infiltration by peoples from Asia and the global south engaged in small wars and insurgencies associated with decolonization.

It is difficult to assess the effect of these articles and images on the officers, because there is no data on the readership of this literature. Nevertheless, it does give us some idea about the organizational culture from a top-down perspective and the political ideologies of the Interior Ministry's staff responsible for editing and publishing the journals. Political cartoons by their very nature are meant to engage in

44 Oberleutnant im BGS Fischer, "Was hat der Westen zu verteidigen? Bericht über die berufsethische Arbeitstagung an der Evangelischen Akademie in Hofgeismar vom 3. bis 6. Dezember 1956," *Die Parole* 7, no. 1 (January 15, 1957): 18.
45 Ibid.
46 Edward Said, *Orientalism* (New York: Random House, 1978), 301.
47 *Die Parole* 8 (August 15, 1963): 2.
48 *Die Parole* 11 (November 15, 1968): 1.
49 *Die Parole* 9 (September 15, 1964): 1.

controversial humor at the expense of their subjects. It might be argued that the images in BGS literature simply underscored Cold War polarization and the ideological divide between East and West. Yet when a professional magazine for a democratic police force deploys racist metaphors and descriptions, it contradicts the ethical behavior the organization supposedly expected of its personnel. After all, border police officers handled foreign travelers and refugees fleeing war and, in many cases, persecution in their home countries. Instead of discouraging racial stereotypes, BGS professional ethics training during the 1950s and 1960s normalized them. These stereotypes, however, existed beyond the early postwar period and also played a role during the asylum debates of the 1980s.

Xenophobia reached new heights in the Federal Republic during the economic downturn of the 1970s and 1980s. According to the migration historian Brittany Lehman, "although many people across West Germany condemned the overt expression of xenophobia, anti-foreigner, anti-Turkish, and anti-Muslim slogans nonetheless appeared across walls and in newspapers as well as in successful political campaigns (including Chancellor Helmut Kohl's)."[50] The BGS played a key role in these debates, because its officers dealt with thousands of migrants attempting to cross the Federal Republic's borders. Between 1978 and 1980, for example, the BGS processed 6,766 persons requesting asylum.[51] Frequently the officers stereotyped migrants and associated them with increased crime and drug trafficking. The February 1981 edition of the BGS Journal, for example, included an article that claimed: "Despite their numerically small group, asylum seekers bring significantly more criminal activity than the local foreigners."[52]

Yet despite the prevalence of these stereotypes and association of migrants with criminality, evidence shows that members of the BGS closely followed the rule of law in dealing with migrants seeking asylum. Article 16a of the Basic Law provided asylum to any persons persecuted on political grounds. Thus officers had very little discretion as long as the individual verbally asserted political persecution as the reason for requesting asylum. The officers had no legal right to challenge the truthfulness of such claims. In helping the men to deal with those fleeing persecution, professional ethics in all command areas during the early 1980s focused

---

50 Brittany Lehman, *Teaching Migrant Children in West Germany and Europe, 1949–1992* (London: Palgrave-Macmillan, 2019), 169.

51 Alexander Dahms, "Asyl aus grenzpolizeilicher Sicht," *Zeitschrift des Bundesgrenzschutzes* 8 (July 1981): 25.

52 Siegfried Bleck, "Polizei-Almanac '80: Asylanten als neues Problem / Rauschgift-Kriminalität weiterhin ansteigend / Gewalttätigkeit und Brutalität nehmen zu," *Zeitschrift des Bundesgrenzschutzes* 2 (February 1981): 8–9.

on the subject of "The Asylum Law and Problems with Aliens."[53] As reflected by Chancellor Angela Merkel's 2015 decision to admit millions of refugees, many of whom fled the war in Syria, West German empathy for political refugees resided in their memories of the Nazi past. As Police Director Alexander Dahms wrote in the July issue of the BGS Journal, "We Germans in particular, who had often found protection from persecution abroad during the time of Hitler's dictatorship, should recognize that the substance of the right to asylum—despite existing abuses—must not be touched."[54]

Dahms, known for his leftist sentiments and later exposed as a Stasi agent, however, did not speak for everyone in the organization. Xenophobic responses to the influx of asylum seekers in the 1980s mirrored similar contradictory reactions to Merkel's policies in 2015. Yet West Germany was a democracy that had by all accounts abandoned the discourse of race and otherness in the aftermath of the Third Reich. The examples from BGS ethics courses, imagery in its institutional literature, and responses to immigration shows that racism persisted long into the postwar era—even if in practice, the border police officers who dealt with migrants kept these opinions to themselves. During the occupation, the Allies intended to reeducate Germany's postwar police officers, but they disregarded the troubling behaviors and examples set by their own forces. To be sure, American, British, and French policy makers could speak about the need for the Federal Republic to democratize while at home they still dealt with their own legacies of racism and segregation. Racism and democracy are not mutually exclusive. Thus, as the historians Rita Chin and Heide Fehrenbach have argued, the West, and America in particular, provided Germans with the best example of how this worked.[55]

Conservative Perceptions of Moral Crisis

Besides the persistence of xenophobia and racism, the professional ethics curriculum reflected innate sociocultural fears of materialism and abandonment of religion that formed part of a wider postwar cultural reaction

---

53 See, "Berufsethische Lehrgänge der GS-Seelsorge 1981," *Zeitschrift des Bundesgrenzschutzes* 1 (January 1981): 29–30.

54 Alexander Dahms, "Asyl aus grenzpolizeilicher Sicht," *Zeitschrift des Bundesgrenzschutzes* 7 (July 1981): 27; In 1991, Dahms was exposed as a Stasi spy; see John O. Koehler, *Stasi: The Untold Story of the East German Secret Police* (Oxford: Westview, 1999), 193.

55 Rita Chin and Heide Fehrenbach, "What's Race Got to Do with It? Postwar German History in Context," in *After the Nazi Racial State: Difference and Democracy in Germany and Europe*, ed. Rita Chin, Heide Fehrenbach, Geoff Eley, and Atina Grossmann (Ann Arbor: University of Michigan Press, 2009), 20.

by conservatives against modernist influences. As Mark Edward Ruff has argued, conservative Christians rejected "materialism, communism, emancipatory gender norms, mass culture, and to a lesser extent, liberalism."[56] However, this brand of what postwar scholars have labeled "restorative conservatism" shaped society during the Federal Republic's early years and endured within the insular organizational culture of the BGS for decades beyond the 1950s. In their ethics teachings, pastors complained that reckless materialism threatened the moral fabric of society and paved the way for West Germany's enemies to destroy its Christian culture.[57] Although this perspective may have resonated with the older "men of the first hour" generation, it did not convince the younger officers or potential recruits to reject the lure of modern lifestyles or the emerging culture of consumption that defined West Germany's economic miracle.

To be sure, conservative fears of a moral crisis emerged as part of a much wider global response by the West to the cultural polarization of the Cold War. Similar attitudes, for example, prevailed among evangelical Christians in the United States. David Settle has suggested that US presidents from Harry Truman to Ronald Reagan publicly expressed using "America's spiritual strength" against communism, while churches and their leaders deployed a rhetoric of warfare to define the east-west polarization.[58] During the Cold War, the BGS used professional ethics to defend Christian conservatism against the challenges of an increasingly secular society. Thus in 1978 when border police instructor Otmar Stöcker described modern developments such as women in the workplace and so called "latch-key" (unsupervised) children as spiritually damaging to German families, he was reaffirming conservative ideas about gender roles prevalent during the 1950s.[59] According to Stöcker, the modern demands of economic wellbeing and the need to conform or "keep up" with others had undermined the "spiritual substance" of the family.

Stöcker, a decorated combat vetean still teaching ethics in the 1980s, based his ideas on the American sociologist David Riesman and his 1950 book, *The Lonely Crowd*. Riesman's philosophies first influenced professional ethics courses in the BGS during the early 1950s. Riesman analyzed American culture using three separate frames of reference:

---

56 Mark Edward Ruff, "Catholic Elites, Gender, and Unintended Consequences in the 1950s" in *Conflict, Catastrophe, and Continuity: Essays on Modern German History*, ed. Frank Biess, Mark Roseman, and Hanna Schissler, 255. New York: Berghahn, 2007.

57 Oberleutnant im BGS Fischer, "Was hat der Westen zu verteidigen?"

58 David E. Settle, *Faith and War: How Christians Debated the Cold and Vietnam Wars* (New York: New York University Press, 2011), 24.

59 Otmar Stöcker, "Die Verantwortung des Erziehers," *Zeitschrift des Bundesgrenzschutzes* 4 (November 1978): 13.

"other-directed," "inner-directed," and "tradition directed."[60] For Stöcker, West German society drifted into the "other directed" category because people mimicked or conformed to the lifestyles of the crowd and lost their individuality. Newspapers, television, and popular culture rather than core family values had a larger influence in shaping people's behavior after the war. He argued that professional ethics training should reemphasize the religious and God-fearing values characteristic of Riesman's "inner-directed" frame of reference.[61] Little had changed in the twenty-three years since Colonel Heinrich Müller made the same recommendations to his men by suggesting they "follow the American sociologist David Riesman's model of an inner-directed man—one that is guided by their own conscience as set by religious and moral principles."[62]

BGS chaplains also focused their efforts on the private lives of the men and their families. To do this, they offered retreats and leisure time so officers could bring their spouses and children to participate. Known as "family camps," the retreats gave the men a chance to take paid leave with their families and visit sites located in the Black Forest, the Alps, the North Sea Coast, and many other destinations. Besides having time for fun activities such as skiing, hiking, and swimming, the participants attended lectures, church services, or bible study groups organized around themes from the ethics curriculum. The chaplains fostered a communal environment and promoted fun activities, but made spiritual and moral lessons the core of their programs. Protestant BGS chaplain Dr. Rolf Sauerzapf, for example, explained: "In addition to the experience and relaxation, our family leisure time is characterized by being together every day under God's word and discussing it." By 1981, more than 1,000 members of the organization took part in these voluntary programs to the extent that it exhausted the available finances the organization allocated to fund them.[63] Still, this did not represent the organization as a whole, because by 1980 it had reached staffing levels that exceeded 15,000 officers.

The retreats and camps of the later postwar decades reflected continuities with the professional ethics curriculum from the 1950s and did

---

60 David Riesman, Reuel Denney, Nathan Glazer, *The Lonely Crowd: A Study of the Changing American Character* (New Haven: Yale University Press, 1950), 24–25; Stöcker's combat record shows he was wounded in action four times, see "LtdPD Otmar Stöcker beging gleiches Jubiläum," *Zeitschrift des Bundesgrenzschutzes* 2 (February 1980): 42.

61 Otmar Stöcker, "Die Verantwortung des Erziehers," 13.

62 Heinrich Müller, "Autorität und Gehorsam im BGS," BArch-K, B106/20765; Heinrich Müller, "Ich Dien' im BGS," July 7, 1955, BA-BA N 848/31.

63 "Familienfreizeiten der GS-Seelsorge finden unvermindert Anklang / Evangelische Seelsorge: 21 Freizeiten mit 1000 Teilnehmen," *Zeitschrift des Bundesgrenzschutzes* 8 (August 1981): 38–39.

not always resonate with the changing lives of BGS members and their families. The chaplains who organized these retreats selected topics that reaffirmed the conservative framing of a society in crisis. Evidence of these continuities surfaced during a program managers conference in Kitzingen in which chaplains decided upon topics to present for the retreats in the calendar year 1982. The motto for the conference, "Life of substance— the Christian Occident is coming to an end," came straight from the 1952 curriculum.[64] Theologians proposed topics for the upcoming year by presenting them to their colleagues first. Dr. Peter Beyerhaus, for example, lectured on the topic "The Crisis of Western Culture from a Biblical Perspective"; Dr. Ulrich Hahn spoke of a "Crisis of Technology, the Crisis of People." The conference concluded with two lectures by Dr. Adalbert Hudak, the first: "Dissidents and Christians in Eastern Europe," followed by: "Threats and Endangerment of the Family: What Can We Do to Help Stabilize it?"[65]

Since the BGS remained an all-male profession until 1987, ethics programs also focused on masculinity and gender relations themes. The Biblical passage that became a popular slogan for the chaplains: "Watch, stand in faith, be manly, and be strong" exemplified patriarchal masculinity to the fullest.[66] Yet as time went on, this framing no longer resonated with the younger generation of police officers even though their commanding officers still felt they had to arm them against the temptations of modern life. In response, ethics instructors tried to adapt by promoting a more civilianized form of masculinity, even though they still referred to the men as troops. The Interior Ministry directed instructors to focus on "the life values of home, emphasizing a civic attitude through service to the community, and helping individuals to live responsibly."[67] Christian conservatism, however, remained at the core of these lessons. In one of his ethics lectures, Heinrich Müller lamented that "Eros has turned into eroticism, even sexology. The picture newspapers, the magazines bear witness to this."[68] Chaplains discouraged promiscuous lifestyles, but the men still engaged in risky behaviors and suffered the consequences

---

64 "Streit um den Frieden—Zerreißprobe für die evangelische Kirche," *Zeitschrift des Bundesgrenzschutzes* 12 (December, 1981): 39.

65 Ibid.

66 "1 Corinthians 16:13," in Robert Carroll and Stephen Prickett, eds., *The Bible: Authorized King James Version* (Oxford: Oxford University Press, 2008), 206; Pfarrer Oskar Rohrbach GSK Süd an den Herrn Bundesminister des Innern: "Tätigkeitsbericht über die evangelische Seelsorge im Bereich des GSK Süd Januar–Juni 1961," München, Ende Juni 1961, BArch-K, B106/20766.

67 See letter exchange between the Grenzschutzkommando Süd and the Bundesministerium des Innern, March 4, 1954, "Berufsethik," BArch-K, B106/20765.

68 Heinrich Müller, "Ich Dien' im BGS," July 7, 1955, BA-BA N 848/31.

of poor decisions that affected other young men in the same age cohort. Border police officers still needed a commanding officer's permission to marry before the age of twenty-seven and many pastors complained that the men frequently filed requests for early marriage. The marriage restriction undermined recruitment efforts and many of the younger officers resigned or requested transfer to the army where they could pursue their romantic interests without oversight. Others, however, still chose promiscuity even though it came with its own set of negative consequences, such as sexually transmitted diseases and unplanned pregnancies.

The records of suicides in the BGS are an indication that in spite of regular professional ethics training and the availability of pastoral care, many police officers struggled to overcome the social problems of their youth, namely, difficulties in romantic relationships and alcoholism. Following a night of excessive drinking, for example, a nineteen-year-old police officer from BGS-Mitte attempted suicide by cutting his wrists, because his new girlfriend left him for a fellow officer.[69] In another more serious case, an intoxicated twenty-two-year-old officer attempted to shoot himself during a visit to a brothel in Lübeck-St. Hubertus. The officer experienced acute depression after a commanding officer denied his request to marry his pregnant girlfriend. In yet another case, a twenty-one-year-old officer shot and wounded himself after learning he caught a sexually transmitted disease from a woman he had been dating. The officer told his supervisor that "I fell apart after learning that I had gotten a venereal disease from the girl I wanted to be engaged to. I was happy to have finally found someone who understood me, but could not face the fact that she was a so-called easy girl."[70] Records for the 1950s and 1960s show that suicides and suicide attempts occurred frequently among men of this age group. In 1958, the records of BGS-South reported suicide attempts in February, March, and June—each case involved single men between the ages of eighteen and twenty-two who reported romantic relationship issues as the motive. The reports also cited excessive alcohol consumption in almost all of the cases. Unfortunately, there are no open archival records for suicide rates beyond 1964, but the trends from the records that do exist show a lower frequency of suicide among the older, married police officers. Moreover, the motives in the few cases of married men that did kill themselves had more to do with career tensions or disciplinary issues rather than relationships. In one case, a happily

---

69 Abteilungsarzt an Kommandoarzt, GSK-Mitte, 12. Februar 1958, "Selbstmorversuch des Gj. S, GSA A Mitte," Ungewöhnliche Todesfälle, Suicide und Suicidversuche.—Einzelfälle, BArch-K, B 106/68375.

70 Abteilungsarzt GSA T Süd an Kommandoarzt GSK-Süd, March 10, 1958, "Besondere Vorkommnisse; hier: Suicid-Versuch des Gj. K," Ungewöhnliche Todesfälle, Suicide und Suicidversuche.—Einzelfälle, BArch-K, B 106/68375.

married forty-year-old officer with children stood in front of a train and ended his life because he had been transferred against his will from the Passport Control Service to the BGS.[71]

The suicides among the younger police officers followed trends across the same demographic of the Federal Republic and in other Western democracies. In a National Health Center report on suicides in the United States for the same time period (1950–1964), statistics show that single men between the ages of twenty and twenty-four had higher rates of suicide than all the other age groups combined.[72] Although the data is insufficient to draw concrete conclusions, the stresses of personal relationships affected the younger officers more than their older, married colleagues. In the BGS, cases of suicide attempts required the evaluation of a clinical psychologist before the officers could return to duty. Unfortunately, however, in their reports of these incidents, physicians and psychologists dismissed suicidal ideation and behaviors as manifestations of "weakmindedness"—a term informed by the widespread belief that male survivors of the war, and veteran soldiers in particular, were "broken."[73]

By 1960, pressure from the BGS Employees' Association and poor recruitment quotas (see chapter. 4) convinced the Interior Ministry to eliminate the marriage ban. Instead, marriage became a normative foil to the pressing concerns of conservatives over the moral dangers they linked to promiscuity.[74] The chaplains tried to adapt by including instruction on topics such as preventing sexually transmitted diseases, birth control through abstinence, the right to life, sexual relations, and what they called the "proper boundaries" in friendships between men and women.[75] The decision to include spouses in the ethics programs through family camps and retreats revealed another way that the organization tried to adapt to changing social conditions. Promoting greater equality in gender relations, and particularly in marriages, showed how BGS chaplains mirrored broader trends among West Germany's conservatives, which as a consequence of war and defeat, found it increasingly difficult to restore prewar

71   Ministierialrat Dr. Hartleben, Referat VI B 3 an das Referat VI C 3 B, March 18, 1958, "Meldung des GSK Süd," Ungewöhnliche Todesfälle, Suicide und Suicidversuche.—Einzelfälle, BArch-K, B 106/68375.
72   US Department of Health, Education, and Welfare, "Suicide in the United States, 1950–1964," Vital and Health Statistics, series 20, no. 5 (1967), available on line, https://stacks.edc.gov/view/cdc/12870.
73   Frank Biess, *Homecomings*, 123.
74   See Dagmar Herzog, *Sex After Fascism: Memory and Morality in Twentieth-Century Germany* (Princeton, NJ: Princeton University Press, 2005), 101–6.
75   Pfarrer Oskar Rohrbach GSK Süd an den Herrn Bundesminister des Innern: "Tätigkeitsbericht über die evangelische Seelsorge im Bereich des GSK Süd Januar–Juni 1961," München, Ende Juni 1961, BArch-K, B106/20766.

notions of the *paterfamilias*. Although professional ethics still emphasized men in the nominal role as head of household, women as co-equals in the family unit began replacing traditional ideals of patriarchal masculinity.[76]

Professional Ethics and Democratic Policing

Besides trying to instill in young police officers the virtues of Christian conservatism, professional ethics also functioned as a medium to teach them their duties and obligations to support democracy. For new recruits this began with the oath of office. According to Pastor Anton Wirtz "The swearing in ceremony is always preceded with a preparatory lesson by BGS pastors ... the aim of which is to make the men aware of the religious meaning and the obligatory significance of the oath of service."[77] Steeped in the traditions of German militarism, the ceremonies took place on the parade grounds of barracks in the presence of the company or division. In the early years, BGS recruits swore loyalty to the constitution and all of West Germany's laws, which revived a practice that began during the Weimar Republic. Later, however, they adopted a revised version of the oath in which they swore to serve "the Federal Republic ... and to bravely defend the rights and freedom of the German people." The revision was intended to broaden the definition of "loyal service" to incorporate people and their civil rights.[78] The pastors who presided over these ceremonies emphasized the seriousness of the oath because it required a solemn promise to God that the men swearing it would serve the democratic state and not a particular political ideology or person—a consequence of the problematic loyalty oaths soldiers swore to Hitler during the Third Reich.[79]

Besides the importance of the oath, pastors and instructors designed lessons to teach the men how to make morally sound decisions. One innovative approach they employed involved showing the men films that dealt with complicated ethical issues to facilitate discussions over what for many must have been uncomfortable topics. During the 1959 winter instruction period, for example, Pastor Oskar Rohrbach showed

---

76 Pfarrer Oskar Rohrbach, "Tätigkeitsbericht über Evangelische Seelsorge GSK-Süd, Januar-Juni 1959," June 1959, BArch-K, B 106/20766; see also Frank Biess, *Homecomings*, 122; Mark Edward Ruff, "Catholic Elites, Gender, and Unintended Consequences in the 1950s," 261–62.

77 Pfarrer Anton Wirtz, "Tätigkeitsbericht, GSK-Süd, 1. Juli-31. Dezember 1958," BArch-K, B 106/20766.

78 See Hans-Peter Stein, *Symbole und Zeremoniell in deutschen Streitkräften vom 18. bis zum 20. Jahrhundert* (Herford: E. S. Mittler und Sohn, 1991), 93.

79 Pfarrer Oskar Rohrbach, "Tätigkeitsbericht über Eevangelische Seelsorge, Januar–Juni, 1959," BArch-K, B 106/20766; Hans-Peter Stein, *Symbole und Zeremoniell*, 90.

the 1949 American film *Lost Boundaries*. The film, starring Mel Ferrer and Beatrice Pearson, is the true story of the Carters, a light-skinned African American family trying to find their way in a Protestant New England town. Scott Carter, played by Ferrer, is a doctor unable to find work because he admitted his African American heritage to prospective employers. Although morally opposed to the advice of friends that he deny his race, Carter eventually acquiesces to find work and fit in with the community. *Lost Boundaries* was a movie ahead of its time in dealing with race in America, but as movie historians Robert Osborne and Donald Bogle aptly pointed out, the producers still avoided African American actors for the title roles.[80] Unlike other films, *To Kill a Mockingbird* (1960), for example, *Lost Boundaries* took place in a New England town whose citizens identified themselves with liberalism rather than in the Jim Crow South. Pastor Rohrbach reported that the movie confronted border police officers with issues of otherness, differences in skin color, race, gender, and social status. While there is no record of how effectively the film resonated with the men, Rohrbach claimed that it sparked "hotly debated topics of conversation."[81]

In another ethics class, Rohrbach showed the 1951 film *Cry the Beloved Country*, starring African American actors Sidney Poitier and Canada Lee. The story is based on a book of the same name by the South African anti-apartheid activist Alan Paton. Like *Lost Boundaries*, the film dealt with themes of race, gender, and class, but in the context of the oppressive apartheid regime. The storyline follows the Reverend Stephen Kumalo, played by Canada Lee, who travels from his remote South African Village to Johannesburg in search of his son, Absalom, whose pregnant girlfriend is forced into prostitution for survival. Kumalo is aided by a local pastor, Theophilus Msimangu, played by Poitier. While searching for Absalom, the pair learn that he participated in the murder of a prominent white social justice activist, a crime for which he is ultimately condemned to death. In addition to race, the film highlighted the struggle of Africans to come to terms with the loss of their traditional lifestyles in the aftermath of colonialism and under the white-settler imposed apartheid system. During the 1950s and 1960s, colonial themes must have resonated with the men as current news highlighted the struggles of decolonization in the developing world. Yet here again there is no specific evidence to analyze how the film affected the police officers who viewed it, but Rohrbach claimed "The subsequent discussion about the meaning

---

80 Robert Osborne and Donald Bogle, *Lost Boundaries*, introductory comments, Turner Classic Movies screening, October 24, 2020, available online at https://www.youtube.com/watch?v=FoRDOIo9or8.

81 Pfarrer Oskar Rohrbach, "Tätigkeitsbericht über evangelische Seelsorge, Januar–Juni, 1959."

of suffering, social justice, equal rights for all people, dignity, guilt and forgiveness were extremely productive."[82]

Other films shown by Pastor Rohrbach included John Steinbeck's epic story, *The Grapes of Wrath*, which scholars and literary critics have suggested contains many underlying Christian and biblical themes, and the 1952 French film, *We Are All Murderers*.[83] Like *Cry the Beloved Country*, *We Are All Murderers* dealt with the moral questions and social injustices of the death penalty. It tells the story of a young man, René Le Guen, who joined the resistance during the war to kill Germans, but ended up condemned to death when he continued to commit murders after the war as a hired assassin. Rohrbach commented in his activity report that the film "was shown in all locations and challenged everyone with moral questions of right and wrong."[84] The idea of emphasizing the moral consequences driven home by these cinematic examples, underscored efforts by chaplains to use professional ethics as an instrument of promoting democratic principles. But commendable as these efforts appeared to be, paradoxically they stood alongside the xenophobic stereotyping of Eastern culture promoted by the same programs and instructors. The coexistence of racialized images attached to Bolshevism on the one hand, and promoting the moral consequences of racism in different contexts on the other, suggests a certain degree of organizational "tone deafness." Thus the BGS could criticize US police officers for their poor treatment of African Americans, as they did for the 1964 race riots in New York, but ignore racism within their own ranks as long as it remained a means to describe their external, communist enemies.[85]

Rohrbach was not the only chaplain using popular cinema in ethics courses. By the late 1950s and 1960s, chaplains from both denominations used films as a matter of routine. Unlike other media, films provided dramatic examples of the subject matter covered in the courses and added an experiential learning element that captured the interest of the students better than lectures and assigned readings alone. For its time, the use of films for law enforcement ethics training broke new ground. California's Commission on Police Officer Standards and Training, for example, did not have anything to match this until it implemented the Sherman Block Supervisory Leadership Institute (SLI) program in 1988. SLI employs experiential learning by using books and films to facilitate difficult moral

82   Pfarrer Oskar Rohrbach, "Tätigkeitsbericht über evangelische Seelsorge," Januar–Juni 1956, BArch-K, B 106/20766.
83   See, for example, Ken Eckert, "Exodus Inverted: A New Look at the Grapes of Wrath," *Religion and the Arts* 13 (2009): 340–45.
84   Pfarrer Oskar Rohrbach, "Tätigkeitsbericht über evangelische Seelsorge," July–December 1959, BArch-K, B 106/20766.
85   See "Rassenkrawalle in Amerika und die Polizei," *Die Parole* 10 (October 15, 1964): 13.

and ethical discussions among police officers preparing for supervisory roles. The program thus "challenges students to learn new ways to resolve issues through group and individual work."[86]

The controversial ethical topics introduced by the films and the discussions that followed their screening evoke the trend of "*Diskussionslust*" that historian Nina Verheyen has identified in her seminal cultural history of West Germany. According to Verheyen, "discussions as a social practice and power technique in West German communication culture experienced an appreciation, formalization and everyday institutionalization from the end of the Second World War to the 1970s."[87] Her findings suggest the influence of "public discourse ethics," a theoretical approach to understanding communicative structures formulated by philosophers Jürgen Habermas and Karl-Otto Apel. Discourse ethics, according to the philosopher William Rehg "offers considerable promise for reflection on the moral bases of cooperation in a society committed to individual initiative and communal bonds," which is precisely how the BGS used its group discussions on controversial moral and ethical topics.[88] Chaplains and instructors hoped to foster respectful debates and healthy conflict between participants in the classroom, in order to arrive at some form of ethical-moral consensus. In other words, the chaplains hoped their students developed sound critical thinking skills. During the Occupation, the Allies formed West German discussion groups in POW camps where they became both an instrument and method of promoting democratization to German soldiers.[89] Although there is no mention of these Allied programs in BGS sources, it is not unreasonable to assume a possible link, since most of the chaplains and a high percentage of the police officers spent time as POWs at the end of the war.

The chaplains and instructors also encouraged dialogue among the men about National Socialism. Yet like other segments of West German society, coming to terms with the Nazi past took decades and often elicited narratives of German victimhood, especially because most of the senior officers in the BGS had been soldiers during the Third Reich. A look at the topics presented during 1960 by the Catholic Dean Helmut Oberle, a veteran artillery officer who served on the Eastern Front, sheds light on the organizational effort to engage police officers with the difficult legacies of their profession. In his activity report for January, for

---

86 See "Sherman Block Supervisory Leadership Institute," available online at https://post.ca.gov/Sherman-Block-Supervisory-Leadership-Institute; the author is a graduate of SLI class number 197.

87 Nina Verheyen, *Diskussionslust: Eine Kulturgeschichte des "besseren Arguments" in Westdeutschland* (Göttingen: Vandenhoeck & Ruprecht, 2010), 14–20.

88 William Rehg, *Insight and Solidarity: A Study in the Discourse Ethics of Jürgen Habermas* (Berkeley: University of California Press, 1997), 2.

89 Nina Verheyen, *Diskussionslust*, 65–74.

example, Oberle lectured on anti-Semitism, while in February he presented a course entitled "The Nature of Dictatorship in the Third Reich." The attempt by BGS chaplains to deal with these issues, however, avoided a thorough reckoning with the Nazi past and instead emphasized soldiers as victims. During a one-week ethics seminar at the Protestant Academy in Hofgeismar, for example, BGS Pastor Dieter Andersen claimed that the virtue of soldiers had been abused by the Nazis when Hitler put his own lust for power ahead of what was good for the people. Andersen suggested that instead of collective guilt or innocence "it would be better to speak of collective shame."[90] The idea of "collective shame" failed to distinguish the differences between victims and perpetrators and obfuscated the role of individuals, many of whom worked in the Federal Republic's higher law enforcement offices. Moreover, the political and civics text used by the BGS explained that the Third Reich was "brought about by the insanity of one man and his clique." Thus even the notion of collective shame could be attributed to one man—Hitler—leaving little room for discussions of how the German people, and the police institution in particular, also contributed to National Socialism. To be sure, the "Germans as victims" narrative, as the historian Robert Moeller has shown in his classic analysis, took hold during the 1950s and prevailed into later decades of the postwar era.[91] This rendering of the Nazi past existed as part of a broader West German memory culture. It also shaped the myth that the Wehrmacht fought a clean war, which emerged during the rearmament debates.

Ethics instructors and chaplains also attempted to deal with the failed July 20 plot to assassinate Hitler as a case study in how police officers should deal with orders from superior officers. The controversial topic divided West Germany's veteran soldiers. In one camp, the traditionalists argued that the army officers involved in the conspiracy committed treason because they violated their oaths to the head of state. In the other camp, however, veteran army officers used the assassination to promote the myth of a clean Wehrmacht as a prelude to rearmament. These veterans tried to find a consensus on the resistance movement that reflected a middle course between right and wrong.[92] In his lecture "I Serve in the BGS," for example, Heinrich Müller exemplified the middle course when speaking about the plot. He told his audience that disobedience to an order rarely became a moral obligation. But in the case of the anti-Nazi

---

90 Pastor Ulbrich, "Erfahrungsbericht: Über berufsethische Lehrgänge auf den evangelischen Akademien Hofgeismar und Friedewald für den Bereich des GSK Mitte," 14. Februar 1955, BArch-K, B 106/20766.
91 See for example, Robert Moeller, *War Stories*.
92 Winifried Heinemann, *Operation Valkyrie: A Military History of the July 20, 1944 Plot* (Oldenbourg: De Gruyter, 2021), 362–63.

resistance movement, he argued that the July 20 conspirators, above all, followed their conscience. Their attempt to assassinate Hitler thus "testified to the fact that, despite everything, the sense of responsibility was alive in the generals."[93] He propagated the myth that the Wehrmacht fought a clean war, but he failed to explain to his students that the July 20 plot was the exception not the rule—the vast majority of army officers either supported or refused to speak out against the regime's criminal policies. By the 1960s, the BGS and Bundeswehr commemorated the attempted assassination, yet still used it to exculpate the complicity of the larger portion of the Wehrmacht with National Socialism.[94]

In spite of extensive efforts and innovative teaching methods, the effect of BGS chaplains and professional ethics on the officers yielded mixed results. In the aftermath of National Socialism, engaging police officers in the larger, more profound ethical questions at the heart of their profession remained important. The use of modern films and the discussions these provoked are one example of how the organization emphasized ethical decision-making as a core principle of democratic policing. While it is difficult to evaluate the precise effects of these lessons and their religious overtones on the individual officers, they nonetheless left no doubt about the expectations for their behavior. Many of the lessons, however, grounded in the influence of Western anti-communism and Christian conservatism, revived the xenophobia and racism that came with the institutional legacies embedded in both churches. The chaplaincy tried to adapt and revise its programs and lessons to deal with changes in West Germany's modernizing society as a whole and its youth in particular, but it still promoted a conservative organizational culture whose values no longer resonated with many of the young men it employed.

93 Heinrich Müller, "Ich Dien' im BGS," BA-MA, N 848/31.
94 Curt-Wolf Roederer, "Zum 20. Juli 1944," *Die Parole* 7 (July 15, 1964): 1,17.

CHAPTER SEVEN

THE DEBATE OVER COMBATANT STATUS AND ITS CONSEQUENCES

ON NOVEMBER 10, 1965, BGS Lieutenant Colonel Hans-Jürgen Pantenius delivered a lecture on the 1944 Warsaw Uprising to a group of his fellow commanding and junior officers in Bonn. The Bundestag had recently passed controversial legislation that designated border police officers as military combatants in the event of an attack on the Federal Republic. The lecture was supposed to provide its leadership cadre with a case study for urban combat in conjunction with the publication of a new "street fighting" manual. Pantenius, a decorated veteran of Nazi Germany's motorized infantry units who also held a PhD in history, fought in Poland, France, and the Soviet Union. At Warsaw he commanded Infantry Regiment 690 of the 337 *Volksgrenadier* Division attached to General Smilo Freiherr von Luttwitz's 9th Army. Although he arrived in the city after the main resistance ended, he remained as an instructor at the Wehrmacht's "Combat School for Street and Fortress Fighting" established in Warsaw's Mokotów district.[1] He trained the Wehrmacht and SS units stationed there that hunted down and massacred the remaining Polish resistance and then destroyed what was left of Warsaw. He told his audience that Warsaw suffered during the original German invasion of 1939, but "compared with the destruction of German cities in 1943 and 1944, this damage was not significant."[2]

---

1   Grenzschutzdienst Bonn, Leiter, Hans-Jürgen Pantenius, "Abschrift Einführung zum Vortrag, 'Der Aufstand in Warschau 1944,' anläßlich der Planuntersuchung 'Straßenkampf' am 25.11.1965," BArch-K, B 106/83898; the 337 Volksgrenadier Division was in Mokotów in September while the last remnants of the resistance were wiped out; see also, Włodzimierez Borodziej, *The Warsaw Uprising of 1944* (Madison: University of Wisconsin Press, 2001),124–25; Alexandra Richie, Warsaw 1944: Hitler, Himmler, and the Warsaw Uprising (New York: Farrar, Straus & Giroux, 2013), 617–27.
2   Hans-Jürgen Pantenius, "Abschrift Einführung zum Vortrag."

A discussion about Nazi Germany's brutal suppression of Polish resistance and criminal destruction of Warsaw as some sort of tactical model for democratic civilian police officers is troubling on many levels. In the twenty years since the Third Reich collapsed, several high-profile criminal cases such as the Frankfurt Auschwitz trials and the Eichmann trial in Jerusalem highlighted the crimes Germany's armed forces perpetrated during the war.[3] So why revive such a terrible example of Nazi violence as some form of lesson, unless as an instruction for what not to do in a democracy? What could the Federal Republic's border police officers possibly glean from a discussion about the wanton destruction of an entire city? To be sure, the 1960s ushered in a paradigm shift in postwar memory culture, where West Germans began focusing more on Holocaust victims rather than their own wartime suffering.[4] But for members of the BGS, the 1960s also brought new fears of communist insurgencies and the possibility of a civil war erupting on the Inner-German border fueled by the conflict in Vietnam and the consequences of decolonization in the developing world. Thus global and transnational tensions abroad also shaped West German responses to security at home.

From this perspective, the Interior Ministry and many commanding officers in the BGS believed they might face execution as partisans if captured during a Soviet or East German attack. Thus they lobbied the Bundestag to legally designate them as military combatants if a war did erupt on the Inner-German border. The debate over the necessity of combatant status is yet another example that divided the organization between advocates against militarization and others who promoted continuities with Germany's authoritarian past. Moreover, those on either side of the debate found useable narratives in competing interpretations of Germany's problematic legacies with militarism and war to justify their stance. Ultimately, the advocates of militarization prevailed, but the debate did not end with the new law. Soon the organization found itself at the center of a public relations backlash, bound up with the emergence of a critical public spere and increased press freedoms. The debate and controversies over combatant status shows how questions about German militarism remained divisive and still hung like a dark cloud over the Federal Republic's BGS in spite of broader societal trends that leaned towards more democratization.

---

3   Daniel Levy and Nathan Sznaider, *The Holocaust and Memory in the Global Age* (Philadelphia: Temple University Press, 2006), 98.
4   Ibid.

Cold War Tensions and Emergency Legislation

Although the division of Germany and threat of nuclear war led to an uneasy integration of both states into antagonistic Cold War blocs, there was still plenty of global tension as the sixties began.[5] In May 1960, a US spy plane was shot down deep inside the Soviet Union and its pilot, Francis Gary Powers, was captured and held prisoner.[6] In April 1961, a proxy force of CIA Cuban Exiles landed at the "Bay of Pigs" and failed in a blundered attempt to overthrow Fidel Castro's communist regime.[7] Later that same year, Berliners awoke to discover that the Soviet backed East German government had begun building a wall to seal off the communist sector of the city. The Berlin Wall was a powerful symbol of Germany's postwar division and an iconic image of the global Cold War. Shortly after construction on the wall began, East Germany integrated its border guard into the National People's Army (*National Volksarmee*— NVA).[8] Then in 1962, the United States and the Soviet Union came the closest they ever had to a nuclear conflict over the deployment of Soviet nuclear missiles in Cuba.[9]

Thus in spite of nuclear deterrence and the strategic stability offered by borders and walls, West Germans, and members of the BGS in particular, believed the prospects of an all-out war with the East remained a significant threat. Opinion polls conducted in the late 1950s, for example, indicated that most Germans feared being caught in a nuclear conflict that would destroy their nation. According to Holger Nehring, although most poll respondents were not pacifists, they had a "profound skepticism

---

[5] The nuclear deterrent effect is discussed at length in John Lewis Gaddis, *The United States and the End of the Cold War: Implications, Reconsiderations, Provocations* (New York: Oxford University Press, 1992), 108–16; See also Marc Trachtenberg, *A Constructed Peace: The Making of the European Settlement, 1945– 1963* (Princeton, NJ: Princeton University Press, 1999), 186; James F. Pasley, "Chicken Pax Atomica: The Cold War Stability of Nuclear Deterrence," *Journal of International and Area Studies* 15, no. 2 (2008): 21.

[6] Francis Gary Powers and Curt Gentry, *Operation Overflight: A Memoir of the U-2 Incident* (Washington, DC: Potomac, 2004).

[7] Howard Jones, *The Bay of Pigs* (Oxford: Oxford University Press, 2008).

[8] Stephan Fingerle, *Waffen in Arbeiterhand? Die Rekrutierung des Offizierkorps der Nationalen Volksarmee und ihrer Vorläufer* (Berlin: Ch. Links, 2001), 211.

[9] See Melvyn P. Leffler, *For the Soul of Mankind: The United States, the Soviet Union and the Cold War* (New York: Hill & Wang, 2008), 151–60; see also Sheldon M. Stern, *The Cuban Missile Crisis in American Memory: Myth versus Reality* (Stanford: Stanford University Press, 2012).

towards the military functions of the state."[10] NATO planners concentrated on the Inner-German border as the likely flashpoint for an east-west conflict. In light of these developments, the Federal Government began working on a series of new laws aimed towards protecting the free democratic order of the state against internal and external security threats. These legal debates culminated with the passage of the *Notstandsgesetze* (Emergency Acts) on May 30, 1968.[11]

In 1960, however, the BGS remained somewhat of an anomaly in West Germany's national security system; was it a police or military force—better suited for internal or external defense? It was these ongoing questions in combination with the debates over emergency legislation that prompted the Interior Ministry to consider how best to use border police officers during a war. The East German government's decision to integrate their border police into the NVA convinced many senior members of the BGS and the Interior Ministry that it was only a matter of time before a civil war erupted along the Inner-German border as a prelude to a larger Soviet invasion. Thus the first proposal for a law authorizing border police officers to fight as combatants was a direct response to East Germany's decision to incorporate police officers into its armed forces.[12] In spite of these developments, Hans Schneppel, head of the Interior Ministry's Police Branch, requested that the Foreign Office and the Federal Ministers of Justice and Defense explore whether the international laws of war protected West Germany's civilian police forces if they

---

10 For information and results of the polls, see Holger Nehring, *Politics of Security: British and West German Protest Movements and the Early Cold War, 1945–1970* (Oxford: Oxford University Press, 2013), 77; See also Michael Geyer, "Cold War Angst," 380–85.

11 The emergency laws and their influence are discussed in greater detail in chapter 7—they were first introduced for debate in 1958, see for example: Michael Schneider, *Demokratie in Gefahr? Der Konflikt um die Notstandsgesetze: Sozialdemokratie, Gewerkschaften und intellektueller Protest 1958–1968* (Bonn: Verlag Neue Gesellschaft 1986), 45–47; Boris Spernol, *Notstand der Demokratie: Der Protest gegen die Notstandsgesetze und die Frage der NS-Vergangenheit* (Essen: Klartext, 2008); Karin Hanshew, *Terror and Democracy*, 62–63; Timothy Scott Brown, *West Germany and the Global Sixties*, 25.

12 Letter from Staatssekretär Dr. Josef Hölzl, Bundesministerium des Innern, to Herrn Staatssekretär des Bundeskanzleramtes, 27. Dezember 1961, Betr.: Entwurf eines Gesetzes zur Ergänzung des Gesetzes über den Bundesgrenzschutz und die Einrichtung von Bundesgrenzschutzbehörden, BArch-K, B136/1928. Fiche no. 1, slides 105–108; Bonner Redaktion, "Grenzschutz darf zurückschiessen: Bonn will umgehend völkerrechtlichen Schutz sicherstellen," *Bremer Nachrichten*, March 16, 1962, 1, BA-MA, BH28-2-257; this was also covered in the Bundesgrenzschutz Journal *Die Parole*, see Regierungsassessor Dr. E. Andrews, "Bundesgrenzschutz und Kombattantenstatus," *Die Parole*, 12, no. 5 (May 15, 1962): 5–6.

engaged with enemy soldiers. Schneppel and others in the BGS feared that they needed combatant status or might otherwise face execution as partisans if captured during a war.[13]

Like so many others at the Interior Ministry, Schneppel had previous law enforcement experience. After attending law school, he began his career as a member of the Prussian Political Police in Berlin and was among the first men to join the newly formed *Gestapo* (secret political police). In the *Gestapo*, Schneppel's specialty was hunting communists, and he was the agent responsible for signing arrest warrants for the two men accused of starting the infamous *Reichstag* fire in 1933.[14] Schneppel requested feedback from the federal ministers about all of West Germany's civilian police forces, but he focused on the BGS since it was part of his ministry. In the event of a war, he wanted to know whether international law protected border police officers.[15] If not, he suggested amending the existing laws or passing new emergency legislation to ensure they were. He insisted it was imperative to address this question because confrontations with enemy soldiers were more likely at border outposts than in West Germany's interior regions. He explained: "A clarification of the international legal position of our police in all conceivable situations is inevitable. The members of the German Police, who during the last war suffered severely from the fact that such a clarification had not taken place at the time, are rightly expecting this to happen."[16]

Schneppel explained that the police "suffered" because of the postwar legal consequences they faced for their participation in anti-partisan warfare. Thus his main concern, besides preventing the men from being treated as partisans by the enemy, was keeping them immune from prosecution if they engaged in combat. After the Second World War, international law played a prominent role in the judgment of Germany's conduct. The trials of Nazi war criminals, first at Nuremburg, but also during many follow-up proceedings, established the criminal behavior of Germany's armed forces. Later, some members of Nazi Germany's security police and those who commanded them were charged with murder for carrying out reprisal killings under the pretext of anti-partisan warfare. Although the perpetrators often evaded conviction or received

---

13 Memorandum: Ministerialdirektor Hans Schneppel an das Auswärtige Amt, den Bundesminister der Justiz, und den Bundesminister für Verteidigung, 3. Februar 1960, Betreff: Kriegsvölkerrechter Status der Polizeien in der Bundesrepublik, BA-MA, BW1/112244.

14 Shlomo Aronson, *Reinhard Heydrich und die Frühgeschichte von Gestapo und SD* (Stuttgart: Deutscher Verlag, 1971), 86. Klaus Wiegrefe, "Flammendes Fanal," *Der Spiegel*, 2001, no. 15 (April 9, 2001): 38–58, here 56.

15 Ministerialdirektor Hans Schneppel, 3. Februar 1960, Betreff: Kriegsvölkerrechter Status der Polizeien in der Bundesrepublik, BA-MA, BW1/112244.

16 Ibid.

light sentences, many of them excused their conduct by pointing out that reprisals were allowed by international laws of war.[17] To be sure, neither the 1907 Hague nor the 1929 Geneva Conventions banned reprisal killings of non-combatants; it was only the revised 1949 Geneva Conventions that outlawed this practice.[18]

The responses of Schneppel's ministerial colleagues reflected the persistence of themes from Germany's authoritarian past on the Federal Republic's police institution. Defense Minister Franz Josef Strauss, for example, praised German police officers for their effectiveness against partisans during the war.[19] He favored recognizing BGS members as military combatants, but suggested they should be distinguished from regular civilian police forces by special insignia or uniforms.[20] Ministry of Justice Director Walter Roemer, another veteran jurist of the Third Reich, agreed with Strauss. Roemer had been a prosecutor for the Bavarian State Court in Munich, where he was responsible for enforcing death sentences, among them, the execution of Sophie Scholl and other members of the White Rose resistance movement. He argued that border police officers were already covered by international law as long as they wore uniforms when hostilities broke out.[21]

Language in both The Hague and Geneva Conventions supported Roemer's conclusion. Article 1 of the 1907 Hague agreements, which was carried over into the 1949 Geneva Conventions and applied to the Federal Republic stated:

> The laws, rights, and duties of war apply not only to armies, but also to militia and volunteer corps fulfilling the following conditions:

17 Luftwaffe General Albert Kesselring used this in his defense for war crimes in Italy; see, for example, Kerstin von Lingen, *Kesselring's Last Battle: War Crimes Trials and Cold War Politics, 1945–1960* (Lawrence: University Press of Kansas, 2009), 51–53; Albert Kesselring, *Soldat bis zum letzten Tag* (Bonn: Athenaeum, 1953), 299.

18 James Crawford, Alain Pellet, Simon Olleson, and Kate Parlett, eds., *The Law of International Responsibility* (New York: Oxford University Press, 2010), 1189; see also Pieter Lagrou, "1945–1955: The Age of Total War," *Histories of the Aftermath: The Legacies of the Second World War in Europe*, ed. Frank Biess and Robert G. Moeller, 287–89 (New York: Berghahn, 2010).

19 Franz Josef Strauss an Hans Schneppel, 15. Februar 1960, Betreff: Völkerrechtlicher Status der Polizeien in der Bundesrepublik; Ihr Schreiben vom 2. Februar 1960/Geheim!, BA-MA, BW1/112244.

20 Ibid.

21 Ministerialdirigent Walter Roemer an Hans Schneppel, 2. März 1960, Betreff: Völkerrechtlicher Status der Polizeien in der Bundesrepublik; Ihr Schreiben vom 2. Februar 1960/Geheim!, BA-MA, BW1/112244; Marc von Miquel, *Ahnden oder amnestieren? Westdeutsche Justiz und Vergangenheitspolitik in den sechziger Jahren* (Göttingen: Wallenstein, 2004), 66–67.

1. To be commanded by a person responsible for his subordinates;
2. To have a fixed distinctive emblem recognizable at a distance;
3. To carry arms openly; and 4. To conduct their operations in accordance with the laws and customs of war.[22]

Moreover, Article 2 permitted anyone, a border police officer, for example, confronted by the sudden approach of an enemy armed force, to spontaneously defend themselves whether in or out of uniform as long as they carried weapons openly in plain sight.[23] So even irregular fighters were protected by international law. Since border police officers wore uniforms at all times, they could not be mistaken for irregular fighters, and thus there was no valid operational reason for the proposed legislation recognizing them as combatants. Yet Roemer's analysis failed to put the matter to rest, because the Interior Ministry still treated the BGS more like an army than a police force, despite their public comments to the contrary. The legacies of Germany's experiences with militarism and war and the postwar trials of its soldiers as perpetrators in mass killings during the Third Reich in particular still held greater sway than the language spelled out in the Geneva and Hague Conventions. Despite the renewed focus on the victims of German atrocities during the 1960s, the notion of "victors justice"—a perception that Germans had been unreasonably subjected to harsh treatment during the Nuremberg trials and denazification—still resonated with many Germans of the war generation. Thus the push for combatant status can also be read as a response to the negative memories of "victors justice" and to leave no question about what is and is not acceptable for police officers caught up in military conflicts.[24]

On June 22, 1960, Siegfried Fröhlich, the head of Public Security at the Interior Ministry, summarized the findings about police officers and the international laws of war.[25] He warned that there was a general lack of consensus between the federal ministries. For Fröhlich and his colleagues, Germany's negative experiences with international law in the aftermath of both world wars weighed heavily on their thinking. They

22 James Turner Johnson and Eric D. Patterson, eds., *The Ashgate Research Companion to Military Ethics* (New York: Routledge, 2016), 315–16; Ingrid Detter, *The Law of War* (Cambridge: Cambridge University Press, 2000), 136.
23 Ibid.
24 Bill Niven, *Facing the Nazi Past: United Germany and the Legacy of the Third Reich* (New York: Routledge, 2002), 94; Jeffrey Herf, *Divided Memory: The Nazi Past in the Two Germanys* (Cambridge, MA: Harvard University Press, 1997), 273–75.
25 Memorandum: Streng-Geheim! Staatsekretär Sigfried Fröhlich an Bundesministerium des Innern: Betrifft: Kriegsvölkerrecht; hier: Völkerrechtlicher Status der Polizeien in der Bundesrepublik," 22 Juni 1960, BA-MA, BW1/112244.

did not want to rely exclusively on competing interpretations of international law, which they claimed, did not protect the officers from prosecution or mistreatment at the hands of enemy soldiers. The Interior Ministry's plans to outline a "military" role for the BGS during a conflict, however, fueled tensions with the state police unions. Federal and State police officials with a stake in the outcome of the debate hired legal experts to support their individual claims. In the process, both sides invoked their own interpretation of Germany's authoritarian past to justify their position on the issue.

Dr. Hans Jess, a CDU representative in the Bundestag who served during the Weimar Republic as the Chief of Police in Schwerin, warned Schneppel to refrain from further secret discussions or inquiries about the matter until lawmakers could weigh in. Jess perceived that the state police unions would protest any move by the federal government to use the BGS militarily. He explained that the unions had always "expressed their support for a clear separation of tasks between the police and the Bundeswehr."[26] Interior Minister Hermann Höcherl also told Schneppel to cease further discussion, because he believed it might present the GDR with fodder for its propaganda campaign against the Federal Republic. In 1962 Jess proposed that the state interior ministers be included in the process so that all of West Germany's police forces could be recognized as military combatants. His intent was to gain the support of the states before the unions could intervene. At a conference in Bad Reichenhall on May 17, 1962, the delegates unanimously agreed with Jess that the proposed legislation should apply to all of West Germany's police officials.[27] Höcherl urged caution and thought it best to "bury" combatant status in the proposed emergency laws where it would be "least noticeable and would provide the fewest possible starting points for propaganda."[28] He and the others knew that such a decision would be controversial. Yet the two issues—combatant status and the emergency laws—never merged into Höcherl's vision for one legislative package.

---

26 Memorandum: Dr. Hans Jess an Hans Schneppel, Federal Interior Ministry, 24. Februar 1960, Geheim! Betrifft: Völkerrechtlicher Status der Angehörigen des Bundesgrenzschutzes und der Polizeien der Bundesrepublik Deutschland, BA-MA, BW1/112244.
27 Memorandum: Geheim! Bundesministerium des Innern, "Völkerrechtlicher Status der Polizei in einem Verteidigungsfall; hier: Niederschrift über die Sitzung der ständigen Konferenz der Innenminister der Bundesländer am 17./18. Mai 1962 in Bad Reichenhall," BA-MA, BW1/316268.
28 Ibid.

The Influence of Trade Union Politics

The failure to "bury" the legislation, as Höcherl suggested, however, made no difference. Both the GdP and the ÖTV learned about the proposal. As predicted, union representatives rejected the Interior Ministry's plan to treat all of West Germany's police forces as combatants. In January 1963, the ÖTV hired Dr. Friederich "Fritz" Berber, a law professor from the University of Munich, to analyze the Interior Ministry's plan. Berber had been a special legal advisor to Hitler's Foreign Minister, Joachim von Ribbentrop.[29] Given his bias towards the police unions, his final report concluded that neither the Hague nor the newly revised Geneva Conventions allowed for civilian police officers to fight as combatants.[30] He also pointed out that Article 5 of the 1949 Geneva Conventions permitted civilian authorities to continue their work on behalf of the local population during a hostile enemy occupation. He explained that police officers who engaged with the enemy forfeited their right to the protections as "civilian authorities" under Article 5 and might be subjected to severe punishment to include execution if captured in battle.[31]

To support his findings, Berber cited Germany's 1914 invasion of Belgium. He blamed the Belgians for the "disastrous consequences" that befell its civilian population during the German invasion and occupation.[32] He reaffirmed the popular postwar myth that Belgian citizens, and their paramilitary Civil Guard in particular, fought an illegal "peoples war" or insurgency against the invading German Army. Of course, he also neglected to say anything about Germany's violation of Belgian neutrality as the pretext for the resistance.[33] Instead, Berber relied extensively on the controversial report by Professor Christian Meurer, a lawyer employed by the German government in 1921 to defend the Army's actions in Belgium. In their seminal study of German atrocities in 1914, John Horne and Alan Kramer argued that Meurer "whitewashed" German

---

29 Michael Stolleis, *Geschichte des öffentlichen Rechts in Deutschland, Vierter Band: Staats- und Verwaltungsrechtswissenschaft in West und Ost, 1945–1990* (Munich: C. H. Beck, 2012), 43.

30 Gutachten von Professor Dr. Friedrich Berber, Vorstand des Instituts für Völkerrecht an der Universität München, "Völkerrechtlicher Status der Polizei in einem Verteidigungsfall," 16. Januar 1963, BArch-K, B106/83869.

31 Ibid.

32 Ibid. Berber was referring here to the German invasion of neutral Belgium at the outbreak of the First World War. The term franc-tireur—or free-shooter—is a French term that refers to guerilla or partisan fighters who resisted German forces during the 1870 Franco-Prussian War; For a comprehensive analysis of these incidents see John Horne and Alan Kramer, *German Atrocities 1914: A History of Denial* (New Haven, CT: Yale University Press, 2001).

33 John Horne and Alan Kramer, *German Atrocities 1914*.

armed forces of any responsibility in the murder of Belgian civilians. According to Horne and Kramer, "for Meurer, Belgian popular resistance had flouted international law and prompted a legitimate German reaction on the grounds of military necessity."[34] Berber argued that designating police officers as combatants would thus turn them into a German version of the Belgian Civil Guard or what Meurer called a "hermaphrodite meddling of the armed forces and the police" that resulted in "the bloody massacre of the Belgian peoples."[35]

The Interior Ministry called upon its own expert, Dr. Heinz Knackstedt, an attorney assigned to the Ministry of Defense, to counter Berber's analysis. Knackstedt argued that "there are no laws that a state must have only one class of armed forces, all of which had to be organized under the same department."[36] Knackstedt explained that a state's civilian police forces could participate in combat operations without belonging to the Ministry of Defense and still be afforded the protections of the international laws of war. He said Berber's comparison to the Belgian Civil Guard was wrong since it fought as a "militia" and was therefore recognized by both the 1907 Hague and 1949 Geneva Conventions. He compared it to the Waffen-SS, military police battalions, the *Reichsarbeitdienst* (Reich Labor Service—RAD), and the *Volkssturm* (home guard), all of which fell under international law during the Second World War.[37] His use of Germany's past reflected yet another example of how competing narratives informed and justified both sides of the combatant status debate.

On January 24, 1963, the Bundestag's Committee for Internal Affairs introduced the bill that recommended revision of the Federal Border Police Act of 1951 to designate BGS members as combatants.[38] The Conference of Interior Ministers for West Germany's *Länder* followed suit and voted unanimously in favor of recognizing all state police officers as combatants.[39] It was this turn of events that motivated the

34   Ibid., 377.
35   Gutachten von Professor Dr. Friedrich Berber, BArch-K, B106/83869.
36   Memorandum: Dr. Heinz Knackstedt to Bundesministerium für Verteidigung, 26. Januar 1963, Betreff: "Kombattantenstatus der Polizei," BArch-K, B106/83869.
37   Ibid.
38   Deutsche Bundestag, Drucksache IV/343, "Schriftlicher Bericht des Ausschusses für Inneres (6. Ausschuss) über den von der Bundesregierung eingebrachten Entwurf eines Gesetzes zur Ergänzung des Gesetzes über den Bundesgrenzschutz und die Einrichtung von Bundesgrenzschutzbehörden," BA-MA, BW1/317989.
39   The provision against subordination to the Bundeswehr was clearly stated in the Standing Conference of the Interior Ministers of West Germany's Federal States on May 17–18, 1962, BA-MA, BW1/316268.

GdP's Chairman, Werner Kuhlmann, to come out against the BGS and in the process, become one of its most vocal critics. As a teenager, he was active in the leftist youth group, *Sozialistische Jugend Deutschlands* (SJD), more popularly known as the Falcons.[40] Like many young men of his generation, he joined the RAD and was later drafted into the *Wehrmacht*. After the war, he joined the North Rhine-Westphalia state police. As a police officer, Kuhlmann continued his political activism and became a prominent trade unionist and member of the SPD. In 1958, he was elected chairman of the GdP and remained head of the organization until 1975.[41] In an open letter to the Bundestag, he declared: "We [GdP] have vigorously opposed this creeping process of the merging of police and military tasks in the interest of a clear delineation. The police institution is, as a matter of fact, just as unsuitable for combat as the Salvation Army!"[42] Representatives of the Bavarian GdP branch also wrote to their Interior Minister, Heinrich Junker, and strongly condemned the Conference of Interior Minister's decision to go along with the federal government's plans.[43]

In March 1963 Kuhlmann published a scathing 32-page condemnation of the combatant status issue, which appeared as a GdP brochure under the title: *Police Must Remain Police!*[44] The cover of the brochure had a glossy photograph of steel-helmeted border police officers firing a mortar and included excerpts of Dr. Berber's findings along with new interpretations by law professors Felix Ermacora and Andreas Hamann.[45] Ermacora and Hamann had divergent backgrounds but held similar opinions. Felix Ermacora, for example, was a liberal Professor of International Law at the University of Innsbruck and a prominent advocate of human rights. Andreas Hamann, on the other hand, was a conservative

---

40 The Falcons socialist youth groups were originally founded in 1909; see, for example, Heinrich Eppe, "100 Jahre sozialistische Jugend in Deutschland im Überblick," in *Sozialistische Jugend im 20. Jahrhundert: Studien zur Entwicklung und politischen Praxis der Arbeiterjugendbewegung in Deutschland*, ed. Heinrich Eppe (Munich: Juventa, 2008), 43–68.

41 Gerd Goch, "Porträt der Woche: Werner Kuhlmann (SPD)," *Landtag intern* 10, no. 32 (December 14, 1979): 15.

42 Unserer Bonner Redaktion, "Völkerrechtler widerspricht Bonn: Professor Berber gibt Gutachten zum Kombattanten-Status für die Polizei," *Deutsche Zeitung* 36, February 12, 1963, 2, BArch-K, B106/83869.

43 Bonn Staff, "Polizei nicht unter Befehl der Bundeswehr: Starke Bedenken der Gewerkschaft—keine militärische Aufgaben," *Bonnischer Anzeiger* (March 3, 1963), 11, BA-MA, BW1/31628.

44 Werner Kuhlmann, "Polizei muss Polizei bleiben: Stellungnahme und Rechtsgutachten zum Kombattantenstatus der Polizei" (Düsseldorf-Benrath: Gewerkschaft der Polizei, 1963), BArch-K, B106/83869.

45 Ibid.

lawyer and professor who had been a member of the Nazi Party and the *Sturmabteilung* or SA.[46] Both men argued that the government's plans violated not only international law but also civil service regulations enshrined in West Germany's Basic Law. They pointed out the absence of references to police officers in either the Hague or Geneva Conventions. Police officers, they argued, were "civilian non-combatants" and should avoid fighting against the enemy at all costs. Moreover, they explained that Article 12 of West Germany's Basic Law—the freedom to choose one's profession—protected the rights of civil servants from action by the government to impose or change working conditions from those existing at the time of employment—giving civilian police officers military duties thus violated both the letter and spirit of Article 12.

Kuhlmann argued:"The police have already been abused in Germany for tasks that are foreign to their lives—this historical example should warn and frighten us. One cannot condemn the abuse of the police during the last war, and at the same time reconsider the circumstances under which military use of police forces can continue in the future."[47] Kuhlmann's protests, along with the analyses of Professors Ermacora and Hamann, made headlines in West German newspapers and professional police journals. The Interior Ministry faced a dilemma because Felix Ermacora, a respected advocate of human rights, called their plans unconstitutional.[48] The idea of human rights as political language shaped the Federal Republic's attempt to remake itself in the aftermath of National Socialism. Lora Wildenthal has argued that by emphasizing human rights across a broad spectrum of institutions "West Germany self-consciously measured their progress away from dictatorship."[49] The unions thus turned to the political language of human rights as a foil to resist and undermine the government's efforts to assign military tasks to its civilian police forces.

Not everyone was moved to act by the GdP's strategic use of human rights. Hanseatic Interior Minister and future SPD Chancellor Helmut Schmidt, for example, criticized the GdP and its "legal experts" for politicizing the issue.[50] Schmidt called Kuhlmann's fear that West Germany

---

46 For biographical details of Felix Ermacora, see Otto Kimminich, "Nachruf für Felix Ermacora," *Archiv des Völkerrechts* 33, no. 3 (July 1995): 305–8; for Andreas Hamann see obituary "Rechtsanwalt Dr. Andreas Hamann," *Neue juristische Wochenschrift*, 17 Jahrgang, Heft 26 (June 1964): 1217.

47 Werner Kuhlmann, "Polizei muss Polizei bleiben," 4.

48 "Kombattantenstatus kein Schutz," *Deutsche Polizei* 121, no. 62 (March 1963): 67–68.

49 Lora Wildenthal, *Human Rights Discourse in West Germany* (Philadelphia: University of Pennsylvania Press, 2013), 6.

50 "Polizei: Kombattanten-Status unter die Soldaten," *Der Spiegel* 17, no. 13, March 27, 1963, 37–39.

would return to policing methods of the past "absurd." He told reporters that awarding combatant status to police officers was not a move towards re-militarization, but simply provided them with the legal authority for their own protection so they could "act within the framework of the laws and carry out their duties in a war without being viewed by the enemy as irregular fighters."[51] An opinion poll by the magazine *Der Spiegel* found that many state police officers opposed the government's plans. Even the local Hanseatic Association of Social Democratic Police Officers (*Arbeitsgemeinschaft sozialdemokratischer Polizeibeamten*) turned against Schmidt and declared that its membership opposed any "return to a position that reflected the years 1933 to 1945."[52]

Dr. Hans-Hugo Pioch, a lawyer at the Interior Ministry's Police Branch, also wrote to the Defense Ministry with suggestions on how to counter the police union experts.[53] Pioch, a veteran of Hitler's Interior Ministry, asked historians at the Institute for Contemporary History and the *Militärgeschichtliches Forschungsamt* (Military History Research Institute—MGFA) for clarification on the use of police officers in past conflicts. Pioch believed that the precedent for legally recognizing police officers as combatants had already been established during the Third Reich.[54] He sent the MFGA copies of orders issued by the chief of the *Wehrmacht* High Command (OKW), Wilhelm Keitel, that explicitly listed uniformed members of the German police as combatants under the terms of the Hague Laws of War on Land.[55] Of course, relying in any manner on the likes of Keitel, a major Nazi war criminal convicted and executed for crimes against humanity among other charges, as support for postwar policies was just as dubious as using the Warsaw Uprising as a case study for teaching police officers about street fighting.

An MGFA historian, Dr. Stahl, sent Pioch a detailed analysis of the role played by Hitler's police battalions in the Second World War, and specifically their use against partisans.[56] Stahl explained that the *Ordnungspolizei* (Order Police—OrPo), SS battalions, and units of the SD (*Sicherheitsdienst*—security service) took part in counterinsurgency

---

51 Ibid.
52 Ibid.
53 Letter with attachments from Dr. Hans-Hugo Pioch to Bundesministerium für Verteidigung, Betr.: "Kombattantenstatus der Polizei im 2. Weltkrieg," February 26, 1963, BArch-K, B106/83869.
54 Ibid.
55 Wilhelm Keitel, Oberkommando der Wehrmacht, "Kennzeichnung der Kombattanten im Sinne der Haager Landkriegsordnung," OKW Nr. 5490/44 AWA/W/Allg. (II c)—WR, 28. August 1944, BArch-K, B106/83869.
56 Militärgeschichtliches Forschungsamt (II—Az.:50-31-05) An Hernn Dr. Pioch, den Bundesministerium des Innern, Betr.: "Kombattantenstatus der Polizei im 2. Weltkrieg," BArch-K, B106/83869.

operations—*Bandenbekämpfung* (Bandit Fighting)—and were thus considered combatants. According to Stahl, there was "no documentary evidence that members of these security police forces were treated any differently from regular soldiers if they were captured."[57] Stahl pointed out that combatant status for these forces was never questioned during or after the war. *Bandenbekämpfung* operations were explicitly military tasks under the jurisdiction of the *Reichsführer-SS* and Chief of the German Police, Heinrich Himmler. Stahl said the problem during the war was "the unfortunate fusion of police and ideological political tasks imposed on the police under Himmler's leadership."[58] Stahl's findings should have given the Interior Ministry cause to reflect, since by advocating combatant status for the BGS, it was trying to impose a fusion of police with military tasks. Pioch's letter and his use of documentary support from the Second World War highlighted the competing use of memory on both sides of the debate. Whereas members of the state police unions pointed to legacies of the Nazi era as part of what they called a "creeping process of militarization," the Interior and Defense Ministries used Nazi police practices to justify their policies.[59]

Kuhlmann's campaign against combatant status and particularly his publication "*Police Must Remain Police*" appeared to have served their purpose. To the dismay of many at the Interior Ministry, legal scholars from both camps unanimously agreed that Article 12 of the Basic Law excluded West Germany's state police officers because assigning them military duties significantly changed their working conditions. The trade unions thus succeeded in blocking the Interior Ministry's proposal to consolidate state police officers into the new legislation.[60] Nevertheless, Kuhlmann refused to back down. On April 5, 1965, he wrote to members of the Bundestag requesting that they also deny combatant status to the BGS on the same grounds.[61] He argued there could never be a mixing of military and civilian law enforcement duties in one organization. He explained that making border police officers military combatants could only be justified by stripping them of all civilian law enforcement duties.[62] He claimed: "It cannot be denied that a motive for giving

   57 Ibid.
   58 Ibid.
   59 Hubert Devlos, "Wird die Polizei militarisiert," *Frankfurter Allgemeine Zeitung*, June 13, 1963, 2.
   60 This was formally removed from the Bundestag draft under Drucksache IV/3003 on January 27, 1965, BArch-K, B136/1928, Fiche Nr. 2, Slide Nr. 247.
   61 GdP Chairman Werner Kuhlmann an die Abgeordneten des Deutschen Bundestag, 5. April 1965, Betr.: "Trennung von Polizei und Bundesgrenzschutz," BArch-K, B136/1928 Fiche Nr. 2, Slides 246–52.
   62 Ibid.

border policemen combatant status is admissible in the interests of their own welfare. The incompatibility, however, comes from the fact that a police force assumes military tasks normally reserved for armed forces and would cause significant uncertainty for those involved."[63] Thus, according to Kuhlmann, the only option for the Bundestag would be to remove the classification of the BGS as a "police force" and place it directly under the armed forces as a resource for external security.[64] For the ÖTV, the central focus of their arguments against the amendment rested upon Article 12 of the Basic Law.[65]

Despite ongoing protests by the police trade unions, on May 12, 1965, the Bundestag voted unanimously to pass the amendment.[66] The law took effect on July 11, 1965. The revision was a rare moment when all of West Germany's political parties seemed to be of one mind on national security matters. The fear of war with East German or Soviet insurgents outweighed the consequences of mixing police and military roles in one internal security force. From this perspective, Germany's authoritarian past, and in particular its campaign against partisans during the Third Reich, played a significant role in how the Federal Republic's lawmakers envisioned the postwar police institution. During the first reading of the law, for example, Representative Artur Anders (SPD) declared: "The purpose of this law is to ensure the welfare and personal safety of BGS members who take part in an armed conflict. We have thus saved our border policemen from being treated as partisans by the enemy in such a conflict and, as such, exposed to all the dangers."[67]

"Helicopters are not *Stukas*":[68] Organizational Tensions over Combatant Status

The 1965 revision of the Federal Border Police Act permitted members of the BGS to "use weapons to defend against military attacks."[69] Now that the BGS could fight in the event of a war, its command staff

---

63 Ibid.
64 Ibid.
65 See Rechtsgutachten von Dr. R. Zippelius, Gewerkschaft Öffentliche Dienste Transport und Verkehr, March 25, 1966, "Die Verleihung des Kombattantenstatus an den Bundesgrenzschutz," BArch-K, B 136/1928, Fiche Nr. 3, Slides 248–261.
66 See Niederschrift der Deutscher Bundestag, 181 Sitzung, 4. Wahlperiode, May 12, 1955, 9106–9109, BA-MA, BW1/317989.
67 Ibid., 9107.
68 See "Einsatz von Hubschraubern im Straßenkampf—Möglichkeiten und Grenzen," BArch-K, B 106/93268.
69 See Bundestag Drucksache IV/343.

intensified the guerilla/small wars training curriculum that Brigadier General Heinrich Müller had secretly implemented when he took command of the organization in 1963.[70] Here again, the tensions between those who advocated for reform and those who insisted upon the status quo exposed the ongoing debate over continuity and change that shaped the organizational identity crises that had troubled the BGS since its inception. Shortly after the law passed, for example, Colonel Karl Winkelbrandt, commander of the BGS school at Lübeck-St. Hubertus, published the organization's "Street Fighting Manual"—a primer for urban combat and house-to-house fighting.[71] Winkelbrandt, with Müller's full approval, drew from the Wehrmacht's 1944 street fighting manual issued by Lieutenant General Rainer Stahel to his troops fighting the Polish resistance at Warsaw. Stahel published the 1944 manual to provide his soldiers with the tactics they needed to destroy what he called the "fanatical Polish bandits" holding out in Warsaw.[72] Winkelbrandt also relied on a book about the uprising by the German historian Hanns von Krannhals, who quoted extensively from Stahel's street fighting manual. Paradoxically, while the BGS used Krannhals's book as a source for Stahel's tactics, prosecutors in Flensburg called Krannhals as a key witness in their war crimes case against SS Commander Heinz Reinefarth for murdering Polish civilians during the uprising.[73]

Since the BGS street fighting manual reproduced the same tactics that members of the Wehrmacht used against the Poles in 1944, it should never have been introduced for use in a civilian law enforcement agency—it did not square with the ideals of democratic policing and the duty of officers to protect life and property. Instead, it instructed officers to toss hand grenades into rooms before entering and when "attacking" houses to "always wait until your own snipers have cleared the roof of the enemy from neighboring houses."[74] The tactics in the manual reflected offensive military actions rather than maintaining law and order. Evidence shows

---

70 Inspekteur des Bundesgrenzschutz Brigadegeneral i. BGS Müller an den BGS Kommandeur des GSK Süd, Mitte, Nord.

71 Oberst i. BGS Winkelbrandt, "Strassenkampffibel für den Bundesgrenzschutz," December 1965, BArch-K, B106/83898; Winkelbrandt was a veteran of Weimar Germany's police forces who also served as a training officer in the Wehrmacht: see "Der neue Kommandeur: Brigadegeneral im BGS Winkelbrandt," *Der Grenzjäger* 3 (March 1967): 5.

72 Generalleutnant Stahel, Merkblatt, Geheim, August 21, 1944, attached to "Einführung des Kommandobesprechung, January 21, 1964," BArch-K, B 106/93268.

73 Hanns von Krannhals, *Der Warschauer Aufstand 1944* (Frankfurt am Main: Bernard & Graefe, 1962).

74 Oberst i. BGS Winkelbrandt, "Strassenkampffibel für den Bundesgrenzschutz," 18.

that Müller and his command staff produced and distributed the controversial manual without approval or insight from the Interior Ministry's legal division. This was a significant and deliberate oversight, but not surprising considering the secret counterinsurgency plans that Müller and his staff had been making since at least 1963. When Dr. Alfred Einwag, head of Department VI B (General Affairs), received a copy of the manual, he requested that it be retracted and revised. He complained that Müller had no authority to publish it and pointed out that the tactics appeared to show "the use of such strong forces and such heavy weapons that the limits of a police operation can very easily be exceeded."[75]

Dr. Einwag's criticisms of the manual shows how some officials at the Interior Ministry recognized the problems of blending law enforcement with military duties and tried to make changes. Yet as long as veteran soldiers like Müller remained in charge, rooting out these problematic themes and tactics proved to be a difficult challenge. Despite their constant public declarations that they were law enforcement officers rather than soldiers, the command staff still treated the BGS more like an army than a police force. In a speech during a 1965 meeting of commanders in Munich, for example, Lieutenant Colonel Teichmann declared: "I don't know whether you noticed, and if you did, whether you thought about it, but when the BGS was set up, it took over the staff structure of the former Wehrmacht, while the Bundeswehr went its own way based on the American Army."[76] The legal designation of their men as military combatants only reinforced these ideals and behaviors—even though border police officers never engaged in the combat that their leaders imagined. Moreover, whereas women joined state law enforcement agencies, the BGS banned them from all but the most basic of administrative jobs, citing the role of its personnel to fight as combatants during a war—a duty forbidden for German women under Article 12 of the Basic Law.

Within the closed organizational spaces of the BGS and among most of its senior command staff in particular, the primacy of military themes and doctrine still took priority over traditional policing duties. The fall war games exercise, code-named *Übung Hessen*, highlighted how the command staff envisioned its role in response to the combatant status legislation.[77] In the after-action report of the exercise, Müller criticized the

---

75 Unterabteilung VI B, Dr. Alfred Einwag an Unterabteilungsleiter VI C, December 13, 1965, "Anwendung unmittelbaren Zwanges durch den Bundesgrenzschutz; hier: Straßenkampffibel für den Bundesgrenzschutz," BArch-K, B 106/83898.

76 Dienstrecht: Oberstleutnant i. BGS Dr. Teichmann, "Kurzvortrag gehalten anläßlich der Besprechung der Kommandeurs des Bundesgrenzschutzes am 24. November 1965 in München," B 106/93268.

77 Der Inspekteur des BGS Brigadegeneral i. BGS Müller an den GSK Süd, Mitte, Nord, Küste, und GS-Schulen, Betr.: "Schlussbesprechung Übung Hessen

performance of his men for failing to "hunt down" partisans, and cited examples from Frederick the Great's campaigns during the Seven Years War. He wrote: "We need commanders who can lead to a Leuthen rather than to a Kunersdorf."[78] Although he claimed that he never intended to "introduce predominantly military thinking in the BGS," this is precisely what he did.[79] His report is thus rife with quotes from Prussian military history that he cited in the lessons he wanted to impart to his subordinates. In criticizing the men's lack of initiative to attack, for example, he quoted Count Alfred Schlieffen who said "the basic principles of leadership remain, and one of these laws is that one cannot defeat the enemy without attack." Besides Schlieffen, he also quoted from the memoirs of Prussian Generals such as Helmuth von Moltke and the anti-democratic former Reichswehr, General Hans von Seeckt.[80] He also argued that the BGS would do well to adapt the "seek and destroy" tactics of American Special Forces in their campaign against the guerillas in Vietnam, reflecting the transnational influences of wars in the developing world on security in the Federal Republic.[81]

The focus on counterinsurgency operations pointed to what could best be described as a sort of moral panic or guerilla-phobia. The obsession with preparing the officers for anti-partisan warfare in the BGS exceeded the boundaries of typical border policing duties. During their regular quarterly Command Staff meetings in the 1960s, for example, senior leaders rarely discussed enforcing laws, but focused instead on relevant secondary literature concerned with guerilla war and counterinsurgency. The Interior Ministry's Security Branch published a comprehensive "subversive war" bibliography and distributed it to all BGS command centers.[82] The recommended readings included classic works by philosophers of guerilla war such as Mao Zedong, Che Guevara, Abdul

---

1965," October 21, 1965, BArch-K, B 106/18019.

78 Ibid., Leuthen and Kunersdorf were battles fought by Frederick the Great during the Seven Years War; At Leuthen, Frederick outmaneuvered and defeated a larger Austrian Army, whereas at Kunersdorf, he was soundly defeated by a combined Russo-Austrian army; On Frederick the Great's battles see Robert Citino, *The German Way of War: From the Thirty Years War to the Third Reich* (Lawrence: University Press of Kansas, 2005), 83–90; See also Russell F. Weigley, *The Age of Battles: The Quest for Decisive Warfare from Breitenfeld to Waterloo* (Indianapolis: Indiana University Press, 1991), 190.

79 Müller: "Schlussbesprechung Übung Hessen 1965," October 21, 1965, BArch-K, B106/18019.

80 Ibid.

81 Ibid.

82 See Bundesministerium des Innern, "Literaturhinweise über Schriftum des subversiven Kampfes," November 11, 1965, BArch-K, B106/93268.

Nasution, and Ho Chi Minh. The Interior Ministry maintained a subversive war library and updated it regularly by purchasing new and out of print titles.[83]

The obsession with, and preparations for, fighting guerillas reflected the tensions between both postwar German states in a phenomenon that some scholars have called a "cold civil war."[84] Thus minor conflicts with NVA border guards and other border security incidents helped to fuel the guerilla-phobia in the BGS. At the quarterly meeting of BGS commanders on November 24, 1965, for example, Major Siegfried Jansch gave a detailed intelligence report about the status of NVA border guards.[85] He emphasized that recent estimates had shown the number of East German police officers stationed at the border exceeded 50,000 men.[86] According to Jansch, in 1963 alone the Border Police Command at Hesse reported some 6,000 minor incidents. Most of these cases, however, were simply visual sittings of NVA troops rather than incidents that led to German-German conflicts. Nevertheless, Jansch described 600 of these incidents as "attacks" where NVA border troops deliberately crossed into disputed West German territory on reconnaissance missions.[87] He pointed out that provocations along the rural border increased in frequency after the Berlin Wall made it more difficult for refugees to flee west through the city. According to Jansch, the Berlin Wall was a decisive development that transferred tensions from the divided city out to the rural regions of the Inner-German border.[88]

GDR intelligence reports show that they engaged in the same type of imagined war with Western security forces and had an excellent understanding of the personnel and strength of the BGS.[89] The East Germans

---

83   See Bundesministerium des Innern Bücherei Bonn, "Partisankrieg," Literaturübersicht nach den Beständen der Bücherei, 12. Januar 1965, BArch-K, B106/93268.

84   Referred to in Franziska Kuschell and Dominik Rigoll, "Broschürenkrieg statt Bürgerkrieg: BMI und MdI im Deutsch-Deutsch Systemkonflikt," in *Hüter der Ordnung*, ed. Frank Bösch and Andreas Wirsching, 378.

85   Major i. BGS Jansch, "Vortrag anlässlich der Zusammenziehung der Kommandeure des BGS am 24.11.1965 in München, Vertraulich! Betr.: Versuch einer vergleichenden Betrachtung der beiderseits der SBZ—DL eingesetzten Sicherungskräfte, unter besonderer Berücksichtigung der NVA Grenz Truppen," BArch-K, B106/93268.

86   Ibid.

87   Ibid.

88   Ibid.

89   Bundesgrenzschutz data was included in the following GDR report from 1960: "Bericht über die Waffen und Geräte der westdeutschen Wehrmacht," BA-MA, DVW1/25814; See also "Bericht über den Bundesgrenzschutz und die Bereitschaftspolizei," Stand: 10. März 1961, BA-MA, DVW1/25825e.

also feared the possibility of a civil-war style conflict erupting at the Inner-German border and expressed particular concern about BGS forces taking part in NATO exercises. For GDR analysts, West Germany's border police officers were just former Nazi soldiers disguised as the police. The analysts concluded that the Federal Republic had "created an additional military formation that, along with the Länder and riot police can be used against its [West German] population at any time." They argued that it "was in a strong position to carry out limited and independent combat operations."[90] GDR analysts called the BGS a civil war army (*Bürgerkriegarmee*). In one report, under the subheading "Role and Importance of the BGS in the War Plans of the Bonn Militarists," analysts described West German border police officers in the following manner:

> German imperialism and militarism began immediately after 1945 with the remilitarization of West Germany. Even after the construction of a new army, the BGS remained and shows that Bonn never had any intention of disbanding it. Our estimates clearly show that German militarism is alive and well in the form of the BGS—a well-trained civil war force, which under the sole command of the [West German] government routinely carries out deliberate provocations and military attacks along the East German and Czech borders. The BGS is thus a fully motorized police army with officers recruited from the ranks of the fascist Wehrmacht and who are indoctrinated and trained in the spirit of fascist and revanchist traditions.[91]

In yet another report, the analyst concluded: "The preparation of the BGS is based on a purely military point of view and its personnel are trained with NATO forces to attack and defend against guerilla forces."[92] The training of border police officers for war on both sides of the demarcation line shows the escalation of mutual fears among the Eastern and Western security forces. Yet evidence also shows that in spite of the détente reflected in the diplomacy of governing elites on both sides of the demarcation line, those at the ground level responsible for security still planned for and imagined a civil war erupting at the Inner-German border.[93]

For the BGS, fears of guerilla warfare not only reflected the idea of a "cold civil war," but also evoked themes tied to global or transnational

---

90 Bericht: "Die Rolle und Aufgaben des Bundesgrenzschutzes in den militärischen Plänen Bonns," BA-MA, DVW1/25771b.

91 Ibid.

92 "Bericht über den westdeutschen Bundesgrenzschutz," 3. Februar 1960, BA-MA, DVW1/25814c.

93 Détente refers to the policy of an easing of tensions between the superpowers and an acceptance of the status quo in regard to Europe's division; see for example Marc Trachtenberg, *A Constructed Peace*, 231.

Cold War tensions. In the 1960s, the United States significantly escalated its military operations in Vietnam and the global decolonization process produced violent insurgencies in Malaya, Algeria, and Kenya—topics that regularly appeared in BGS literature and training.[94] The articles in organizational magazines like *Die Parole*, *BGS Zeitschrift* and *Der Grenzjäger* highlighted the fears of West Germany's conservatives about immigration from regions of the developing world, and the global south in particular.[95] Lora Wildenthal has argued that West Germany's New Left formed "solidarities with non-Germans such as foreign students, foreign guest workers, and anti-national liberation movement activists."[96] The link between the New Left and these movements alarmed conservatives who found their open reverence for iconic revolutionary figures such as Fidel Castro and Che Guevara unsettling.[97] Since BGS commanders and the majority of their personnel identified with Christian conservatism, they linked the peoples and movements in the developing world to their base fears of guerilla war and insurgency. Thus Brigadier General Müller often invoked Indonesian counterinsurgency expert Abdul Nasution, who proclaimed: "Guerillas move like lice among the population."[98]

Backlash: West Germany's Emerging Critical Public Sphere

Despite strong parliamentary support for recognizing BGS members as military combatants, militarized police forces still upset most West

---

94 See Michael Burleigh, *Small Wars, Faraway Places: Global Insurrection and the Making of the Modern World, 1945–1965* (New York: Penguin, 2014), 6; William J. Lederer, "Der Guerillakrieg, den Roten verloren: Das Beispiel des Malaiischen Bundes zeigt, dass die Kommunisten in Asien keineswegs unbesiegbar sind," *Die Parole* 12, no. 11 (November 15, 1962): 13–15, 25.

95 These are just a few representative examples of the many articles focused on subversive warfare: See, for example, "Kampf gegen Banden und Agenten," *Die Parole* 12, no. 11 (November 15, 1962): 3–4; "Rote Methoden im Kampf um Asien: Flugblattbomben, Perfekter Terror, Wirtschaftshilfe, Ideologie, Revolution," *Die Parole* 12, no. 8 (August 15, 1962): 17–18.

96 Lora Wildenthal, *The Language of Human Rights*, 11.

97 *Die Parole* magazine in particular featured numerous articles and politicized cartoons that reflected this linkage; Russell Duncan, "The Summer of Love and Protest: Transatlantic Counterculture in the 1960s," in *The Transatlantic Sixties: Europe and the United States in the Counterculture Decade*, ed. Grzegorz Kosc, Clara Juncker, Sharon Monteith, and Britta Waldschmidt-Nelson (Bielefeld: Transcript Verlag, 2013), 149.

98 Abdul Nasution, *The Fundamentals of Guerilla Warfare and the Indian Defense System Past and Future* (Djakarta: Indonesian Army Information Service, 1953).

Germans. Citing "political reasons," Müller instructed his staff to keep all discussions and plans about military tactics confidential.[99] It did not take long, however, before the BGS found itself at the center of a press scandal over its military equipment and organizational culture. The burdens and legacies of the Nazi past continued to shape public opinion about themes linked to militarism and war. The problem emerged after the popular weekly magazine *Stern* published a photo essay that appeared to show teenage boys playing with weapons at a BGS barracks in Lüneburg. The boys, who were members of the Berlin chapter of the Association of Returnees, POWs, and MIAs, had elected to spend a portion of their annual summer camp living in the barracks, where they could learn more about a career in the BGS.[100] The photos showed the boys carrying semi-automatic rifles, dressed in camouflage smocks and wearing Wehrmacht-style steel helmets. In one of the photos, the boys appear to be the victims of a mock execution in front of a BGS firing squad. The boys wrote about their experiences in essays that *Stern* editors reprinted in the article under the title: "My Best Vacation Experience with the BGS." In the essays, the boys wrote how powerful they felt while holding the rifles and one of them said he "felt strong enough to conquer Russia if necessary."[101]

The emergence of a critical public in West Germany after the war was a consequence of its democratization. According to Christina von Hodenberg, "the long sixties became the decade of media-political affairs" and there was certainly no shortage of controversy surrounding the BGS and the Federal Republic's new armed forces.[102] In 1955, for example, *Der Spiegel* (The Mirror) published a sensational story that forced former Wehrmacht Colonel Bogislaw von Bonin to resign from the Blank Office because of comments he made about using BGS units for territorial defense. In 1962, *Der Spiegel* also exposed NATO plans to use tactical nuclear weapons during a conflict with the Soviets.[103] In what the media

---

99 Inspekteur des Bundesgrenzschutz Brigadegeneral i. BGS Müller an den BGS Kommandeur des GSK Süd, Mitte, Nord, Küste, und GS-Schulen, "Zusätze zur "Einsatzmöglichkeiten des Bundesgrenzschutzes," BArch-K, B106/18019.

100 Letter from Herr Duchstein, Verband der Heimkehrer, Kriegsgefangenen und Vermisstenangehörigen to the Bundesministerium des Innern, May 13, 1965, BArch-K, B106/373627.

101 Ralf Döring and Henri Nannen, "Mein schönstes Ferienerlebnis," *Stern*, no. 33, August 15, 1965, 12–16.

102 See Christina von Hodenberg, *Konsens und Krise: Eine Geschichte der westdeutschen Medienöffentlichkeit* (Göttingen: Wallstein, 2006), 293; see also Jürgen Bellers and Maren Königsberg, eds., *Skandal oder Medienrummel?* (Münster: LIT, 2004), esp. 51 "Die Spiegel-Affäre 1962."

103 For a collection of articles on all aspects of the Spiegel Affair, see *Die Spiegel-Affäre: Ein Skandal und seine Folgen*, ed. Martin Doerry and Hauke Janssen (Munich: Deutsche Verlags-Anstalt, 2013); See also Justin Collings,

dubbed the "*Spiegel Affair*," Defense Minister Franz Josef Strauss retaliated by ordering police raids on the magazine's Hamburg offices and the personal homes of its editorial staff. When Strauss lied to the Bundestag about his order to arrest the author of the article, Conrad Ahlers, he was forced to resign.[104]

Stern magazine's editor-in-chief, Henri Nannen, was no stranger to sensationalism. He had been a loyal National Socialist and during the war served with a special propaganda unit—the *SS-Standarte Kurt Eggers*—in occupied Italy. He had also been a narrator for Leni Riefenstahl's 1938 Nazi propaganda film *Olympia*.[105] On July 13, 1965, just two days after the Bundestag passed the combatant status legislation, Nannen sent his newest reporter, Ralf Döring, to the Lüneburg barracks with the purpose of writing a story about the boys visiting the BGS. What transpired after Döring's arrival can be reconstructed from the Interior Ministry's investigation, transcripts of interviews, and the correspondence of those involved.[106] During the visit, Döring found the boys under the supervision of Sergeant Hans Völzke. Lüneburg barracks was part of BGS-North, which at the time was commanded by Brigadier General Siegfried Noffke, a veteran of the Prussian *Schutzpolizei* and Nazi Wehrmacht. Döring asked if he could take pictures of the boys on the rifle range for his article, but Völzke denied the request on the grounds that the boys were only allowed to shoot air rifles. Völzke left Döring with the boys for approximately thirty minutes while he attended to other duties. It was a brief break that he would later come to regret. While Völzke was away, Döring flagged down some younger border police officers returning from training and enlisted their help to get the pictures he wanted. He allegedly told the unsuspecting officers that he only wanted to take photos of the boys with rifles and dress them in military uniforms as a joke, and they agreed to help.[107]

Democracy's Guardians: A History of the German Federal Constitutional Court, 1951–2001 (Oxford: Oxford University Press, 2015), 80–82.

104 Justin Collings, *Democracy's Guardians*, 81.

105 Hermann Schreiber, *Henri Nannen: Drei Leben* (Munich: Bertelsmann Verlag, 1999), 136; Taylor Downing, *Olympia*, 2nd edition (London: Palgrave Macmillan, 2012), 127; Nannen was also a key figure in the scandal surrounding the forged Hitler diaries during the 1980s. See Charles Hamilton, *The Hitler Diaries: Fakes that Fooled the World* (Lexington: University Press of Kentucky, 1991), 98–99.

106 Eberhard Barth, "Bericht über Prüfung der Vorfälle, die sich bei der Aufnahme der Berliner Ferienkinder durch den Bundesgrenzschutz ereigneten und Anlass von Presseveröffentlichungen waren," September 10, 1965, BArch-K, B106/373627.

107 Statement of *Stern* Reporter Ralf Döring given to Dr. Eberhard Barth, September 1, 1965, BArch-K, B106/373627; statement of Sergeant Völzke to

When Nannen saw Döring's photos, he recognized the sensational effect they would have in light of the recent controversial combatant status debate. Thus he instructed Döring to return to Lüneburg and get the boys to write essays about their experiences. The boys wrote the essays, but *Stern's* editorial staff complained to Döring that they were "not what they had hoped for."[108] Apparently, in the first drafts the boys wrote more about their typical summer camp days in Lüneburg, which included swimming and miniature golf. To be sure, Nannen and his staff wanted them to write more about handling the rifles and ordered Döring to help them craft the essays to match the photos. Nannen later denied he told Döring to coach the boys, but his narrative that accompanied the published photo-essay shows otherwise. In captions under the photos, Nannen wrote that the boys in Lüneburg were "Just like the Führer's werewolves—hungry children in oversized uniforms with courage and fear in their eyes standing in the courtyard of the Reich Chancellery waiting for him to pin the Iron Cross on their tunics before returning to the front, where lying in wait for Russian tanks, their childish bodies would be shredded."[109] On the heels of the recent combatant status debate, Nannen hoped to capture the emotional impact of images depicting children "playing" war and those of the mock executions in particular.

Brigadier General Noffke dismissed the article and photos as a calculated effort by *Stern* reporters and their editors to smear the BGS. He filed a criminal complaint against Nannen alleging that he violated section 164 of the West German Criminal Code, which made it illegal to falsely accuse a public official of unlawful acts.[110] Interior Minister Höcherl called for an investigation and assigned it to Eberhard Barth, a former Nazi and retired attorney from the Ministry of Defense. Barth's analysis of the incident placed the majority of the blame on Henri Nannen. According to Barth, as *Stern's* Editor-in-Chief, Nannen, should not have assigned the story to Döring, who only recently had completed his training as a journalist. Barth said that while he could not prove Nannen ordered Döring to stage the photos or alter the boys' essays, as the lead editor and author of the article, Nannen was solely responsible for its content and publication. Barth also blamed the junior officers of the BGS for leaving a reporter alone with the boys. He pointed out that border police officers

---

Dr. Eberhard Barth, August 25, 1965, BArch-K, B106/373627.
108 Döring to Dr. Barth, BArch-K, B106/373627.
109 Ralf Döring and Henri Nannen, "Mein schönstes Ferienerlebnis," 12–16.
110 W. Schöttler an Brigadegeneral Noffke, August 16, 1965, "Reportage im Stern," BArch-K, B 106/373627; Michael Bohlander, *The German Criminal Code: A Modern English Translation* (Oxford: Hart, 2008), 127.

at all levels of the organization would benefit from additional public relations training.[111]

Höcherl felt vindicated by Barth's findings and sent a copy of the final report to Nannen, calling the story about the boys playing war "objectively false" and demanded he immediately publish a correction. The father of one of the boys came to the defense of Noffke and accused Nannen and his staff of "abusing the freedom of the press for purposes of sensationalism."[112] For his part, Nannen refused to back down and threatened to publish the portions of Barth's report that criticized the border police officers for failing to supervise the children under their care. Nevertheless, it was the criminal complaint filed by Brigadier General Noffke that finally brought the matter to a close. In the meantime, Paul Lücke replaced Höcherl as the new Interior Minister. Facing criminal prosecution by Noffke, Nannen wrote to Lücke and claimed he never intended to harm the reputation of the BGS. He suggested that if Noffke dropped his case, he would write a corrective article that blamed the incident on "a combination of factual and human errors." At first, Noffke was intransigent and refused any suggestion that he should back down. In the interest of bringing the negative press to a halt, however, Heinrich Müller persuaded Noffke to drop his criminal complaint against Nannen. Noffke made it clear to Müller that he agreed to do so "with a heavy heart only out of my respect and confidence in you personally."[113] With Noffke's agreement to withdraw his complaint against Nannen, the press lost interest.

Although it could be argued that Barth's investigation was far from impartial, both sides in the controversy bore responsibility for what transpired with the boys. Nannen was certainly well-versed in the uses of propaganda and wielded his skills effectively to produce a sensational story that captured the public's attention. He could and should have done more to scrutinize the details in the story before publishing it. The East Germans capitalized on the article, and Radio Berlin International used it to report that Nazism was alive and well in West Germany's first post-Hitler generation because it armed rather than educated its children.[114]

---

111 Eberhard Barth, "Bericht über Prüfung der Vorfälle."

112 Letter from Interior Minister Hermann Höcherl to *Stern* Chief Editor Henri Nannen, September 20, 1965, BArch-K, B106/373627; Letter from Reinhold Reichardt to Brigadier General Noffke, August 14, 1965, BArch-K, B106/373627.

113 Correspondence between BGS Inspekteur Heinrich Müller and Brigadier General Noffke, January 17, 1966, BArch-K, B106/373627; Nannen did publish a correction: see Henri Nannen, "Kind ans Gewehr?" *Stern* 35 August 29, 1965, 16–20.

114 Transcript of Radio Berlin Broadcast, August 13, 1965, Presse und Informationsamt der Bundesregierung: Nachrichtenabteilung, "Sowjetzonen-Spiegel

The story and its protagonists have largely been forgotten, but the scandal showed how even two decades later, images of boy soldiers revived disturbing memories of the war and struck a nerve with West Germans. For its part, the BGS learned a bitter lesson that highlighted its challenges in adapting to the popular opinion and critical public sphere that came with democratization. By the early 1960s, the military symbolism and ceremony that had come to define its organizational culture began to lose touch with the democratic values ingrained in the Federal Republic's civil society. Thus, as insignificant as the scandal might have been to the BGS as a whole, it forced its leaders to look inward despite ongoing tensions between continuity and change and the persistent reluctance by many in its command staff to make substantive changes. Still, the proverbial writing was on the wall, and to echo Bob Dylan's hit song of that time: "*You better start swimmin' or you'll sink like a stone, For the times they are a-changin'.*"[115]

(Rundfunk, Fernsehfunk, und Agenturmaterial), Nr. 187/65, BArch-K, B106/373627.

115 Bob Dylan, "The Times They Are A-Changin'," 1964, available online at https://www.bobdylan.com/songs/times-they-are-changin.

PART III

MODERNIZATION: BECOMING A FEDERAL POLICE AGENCY, 1968–2005

CHAPTER EIGHT

BONN'S "PROBLEM CHILD": THE STRUGGLE TO MODERNIZE THE BGS

On April 19, 1967, after years of declining health, Konrad Adenauer passed away at his home in Rhöndorf on the Rhine River. The chancellor's death struck a chord with senior BGS commanders, who fondly recalled his tireless advocacy and promotion of their organization. But as the chancellor was laid to rest, the Federal Republic, and the BGS in particular, which the press began calling Bonn's "problem child," faced new challenges.[1] In 1966, the booming economic miracle that came to define the Adenauer era finally came to a grinding halt during West Germany's first postwar recession. As a result of the economic crisis, Adenauer's successor Ludwig Erhard resigned and his government collapsed. Facing significant budget cuts, the BGS struggled to overcome staffing shortages still lingering after many of its personnel transferred to the army in 1956. Despite spending millions on recruitment, the organization never reached its authorized strength of 20,000 men. Moreover, the federal government was mired in an ongoing political debate over emergency legislation that contributed to the extra-parliamentary opposition (APO) crisis and student protests that rocked West Germany in the late 1960s. State and local police forces were pushed to their limits dealing with the crowds, and many of them responded violently against the demonstrators.

During the crisis of the late 1960s, many border police officers lost faith in the organization and complained to their unions that it needed to be modernized.[2] In 1962 the revised compulsory service law enabled men to waive mandatory military service if they elected to serve at least eighteen months in the police instead. The change, however, only offered a short-term solution to the staffing issues, since most of the men that took advantage of it left when their terms expired or transferred to the

---

1 Leopold Habicher, "Sorgenkind der Regierung: Bundesgrenzschutz soll verstärkt warden," *Göttinger Tageblatt*, September 19, 1968.
2 BGS Oberleutnant Karl Heinz Müller, "Bundesgrenzschutz—Noch notwendig?" *FAZ*, August 15, 1970, BA-MA, BH 28-2-257.

state police, which offered better career and promotional opportunities. Candidates had no incentive to remain in the BGS, because the state police or other civil service professions did not give credit or offer incentives for their experiences guarding borders.[3] By the end of the 1960s, the BGS continued to struggle against complaints that it was really just an army posing as a police force. Of course, the organization contributed to this image with its public ceremonies and parades of militarized equipment and vehicles. GdP Chairman Werner Kuhlmann, one of its chief critics, attracted attention with his renewed accusations and calls for the organization to be disbanded. The 1969 arrest of a BGS colonel for war crimes did little to help its flagging public image.[4]

On the diplomatic front, Willy Brandt became the first SPD Chancellor of the postwar era. His *Ostpolitik* campaign, an effort to engage with the Federal Republic's eastern neighbors, helped to reduce Cold War tensions. The 1971 four-power Berlin Agreement, for example, re-established travel between the divided sectors of the city and assured mutual respect of joint rights and responsibilities. The Basic Treaty that followed in 1972 opened up diplomatic relations between the two German states and relaxed the prospect of a civil war on the Inner-German border, which had been such a focal point for border police officers during the 1950s and 60s. By 1973, a border commission composed of members from both states met to iron out territorial disputes over the course of the demarcation line, using diplomacy instead of violence.[5] Although border incidents still occurred, the future looked uncertain for the BGS. Despite improved relations and the easing of tensions attributed to Brandt's *Ostpolitik*, incidents on the Inner-German border still created enough problems to make security a high-priority for West German politicians. To be sure, many lawmakers saw the BGS as an instrument of détente because it functioned as a "buffer" to diffuse potential conflicts between Soviet and NATO forces. Moreover, the rise of violent crime, terrorism, and the increased demand for security at the Federal Republic's airports often strained the operational capabilities of state police forces. Because of these emerging security challenges and the declining interest

---

3   Ibid.
4   "Fall Radtke ist Teil grösserer Ermittlungen," *Die Welt*, October 17, 1969, 1, BA-MA, BH28-2-527; Radtke avoided prosecution by claiming he was not medically fit to stand trial; see Beschluss: Radtke Wilhelm, geb. 16. Mai 1913, wohnh. in Pfreimd, wegen Mordes (NSG), October 25, 1971, StA-M 35279/5.
5   The Berlin Agreement guaranteed unhindered transit between East and West Berlin, while the Basic Treaty recognized East Germany and banned threats or uses of force in the relations between the two German states;, eds., *Uniting Germany: Documents and Debates, 1944–1993*, ed. Konrad Jarausch and Volker Grasnow, 20–22; Klaus Emmerich, *Die Grenzkommission beider deutscher Staaten: Aufgaben, Tätigkeit und* Dokumente (Norderstedt: Books on Demand, 2014).

of young men in joining the force, the Interior Ministry, state officials, the trade unions, and lawmakers worked collaboratively to overhaul the organization. Their efforts culminated in the first major revision of the Border Police Act since its passage in 1951, and set the BGS on a course to becoming a modern law enforcement agency.

The Emergency Acts: A First Step toward a Reformed BGS

The debate over what were collectively referred to as the "emergency acts" was a consequence of the 1954 Paris Treaties, which tentatively ended West Germany's status as an occupied nation.[6] As proposed, the laws created new security duties for the BGS that allowed the government to deploy it beyond the borders—even though it had already been unofficially doing this for years. Before granting full sovereignty, the Allies required the Federal Republic to pass emergency legislation as a security guarantee for their troops stationed on German soil.[7] Members of the Bundestag needed a two-thirds majority vote to pass the new laws. The Paris Treaties symbolically ended the occupation, but the process lasted more than a decade because of internal political bickering.[8] As early as 1958, Interior Minister Gerhard Schröder had tried to force the passage of emergency legislation that empowered the executive branch. The SPD rejected this early proposal because they feared granting such powers might be used to curtail the rights of trade unionists and specifically their right to strike.[9] As a "militant democracy," the burdens of the Nazi past and the shadow of Weimar's collapse still hung like an ever-present shadow over these debates. Karrin Hanshew has argued that legacies of democratic failure and the rise of Nazism in 1933 "assured that democratic stability would remain a topic of postwar discussion."[10] Thus the framers of West Germany's Basic Law treated executive power cautiously, since the National Socialists used it under Article 48 of the

---

6 For a recent analysis of the emergency legislation debate, see Martin Diebel, *Die Stunde der Exekutive: Das Bundesinnenministerium im Konflikt um die Notstandsgesetzgebung, 1949–1968* (Göttingen: Wallstein Verlag, 2019).
7 Karen Hanshew, *Terror and Democracy*, 62–63.
8 Justin Collings, *Democracy's Guardians*, 100.
9 See Michael Schneider, *Demokratie in Gefahr?*, 47; see also Gerard Braunthal, "Emergency Legislation in the Federal Republic of Germany," in *Festschrift für Karl Loewenstein: Aus Anlass seines achtzigsten Geburtstages*, ed. Henry Steele Commager, Günther Doeker, Ernst Fraenkel, Ferdinand Hermes, William C. Harvard, and Theodor Maunz, (Tübingen: J. C. B. Mohr, 1971), 78.
10 Karrin Hanshew, *Terror and Democracy*, 6.

Weimar Constitution to suspend and ultimately overthrow Germany's first democracy.

The ongoing struggle by lawmakers to find a permanent solution to the problem exposed West Germany's domestic political fault lines. For the SPD, Schröder's proclamation that a national emergency triggered what he referred to as "the hour of the executive" sounded too similar to the authoritarian principles and writings on executive power of the controversial Nazi political theorist Carl Schmitt.[11] In 1961, when Hermann Höcherl replaced Schröder as Interior Minister, the issue returned to the forefront of parliamentary politics, fueled in part by East Germany's surprise construction of the Berlin Wall.[12] At first, Höcherl rejected Schröder's hardline approach to executive power. Instead, he dealt directly with the SPD and West Germany's largest trade union—the *Deutsche Gewerkschaft Bund* (DGB) to try and find a consensus. While social democrats and trade unionists welcomed his willingness to negotiate, they remained skeptical. They appreciated his public statements that emergency legislation should protect rather than prohibit the right to strike.[13] Yet despite Höcherl's willingness to reach across political lines, he jeopardized the negotiations when he lost his temper during a debate over the laws in the Bundestag and accused a member of the SPD of being a "liar like Strauss." During the heated exchange, several Bundestag members came close to exchanging blows. Thus the Bundestag remained bitterly divided and no closer to reaching a consensus than they had been under Schröder.[14]

By 1966 the government of Adenauer's successor, Chancellor Ludwig Erhard, collapsed because of ongoing economic tensions and power struggles between Erhard, the Free Democrats (FDP), and those within his own party who had lost confidence in his leadership.[15] Kurt Georg Kiesinger, the former CDU Minister-President of Baden-Württemberg, replaced Erhard and formed a coalition government with the SPD, CDU, and CSU. Paul Lücke, a moderate CDU politician known for working cooperatively with the SPD, took over as Interior Minister. The coming together of socialist and conservative lawmakers in this "Grand Coalition," however, had more to do with the economic turmoil of the times than emergency legislation. Moreover, Kiesinger's policy goals

---

11 See Jan-Werner Müller, *A Dangerous Mind*, 64; Carl Schmitt, *The Crisis of Parliamentary Democracy*, 43.
12 Michael Schneider, *Demokratie in Gefahr?*, 81.
13 Ibid.
14 See, "Notstand Sie! Sie!," *Der Spiegel* 26, June 22, 1965, 19; Höcherl's accusation that the SPD member lied like Strauss referred to Defense Minister Franz Josef Strauss and the Spiegel Affair.
15 See Ronald J. Granieri, *The Ambivalent Alliance: Konrad Adenauer, the CDU/CSU, and the West, 1949–1966* (New York: Berghahn, 2002), 220.

emphasized economic reform and made no mention of emergency laws. Yet without the Grand Coalition, the government would have been no closer to passing the laws than they had been in 1965. Both sides in the debate had long recognized the need to compromise if they wanted the Allies to lift their reserved powers.[16] Although many junior members of the SPD criticized their party elders for entering into a government with its conservative adversaries, it also forced the CDU to make its own compromises. The SPD's "Right to Resist" (*Widerstandsrecht*) provision, for example, granted all Germans the right and duty to resist against "any threat to the free democratic order." With the compromises in place, the emergency acts finally gained the elusive two-thirds majority and took effect on May 30, 1968.[17]

The legal changes opened a new chapter for the BGS that outlined new duties beyond just guarding the Federal Republic's borders. The emergency laws set it on course to becoming the federal police force the government had always claimed it to be. Article 91 paragraphs 1 and 2 (the federal emergency law), for example, now included language that allowed border police officers to support the state police whenever the free democratic order of the nation or a particular state was in "imminent danger."[18] The new language legalized what had already been an unofficial practice of using the BGS to support the state police; it transformed it into a mobile police reserve that could respond anywhere it was needed. The emergency laws also revised Articles 35 and 115 (f) of the Basic Law. Article 35 allowed border police officers to aid the state police during natural disasters, and article 115 (f) reaffirmed its controversial combatant status, but now extended it to cover operations within the Federal Republic's borders. Moreover, in January 1969, the Bundestag amended section 42 of the Compulsory Military Service Act, which allowed young men to serve two years in the BGS or three years in the state police as a substitute for their two-year military service obligation. Later that year, the Bundestag added border protection to the list of duties covered by Section 42.[19]

Conscription, however, remained a short-term solution, because young men joined as a means to avoid military service, and most recruits had no allegiance to the organization. Influenced by the youth counterculture of the late 1960s, some conscripts defied disciplinary standards

16 Martin Diebel, *Die Stunde der Exekutive*, 157–58; Michael Schneider, *Demokratie in Gefahr?*, 194.
17 Karrin Hanshew, Terror and Democracy, 63–67.
18 See "Grundgesetz für die Bundesrepublik Deutschland," Textausgabe Stand: August 2006 (Berlin: Bundeszentrale für politische Bildung, 2006), 55.
19 "Nach Verabschiedung der Notstandsgesetze: der Bundesgrenzschutz rüstet sich für neue Aufgaben," *Die Welt*, August 2, 1968, 1, BA-MA, BH28-2-257.

they found too rigid. In a 1971 case, for example, border police conscript Michael Meister and eleven of his colleagues refused an order to cut their long hair. As punishment, their commanding officer revoked their right to serve in the BGS and sent them to the army for the remainder of their terms. Meister and his colleagues joined the BGS to avoid military service and retained an attorney to fight the charges. The men told reporters that they wondered what the border police had against "fashionable hairstyles" and alleged the organization discriminated against them because they were conscripts. The men claimed that the voluntary border police officers were allowed to grow their hair long "if it could be pinned up or contained by a hairnet."[20] Although the men eventually agreed to cut their hair in order to remain police officers, they still had to pay fines through payroll deductions of up to 30 DM each. As minor or anecdotal as the haircut issue might first appear, it reflected continual internal tensions in the organization between those who advocated liberalization and those who favored the status quo or militarized model of policing, where draconian punishments are meted out for minor infractions. Moreover, it also revealed how career officers looked down on conscripts and engaged in selective enforcement of grooming standards depending upon someone's status in the organization.

The organizational divide showed that the BGS sometimes stood in its own way by alienating potential recruits at a time when they needed personnel to guard the borders and assume the new tasks that came with the emergency laws. The recession of 1967 increased the number of applicants and helped the force reach a strength of 18,121 men, but the poor economy worked both ways. Because of shrinking budgets, the Interior Ministry had to cut its strength to 17,500 men. After the passage of the emergency laws, the force had 15,765 of its 20,000 vacancies filled. Besides personnel shortages, the BGS suffered from a lack of leadership posts. By the fall of 1968, it recorded a 58 percent attrition rate among junior officers—the *Hundertschaftsführer*—a line-level supervisory rank vital to its daily operations.[21] The new duties also posed massive organizational and logistical challenges. Since 1951 it had stationed the majority of its personnel near the Inner-German border and now had to contend with transferring units to offer better coverage for interior regions of the country. Border Group 1 stationed at the Czech border, for example, had

---

20 See Ulla Küspert and Erika Krauss, "Grenzer mit Mähne 'strafversetzt' zur Bundeswehr," *Hamburger Morgenpost*, September 20, 1971, 1, BA-MA, BH 28-2-237.

21 Dr. Alfred Einwag, ÖS II, Bundesministerium des Innern, "Aktennotiz M 130 040/24: Einsatz des BGS zur Unterstützung der Länderpolizei," November 25, 1968, 11, BArch-K, B 106/83920.

only 664 of its 1,823 posts staffed during the mass influx of refugees fleeing the Soviet crackdown on Prague in 1968.[22]

At its annual meeting in 1969, the command staff discussed many of these organizational challenges and how they might try to address them. During the meeting, Public Security Branch Chief at the Interior Ministry Karl Gumbel delivered a keynote address titled, "The Bundesgrenzschutz Today and Tomorrow." Gumbel shared complaints brought to the Ministry's attention in 1968 by the BGS Employees' Association.[23] He argued that "considerable personnel problems have piled up over the years" and complained that the BGS failed to offer career options or incentives that were comparable to those available to state police officers.[24] Gumbel acknowledged that conscription had turned the BGS into what he called a "training organization for short-duty personnel"— or in other words, an option to avoid military service. Despite increased recruitment budgets, the ratio of applicants to vacancies remained below what the organization needed to reach its authorized strength.[25]

The BGS and Protest Policing

Although the passage of the emergency acts is often heralded as the catalyst for West Germany's student uprisings in 1968, popular resentment about the war in Vietnam played a larger role. The Federal Republic's support for the United States and the stationing of its troops on German soil angered more than just its university students. Many West Germans questioned how a liberal democracy could perpetrate what many viewed as a classic war of aggression in the developing world. Thus the passage of the emergency laws may have "radicalized" the student movement, but the expansion of the US war in Vietnam and especially its bombing campaign in 1965 played a greater role. Student activists viewed their government

---

22 See 1970 Interior Ministry Report, "Logistische Folgerungen aus dem BGS-Programm," BArch-K, B 106/370091; Ministerialrat Alfred Einwag, ÖS II 1, Aktennnotiz M 130 040/23, "Verstärkung des Bundesgrenzschutzes," September 25, 1968, 1, BArch-K, B 106/83920; "Bundesgrenzschutz ist zu schwach: Die Ereignisse in der CSSR bringen es in Erinnerung," *Hannoversche Rundschau*, September 3, 1968.

23 Bundesvorsitzender Bundesgrenzschutz-Verband e.V. an Herrn Bundesminister des Innern Ernst Benda, September 16, 1968, "Um die Zukunft des Bundesgrenzschutz: Gedanken und Vorschläge des Bundesgrenzschutz-Verbandes e.V." BArch-K, B106/88821; Staatssekretär Karl Gumbel, Kommandeurtagung Duderstadt, "Vortrag des Herrn Staatssekretär über das Thema Bundesgrenzschutz heute und morgen," January 13, 1969, BArch-K, B 106/93269.

24 Staatssekretär Karl Gumbel, "Bundesgrenzschutz heute und morgen," BArch-K, B 106/93269.

25 Ibid.

as an authoritarian instrument of ruling elites, many of which, as they correctly pointed out, were former Nazis. The student uprisings of the late 1960s represented a significant challenge for the Federal Republic's police forces, and they often resorted to military tactics and violence in trying to bring the crowds under control.[26]

West German students also found solidarity with the global anti-authoritarian movements spreading throughout the developing world. In 1967, for example, tensions rose in many West German cities as the divisive Iranian Shah, Reza Pahlavi, began a nine-day state visit in May. The authoritarian Shah was a symbol of oppressive, corrupt, and dictatorial regimes around the world that derived their support from Western governments, and the United States in particular.[27] Protests took place in several cities during the Shah's stay, but the contrasts in how the police responded often determined their outcome. On June 2, 1967, the Berlin police violently attacked the crowds lining the Shah's motorcade route. The officers, with the support of Iranian Security Services, used truncheons and critically wounded many of the protestors. In the ensuing chaos, a student, Benno Ohnesorg, was shot and killed by Karl-Heinz Kurras—later revealed to be a Stasi agent posing as a Berlin police sergeant.[28]

The Munich Police watched the events in Berlin closely as they prepared for the Shah to visit their city on June 7. Munich's police chief, Manfred Schreiber, an advocate of de-escalation, assumed command in 1962 following a series of youth riots that shook the Schwabing neighborhood.[29] Schreiber emphasized verbal communication over violence as a better method for dealing with unruly crowds. He enlisted psychologists to train his police officers in the art of communication they needed to de-escalate the crowds. Thus instead of seeking out and forcibly arresting agitators, Schreiber's officers left protestors alone unless forced to

---

26 Geoff Eley, *Forging Democracy: The History of the Left in Europe, 1850–2000* (New York: Oxford University Press, 2002), 344; Michael Schneider, *Demokratie in Gefahr?*, 188; see also Wilfried Mausbach, "Wende um 360 Grad? Nationalsozialismus und Judenvernichtung in der 'zweiten Gründungsphase' der Bundesrepublik," in *Wo "1968" liegt: Reform und Revolte in der Geschichte der Bundesrepublik*, ed. Christina von Hodenberg and Detlef Siegfried, (Göttingen: Vandenhoek & Ruprecht, 2006), 15.

27 Eckard Michels, *Schahbesuch 1967: Fanal für die Studentenbewegung* (Berlin: Ch. Links, 2017), 102–3; see also Douglas Little, *American Orientalism: The United States and the Middle East since 1945*, 3rd edition (Chapel Hill: University of North Carolina Press, 2008), 220; and Uwe Soukoup, *Ein Schuss, der die Republik veränderte: Der 2. Juni 1967* (Berlin: Transit, 2017).

28 Ibid., 161.

29 Ibid., 162–63; As the Munich police chief, Schreiber later played a significant role in the security of the Munich Olympic Games in 1972.

act in life-threatening situations. His officers deployed cameras in order to film acts of vandalism and property crimes committed by demonstrators in order to charge them for their crimes at a later time away from the heightened emotions of the protests. What came to be known as the "Munich Model" promoted de-escalation and helped officers to deal with the crowds non-violently. In contrast to the bloody protests in Berlin, the Shah's visit to Munich took place without incident.[30]

The demonstrations against the Shah were the beginning episode of the mass student protests that followed. A leading force of the grassroots student opposition, the Socialist German Student Union (SDS), led many of the larger protests.[31] During the 1960s, SDS activists took issue with the conservative Axel Springer publishing house. Many of Springer's articles attacked students and branded them as traitors, but the publisher was also emblematic for everything they stood against—authoritarian elites compromised by their Nazi pasts. Many of Springer's articles spoke favorably of West Germany's support for American efforts in Vietnam.[32] The ideological struggle between the SDS and Springer came to a head on April 11, 1968, after radical right-wing activist, Josef Bachmann, shot and gravely wounded the charismatic SDS leader Rudi Dutschke in Berlin.[33] Spontaneous protests known collectively as the "Easter Riots" erupted all over West Germany. In Berlin, students surrounded Springer's headquarters and attacked newspaper delivery vans and employees with rocks and bottles. The SDS blamed Springer for fomenting the radical right-wing rhetoric that motivated Bachmann to shoot Dutschke. In Hamburg, 58 students were arrested while two police officers and two citizens suffered serious injuries. In Frankfurt, the police used high-pressure water cannons and batons to subdue a crowd of 7,000; 42 protestors and two police officers were severely injured.[34] In Munich, despite Schreiber's call for de-escalation, newspaper photographer Klaus Frings and a student,

30 Ibid.
31 Sean A. Forner, *German Intellectuals and the Challenge of Democratic Renewal* (Cambridge: Cambridge University Press, 2014), 325; Michael Schmidtke, *Der Aufbruch der jungen Intelligenz: Die 68er Jahre in der Bundesrepublik und der USA* (Frankfurt am Main: Campus, 2003), 132; Martin Klimke, *The Other Alliance: Student Protest in West Germany and the United States in the Global Sixties* (Princeton, NJ: Princeton University Press, 2010), 33.
32 Ingo Cornils, *Writing the Revolution: The Construction of "1968" in Germany* (Rochester: Camden House, 2016), 157.
33 Nick Thomas, *Protest Movements in 1960s West Germany: A Social History of Dissent and Democracy* (Oxford: Berg, 2003), 169–73.
34 "Verlaufs- und Erfahrungsbericht der Schutzpolizei über die polizeilichen Massnahmen vom 11. bis 15.4.1968 anlässlich der Aktionen der 'ausserparlamentarischen Opposition' im Zusammenhang mit den Schüssen auf Rudi Dutschke," Berlin, May 4, 1968, BArch-K, B106/83892.

Rudiger Schreck, died during clashes with the police. Both men suffered blows to the head from an unknown assailant, but medical examiners never determined whether the police or rocks thrown by other protestors caused their deaths. No witnesses to the crime came forward, but doctors who treated Schreck noted he had two severe head wounds indicating he had been struck at least twice—once on each side of his head. Schreck's injuries, they believed, seemed to be more consistent with a metal police baton rather than a rock.[35]

Despite the violent nature of these demonstrations, the government did not send BGS units to assist the state police in their direct confrontations with the crowds. On the one hand, this could be interpreted as a sign of remarkable restraint by West German officials, since militarized border police officers might escalate the violence. After all, its officers trained for urban combat and house-to-house fighting rather than keeping the peace during a public exercise of the constitutional right to protest. In fact, at the time of the Easter Riots, the BGS had neither crowd control training nor the appropriate equipment to carry out these typical law enforcement duties. Instead, its personnel had weapons and equipment more suitable for warfare than protest policing. On the other hand, however, it also exposed the conundrum West Germany's government found itself facing with a peculiar force like the BGS in which the duties of policing and fighting wars came together in one organization—a persistent problem that had come to both define and hinder the organization since its inception. Again, if it had been strictly a law enforcement agency, as the Interior Ministry claimed, then why did it fail to prepare its personnel for one of the most fundamental and typical functions of the police in a democracy?

Because of this dilemma, BGS platoons performed largely symbolic roles as a show of force, while state and local police bore the brunt of the protests. During the spontaneous outbreak of violence in Bonn, for example, the BGS Watch Battalion at the Chancellery mobilized to protect the federal offices in the government quarter as more than 8,000 protestors took to the streets.[36] A BGS reserve force also stood ready in Duisdorf to deploy by helicopter if necessary. Yet its lack of preparation or proper equipment raises the question of what the Interior Ministry expected these men to do if actually forced into confrontations with the protestors.

---

35 Letter from Bavarian Interior Ministry to Staatsekretär Siegfried Fröhlich, April 18, 1968, Betr: "Tod des Studenten Rudiger Schreck," Fiche Nr. 1, Slide Nr. 239; see also letter from Staatsekretär Siegfried Fröhlich to Bundeskanzler Kiesinger, April 18, 1968, Betr: "Tod des Studenten Rudiger Schreck," Fiche Nr. 1, Slide Nr. 242, BArch-K, B136/5035.

36 Bericht vom Dr. Roesch, Bundesministerium des Innern, Betr: "Zusammenfassung der Meldungen über Demonstrationen am 15. April 1968," BArch-K, B136/5035, Fiche Nr. 1, Slide Nr. 239.

They lacked the training and skills of their state police colleagues in the methods of de-escalation and as a result could not carry weapons other than batons and tear gas pistols while assigned to protests.[37] While the decision to prohibit firearms reflected a cautious approach by the officials in charge of the federal government's response, it also exposed their lack of confidence in the officers to behave appropriately given the circumstances. Thus calling the BGS a law enforcement agency could not have been further off the mark.

Internal correspondence between the Interior Ministry and its border police command staff sheds light on their training deficiencies. In the aftermath of the Easter Riots, Brigadier General Heinrich Müller instructed his staff to immediately formulate and implement more training in crowd control tactics.[38] Moreover, in a confidential internal memorandum, State Secretary Gumbel admitted that "It should be taken into account that this type of operation means completely new territory for the border police officers."[39] Thus its leaders found themselves relying upon the BePo for crowd control training when according to the new emergency laws, the BGS was supposed to reinforce the BePo in a national emergency.[40] On a positive note, however, since protest policing was an entirely new duty, the Interior Ministry had the benefit of teaching border police officers how to respond based upon the mistakes of other police agencies, and particularly the violent shootings of Benno Ohnesorg and Rudi Dutschke. The Interior Ministry, for example, used the Berlin Police Department's after-action report of the riots that followed Dutschke's shooting and distributed it to all BGS commanders as a case study in how not to confront crowds.[41] The report showed that while the Interior Ministry advocated de-escalation and restraint, Berlin Police commanders praised their officers for responding violently. According to the Berlin Police "hardness was required" to foil the rioters and this promoted a positive "sense of belonging and camaraderie among the officers within the units." The report also took aim at the press for what it called their "derogatory depictions" of the police.[42]

---

37 Letter from Staatssekretär Koester, Referat I/2 Bonn, to Bundeskanzler Kiesinger, 16. April 1968, BArch-K, B136/5035 Fiche Nr. 1, Slide Nr. 219.

38 BGS Inspekteur Heinrich Müller, "Gedanken über die Bewältigung der jüngsten Demonstrationswellen, sofern ein Einsatz der Exekutive notwendig wird," May 24, 1968, BArch-K, B106/83892.

39 Letter from Unterabteilungsleiter ÖS III (Keidel) to Staatssekretär Gumbel, "Erabeitung von Richtlinien für den Einsatz bei inneren Unruhen," June 7, 1968, BArch-K, B106/83892.

40 Ibid.

41 See footnote 31 above, "Verlaufs- und Erfahrungsbericht Schüssen auf Rudi Dutschke," Berlin, May 4, 1968, BArch-K, B106/83892.

42 Ibid.

The Berlin Police response to the Easter Riots showed little change from their violent treatment of the crowds during the Shah's visit.[43] The Interior Ministry, however, rejected this approach and instead developed riot control tactics more closely aligned with the Munich Model of Manfred Schreiber. BGS commanders also tried to avoid the negative press and criticism they endured during the combatant status debate. By 1968, Brigadier General Detlev von Platen replaced Heinrich Müller as head of the organization and made more of an effort to focus on improving its public image. He claimed that those who called the BGS a civil war army were "stalwarts who believe we are still beholden to so-called militaristic ideas."[44] The truth of the matter, however, was somewhere in the middle of the contradictions that had come to define the BGS. Despite his plea to the contrary, von Platen, a veteran of the Nazi General Staff, still promoted a culture of militarization by continuing to train his officers for combat while advocating their need for infantry weapons to include heavy mortars. Nevertheless, his concerns over the public image of the BGS also showed the growing influence of a critical press that had begun to shape its organizational behaviors and policies.[45]

The BGS first employed its new crowd control training when it was sent to support the North Rhine Westphalia state police during the "March on Bonn," a nationwide protest that erupted after the formal passage of the Emergency Laws. Hans Schneppel, director of the Police Branch at the Interior Ministry, outlined the mission and rules of engagement for the border police units deployed in and around Bonn.[46] During the demonstrations, BGS personnel protected critical buildings in the government quarter. The officers had barricades, tear gas, and water trucks to use against any protestors who might attempt to enter protective zones established around each of the buildings.[47] Schneppel made it clear to his subordinates that any action taken against protestors must be proportional and measured. He emphasized strict restraint and recommended that the officers use verbal commands with loudspeakers to

---

43 This was outlined by Eckard Michels in his comparative analysis of tactics used by the Berlin and Munich Police during the Shah's visit; see Eckard Michels, *Schahbesuch 1967*, 102–3.

44 Detlev von Platen, "Über die Aufgaben des BGS: Aus seiner Ansprache in Fulda," *Die Parole* 18, no. 12 (December 15, 1968): 2.

45 See Christina von Hodenberg, *Konsens und Krise*, 68.

46 Memorandum from Hans Schneppel, Polizei Abteilung, Bundesministerium des Innern to Grenzschutz Mitte, Bonn, Betr: "Sternmarsch auf Bonn; Einsatz von Verstärkungskräften des Bundesgrenzschutzes in den Bewachungsobjekten in Bonn am 10. und 11. Mai 1968 (mündlich und fernmündlich voraus)," May 10, 1968, BArch-K, B106/83892.

47 Ibid.

de-escalate the crowds rather than physical violence in gaining compliance. He explicitly cautioned that "the use of firearms is permitted only in the case of self-defense and then only after the attacker has been warned. All efforts to protect the attacker must be taken. If using a firearm is unavoidable, then officers must aim for the attacker's legs in order to minimize any injuries."[48]

Schneppel's instructions revealed that contrary to what critics feared about deploying a militarized force like the BGS during protests, its response to the crowds in Bonn reflected a measured approach. Like the orders against carrying firearms during the Easter Riots, it demonstrated that the Interior Ministry recognized the need for additional training to bring the BGS in line with law enforcement principles. Schneppel's warnings also reflected the realization, at least at the administrative level of the organization, that militarized policing no longer suited the duties they expected its officers to carry out, despite those that still insisted on the need for infantry weapons and training.[49] As a result of the new training, the protests in Bonn ended without significant violence or property damage. According to Thomas Etzemüller, during the uprisings of the late 1960s, the BGS actually proved itself to be a taming influence on state and local police forces that still employed civil war fighting tactics against protestors.[50] While Etzemüller is correct to point this out, the Interior Ministry also had the benefit of time and indeed the prudence to study what worked and what did not to prepare the BGS before deploying it for major crowd control events.

"We Want to Dare More Democracy!"

In the immediate aftermath of the student uprisings, the BGS Employee's Association complained to the Interior Ministry that its officers lacked the capability to carry out the additional duties that came with the passage of the emergency laws.[51] The memorandum outlining their grievances

48 Ibid.
49 Dirk Schumann, *Political Violence in the Weimar Republic*; Hsi-huey Liang, *The Berlin Police Force in the Weimar Republic*; Belinda Davis, "Polizei und Gewalt auf der Strasse: Konfliktmuster und ihre Folgen im Berlin des 19. und 20. Jahrhunderts," in *Polizei, Gewalt und Staat im 20. Jahrhundert*, ed. Alf Lüdtke, Herbert Reinke, and Michael Sturm (Wiesbaden: Springer, 2011); Hans Schneppel, "Sternmarsch auf Bonn; Einsatz von Verstärkungskräften des Bundesgrenzschutzes in den Bewachungsobjekten in Bonn am 10. und 11. Mai 1968."
50 Thomas Etzemüller, 1968—*Ein Riss in der Geschichte: Gesellschaftlicher Umbruch und 68er-Bewegungen in Westdeutschland und Schweden* (Konstanz: UVK, 2005), 139.
51 Bundesvorsitzender Bundesgrenzschutz-Verband e.V. an Herrn Bundesminister des Innern Ernst Benda, September 16, 1968, BArch-K, B106/88821.

suggested that the BGS be further developed into an internal security force. While the memorandum emphasized concerns over working conditions and pay, it also included many useful suggestions on how the force could be re-imagined and reformed. In her study of the BGS, sociologist Patricia Schütte-Bestek has suggested that the emergency laws created "conditions at the political level which permanently secured the legitimacy of the BGS for the support of the state police."[52] But the changes that came with the emergency laws did not go far enough; the process of securing its legitimacy took an additional four years and involved significant legislative revisions. West Germany's state police forces, however, could not handle every large incident of internal unrest or national emergency alone. The Basic Law prohibited the deployment of the army for domestic emergencies unless during a war or massive natural disaster.[53] For the Interior Ministry, the BGS offered an interim solution—stronger than the state police, but less intrusive than using the army. An article in the May 1968 edition of *Die Parole* was explicit on this point: "The stronger the BGS, the less need there is for the army in such cases."[54] According to Brigadier General von Platen, the emergency laws provided a "concretization" of the organization's role in securing West Germany's democracy. He emphasized that "above all, it [BGS] will not and cannot be used against its own population, but rather for their protection should this become necessary."[55]

Although passage of the emergency laws paved the way for the BGS to gain additional duties, the comprehensive internal security program that followed led to a massive coordination of all West German security forces. Between 1965 and 1971, despite a few lean years, the BGS budget increased on average from 300 to 500 million DM per year.[56] The increases and grassroots attempts to redefine the organization and its place in the Federal Republic gained momentum just as Willy Brandt took over as the first Social Democratic Chancellor of the postwar era. Brandt's leadership style ushered in a new approach to government that favored more centralization. It was Brandt who during his "Government

52 Patricia Schütte-Bestek, *Aus Bundesgrenzschutz wird Bundespolizei: Entwicklung einer deutschen Polizeiorganisation des Bundes aus organisationssoziologischer Perspektive* (Wiesbaden: Springer, 2015), 116.

53 The army was generally prohibited from being used in a domestic emergency. See Article 87a Grundgesetz—Bundeszentrale für politische Bildung, "Grundgesetz für die Bundesrepublik Deutschland," 51.

54 Staff, "BGS und Notstandsverfassung," *Die Parole* 18, no. 5 (May 15, 1968): 2.

55 Detlef von Platen, "Über die Aufgaben des BGS: Aus seiner Ansprache in Fulda," *Die Parole* 18, no. 12 (December 15, 1968): 2.

56 See "Schwerpunktprogramm Innere Sicherheit," *Die Parole* 22, no. 4 (April 1972): 3.

Policy" declaration to the Bundestag called for a comprehensive "modernizing and intensifying of the fight against crime" and the formation of an immediate "Program for Internal Security."[57] Brandt, known as the "Chancellor of Domestic Reform," modernized governmental agencies and advanced democratization to a greater extent than at any point in the postwar era.[58] From a foreign policy perspective, his *Neue Ostpolitik*—a policy of rapprochement and détente with Eastern Bloc countries—was underscored by his solemn act of kneeling at the monument to the victims of the Warsaw Ghetto Uprising.[59] The new spirit of détente combined with the hardened security measures along the Inner-German border relaxed the "cold civil war" between East and West Germany and threatened the continued relevancy of the duties upon which the BGS was founded in 1951.

In 1969 the ÖTV reacted to Brandt's call to modernize the fight against crime by publishing a study outlining their own proposals for reform in the BGS. ÖTV chairman Gerhard Schmidt sent a pamphlet called *The Modern Bundesgrenzschutz* to West Germany's new Interior Minister, Hans Dietrich Genscher.[60] Citing Brandt's *Neue Ostpolitik*, the report emphasized that "the agreement of the great powers to the status quo and the respect of the mutual spheres of influence made violent border incidents ever more improbable." In addition, the report claimed that fortifications on both sides of the demarcation line had reached an extent to where cross-border attacks were less likely.[61] The ÖTV revived its longstanding opposition to border police officers having combatant status and demanded an immediate end to this policy. ÖTV representatives argued that because of its combatant status, "for the first time in the Federal Republic, military tasks were transferred to a police organization the mixture of which created a dangerous situation and increasingly

---

57 "Regierungserklärung von Bundeskanzler Willy Brandt vor dem Deutschen Bundestag in Bonn," October 29, 1969, transcript available online at https://willy-brandt-biografie.de/wp-content/uploads/2017/08/Regierungs erklaerung_Willy_Brandt_1969.pdf.

58 Bernhard Gotto, "Von enttäuschten Erwartungen: Willy Brandt's "Mehr Demokratie wagen" und Valéry Giscard d'Estaing's "Démocratie française," in *Nach "Achtundsechzig": Krisen und Krisenbewusstsein in Deutschland und Frankreich in den 1960er Jahren*, ed. Bernhard Gotto, Horst Möller, Jean Mondot and Nicole Pelletier (Munich: Oldenbourg Wissenschaftsverlag, 2013), 43.

59 See Katarzyna Stoklosa, *Polen und die deutschen Ostpolitik, 1945–1990* (Göttingen: Vandenhoeck & Ruprecht, 2011), 187.

60 ÖTV Chairman Gerhard Schmidt to Interior Minister Hans Dietrich Genscher, December 29, 1969, Anlage: "Der Moderne Bundesgrenzschutz: Die Gewerkschaft Öffentliche Dienste, Transport und Verkehr: stellt zur Diskussion," BArch-K, B106/88821.

61 Ibid.

pushed police duties into the background." Border police officers, they complained, should arrest perpetrators under the democratic rule of law rather than attack them like soldiers.[62]

The ÖTV also criticized the BGS for its militarized training and infantry weapons. Thus instead of mortars and machine guns, they suggested that its personnel would be better served by mastering the use of data processors and electronic devices to aid in the capture of criminal fugitives. The report also recommended a complete abandonment of the traditional military-style uniforms and rank structures. The old Wehrmacht-style steel helmets and military uniforms, strong symbols of Germany's authoritarian past, however, remained in service until the early 1990s and despite minor modifications looked essentially the same. According to the authors of the report "it is only when the federal border police is released from its military mission that, as a true federal police force, it can be fully used for policing tasks, which is now all the more urgently needed for the fulfillment of internal security duties."[63]

In February 1970, the *Stuttgarter Zeitung* wrote about the ÖTV report and quoted its chairman, Gerhard Schmidt, who claimed that the BGS needed to be psychologically and materially disarmed.[64] Schmidt also argued for reforms that were guided by the principle of what he called "internal and external democratization." He wanted to strip Border police officers of all their military equipment, uniforms, and training in order to bring their organization into line with other West German police forces.[65] The article irritated Inspector Detlev von Platen, since he wanted to change what he believed were false perceptions about the BGS as a military force in disguise. It also angered members of its Employees' Association, who rejected the ÖTV's claims and argued that their weapons were necessary to keep them safe at the border. They pointed to a recent dramatic rescue by members of the BGS who risked their lives to save seventeen-year-old Bernd Geis. Geis stepped on a landmine in the so-called death strip on the Eastern side of the Inner-German border. If not for the quick thinking BGS patrol that heard his pleas and illegally entered GDR territory to save him, Geis would certainly have bled to death.[66]

62 Ibid.
63 "Der Moderne Bundesgrenzschutz."
64 "ÖTV wünscht keine Grenzschutz-Generäle," *Stuttgarter Zeitung*, February 6, 1970, 1, BArch-K, B106/88821.
65 Ibid.
66 "Unter der Lupe: Grenzschutz entwaffnen?" *Der Grenzjäger* 3 (March 1970): 2; "West German Border Guards Rescue Youth Hurt by Mine," *New York Times*, January 3, 1970, 14; "Grenzschutz/DDR-Flucht: Holt ihn raus," *Der Spiegel* 3, January 11, 1970.

Von Platen took the issue to Genscher and complained that Schmidt's criticisms of the military-style equipment and training had nothing to do with democratization. He emphasized that the "Bundesgrenzschutz was already firmly grounded in our democracy and is legally bound by the Basic Law; anyone who suggests otherwise is mistaken."[67] Yet like his predecessors, behind the scenes von Platen still considered the BGS to have more of a military than a police role. In setting the agenda for the 1970 commander meeting, for example, he asked his staff for recommendations re new anti-tank weapons. Although he explained that the weapons "must be kept within the narrow limits of what is possible for the Federal Border Police" he still suggested that they should be trained and armed with long-range rifle grenades, guided missiles, and artillery to counter Soviet tanks.[68] The use or discussion of anti-tank weapons was precisely what the ÖTV and other critics cited as evidence that it was not really a police force.

Genscher followed a steady line of Interior Ministers, beginning with Robert Lehr, who defended the BGS and treated it like their own private armed force. He told Schmidt: "The members of the BGS already stand clearly and unambiguously on the very soil of our democracy; I was thus astonished and dismayed that you think otherwise."[69] Caught off-guard, Schmidt later apologized for the misunderstanding and blamed the *Stuttgarter Zeitung* for misconstruing what he said. But Schmidt still used the opportunity to complain about the recent introduction of conscription to address personnel shortages. He argued that "The ÖTV trade union cannot agree with the maintenance of combatant status and the introduction of conscription to fill vacant positions, which simply cannot be reconciled with the police and the 'alleged' police character of the Bundesgrenzschutz."[70] Schmidt's use of the phrase "alleged police character" shows what he really thought about the Interior Ministry's claims. Genscher responded that it made no sense to criticize the equipment, training, or combatant status of the BGS, since all of these things

---

67 Letter from BGS Inspekteur Detlev von Platen to Bundesminister des Innern, Hans Dietrich Genscher, February 11, 1970, Betr: "Angriff der ÖTV auf die demokratische Grundhaltung des Bundesgrenzschutzes, Stuttgarter Zeitung vom 6. Febr. 1970," BArch-K, B106/88821.

68 Der Inspekteur des Bundesgrenzschutzes (von Platen) to all BGS Commands, BGS II—654 002—½, Bonn, February 16, 1970, BArch-K, B 106/93267.

69 Letter from BMI Hans Dietrich Genscher to ÖTV Chairman Gerhard Schmidt, February 20, 1970, BArch-K, B106/88821.

70 Letter from ÖTV Chairman Gerhard Schmidt to BMI Hans Dietrich Genscher, March 6, 1970, BArch-K, B106/88821.

were authorized and regulated by the Bundestag.[71] Moreover, Genscher rejected Schmidt's assessment of conscription, arguing "I cannot support your remarks about allegedly increasingly noticeable military tendencies in the Bundesgrenzschutz—to me, the reasoning you give for your fears seems largely unconvincing ... under the present circumstances, there are no alternative solutions to conscription to reach these staffing goals."[72]

Revising the 1951 Border Police Act

On May 8, 1971, Genscher spoke about his plans to expand the internal security duties of the BGS, during a speech he gave in Lübeck commemorating its twentieth-anniversary. He talked about a need for what he called a "cooperative federalism" whereby border police officers could be sent to support rather than supplant the state police. He proclaimed: "In order to safeguard the police character of the BGS ... I believe it is important to ensure, through the new draft law, that the BGS, whose existence has been repeatedly questioned in the past, is preserved."[73] The new "draft law" Genscher referred to was his proposed revision of the 1951 Federal Police Act, which incorporated many of the recommendations identified by State Secretary Gumbel in his 1969 lecture about the organization's future. Genscher's predecessor, Interior Minister Ernst Benda, first proposed a new BGS law since the passage of the emergency laws added duties not covered by the original 1951 legislation. At the time, however, Benda decided to postpone further action until the extra-parliamentary crisis subsided.[74]

In 1970, Genscher revived Benda's plans and, in the spirit of Brandt's modernization campaign, presented them to the Conference of Interior Ministers and Senators in Working Group II—Internal Security (*Arbeitskreise II—Innere Sicherheit*).[75] Formed in 1954 to deal with cross-state political issues, the conference included six permanent working groups, to include one for internal security. The Federal Minister of the Interior held a permanent, non-voting post on the conference.

---

71 Letter from BMI Hans Dietrich Genscher to ÖTV Chairman Gerhard Schmidt, April 24, 1970, BArch-K, B106/88821.

72 Ibid.

73 Ansprache: des Bundesministers Hans-Dietrich Genscher vor Angehörigen des Bundesgrenzschutzes anlässlich des 20-jährigen Bestehens des BGS in Lübeck, Bonn/Lübeck den 8. Mai 1971, BArch-K, B106/83890.

74 For a thorough analysis of the draft law, see David Parma, *Installation und Konsolidierung des Bundesgrenzschutzes*, 378, 389–95.

75 See "Massnahmen zur Verbesserung der Inneren Sicherheit: Bericht der Arbeitsgruppe 'Innere Sicherheit-Bund' beim Bundesminister des Inneren vom 10. Dezember 1971," VS-Vertraulich amtlich geheimgehalten, BArch-K, B443/807.

The proposed revisions attempted to codify the changes contained in the emergency acts of 1968 and intended to transform the BGS into a national law enforcement agency aligned with the police departments in West Germany's federal states. The draft of the revised law included 74 paragraphs and reflected the largest effort to define a permanent law enforcement role for the organization since its foundation in 1951.[76]

Genscher wanted to standardize BGS training, equipment, and procedures to the extent that its members were interchangeable with their counterparts in West Germany's state and local law enforcement agencies. The changes included more training for the BGS in law enforcement and crime detection duties, revised pay scales, better equipment, and a new rank structure based on police rather than military titles. In short, if passed, the law would completely overhaul the BGS by legalizing duties it had been already carrying out pursuant only to Interior Ministry instructions.[77] More importantly, it allowed border police officers to attend the same police schools, take the same promotional exams, and meet the same standards as their state police colleagues. The Interior Ministry hoped the coordination of qualifications for state and federal officers would solve their staffing problems, since young men who began their career in the BGS could now qualify for employment in the state police. Thus candidates now had an incentive to remain in the BGS for the advantages it gave them for later careers in the state police forces. The legislation also banned mortars—an infantry weapon—from use by the BGS, signaling a recognition by the government that they were inappropriate for civilian law enforcement duties. Instead, the Interior Ministry equipped the BGS with water cannons for use during riots. Germany first deployed water cannons for crowd control in the 1930s. Although better than mortars, water cannons, like other allegedly "less-lethal" police force options, still had the potential to cause serious injuries and even death.[78]

The proposed revisions also gave the BGS jurisdiction over the security of federal buildings and sites around Bonn's government quarter, which had been guarded by border police officers since 1951 pursuant to

---

76 See "Ständige Konferenz der Innenminister und -senatoren der Länder: Aufgaben und Arbeitsweise," online at https://innenministerkonferenz.de/IMK/DE/aufgaben/aufgaben-node.html; see also David Parma, *Installation und Konsolidierung des Bundesgrenzschutzes*, 377–78.

77 For the draft submitted to the Bundestag see Staatssekretär Dr. Rutschke, "Folgerungen aus dem BGS-Gesetz für den BGS, Weisung vom 20. Januar 1972," BArch-K, B106/83883.

78 Dr. Rutschke, "Folgerungen aus dem BGS-Gesetz für den BGS, Weisung vom 20. Januar 1972"; for water cannons, see Vincent Iacopino, MD, and Rohini J. Haar, MD, "Lethal in Disguise: The Health Consequences of Crowd-Control Weapons," *Physicians for Human Rights* (March 1, 2016), online at https://phr.org/our-work/resources/lethal-in-disguise/.

a simple ministerial instruction. By including the legal provision for security in Bonn, the Interior Ministry finally resolved longstanding grievances between officials from the state of North Rhine Westphalia and the federal government over who had jurisdiction for security at these key sites.[79] Moreover, Genscher's proposal also gave border police officers a security role in West Germany's airports, a duty they had been carrying out for some time in Frankfurt, Hamburg, Hanover, Bremen, Stuttgart, and Cologne. It also formalized the practice of sending border police officers abroad to guard German embassies and the offices of its national airline, Lufthansa.[80] The beginning of the jet age and expansion of global travel made airports a central hub for international crime and a favorite target for terrorists. During the 1960s and early 1970s, aircraft hijackings and attacks on airports increased. On February 10, 1970, for example, members of the Popular Front for the Liberation of Palestine (PFLP) attacked an *El Al* airlines passenger bus and terminal at Munich's Riem Airport, killing one and injuring twenty-three others.[81] The passage of the 11th Criminal Law Amendment Act, which took effect on December 19, 1971 included a resolution that called on the federal government to immediately strengthen airport security measures. Genscher thus looked to the BGS to fulfill this new role, because it already had officers of the GSE handling passport checks at all of the major airports.[82]

The urgency with which members of Genscher's Interior Ministry lobbied to pass these revisions shows how they recognized that the BGS needed to become more like a true law enforcement agency in order to remain relevant. Evidence for this urgency is apparent in State Secretary Siegfried Fröhlich's confidential speaking points for his presentation about the proposed revisions to the Conference of Interior Ministers, which had been reviewing a draft of the new law since April, 1971.[83] Fröhlich's efforts to justify the draft reflected an organization struggling to find a

---

79   Dr. Rutschke, "Folgerungen aus dem BGS-Gesetz für den BGS, Weisung vom 20. Januar 1972"; see also David Parma, *Die Personen- und Objektschutzaufgaben der Polizeien des Bundes: Eine rechtshistorische Betrachtung unter besonderer Berücksichtigung der verfassungsrechtlichen Zulässigkeit* (Hamburg: Verlag Dr. Kovač, 2019), 9–12, 38.

80   "Bundesgrenzschutz unterstützt Bodenkontrollen der Lufthansa," *Neue Hannoversche Presse* November 3, 1972, 1, BA-MA, BH 28-2-387.

81   David Binder, "Grenades Miss Dayan Son in Arab Attack in Munich," *New York Times*, February 11, 1970, 1; Stefan M. Aubrey, *The New Dimension of International Terrorism* (Zurich: VDF Hochschuleverlag, 2004), 27.

82   Genscher to Bavarian State Interior Minister Bruno Merk, February 15, 1972, BArch-K, B 106/83929.

83   Staatssekretär Fröhlich, "Entwurf: Eines Sprechzettels für die Besprechung mit der Fünferkommission der Innenminister der Länder," May 24, 1971, BArch-K, B 106/83876.

place in West Germany's internal security system. He was convinced that should the ministers reject the draft, the BGS would become obsolete and certainly be disbanded. In his notes, he made a point to explain to the ministers that despite recent rumors, the draft was not an attempt to undermine the police power of the federal states or increase their burden for internal security. Instead, Fröhlich reiterated that the purpose of the legislation was to ensure the "continued existence and viability of the BGS." He explained: "It is my firm conviction that the BGS must be preserved not only as an instrument for border security, but above all as a factor in internal security ... it would be irresponsible to write it off."[84]

Fröhlich's notes also revealed many of the structural problems that plagued the BGS since its inception and its problematic blending of police and military duties in particular. He claimed that a failure of the ministers to finally resolve its ambiguous legal standing—was it a police or military force—threatened its very existence. Moreover, he argued that "A clear concept for the BGS can only be achieved by freeing it from its hybrid position between the police and Bundeswehr ... in the long run, there are only two alternatives to choose from: either fully deploying it to the military defense of the country, or in the absence of a sensible concept, writing it off and disbanding it."[85] For these reasons, Fröhlich recommended that the ministers approve the draft, which emphasized law enforcement duties and recognized it as a federal police force. He concluded that the draft gave the ministers an opportunity to "make a real an effective contribution to improving public safety and order at the federal and state level ... the situation in the field of public safety requires a healthy BGS, not a sick one."[86]

West Germany's Police Unions and Competing Visions for the *New* BGS

Border Police officers that joined and participated in trade unions belonged to a fragmented combination of the DGB, the ÖTV, or the BGS Employee's Association. None of them, however, belonged to the GdP. While the DGB, ÖTV, and BGS Employees' Association disagreed over various minor points in the proposed reforms, the GdP called for the organization to be completely disbanded. At a press conference on May 18, 1971, GdP Chairman Werner Kuhlmann suggested that members of the GSE be transferred to the state police, that all paramilitary formations in the BGS be disbanded or integrated into the armed forces, and if that was not possible, the entire BGS should be transferred to the Ministry of

84 Ibid.
85 Ibid.
86 Ibid.

Defense, which he argued other European nations had already done with their paramilitary security forces.[87] The Interior Ministry often claimed the BGS was a West German version of the Italian Carabinieri, the Dutch Marechaussee, and the Austrian Gendarmerie, yet these paramilitary forces all answered to their respective defense ministries instead of their civilian interior ministries. Genscher rejected Kuhlmann's suggestions, however, and said that his unreasonable demands contradicted the federal government, the Bundestag, and the trade unions that represented BGS employees.[88]

The press conference did not end the GdP's campaign to stop the Interior Ministry from moving forward with the revisions. Kuhlmann wrote directly to Genscher and provided him with a lengthy report describing his plans to turn the BGS into a national police force as unconstitutional, "politically dangerous, and highly explosive."[89] Many of the arguments outlined in the report revived Kuhlmann's longstanding criticisms of the BGS as an army disguised as a police force. He condemned, for example, its military character and its equipment and weapons in particular. He argued: "Anyone who, under these circumstances, speaks of the BGS as a 'police force' is abusing the term police." Moreover, he said that those who considered it a police force had about as much credibility as someone who "described the features of a tiger and then claimed it was an angora kitten."[90] He also pointed out that the federal government already had a "real" national police force, the BKA, and thus did not need another one. Kuhlmann warned that using a militarized police force with combatant status for internal security was an abuse of power by the federal government, which might turn it loose in labor disputes or against striking workers. Without regard to its measured response during the protests in Bonn, GdP spokesman Adalbert Halt resorted to hyperbole when he claimed: "We have learned a lot from the incidents of 1968 … sending militarized police forces like the BGS to demonstrations could easily result in murder and manslaughter."[91] In reality, it was the GdP's state police forces and not the BGS who used violence to subdue unruly crowds during the protests in 1968.

In a GdP press communique, Kuhlmann challenged the very foundation of the BGS as unconstitutional. He claimed that the federal

---

87 Siegfried Fröhlich, "Forderungen der GdP auf der heutigen Pressekonferenz in Düsseldorf," May 18, 1971, BArch-K, B 106/83876.
88 Ibid.
89 Werner Kuhlmann to Hans-Dietrich Genscher, "Stellungnahme zum Entwurf eines neuen BGS-Gesetzes," May 24, 1971, 8, BArch-K, B 106/83876.
90 Ibid., 5.
91 Ibid., 8; Hans Wüllenweiler, "Der Grenzschutz bleibt Militär: Polizeigewerkschaft ist gegen Einsatz be Demonstrationen," *Weser-Kurier* (July 3, 1972), BA-MA, BH 28-2-387.

government violated the original intent of the Allies and the Bundestag, which when ratifying the Basic Law, intentionally deleted the word "police" from Article 87, the clause used to establish the BGS. In their "police letter" of April 14, 1949, the Allies explicitly allowed the federal government to establish border and customs authorities to deal with smuggling, but denied Adenauer's request to form separate national police forces (see chapter 1).[92] Kuhlmann reiterated that pursuant to the Basic Law, sovereignty over policing in the Federal Republic still rested with its states. He quoted the 114th Bundestag session during which the lawmakers declared that "In federalist Germany, all police functions rest solely and exclusively with the federal states." He explained that the lawmakers did this on the grounds that they wanted to decentralize the police as a "deliberate departure from the situation under the National Socialist regime." Thus, he argued, it was the clear intention of the constitutional framers that the federal government should have neither separate police powers nor the right to set up a national police force.[93]

Kuhlmann's statement struck right to the core of the structural and constitutional issues that the Interior Ministry was trying to correct by revising the original 1951 Border Police Act. From a legal perspective, his argument made sense. The BGS was an anomaly in the Federal Republic that if left in its present configuration might become a pariah and lose relevancy. Yet it had been the only instrument of executive power the federal government had at its immediate disposal in the years before the Federal Republic established the Bundeswehr. In the aftermath of the Korean War, the Allies welcomed the new force as an interim solution to full rearmament and a concession to keep Adenauer's government politically aligned with the West. The Allies chose not to intervene in what they considered to be a domestic political issue. Besides, at the time the Allies and many West Germans believed the force would be replaced once they formed a new army. The legal and structural problems emerged in 1956 after many border police officers decided against joining the army, and the government, under the mistaken belief that most of the men wanted to be soldiers, had no concrete plans for the organization's future. State Secretary Fröhlich admitted as much when he told the Council of Interior Ministers that "after the BGS was called upon to build up the Bundeswehr, it was not given a clear and contradictory position in the security system of the Federal Republic."[94]

---

92 Press, Rundfunk, Fernsehen, Gewerkschaft der Polizei, "BGS-Gesetzentwurf verfassungswidrig," May 18, 1971, BArch-K, B 106/83876.
93 Ibid.
94 Staatssekretär Fröhlich, "Entwurf: eines Sprechzettels," 2, BArch-K, B 106/83876.

Although factually correct, Kuhlmann's complaints about the legal position of the BGS also revealed federalist tensions over jurisdiction and jobs. At the time of its foundation, constitutional concerns about the potential encroachment of federal officers into state policing matters created the most debate during the draft's first reading in the Bundesrat (Federal Council).[95] Kuhlmann's opposition to Genscher's proposed revisions was the latest chapter in an ongoing campaign he had been waging against the BGS for many years. An Op-Ed in the conservative weekly *Christ und Welt* accused Kuhlmann of targeting the BGS because he had failed to gain a foothold in the organization for the GdP.[96] More likely, however, he feared a newly reformed BGS might supplant state police forces or intrude upon state affairs during a national emergency. Thus his criticism can be attributed more to his role as an advocate for his own constituents rather than his belief that the BGS might undermine West German democracy. Moreover, his complaints about its military equipment and combatant status were less convincing and somewhat disingenuous, considering that state police forces still used infantry weapons. The state police also employed former Nazis and promoted militarized tactics. Riot Police chief Carl Boysen, for example, had been a high-ranking Nazi police officer during the war. In 1967 Boysen requested, and the Conference of Interior Ministers approved, an equipment list that included high-explosives, hand grenades, mortars, and machine-guns.[97]

Cooperative and Constructive Federalism

Another factor that undermined Kuhlmann's complaints about the BGS was Genscher's willingness to collaborate on the draft with his counterparts in West Germany's state interior ministries. Thus from the start Kuhlmann lacked political support from key state officials who led the departments he represented, or from anyone serving on the Conference of Interior Ministers. Only representatives from Bavaria and Hesse challenged the proposed revisions during the bill's first reading at the Bundesrat. The Bavarians, motivated by a desire to preserve their own border guard, questioned any legal changes they believed might jeopardize its jurisdiction. The Hessians argued that the draft was

---

95 David Parma, *Installation und Konsolidierung des Bundesgrenzschutzes*, 396–98.
96 Wolfgang Höpker, "Bundesgrenzschutz—Bonns Feuerwehr: Neue Aufgaben für die Eingreifreserve des Bundeswehr," *Christ und Welt* (June 23, 1972).
97 Inspector Boysen ÖS II 3—M 640 205/9, "Ausbildung und Ausstattung der Polizei im Hinblick auf Artikel 87a GG, Berichterstattung: Nordrhein-Westfalen," June 20, 1968, 1, BArch-K, B 106/83920; Klaus Weinhauer, *Schutzpolizei in der Bundesrepublik*, 298–302, 141–66.

unconstitutional and invalid without significant amendments to the Basic Law. Nevertheless, in spite of their challenges, neither the Bavarian nor the Hessian motions to dismiss the law gained support.[98] Once the draft finally reached the Bundestag on June 22, 1972, it passed unanimously. During the second reading, Heinz Schwarz, the state Interior Minister from Rhineland-Palatinate called the draft "An important contribution to a security concept that meets the requirement of our time."[99]

How did Genscher and his Interior Ministry manage to gain such overwhelming support for a law that gave the federal government the most emergency police powers it had wielded since the Third Reich? Even the controversial combatant status provision survived the final reading. Not everyone, however, believed deploying the BGS for internal security was a good idea. An Op-Ed in the *Deutsches Allgemeines Sonntagsblatt*, for example, complained: "The exception has become the rule and the state of emergency has become the norm."[100] Genscher succeeded in large part because he collaborated with the states and ensured that no part of the law infringed upon their sovereignty in police matters. The growing fears of the population about rising crime and terrorism, exemplified by the RAF's recent bombings and high-profile attacks, made consolidating the state's internal security forces a matter of great urgency.

Years in the making, the new law finally took effect on August 19, 1972. Less than a month later, however, West Germany's internal security faced its darkest hour as PFLP terrorists took members of the Israeli wrestling team hostage during the Olympic Games in Munich.

---

98 David Parma, *Installation und Konsolidierung des Bundesgrenzschutzes*, 398–400.
99 Protocol, Deutscher-Bundestag, 195 Sitzung, June 22, 1972, 11460.
100 Bernd C. Hesslein, "Bürgerschutz mit Mörsern und Panzern," *Deutsches Allgemeines Sonntagsblatt* (July 16, 1972).

CHAPTER NINE

FROM MUNICH TO MOGADISHU: FIGHTING TERRORISM AT HOME AND ABROAD

The Federal Republic's new Program for Internal Security faced an extreme test just thirteen days after the revised Border Police Act took effect. Eight Palestinian terrorists from Black September attacked the Israeli team during the Olympic Games in Munich. The attackers killed weightlifter Yossef Romano and wrestling coach Moshe Weinberg while holding the rest of the athletes hostage at their Olympic Village quarters. The terrorists threatened to kill the hostages unless Israel released 234 Palestinian prisoners; they also demanded that the Germans release jailed RAF leaders Andreas Baader and Ulrike Meinhof. In the words of ABC Sportscaster Jim McCay "The Olympics of serenity have become the one thing the Germans didn't want them to be, the Olympics of terror."[1] The attack caught the Federal Republic's security services and their leaders completely by surprise. Interior Minister Genscher's high hopes for a spirit of cooperative federalism were crushed by the bureaucratic gridlock reflected in the blundered rescue attempt and murder of all the Israeli athletes.

Although scholars have focused extensively on Germany's first Olympic Games since the Third Reich, and their tragic ending in particular, the involvement of border police officers in these pivotal events is missing from most of these accounts.[2] To be sure, one of Genscher's main

---

1   Diane Bernard, "50 years after Munich Olympics attack, victims' families are compensated," *Washington Post* (September 5, 2022), available online at https://www.washingtonpost.com/history/2022/09/05/munich-olympics-terrorism-1972/.

2   See for example, David Clay Large, *Munich 1972: Tragedy, Terror, and Triumph at the Olympic Games* (New York: Rowan & Littlefield, 2012); Kay Schiller and Christopher Young, *The 1972 Munich Olympics and the Making of Modern Germany* (Berkeley: University of California Press, 2010); Bernhard Fischer, "Die Olympischen Spiele in München: Sicherheitskonzept und Attentat im Spiegel der Akten des Sicherheitsbeauftragten im Bayerischen Staatsministerium des

justifications for revising the Border Police Act in 1972 was to use the BGS as a reserve that could support the state police in national emergencies just like the attack in Munich. Border police officers had proven their usefulness during nationwide manhunts that helped state police forces capture the RAF's leaders. The violence perpetrated by the RAF in the years leading up to the Olympics convinced West Germany's politicians to support Chancellor Willy Brandt's call for more Internal Security.[3] Yet at a time when they needed them most, Genscher and Munich Police chief Manfred Schreiber kept the BGS sidelined. Instead, they sent Munich Police officers who lacked the proper weapons and tactical training to carry out a high-stakes hostage rescue operation.

Despite the Federal Republic's reputation as a successful liberal democracy, terrorism pushed it closer than it ever had been during the postwar era to an authoritarian national security state. Its militant democracy became more militant. As sociologists Ian Loader and Neil Walker have suggested "States—even those that claim with some justification to be liberal or democratic—have a capacity when self-consciously pursuing a condition called security to act in a fashion injurious to it ... they proceed in ways that trample over the basic civil liberties of citizens ... or that extend the coercive reach of the state ..."[4] West Germany faced this same dilemma during its response to terrorism during the 1970s. The violent attacks by the RAF in the years before the Olympics and its alliance with Palestinian and other leftwing militant groups conjured fears of the political violence that brought down the Weimar Republic. The challenge for West Germany's politicians was to find ways to preserve democracy without destroying it in the process—or, as Chancellor Willy Brandt warned, trying to "withstand hysterical reactions and allow as little injury as possible to the constitutional state."[5]

In West Germany, as in the United States in the aftermath of the 9/11 attacks, terrorism produced a sense of panic and fear that underscored the

---

Innern und der Staatsanwaltschaft München I" (Diplomarbeit: Universität München, 2006).

3 J. Smith and André Moncourt, eds., *The Red Army Faction: A Documentary History, Volume I: Projectiles for the People* (Montreal: Kersplebedeb, 2009), 178; See also "Blasts at US Base in Germany Kill 3," *New York Times*, May 25, 1972; Hans-Anton Papendieck, "Schatten über der heilen Welt des Bundesgrenzschutz: Beim BGS-Kommando Nord keine Ausbildungsübertretungen festgestellt, Gespräch mit Generale Kühne," *Hannoversche Allgemeine Zeitung*, March 19, 1973, 1, BA-MA, BH 28-2-387; Karrin Hanshew, *Terror and Democracy*; Stefan Aust, *Baader-Meinhof: The Inside Story of the R.A.F.* (New York: Oxford University Press, 2008).

4 Ian Loader and Neil Walker, *Civilizing Security* (New York: Cambridge University Press, 2007), 7.

5 Willi Brandt, *My Life in Politics* (New York: Viking, 1992), 262.

robust security measures that followed. The Federal Republic responded by introducing unprecedented levels of state intervention and police surveillance into the everyday lives of West German citizens.[6] The BGS played a key role in the government's responses and this cemented its permanent place in the Federal Republic's Internal Security infrastructure. After the Munich attacks, for example, Genscher created an elite BGS counterterrorism unit—Grenzschutzgruppen-9 (GSG-9). The idea for the new unit came from his charismatic adjutant, Ulrich Wegener, who was by his side during the botched rescue attempt in Munich. Modeled on the Israeli Special Forces, GSG-9 immediately raised suspicions on the left, since the idea of "elite" units summoned images of Nazi Germany's SS and police troops. GdP Chairman Werner Kuhlmann called GSG 9 an assassination squad and renewed his demand that the BGS be eliminated altogether. Kuhlmann's accusations, however, had little effect on most West Germans, who demanded more security in the wake of these violent terrorist attacks. In 1977, GSG 9's dramatic rescue of hostages aboard a hijacked Lufthansa airliner in Mogadishu symbolically righted the wrongs at Munich and turned Wegener's men into national heroes. Even the press began calling them "Bonn's Fire Brigade."[7] Although Kuhlmann failed to turn politicians and citizens against the BGS, he still succeeded in exposing its militarized training and practices to the public—a fact that the Interior Ministry could no longer ignore. Thus, like the press, Kuhlmann's GdP formed another institution of the critical public sphere—a "watchful observer" that engaged the state in a discursive process of "contestation" and helped tame the authoritarian impulses of its response to terrorism.[8]

The BGS and Security at the Olympic Games in Munich

For all the effort and debate between 1968 and 1972 about the use of BGS units to support the state police, it would seem that an event like the Olympics would be an ideal opportunity to use them. The games were symbolically important for West Germany. It was the first time a German city had hosted the Olympics since 1936, when Hitler's Third Reich was in power. Bruno Merk, the Bavarian Interior Minister, had jurisdiction

6   Karrin Hanshew, *Terror and Democracy*, 146–47.
7   In 1971 BGS units helped rescue hostages and captured the suspects in a violent bank robbery in Cologne: see UPI, "Cologne Bank Robbed; Police Hostages Freed," *New York Times*, December 28, 1971, 5; Wolfgang Höpker, "Bundesgrenzschutz—Bonns Feuerwehr: Neue Aufgaben für die Eingreifreserve des Bundeswehr," *Christ und Welt*, June 23, 1972, BA-MA, BH 28-2-387.
8   Ian Loader and Neil Walker, *Civilizing Security*, 221–23.

over security for the Olympics, but the architect of the security plan was his subordinate, Munich's Police President Manfred Schreiber. Schreiber was already well known for his low-key approach to law enforcement and use of de-escalation.[9] His security plans for the Olympics, however were based on promoting a "cheerful" image of the games to the outside world instead of focusing on contingencies for dealing with violent incidents. He and others on his team ignored intelligence shared by the BfV concerning potential terrorist attacks and he later claimed these warnings were so routine that he could not act on each one.[10]

The BGS joined police forces from all over West Germany that were called upon to support the Munich Police during the Olympics. Schreiber, however, was reluctant to use border police units, because he feared they would personify the militarized images that he tried so hard to avoid. The BGS with their military uniforms, Wehrmacht-style helmets, and armored vehicles looked and acted more like soldiers than police officers. Schreiber expressed these concerns in a letter to the Interior Ministry and, as an example, pointed to the recent Hans-Braun sports festival, where heavily armed security personnel with police dogs patrolled the venues.[11] His solution to prevent such displays in Munich was to create a special unit called the *Ordnungsdienst* (Security Service). The unit included police officers from all over West Germany who volunteered to serve on paid leave from their regular assignments and were temporarily placed under the command of the Bavarian state police. The Security Service included 900 border police officers.[12]

Schreiber's vision for the Security Service followed his preference for keeping police officers out of sight. He wanted officers who were athletes so that they could seamlessly blend in with competitors and guests. He also recruited fifty women from the Federal Republic's State Criminal Police forces for the Security Service, because he believed they had better

9 Eckard Michels, *Schahbesuch 1967*, 162.
10 See Schreiber's post-attack interview, "Mal der eine Falke, mal der andere Taube," *Der Spiegel* 38, September 10, 1972.
11 Letter, Dr. Manfred Schreiber, Organisationskomitee für die Spiele der XX. Olympiade München 1972 an Oberstleutnant im BGS Krassmann, Bundesministerium des Innern, "Verhalten und Erscheinungsbild von Ordnungskräften im weiteren Sinne bei Strassenwettbewerben," September 20, 1971, BArch-K, B106/371832, Band III; "Viel Polizei—wenig Organisation: Drei bekannte Sport-Journalisten kommentieren den vorolympischen Test," *Münchner Merkur*, September 7, 1971; Martin Maier, "Klischeebilder," *AZ Zürich Sport*, August 14, 1970.
12 See "Vereinbarung über die Abstellung von Angehörigen des Bundesgrenzschutzes zum Ordnungsdienst des Organisationskomitees für die Spiele der XX. Olympiade München 1972," BArch-K, B106/371832, Band II.

verbal communication skills than their male colleagues.[13] Schreiber also hired officers who could speak foreign languages, because he wanted members of the Security Service to be "ambassadors" for West Germany's international guests. Olympic Committee Chairman Willy Daume wrote to the police officers that volunteered for the Security Services and reminded them : "The awarding of the Twentieth Olympiad to us reflects worldwide trust. There have not been many examples yet for the world to restore this trust. And the land in which we live still has some room to improve. The games are a great opportunity for the world to know a different Germany than the one that many of our guests may still remember. A peace-loving Germany that would like to spread friendship and goodwill throughout the world."[14]

Remarkably, Schreiber prohibited members of the Security Service from carrying firearms. The officers had no police or arrest powers, and wore light-blue tracksuits instead of uniforms. Each member was assigned a pistol, but they remained in storage in their quarters at the *Werner Kaserne*, seven kilometers away from the Olympic Village.[15] BGS officials raised the alarm about the risks of these policies and criticized the general low-key approach of Schreiber's security plan. Genscher's adjutant, Colonel Ulrich Wegener, for example, claimed that even senior members of the Munich Police thought that outfitting the Security Service in what he called "weird" tracksuits and prohibiting them from carrying firearms was foolish. In an emergency, how were the officers to access pistols stored seven kilometers away? BGS officials at the Interior Ministry also questioned the wisdom of placing border police officers in units with their state police colleagues because they had been trained differently.[16]

---

13 Protokoll, Sitzung der Arbeitsgruppe Polizei-Führungsstab: Ordnungsreferent Hermann Wöhrle, Abteilung XIII, July 15, 1971, "Aufgaben, Organisation und Arbeitsweise des Ordnungsdienstes und seine Abgrenzung zur Polizei," BArch-K, B106/371828.

14 For Willi Daume's personal letter to members of the Ordnungsdienst see Hermann Wöhrle, Organisationskomitee für die Spiele der XX. Olympiade München 1972, Abteilung XIII: Der Ordnungsbeauftragte, "Lehrprogramme für den Ordnungsdienst," 13. April 1972, BArch-K, B106/371828.

15 See "Grenzschutzkommando Süd: Einsatz des BGS während der XX. Olympischen Spiele 1972 in München—Organisationsübersicht: 1. GSOD (Grenzschutzordnungsdienst), Ausrüstung, Geräte, Waffen," January 27, 1972, BArch-K, B106/371830.

16 Ulrich Wegener, Ulrike Zander, and Harald Biermann, *GSG 9: Stärker als der Terror* (Berlin: Lit Verlag Dr. W. Hopf: 2017), 36; minutes from Olympic Committee Meeting, September 5, 1970, "Besprechung: über Probleme der Abstellung von Polizeibeamten zur Verstärkung der örtlichen Polizeikräfte und für den Ordnungsdienst des Organisationskomitees," 3, BArch-K, B 106/371830.

Schreiber refused to consider allowing the BGS to operate independently of the Bavarian Police authorities or reverse his policies against firearms. To address the Interior Ministry's concerns regarding training, he required that all Security Service members attend a mandatory five-day seminar at Munich's Police Training Institute.[17] The seminar had little to do with security or what to do in the case of a violent incident. Instead, the topics covered the history of the Olympics, basic psychology, and de-escalation techniques for crowd control, which the organizers believed would be their biggest security challenge of the games. Schreiber, the resident expert on de-escalation, taught a course on using verbal skills to defuse potential conflicts.[18] Instead of firearms, Schreiber armed members of the Security Service with whistles and air horns to distract potential demonstrators. The use of police officers in this manner—as docents rather than executors of the state's coercive powers—might have worked for diffusing protestors, but rendered them useless against violent attackers. In their study of the Munich Olympics, Kay Schiller and Chris Young emphasized that the Security Service was largely effective given its instructions for a soft approach to security, but Schreiber's decision to use it to "charm the public and execute its duties with a light touch certainly assisted the terrorists in the first instance."[19]

Interior Minister Genscher claimed that he had complete confidence in Schreiber, and because of his reputation in Munich, he called him the "right man" for the job.[20] But Schreiber put too much emphasis on avoiding embarrassing security displays and not enough on what to do in the case of a violent incident. Without question, he was under intense pressure from International Olympic Committee Chairman, Avery Brundage, and its Organizing Committee Chair, Willy Daume, to promote a spirit of openness and cheerfulness. Instead of using the BGS for its strengths—better weapons and tactical training—Schreiber kept it concealed. Its only visible presence was its helicopters, which the Bavarians relied upon to move dignitaries and VIPs between the different venues.[21] Besides the border police officers who volunteered for the Security Service, the BGS contributed one alert company (100 men) that was placed on reserve in

---

17 Dr. Manfred Schreiber to Herr Gründemann at the Interior Ministry, "Seminare für die Führungskräfte des Ordnungsdienstes," March 15, 1972, BArch-K, B106/371830.
18 Ibid.
19 Kay Schiller and Chris Young, *The 1972 Munich Olympics*, 308–9.
20 Hans-Dietrich Genscher, *Erinnerungen* (Munich: Verlag, 1995), 148.
21 Bavarian Interior Ministry Director Dr. Stroll to Federal Interior Ministry, November 19, 1971, "Vorbereitung der Olympischen Spiele 1972," BArch-K, B106/371842.

the Munich region.[22] This company had armored cars and heavy weapons, but it was 90 minutes driving time from the Olympic Village, and its personnel were only available between the hours of 8:00 am and 8:00 pm. Border police command south (GSK-Süd) also had two full divisions with over 1,000 men stationed at various locations throughout the Bavarian region, which could be called up if needed.[23]

Overall, the Olympic games proceeded on schedule with few disruptions and seemed to be on course to achieve the objective of showcasing all that was good about modern West Germany. It thus came as a complete shock to Schreiber and his security team on September 5 when they first learned that eight heavily armed Palestinian terrorists had scaled the flimsy perimeter fence of the Olympic Village and attacked the Israeli athletes quartered at 31 Connolly Strasse.[24] The terrorists killed Moshe Weinberg and Yossef Romano when they tried to fight back, and then barricaded themselves in the apartment, threatening to kill all the remaining hostages unless their demands were met. Bavarian Interior Minister Bruno Merk managed the incident and set up a "crisis staff" to negotiate with the terrorists. The staff was led by Manfred Schreiber, but also included, Genscher, Israeli Ambassador Eliashiv Ben-Horin, and other officials.[25] Israeli Prime Minister Golda Meir made it clear from the beginning that there would be no deal with the terrorists. Meir placed Israel's elite counterterrorism unit, the Sayeret Matkal, one of the very few forces capable of hostage rescue operations, on alert. She also dispatched the head of Israel's Mossad (secret services), Zvi Zamir, and his assistant, Victor Cohen, to Munich.[26] In his memoirs, Genscher claimed that he asked Zamir repeatedly to use Israel's forces for the rescue attempt, but he refused. Zamir denied ever being asked by anyone on the German side to intervene and recalled that the Bavarians in particular "were extremely hostile to us throughout, literally refusing to talk to us. Genscher and our Ambassador in Bonn [Ben-Horin], had to intervene again and again."[27]

---

22 See letter from BGS-Inspekteur Grüner to Bundesministerium des Innern, June 27, 1972, "Entsendung von Verbanden des Bundesgrenzschutzes zur Verstärken der bayer. Polizei aus Anlass der Spiele der XX. Olympiade in München in 1972," BArch-K, B106/371832, Band II.

23 See letter from BGS Oberstleutnant Thelen to Bundesminsterium des Innern, July 2, 1972, "Vorbereitung der Olympischen Spiele 1972," BArch-K, B106/371832, Band II.

24 For the attack see David Clay Large, *Munich 1972*, 242; see also Simon Reeve, *One Day in September: The Full Story of the 1972 Munich Olympics Massacre and the Israeli Revenge Operation Wrath of God* (London: Faber and Faber, 2005).

25 David Clay Large, *Munich 1972*, 238.

26 Simon Reeve, *One Day in September*, 94.

27 Genscher, *Erinnerungen*, 151; Reeve, *One Day in September*, 94.

FROM MUNICH TO MOGADISHU ♦ 235

What happened in the hours that followed the seizure of the Israeli hostages has been the subject of numerous books and movies.[28] Despite repeated attempts to negotiate with the terrorists, the crisis team could do no more than stall for time because they had nothing to offer in return for the hostages. When they ran out of options, Schreiber decided to mount a rescue attempt, but made a series of disastrous mistakes in how they would carry it out.[29] Finally, the crisis team decided to allow the terrorists to move with their captives to Fürstenfeldbruck airfield on the false promise that they would be allowed to fly to Egypt. BGS helicopters flew them from Connolly Strasse to the airfield. Schreiber planned for a surprise assault on the terrorists at the airfield. In his study of the attempt, David Clay Large described it as "a masterpiece of incompetence, a veritable textbook demonstration of how *not* to conduct operations of this sort." Colonel Ulrich Wegener, who witnessed the blundered operation with Genscher from the control tower, called the plans by the Munich police "A complete joke."[30] When the terrorists arrived at the airfield, they left the athletes restrained in the helicopters and walked out onto the field to inspect the jet parked nearby. When Munich police officers opened fire, they only managed to hit one terrorist. In the deadly firefight that ensued, the terrorists murdered all the Israeli athletes.[31]

In the aftermath of the incident, the Munich Police finally activated the BGS alert company, but only to guard the bloody crime scenes on Connolly Strasse and the Fürstenfeldbruck airfield. The company also provided security for West German and Israeli officials attending the memorial services for the victims held on September 6.[32] Why did neither Schreiber nor Genscher call upon members of the BGS during the incident? Border police officers had spent years training to fight insurgents and were certainly better qualified than the Munich Police to attempt such a dangerous assault. Moreover, twenty-two border police officers from the Security Service were competitive sharpshooters and had better rifles than those used by the Munich Police.[33] The failure of anyone

---

28 Steven Spielberg's controversial 2005 film, *Munich*, as well as a documentary based on Simon Reeve's book, *One Day in September*, are only two examples of the interest generated by the 1972 events.

29 For a full description of these decisions, see David Clay Large, *Munich 1972*, 276–94; see also Simon Reeve, *One Day in September*.

30 Ibid., 238; Ulrich Wegener, *GSG 9: Stärker als der Terror*, 37.

31 Ibid.

32 Oberleutnant i. BGS Prasse, Grenzschutzabteilung II/1 Nabburg, 4. Januar 1973, "Erfahrungsbericht über den Einsatz der I. GSA zur Unterstützung der Polizei anlässlich der Spiele zur XX. Olympiade in München," BArch-K, B106/371829.

33 See personnel rosters attached to a letter from Staatssekretär Fröhlich to all BGS Commands, "Olympische Spiele 1972 in München, Bereitstellung von

Figure 9.1. Aftermath: September 5, 1972, one of two BGS helicopters in which the Israeli athletes were murdered during the bloody firefight at Munich's Fürstenfeldbruck Airfield. Photo by Heinz Gebhardt, courtesy of IMAGO.

on the crisis team to consider deploying BGS units, or for that matter, Genscher's reluctance to insist upon it, laid bare the fallacy of his ideas about cooperative and constructive federalism. Ongoing tensions over police sovereignty between the state and federal government stood against the chances of a successful outcome to the crisis. The federal government's fear of treading on state jurisdiction outweighed the logic of using the best trained personnel for the rescue. Although Mossad Chief Zamir believed it was Chancellor Brandt who ultimately decided against using Israeli special forces for the assault, he also observed that Genscher let the Bavarian officials run the operations.[34]

Bavaria's politicians had a history of resisting the federal police concept because they believed it might supplant their own state police. They voted against any laws that proposed using the BGS for state police matters, most recently, by joining Hesse to oppose the 1972 revisions to the Border Police Act. Yet since the new law only took effect three weeks before the Olympics began, neither the Interior Ministry nor officials

---

Verbänden des BGS für Aufgaben der Bayerischen Polizei und Entsendung von Angehörigen des BGS zum Ordnungsdienst," BArch-K, B 106/88817; see also BGS Oberstleutnant Naujokat, "Mit modernen Polizeiwaffen," *Die Parole* 5 (May 28, 1961): 12.

34 Simon Reeve, *One Day in September*, 95.

from West Germany's states considered how the changes might affect an actual emergency. Section 8 of the law still required a state's consent before the BGS could be deployed, and this helps to explain the bureaucratic quagmire that Genscher struggled with during the hostage crisis. According to David Clay Large, the Bavarians "were extremely prickly in matters of state sovereignty in general and control over the Munich Games in particular."[35] Moreover, Schreiber finalized his security plan long before the new law passed. Wegener recalled telling Genscher that the Bavarian plans for the rescue mission "contradicts all the basic tactical rules," but Genscher simply told Wegener that "a lot of the police don't know about that."[36] Thus the tensions over police sovereignty and jurisdiction is the most plausible explanation for why BGS units remained in their barracks during the crisis. The horrific murder of the athletes resulted from a complete systemic failure rather than any one thing or person in particular. Genscher later explained that the federal government had "no police responsibility in this case. That's why I could only support the authorities of the City of Munich and the Free State of Bavaria ... the police operation in Munich and in Fürstenfeldbruck was the sole responsibility of the Bavarian state government." Yet at the same time he also felt personally responsible for the outcome and offered to resign for not intervening. But Chancellor Brandt refused and explained that, "... the federal government was not responsible in view of the police sovereignty of the federal states."[37] Wegener observed this bureaucratic nightmare firsthand during the firefight on the airfield, when he pleaded with the head of Bavaria's Riot Police to intervene and save at least some of the hostages, to which he replied, "I have no orders, I have to wait for someone to come and give me an order." Wegener recalled that watching from the control tower as the Israeli's were murdered was one of the most "traumatic events of my career."[38]

"We have to make sure nothing like this ever happens again!"

The news of the failed rescue and death of all the Israeli hostages shocked those around the world who were watching as ABC news anchor Jim McKay solemnly corrected reports that the athletes had been saved and confirmed the horrific news that they were "all gone."[39] Wegener said he

35   David Clay Large, *Munich 1972*, 288.
36   Ulrich Wegener, *GSG 9: Stärker als der Terror*, 37.
37   For Genscher's explanation and Brandt's response, see Genscher, *Erinnerungen*, 150, 158–60.
38   Ibid.
39   Kay Schiller, and Chris Young, *The 1972 Munich Olympics*, 309.

had "seldom seen Genscher so upset ... it affected him very much that he had not been able to use his own will to prevent the catastrophe." Genscher told Wegener "I have to report this to the Chancellor and we must now consider what we must do ... we have to make sure nothing like this ever happens again!"[40] Wegener took the opportunity to propose the formation of a West German counterterrorism force, to which Genscher readily agreed. Wegener suggested that the new force should come from the BGS and volunteered to lead it. Wegener told Genscher "We don't need any more criminalists, we need a special unit that can take troop action against these terrorists." On September 26, 1972, Genscher gave the order to form the unit. Since there were eight border guard groups (*Grenzschutzgruppen*—GSG), the new unit was designated as its ninth, or GSG 9. A few days later, Colonel Wegener was on his way to Israel to work with its special clandestine counterterrorism forces—Mossad and Sayeret Matkal—from which, among other international examples, he developed the concept for GSG 9.[41] Building the new unit took time, and it was not ready for action until mid-1973.

Genscher later said his decision to strengthen the police and create GSG 9 followed his belief: "The response of the free constitutional state will be all the more effective the less the free constitutional state allows itself to give up its principles in whole or in part."[42] Yet his response to terrorism in the years leading up to Munich stood in stark contrast to such claims. In January 1972, for example, the Conference of Interior Ministers passed the Anti-radical decree (*Radikalenerlaß*) banning anyone belonging to specific organizations from the civil service. The controversial decree also required civil service applicants to undergo invasive background checks, even for jobs that did not need security clearances.[43] Genscher's Interior Ministry, in cooperation with the state governments, and the BKA also carried out nationwide manhunts targeting the RAF and its supporters or, for that matter, anyone considered to be affiliated with leftwing political views. By contrast, no operations of this scale were implemented to deal with groups on the radical right. Yet during the 1970s, groups such as the *Wehrsportgruppe* Hoffmann (Military Sports Group—WSG) also carried out violent terrorist attacks. Unlike the RAF, however, these groups operated clandestinely and thus

40   Hans-Dietrich Genscher to Ulrich Wegener on the formation of GSG 9, quoted in Ulrich Wegener, *GSG 9: Stärker als der Terror*, 40.
41   He also studied the US Special Forces, the FBI, and the British SAS, See Ulrich Wegener, *GSG 9: Stärker als der Terror*, 43.
42   The dialogue quoted between Wegener and Genscher comes from Ulrich Wegener, *GSG 9: Stärker als der Terror*, 39–40.
43   Gerard Braunthal, *Political Loyalty and Public Service in West Germany: The 1972 Decree against Radicals and Its Consequences* (Amherst: University of Massachusetts Press, 1990), 23–28.

avoided the spotlight, relieving the government of public pressure to act. In 2012, newly declassified documents proved that two Neo-Nazis provided direct support to the Black September terrorists who carried out the Munich attacks.[44]

During the RAF's May 1972 offensive, the BGS deployed thousands of officers as part of a *Sondersicherheitsgruppe* (Special Security Group) of 14,930 police officers under the overall command of BKA Chief Horst Herold. The BGS also contributed 34 helicopters and hundreds of vehicles to support this massive operation.[45] Border police units set up checkpoints on the autobahns and used helicopters to move officers anywhere they might be needed.[46] The massive operations targeting the RAF and other leftwing groups represented the largest use of civilian police power in postwar West Germany. The surge of police officers, and the checkpoints along the autobahns in particular, subjected West Germans to unprecedented levels of state intervention and surveillance. The presence of so many officers prompted accusations by the left that the Federal Republic had become an authoritarian or fascist police state. Brandt's administration was caught between calls by conservatives for more security and complaints by leftwing Social Democrats and student groups that the state had become fascist.[47] It was not too difficult to see why critics accused the state of overreach. During the extensive manhunts, border police officers were given specific instructions to profile drivers and their vehicles for random detentions. For example, officers detained any persons in vehicles with, among many other features, two radio antennas or any emblems they deemed to be suspicious.[48] As a result, the BGS conducted 210,218 vehicle and 254,199 person searches across more than 1,258 checkpoints. The officers, however, often exceeded the mission of searching for RAF suspects and took the opportunity to seize cars, weapons, jewelry, radios, and cash from crimes that had nothing to do with terrorism.[49] The searches had a powerful effect on the thousands of

---

44 Daniel Koehler, *Right-Wing Terrorism*; Barbara Manthe, "On the Pathway to Violence: West German Right-Wing Terrorism in the 1970s," *Terrorism and Political Violence* 33, no. 1 (2021): 56.

45 See memorandum from BGS Inspektor Rudolf Grüner to all BGS Commands, May 31, 1972, "Fahndung im Bundesgebiet," BArch-K, B106/371806.

46 Telex from Bundesministerium des Innern, May 31, 1972 to BGS II, BArch-K, B106/371806.

47 Timothy Scott Brown, *West Germany and the Global Sixties*, 35; Karrin Hanshew, *Terror and Democracy*, 4–5, 121.

48 See "Hinweise für Kfz.- und Personenüberprüfungen bei der Großfahndung nach anarchistischen Gewalttätern," BArch-K, B 106/391705.

49 For a detailed breakdown of these searches and police/BGS resources, see Inter-office memorandum, May 6, 1972, Bundesministerium des Innern—BGS II 1, Gründemann, BArch-K, B106/371806, 1.

citizens caught in their web, not the least of which meant their travel was delayed or disrupted. As criminologists Leanne Weber and Ben Bowling have emphasized, "stop and search" tactics by the police are "a visceral manifestation of coercive and intrusive power and the most publicly visible interaction between state agent and citizen."[50]

Besides the manhunts, BGS telecommunications specialists assigned to its secret "*Gruppefernmeldewesen*" (Telecommunications Group/Group-F) unit, employed more invasive measures to target and root out the RAF. Group F, which Interior Ministry officials simply referred to as "the engineers," remained classified and unknown to West German citizens or politicians until the 1990s. The unit was formed in 1955 by veterans of the Gehlen Organization for counterespionage operations and surveillance of East German troops along the Iron Curtain. Since it operated clandestinely, it was free of parliamentary oversight that regulated the wiretapping activities of other West German security agencies.[51] In the 1970s, Group F engaged in wiretapping operations and used its powerful radio equipment to monitor the open communications of West Germans believed to be involved with or supporting members of the RAF and other leftist factions. The practice took on greater urgency when officials learned that RAF members had been monitoring police radio networks.[52] Although records of its activities remain largely classified, evidence suggests that Group F shared the personal data it collected with the Federal Republic's law enforcement and intelligence services. A confidential Interior Ministry memorandum shows that Group F leaders Saborowski and Idolski met with BKA Chief Horst Herold on July 19, 1972. Along with this memorandum, transcripts in the same archival collection show that Group F monitored RAF walkie-talkie broadcasts and telephone calls they intercepted from the Federal Post Office's telecommunications networks.[53] During 1994 Bundestag hearings, the government released

50 Leanne Weber and Ben Bowling, eds., *Stop and Search: Police Power in Global Context* (New York: Routledge, 2013), 1.

51 "Bundesgrenzschutz—Geheime Horchtruppe, *Der Spiegel* 20, May 15, 1994: "Die Nacht von Stammheim: Was wussten die Geheimdienste?" *Der Spiegel*, September 8, 2007; see also Stefan Aust, *Baader-Meinhof*, 428–29; for wiretapping laws, see James G. Carr, "Wiretapping in West Germany," *American Journal of Comparative Law* 29, no. 4 (Autumn 1981): 607–13.

52 Memorandum from Interior Ministry Public Security Branch to BGS Department Head, Dr. Karl Reuter, "Illegaler Fernmeldeverkehr von Mitgliedern der Baader-Meinhof-Bande," December 23, 1971, BArch-K, B 106/391705.

53 Interior Ministry Telecommunications Division, "Besprechung mit dem Leiter des *Bundeskriminalamtes* Herrn Dr. Herold am 19.7.1972 in Wiesbaden," participant list includes O. Saborowski and M. Idolski, Gruppe F; for reference to Federal Postal networks, see Dr. Fritsch, BKA to Interior Minister Genscher, "Illegaler Fernmeldeverkehr," December 2, 1972, BArch-K, B 106/391705.

a statement denying that Group F shared data with either the BND or BfV, but claimed in part that "All processes containing details of the organization, tasks and cooperation between the Federal Border Police telecommunications group and the Federal Office for the Protection of the Constitution are classified as Top Secret or Confidential, and thus questions can only be answered in accordance with public accessibility."[54]

While BGS Group F operated in the shadows, the automation of surveillance and intelligence gathering methods centralized police resources in the fight against the RAF. As Karrin Hanshew has suggested, the groundwork for these innovations had already been established long before the RAF began its attacks. Combating terrorism, however, gave BKA Chief Herold the edge in his struggle to centralize criminal intelligence over the resistance of West Germany's states, which favored their own fragmented systems.[55] BGS officers working in airports, manning checkpoints, and staffing border crossings became instruments in Herold's rational approach to crime fighting, which focused on gathering and storing massive amounts of personal data. Herold favored automated data collection so it could be easily accessible to officers in the field. In this way, security forces could locate terrorists and solve crimes using predictive patterns developed from the scientific analysis of data.[56] Thus BGS officers were linked by telex, computer networks, and VHF radios, which improved their ability to capture fugitive terrorists traversing through their checkpoints.

After the Olympic tragedy, and especially because of the link between Black September and the RAF, West Germany's counterterrorism campaign intensified. On September 8, 1972, just three days after the Munich attacks, Genscher called an emergency meeting that brought together all of his Public Security Department Heads with BGS Chief, Brigadier General Rudolf Grüner, and members of his staff.[57] Genscher rolled out a comprehensive security plan that targeted West Germany's Arabic population. He assigned Border police officers to assist BKA personnel guarding West German politicians and their families. They were also sent

---

54 Deutscher Bundestag 12. Wahlperiode, Drucksache 12/7290, "Überwachung des Funk- und Fernmeldeverkehrs durch den Bundesgrenzschutz," Antwort des Bundesregierung, 15. April 1994.

55 Karin Hanshew, *Terror and Democracy*, 116.

56 Matthew G. Hannah, *Dark Territory in the Information Age: Learning from the West German Census Controversies of the 1980s* (London: Routledge, 2010), 13–16; Dieter Schenk, *Der Chef: Horst Herold und das BKA* (Hamburg: Spiegel-Buchverlag, 1998), 230–38.

57 Referat ÖS 6, Niederschrift: "Terroristische Aktivitäten arabischer Untergrundorganisationen: Dienstbesprechung unter Vorsitz von Herrn Minister in München aus Anlaß des Anschlags auf die israelische Olympiamannschaft am 5.9.72," September 8, 1972, BArch-K, B 106/371829.

abroad to protect foreign missions and the offices of its national airline, Lufthansa.[58] Some of the more problematic measures focused on commercial airlines and airports. Genscher ordered, for example, that "all passengers from Arab countries" be banned from air travel, and also "the immediate termination of employment of all workers from Arab countries who are employed in aviation." All Arabs residing in West Germany illegally and any of those suspected of political activities were to be immediately deported. He banned all Palestinian Student and Workers Clubs (GUPA/GUPS) based in the Federal Republic. The Interior Ministry ordered border police officers to increase their surveillance of "foreigners of Arabic origin residing in federal territory and prevent the uncontrolled entry of all persons of Arabic origin"[59]

When democracies are attacked, the civil liberties-national security scale tilts towards a robust response; it is during these critical moments where the democratic rule of law is at its greatest peril. Ian Loader and Neil Walker's idiom that "Anxious citizens make bad democrats" certainly held true for the Federal Republic during its fight against terrorism. Something had to be done, but the intensification of security measures, data collection, and invasive surveillance threatened the civil liberties of its citizens. During the RAF's May 1972 offensive, for example, plain-clothes police officers in Stuttgart shot and killed 34-year-old Iain Macleod, an unarmed British salesman with no known ties to the terrorists. Macleod was sleeping when officers in civilian clothes covertly entered his apartment and surprised him. He was shot twice in the back through a bedroom door he had closed in a panicked attempt to escape. The Stuttgart police, in their haste to deal with recent RAF bomb threats, cut corners in their investigation and zeroed in on Macleod because RAF members rented his former apartment in the city center. Unfortunately, his name remained on the apartment's mailbox and he was still registered to the phone line. Archival evidence shows that the officers who killed Macleod may have acted in part on wiretap intelligence from his old phone line supplied by BGS Group F.[60] Although police officials initially stuck to the claim that Macleod was an RAF supporter, they eventually admitted there was no connection and that the officers who shot him overreacted.[61]

58 Ibid., 4.
59 Ibid., 4–6.
60 See Interior Ministry Telex no. 9258 2606 1425, Minister Genscher, State Secretary Rutschke, Director Smoydzin, "Lagebericht: stand June 26, 1972," BArch-K, B 106/391705; handwritten in blue ink on the Telex it states: "Meeting with Dr. Herold for the week of July 3–7, 1972, with GR-F (Gruppe-F), Idolski."
61 Hans Scheuler, "Der Fall Macleod: Stunde der Anfechtung," *Die Zeit*, July 28, 1972; Robert Chesshyre, "Shot Briton's friends accuse police," *Observer*, July 2, 1972, 4; "Ein brennendes Gefühl im Unterbauch: Spiegel-Interview mit

Fortunately, tragic incidents like the mistaken killing of Iain Macleod were exceptional, but the Federal Republic's response to terrorism, and its use of the clandestine BGS-Group F in particular, became pervasive. To understand how this happened in West Germany's democratizing postwar society, Ian Loader and Neil Walker's theories on "civilizing security" are once again instructive. Loader and Walker point to what they suggest are "pathologies" or conditions imbedded within modern policing and security "that variously help to give security its pervasive, uncivil forms …"[62] While critics on the left accused West Germany's government of eroding liberal democracy with authoritarian or fascist security policies, a better explanation frames its response to terrorism somewhere between the security conditions known as "paternalism" and "authoritarianism." Paternalistic states are those where professionals or government officials determine what security measures are in the best interests of keeping citizens safe without public input or oversight.[63] When left unchecked, a paternalistic state, such as the Federal Republic became in response to domestic terrorism, might become authoritarian because, as Loader and Walker argue "By seeking to act in the interests of citizens who cannot thereby be treated as equal partners in dialogue, paternalism lacks an adequate brake upon its pathological propensity to become opaque and self-corroborating … in ways that may not necessarily coincide with the values, concerns or interests of those whom it purports to serve."[64]

The Civilizing Effect of Kuhlmann's GdP

The intensification of security, and Genscher's establishment of GSG 9 in particular, are precisely what critics on the left pointed to as evidence that West Germany's counterterrorism policies had gone too far. On February 7, 1973, GdP Chairman Werner Kuhlmann told Genscher he had credible evidence to prove BGS instructors had committed criminal acts during training exercises. His allegations focused on information he obtained from twenty former border police officers who complained of harsh treatment by US Special Forces during the controversial 1964 military exercise—Operation South-Bavaria (*Übung Südbayern*—see chapter 5). At the time, Interior Ministry officials ignored the men's complaints and, without further inquiry, accepted the explanation of BGS Lieutenant

---

Stuttgarts Polizeipräsident Rau und Kripochef Frey über den Tod von Iain Macleod," *Der Spiegel* 28, July 2, 1972, 52–53.
62 Ian Loader and Neil Walker, *Civilizing Security*, 196–97.
63 Ibid., 199.
64 Ibid., 200.

Colonel Franz Sleik that they were exaggerating the extent of the incident.[65] Kuhlmann also reported that its chief helicopter training pilot, Colonel Erwin Knorr, had verbally and physically abused his trainees for years. According to statements by witnesses, Knorr often beat his trainees, causing significant physical injuries. Kuhlmann learned of Knorr's behavior from state police pilots who trained at the BGS flight school in Hangelar, where Knorr's nickname was "The Hangman of Hangelar." The magazine *Der Spiegel* also reported that it had obtained secret documents in which GSG 9 would be tasked to "Annihilate" rather than "Paralyze" terrorists.[66]

Kuhlmann publicized these allegations during a press conference on February 28, 1973, but refused to identify the officers that had been victimized, because he claimed the men feared retaliation. Genscher, who by this point was fed up with what seemed like Kuhlmann's endless complaints, worried that he might have discovered something that might cause a scandal. He told BGS Inspector Grüner that it "could not be ruled out" that Kuhlmann might have the evidence to prove some of his allegations.[67] On March 1, Genscher hired the former Ministry of Justice official Dr. Hermann Maassen to investigate the allegations and then requested an immediate audience with the Bundestag's Internal Affairs Committee to block Kuhlmann's demand for parliamentary hearings. Genscher did not take the allegations seriously because he told the members of the Internal Affairs Committee that Maassen's report would already be in his hands by March 20.[68]

Colonel Knorr, a decorated World War II fighter pilot, was somewhat of a legendary figure in the BGS. In 1957, he established its aviation unit and had been Chancellor Adenauer's personal pilot. Knorr was also one of the helicopter pilots who flew the Israeli athletes to the airfield before the doomed rescue attempt, an act for which he received the Federal Republic's highest award for bravery. He denied the allegations

---

65 Grenzschutzabteilung I/1, Lieutenant Colonel Franz Sleik, Nr. 114/64, VS-Nur für den Dienstgebrauch, to Grenzschutzkommando Süd, München, June 11, 1964, "Übungsüdbayern Erfahrungsbericht," BArch-K, B 106/83904; See also Ch. 5.

66 "Bundesgrenzschutz: Kleine Schwinger: Ein Geheimpapier gibt dem Streit um BGS-Ausbildungsmethoden einen neuen Stellenwert," *Der Spiegel* 12, March 18, 1973.

67 Confidential memorandum from BGS Inspector Grüner to Genscher, "Vorwürfe des Vorsitzenden der Gewerkschaft der Polizei gegen den Bundesgrenzschutz, Fernschreiben des Herrn Kuhlmann vom 2. März 1973," BArch-K, B 106/83904.

68 Genscher, "1. Bericht des Bundesministers des Innern vor dem Innenausschuß des Deutschen Bundestages am 14. März 1973, zu Vorwürfen gegen den Bundesgrenzschutz," 5, BArch-K, B106/83904.

against him and grounded himself from all flight operations pending the outcome of the case. Genscher, who held Knorr in the highest esteem because of his heroism at Munich, was not interested in getting to the truth of the matter. Instead, he viewed Kuhlmann's allegations as just the latest round in his ongoing effort to eliminate the BGS. In his memoirs, he admitted that without question he believed Knorr and hired Dr. Maassen to "quickly clear the smokescreen of those accusations."[69] Thus, from the outset Maassen's inquiry served to confirm Genscher's preconceived beliefs about Knorr's innocence rather than following a fact pattern from the evidence. Moreover, it took him just nineteen days to complete and submit his final analysis, in which he concluded "that there could be no question of a scandal."[70]

During his inquiry, Maassen did not speak with independent witnesses about the allegations. Instead, he relied on Interior Ministry documents such as Lieutenant Colonel Sleik's 1964 after-action report for Operation South Bavaria.[71] Maassen agreed the men in question had been criminally assaulted, but blamed US Special Forces and agreed with Sleik that they exaggerated the extent of their mistreatment. He spent a greater amount of time on the allegations against Knorr, but again, did not speak directly to the victims or seek independent witnesses. Instead, Maassen spoke with or received written statements from 42 graduates of the most recent helicopter training course in Hangelar (which Knorr did not teach). He also spoke to instructors from civilian flight schools and officials from West Germany's Federal Aviation Office. In summary, he found no evidence of harsh training methods or a pattern of violence. He argued that Knorr and the other instructors occasionally "tapped" or "nudged" their students to prevent them from making dangerous mistakes, which at times may have exceeded acceptable limits. Maassen also found that foul language was endemic in the flight school and suggested the instructors tone it down because "Greater restraint seems desirable for superiors."[72]

On the same day that Genscher received Maassen's final report, he shared its findings with the Internal Affairs Committee.[73] He also used the opportunity to address the allegation by Kuhlmann and *Der Spiegel* that GSG 9 intended to kill rather than arrest perpetrators. According to

69 Hans-Dietrich Genscher, *Erinnerungen*, 164.
70 Dr. Hermann Maassen, "Bericht betreffend die Vorwürfe der Gewerkschaft der Polizei gegen den Bundesgrenzschutz," March 20, 1973, 19, BArch-K, B 106/83904.
71 Ibid., 3.
72 Ibid., 18.
73 Genscher, "2. Bericht des Bundesministers des Innern vor dem Innenausschuß des Deutschen Bundestages am 20. März 1973, zu Vorwürfen gegen den Bundesgrenzschutz, BArch-K, B 106/83904.

Genscher, the claims about GSG 9 as some sort of "assassination squad" were taken out of context from fragments of leaked documents produced at a meeting with the Conference of Interior Ministers on September 15, 1972. During the meeting, BKA Chief Dr. Herold spoke about the murder of the Israelis in Munich and suggested that in the future, a terrorist might have to be killed if all other measures to resolve a given situation fail. Genscher explained that Herold's comments concerned a purely hypothetical scenario and did not reflect official policy.[74] He also took direct aim at critics of the BGS and commended its personnel for their dedicated service protecting West Germany's citizens. He reminded the committee that although the Federal Republic was a democracy and border police officers were not free of criticism, he "rejected any attempt to question the BGS since just under a year ago, all the parliamentary groups in the German Bundestag and the federal states committed themselves to it." His comments reflected that West Germany's response to terrorism fit Loader and Walker's model of a paternalistic approach/attitude towards security. This is all the more evident from Genscher's own recollection of these events, in which he claimed that: "In truth, therefore, the chief danger is the indolent majority, enjoying the blessings of our libertarian order, but leaving it to others to champion that order."[75]

Despite Maassen's report clearing Knorr, Bonn's Public Prosecutor's Office indicted him on 5 counts of assault under the color of authority.[76] Knorr pled not guilty and the case went to trial in 1975. The indictment was based on statements from five police pilot trainees who suffered visible injuries that included bruises and abrasions on their hands and faces, which prosecutors claimed could not have resulted from normal training practices. The accusations against Knorr covered a period of ten years, but due to the statute of limitations he could only be charged for crimes that occurred between 1969 and 1973. Prosecutors interviewed 120 border police officers and called more than twenty witnesses to testify at the trial, which was presided over by Helmut Quirini, a conservative magistrate and veteran soldier who also served as a prosecutor on the Nazi District Court in Cologne.[77]

The trial, which ended in Knorr's acquittal on all charges, exposed the tensions between conservatives and the left over the extent to which the government's responses to terrorism undermined its democracy. It

---

74 Ibid., 5.
75 Genscher, *Erinnerungen*, 170.
76 Hans Wüllenweber, "Staatsanwalt klagt Oberst Knorr an: Grenzschutz-Ausbilder soll Flugschüler geschlagen haben," *Weser-Kurier* (March 30, 1974), BA-MA, BH 28-2-387.
77 For Quirini's biography, see "Quirini: Bütt im Tribunal," *Der Spiegel* 36, September 3, 1959, 40–42.

also showed how legacies of the Nazi past and the collapse of Weimar Germany continued to inform and shape the attitudes of West Germans on both sides of the national security debate. For those on the left, Knorr's behavior reflected everything problematic about Genscher's Interior Ministry and the BGS in particular—an uncomfortable reminder of Nazi Germany's paramilitary forces. The revelations that border police officers participated in war games involving allegations of torture and that GSG 9 trained to "annihilate" its opponents were warning signs for Germans on the left. They fought back to avoid repeating mistakes of the past that ultimately paved the way for dictatorship and war. For conservatives and others on the political right, however, the Weimar Republic served as a warning that to preserve democracy, political violence in any form had to be crushed. To those on the right, West Germans who questioned the tough security policies that kept them safe were treasonous. In reporting on Knorr's acquittal, for example, the *Bild am Sonntag*, a popular weekly newspaper published by the conservative Axel Springer House, depicted Knorr as a martyr victimized by a leftist smear campaign that in the end made West Germany more vulnerable to its enemies. Judge Helmut Quirini's verdict acquitting Knorr captured this strand of conservatism when he called him, "An irreproachable officer" while referring to his alleged victims as "puppets" of the GdP.[78]

After Knorr's acquittal, Kuhlmann's campaign against the BGS lost momentum and conservatives dismissed his further criticisms as a by-product of trade union politics. Kuhlmann was motivated by a desire to block the Interior Ministry from treading on the police sovereignty of West Germany's states. Yet the challenges of dealing with terrorism often proved too much for state police authorities to handle alone, and they welcomed the BGS as a useful resource they could rely upon. Genscher convinced the Conference of State Interior Ministers and most West Germans that terrorism reflected a greater threat to their democracy than dangers posed by the militarized security forces deployed to fight it. He also had strong support from key political allies such as Willi Weyer (FDP) and Heinz Ruhnau (SPD), who shared his vision for the BGS.[79] Although Kuhlmann annoyed Genscher, his GdP was another institution of democratic accountability, which like the free press, kept the Federal Republic's paternalistic approach to national security from drifting closer to authoritarianism. When viewed through the sociological lens of the "principle of recognition," the GdP functioned as a tier in the public sphere that produced an example of what Loader and Walker suggest were "watchful observers and critical scrutinizers of state practices as well as being a conduit through which the state can engage in

78 Hans Wüllenweber, "Staatsanwalt klagt Oberst Knorr an."
79 Genscher, *Erinnerungen*, 163.

dialogue about what it means to think about and seek to realize security as a public good."[80] Thus, regardless of its final outcome, Knorr's indictment and trial were only possible because of the GdP. In an authoritarian state, Kuhlmann could have been jailed and his GdP banned. In the Federal Republic, however, he was a force its government had to reckon with. At the same time, even if his allegations against Knorr were part of a union motivated smear campaign, as some conservatives alleged, Knorr still exercised his own democratic rights to due process and cleared his name nonetheless.

GSG 9: We Can Deal with Any Situation

In spite of the accusations by Kuhlmann and other leftwing politicians that GSG 9 was intended to be an assassination squad, evidence shows that Wegener implemented processes to prevent that. Starting with a budget of 6.3 million DM, he set out to model GSG 9 on the counterterrorism units he studied during his trips to Israel, England, and the United States. He tried to create a special unit that could prevent another Munich tragedy, but intended that its personnel should be capable of handling any form of terrorism. Wegener, an avid reader, spent a significant amount of time learning about the motivations and tactics of the militant groups he might have to face. He read, for example, Carlos Marighella's influential *Manual for the Urban Guerilla* and also the writings of Ulrike Meinhof and Frantz Fanon.[81] His first priority was to select police officers who were not just physically fit and excellent sharpshooters, but could perform efficiently under the most extreme circumstances. Thus, in addition to the tough physical fitness exams, candidates for GSG 9 had to pass stringent psychological evaluations. The Interior Ministry contracted with the firm Studio-Z to screen the applicants.[82] The type of men Wegener sought to join his elite unit differed significantly from the masculine ideals the BGS emphasized for its personnel during the 1950s and 1960s, which were shaped by the influences of its Wehrmacht generation. Instead, he selected men who had what he describes as "psychological strength, good self-esteem and a stable identity." Nevertheless, for many West Germans, elite units still produced negative legacies of the Nazi past.[83]

---

80   Ian Loader and Neil Walker, *Civilizing Security*, 221.
81   Ulrich Wegener, *GSG 9: Stärker als der Terror*, 48.
82   See Letter from Herr Günther, Studio für Psychologische Unternehmens- und Behördenberatung, to Interior Minister Hans-Dietrich Genscher, "Psychologische Beratung der Spezialeinheit GSG 9: Angebot eines Beratervertrages," November 21, 1972, BArch-K, B106/88881.
83   Ulrich Wegener, *GSG 9: Stärker als der Terror*, 56; Karrin Hanshew, *Terror and Democracy*, 124.

With GSG 9, West Germany had a counterterrorism response unit similar to those in the Israeli Defense Forces, but the Interior Ministry still exercised great restraint in deploying it. According to Ulrich Wegener, "despite the internal security problem within the FRG, the establishment of GSG 9 did not guarantee universal acceptance of the unit—quite simply, it had to prove itself."[84] After Munich, many of the Federal Republic's state police forces began forming their own elite tactical units—*Spezialeinsatzkommandos* (SEK's)—which were comparable to the Special Weapons and Tactics Teams (SWAT) established by US police forces during the 1970s.[85] The states preferred to use their own SEK units and avoided calling upon GSG 9. In 1974, the Hamburg Police requested GSG 9 to support its security operations at the funeral of RAF prisoner Holger Meins, who died in prison after a hunger strike.[86] Wegener's unit also travelled with West Germany's Olympics Teams to provide security at the 1976 games in Innsbruck and Montreal. Yet the federalist tensions that proved so disastrous at Munich remained problematic. During the Olympics in Innsbruck, for example, Bavarian officials refused to house or support GSG 9 security personnel in order to discourage the federal government from sending them. According to a memorandum from the Interior Ministry's Security Branch "The Bavarian Interior Ministry will wait until there is an actual emergency before it will call GSG 9."[87]

During the 1970s, the Federal Republic continued its focus on commercial aviation and airport security measures. During 1975 alone, there were 151 airport security incidents in West Germany, including six that involved the taking of hostages. Most of these were still handled by state

---

84 Ulrich Wegener, "The Evolution of Grenzschutzgruppe (GSG) 9 and the Lessons of 'Operation Magic Fire' in Mogadishu," in *Force of Choice: Perspectives on Special Operations*, ed. Bernd Horn, J. Paul de B. Taillon, and David Last (Montreal: Queens University School of Policy Studies, 2004), 112.

85 SWAT—or special weapons and tactics teams were formed by the Los Angeles Police Department in the early 1970s to combat leftist terror cells like the Symbionese Liberation Army (SLA).

86 See letter from Hamburg Staatsrat Dahrendorf to Bundesministerium des Innern Staatssekretär Dr. Fröhlich: "Einsatz von Kräften des Bundesgrenzschutzes in Hamburg anläßlich der Beerdigung des Holger Meins am 18. November 1974," November 21, 1974, BArch-K, B106/371613.

87 See memorandum: BGS Referat ÖS 1, Streicher, to Bundesministerium des Innern, "Olympische Spiele 1976 in Innsbruck; hier: Sicherheitsmassnahmen," January 9, 1976; See also Memorandum: BGS Referat II 1, Krassmann to Bundesministerium des Innern Referat SM I 1, "Schutz des deutschen Olympische Mannschaft Montreal 1976," January 19, 1976, BArch-K, B106/371815.

police forces.[88] Terrorists and criminals also focused on other high-profile targets. On March 10, 1976, for example, 24-year-old Rudi Manz entered the Frankfurt state court and took two hostages. Manz demanded the release of the high-profile bank robbery suspect Gerhard Linden, ransom money, and a flight to Cuba. The Frankfurt police called on GSG 9 for technical support, because the building housing the courtrooms had multiple levels. The incident finally ended when the hostages overpowered Manz and shot him in the hip with his own firearm.[89] The Hessian Minister of Justice, Herbert Günther wrote a personal letter of thanks to Colonel Wegener and the Interior Ministry for the operational support and assistance they provided during the standoff.[90] Günther explained that "even though the use of Bundesgrenzschutz officers was not required by the course of the action, the local operational management still felt the support and good cooperation with GSG 9 was very helpful."[91] Wegener, irritated with the manner in which the situation evolved, argued that GSG 9 should have been notified much earlier than it was. He was frustrated and found it "unimaginable" that West Germany's states still hesitated to call on his unit for dangerous situations like those in Frankfurt.[92] All this was about to change, however, as the Interior Ministry called on Wegener's unit to face its most difficult challenge yet.

Operation Magic Fire: "Now We Have Heroes Again"

The government's reluctance to use GSG 9 finally ended in 1977 during the *Deutscher Herbst* (German Autumn), a new phase in the RAF's domestic terror campaign, in which its second generation launched a new series of violent attacks aimed at securing the release of their jailed leaders. On April 7, 1977, RAF assassins on a motorcycle shot and killed Attorney General Siegfried Buback and two others in his vehicle when

---

88 See p. 19, section C "Unterstützung der Polizeien der Länder durch Bundesgrenzschutz," Bundesministerium des Innern, "Tätigkeitsbericht des Bundesgrenzschutzes (BGS) 1975," Bonn, 3. Februar 1976, BArch-K, B122/16347.

89 See Staff, "2 Hostages Attack Frankfurt Gunman and Overcome Him," *New York Times*, March 11, 1976.

90 Letter from Hessischen Minister of Justiz Dr. Herbert Günther to OTL Ulrich Wegener, March 11, 1976, BArch-K, B106/371613.

91 Letter from Hessischen Minister des Innern an Bundesminister des Innen Dr. Maihofer, March 19, 1976, "Polizeilicher Einsatz anlässlich der Geiselnahme am 9. 10. März 1976, in Frankfurt Main," BArch-K, B106/371613.

92 Gesprächsvermerk: "Gespräch über GSG 9 am 29. März 1976, 15.00 Uhr," 1. April 1976, BArch-K, B106/371613; see also Ulrich Wegener, GSG 9: *Stärker als der Terror*, 58–59.

they stopped for a red light in Karlsruhe. On July 30, they murdered Dresdner Bank Chairman Jürgen Ponto in his home during a botched kidnapping attempt.[93] Then on September 5 they kidnapped industrialist Hanns-Martin Schleyer in Cologne. The attackers used an elaborate ruse, pushing a baby carriage into the path of Schleyer's vehicle and then catching his security detail by surprise, machine-gunning his driver and three police bodyguards.[94] The brazen crime shocked West Germans and shattered the confidence of other executives that they were safer with police bodyguards. The kidnappers held Schleyer hostage and demanded the release of RAF leaders Andreas Baader, Gudrun Ensslin, and others jailed in Stuttgart's notorious Stammheim Prison.

Chancellor Helmut Schmidt (SPD) was fed up with what he called "the bloody provocation against us all." CDU chairman and future chancellor Helmut Kohl also proclaimed: "we must now all understand that it is 5 minutes to midnight and we have to use all the means of power at the disposal of our democratic state to fight this intolerable threat to our peace and inner freedom."[95] Interior Minister Werner Maihofer, Genscher's successor, activated GSG 9 and thousands of additional border police personnel in the hours following Schleyer's kidnapping.[96] Like the nationwide manhunts of 1972, thousands of border police officers joined the state police in a massive effort to locate and rescue Schleyer.[97] The West German government refused to release the Stammheim prisoners or negotiate with the RAF in exchange for Schleyer. Matters took a turn for the worse on October 13, when four terrorists from the PFLP and RAF hijacked Lufthansa Flight 181 as it flew from Majorca, Spain, to Frankfurt. The terrorists used the hijacking as a means to increase the pressure on West Germany to release the prisoners in Stammheim and Palestinians held in Turkey.[98] Whereas the Schleyer kidnapping remained a national incident, the hijacking of the Lufthansa flight gained international attention. Like Munich, the whole world was watching.

---

93 For descriptions of the Buback and Ponto murders see Stefan Aust, *Baader-Meinhof*, 286, 293–94.

94 See Anne Ameri-Siemens, *Ein Tag im Herbst: Die RAF, der Staat und der Fall Schleyer* (Berlin: Rowohlt, 2017), 152–58.

95 See Staff, "Blutige Provokation gegen uns alle: Die Parteien verurteilen die Gewalt; Diskussion politischer Konsequenzen," *Frankfurter Allgemeine Zeitung*, September 6, 1977, 1.

96 Referat BGS II 1, Krassmann to Staatssekretär Dr. Fröhlich, October 13, 1977, "Reduzierung von Einsatzmassnahmen des BGS aus Anlass der Schleyer-Entführung," BArch-K, B106/371953.

97 Schnellbrief from Bundesministerium des Innern an GSK, October 21, 1977, "Einsatzmassnahmen des BGS aus Anlass der Schleyer-Entführung," BArch-K, B106/371953.

98 Ulrich Wegener, "The Evolution of Grenzschutzgruppe (GSG) 9," 114.

Schmidt wasted no time in calling on GSG 9 to deal with the unfolding crisis. It was just the sort of operation Wegener had been preparing for. In 1976, he had assisted the Israelis at Entebbe airport in Uganda during "Operation Thunderbolt," the rescue of hostages from El Al Airlines flight 139, hijacked by RAF and PLFP terrorists.[99] Moreover, as luck would have it, he and his men had just completed a series of practical training exercises in Nuremberg, where they simulated hostage rescue scenarios using a Boeing 737 aircraft—the very same fuselage configuration of Lufthansa Flight 181. Wegener knew he and his unit could deal with the situation.[100] There were 91 souls aboard Flight 181. Once the terrorists seized control of the aircraft, they flew to Rome and then made stops in Dubai and Aden. In Aden, the hijackers murdered pilot Jürgen Schumann. Wegener called Schumann's murder a turning point because the killing of one hostage might be the first step in killing them all.[101] The time for decisive action was running out. After killing Schumann, the terrorists ordered co-pilot Jürgen Vietor to fly the aircraft to Mogadishu in Somalia.

Wegener decided he would initiate his rescue plan—code-named Operation Magic Fire—in Mogadishu. The terrorists refused further negotiations and threatened to begin murdering the hostages every hour until their demands were met. Wegener also knew they had explosives aboard and worried they might try to detonate the entire aircraft. Thus in the early morning hours of October 18, Somali armed forces set fire to a bundle of tires on the runway in front of Flight 181's cockpit to distract the terrorists. Assault teams from GSG 9 moved into position and used explosive breaching charges to blow open the aircraft doors while British Special Air Service (SAS) personnel set-off "flash-bang" stun-grenades outside the aircraft as a diversion.[102] Wegener's plan worked and his men caught the terrorists completely by surprise. The assault ended in less than five minutes with three of the four terrorists killed and the fourth severely

99 See J. Paul de B. Taillon, *Hijacking and Hostages: Government Responses to Terrorism* (Westport: Praeger, 2002) 109, 143; see also Saul David, *Operation Thunderbolt: Flight 139 and the Raid on Entebbe Airport, the Twentieth Century's Greatest Special Forces Mission* (New York: Hachette Book Group, 2015).

100 Ulrich Wegener, GSG 9: *Stärker als der Terror*, 59.

101 Ulrich Wegener, "The Evolution of Grenzschutzgruppe (GSG) 9," 115.

102 "Flash-Bang" grenades are light-sound diversionary devices that emit loud explosions and extremely bright flashes from phosphorus—they were developed by the British Special Forces and the GSG 9 Mogadishu rescue was the first time they were ever used in an actual operation—they are still used by police tactical and special operations forces around the world; see Ulrich Wegener, "The Evolution of Grenzschutzgruppe (GSG) 9," 116.

wounded. Two hostages and one GSG 9 operator suffered minor injuries; otherwise all passengers and remaining crewmembers were unharmed.[103]

Unfortunately for Schleyer, the rescue of passengers on Flight 181 sealed his fate. His captors murdered him and left his body in the trunk of a car abandoned just over the French border near the city of Mulhouse. Baader, Ensslin, and Raspe committed suicide in their jail cells after learning of the Mogadishu rescue. The hardcore element of the RAF and many others on the radical left refused to accept that their leaders had committed suicide. Instead, they accused the government of murdering the prisoners and later generations of the RAF remained active well into the 1990s.[104]

When news of the successful rescue operation in Mogadishu reached Bonn's Federal Press Office, an observer proudly exclaimed: "Wir haben jetzt wieder Helden!" (We now have heroes again).[105] Overnight, Wegener and his men made it possible again for Germans to have pride in the actions of their armed forces—in this case, civilian border police officers rather than soldiers. On October 17, 1977, Interior Minister Werner Maihofer decorated Wegener with the Federal Republic's highest honor, the Grand Service Cross (See Fig. 9.2). According to Karrin Hanshew, the men of GSG 9 differed from the specialized police officers of Germany's past. The young men in their contemporary clothing and hairstyles were—as she aptly described them, "Rocker cops" in blue jeans and leather jackets.[106] That is to say that they had begun to reflect the modern trends and styles of the society they served—a distinct paradigm shift from the conservative traditions and symbolism of the old Wehrmacht reflected by the founding "men of the first hour" generation. A *Frankfurter Allgemeine Zeitung* reporter called the Mogadishu operation Germany's "Entebbe" and euphorically asked "what is this man, and what are these men, the Bundesgrenzschutz officers, who with determination and skill ended a nightmare that had gripped an entire nation?"[107]

Operation Magic Fire erased some of West Germany's national shame over the blundered rescue attempt at Munich and cemented the BGS as a valuable asset in the campaign against terrorism. GSG 9 proved that when all else failed, the Federal Republic could defend its democracy by using measured, precise applications of force. Still, nagging questions

103 Ulrich Wegener, *GSG 9: Stärker als der Terror*, 88–92.
104 Ulrike Meinhof had already committed suicide in 1976; See Stefan Aust, *Baader-Meinhof*, 258, xviii.
105 Karl Feldmeyer, "Wir haben jetzt wieder Helden! Die Spezialtruppen aus Mogadischu," *Frankfurter Allgemeine Zeitung*, October 19, 1977, 5.
106 Karrin Hanshew, *Terror and Democracy*, 233.
107 Entebbe was a reference to the successful Israeli rescue of hostages from a hijacking in 1976; Adelbert Weinstein, "Der Chef der GSG 9," *Frankfurter Allgemeine Zeitung*, October 19, 1977, 12.

Figure 9.2. October 17, 1977: Interior Minister Werner Maihofer decorates GSG 9 Commander Ulrich Wegener with the Grand Service Cross for his actions in the rescue of hostages aboard Lufthansa flight 181 in Mogadishu. Photo by Sven Simon, courtesy of IMAGO.

loomed over the future of the BGS and how it might be better incorporated into the Federal Republic's responses to domestic emergencies and crime. While West Germans welcomed its use for exceptional cases like the hijacking of Lufthansa Flight 181, they were less certain and even critical of its use for routine policing duties. Controversies remained, for example, regarding its invasive surveillance and data-collection measures during the ongoing campaign against the RAF's later generations. Moreover, some of its more senior members still promoted a militarized organizational culture and pushed back against internal reform efforts that sought to abandon infantry weapons and training in order to align it with the Federal Republic's state police forces. Nevertheless, the struggle against terrorism proved that the organization was here to stay; now it was up to officials at the Interior Ministry to transform it into the national police force they had always claimed it to be.

CHAPTER TEN

MORE THAN GUARDING BORDERS: FROM BGS TO BUNDESPOLIZEI

GSG 9's DRAMATIC RESCUE of the hostages aboard Lufthansa Flight 181 did not end the Federal Republic's ongoing struggle against terrorism or the questions its responses raised about the ethics of security in a democracy. The success of GSG 9 was tempered by the failure of West Germany's security forces to locate and rescue Hanns-Martin Schleyer before he was murdered by the RAF. Former Interior Minister Hermann Höcherl investigated the failed attempt to find Schleyer and in his final analysis, recommended more coordination between the Federal Republic's security agencies.[1] Six weeks after Colonel Wegener and his men returned in triumph, however, the BGS faced accusations that the government's security policies had gone too far. Border police officers assigned to the Munich Airport detained Bundestag Deputy Eckart Kuhlwein (SPD) during a routine pre-boarding security check. His complaints about his treatment renewed the public debate about the nature of the government's collection of personal data from travelers, and, more important, which agencies it was sharing it with.[2] Interior Minister Werner Maihofer, who replaced Genscher when he became Minister of Foreign Affairs in 1974, faced problems of his own over invasive security policies. In 1977, *Der Spiegel* revealed that he had authorized a secret wiretapping operation against nuclear physicist Klaus Traube, whom he suspected of having ties to the RAF. When he failed to produce evidence linking Traube to the RAF, Maihofer resigned. Gerhart Baum, a liberal member of the FDP, replaced him.[3]

Baum brought a new approach to the post of Interior Minister, and his progressive policies were a moderating influence on the BGS. The

---

1 "Diese Narren: Der frühere CSU-Innenminister Höcherl steht in dem Verdacht, er wolle der sozialliberalen Regierung helfen," *Der Spiegel* 21 (May 21, 1978), 122–25.

2 Eckhart Kuhlwein, "Factual Statement," Fragesstunde im Deutschen Bundestag, June 5, 1978, 1, BArch-K, B 106/107449.

3 For the Traube Affair, see "Der Minister und die Wanze," *Der Spiegel*, 10 February 28, 1977, 19–35; Karrin Hanshew, *Terror and Democracy*, 166–67.

1972 revisions to the Border Police Act had set the organization on a path towards modernization and in the years that followed led to greater integration of its personnel with West Germany's state police forces. Because of these reforms, by 1973 the BGS reached and exceeded its full strength of 20,000 men for the first time in its history. The Interior Ministry no longer needed conscripts to maintain adequate staffing. The passage of a new Personnel Structure Act in 1976 equalized the pay, benefits, and training of border police officers with their state police colleagues. Moreover, the Federal Republic's state police forces now hired twenty percent of their recruits from the BGS, providing its members with greater career incentives and better prospects for advancement. The revisions also came at a key moment in the organization's evolution, when most of its older Wehrmacht generation began to retire. Brigadier General Kurt Schneider, the last "man of the first hour" to lead the organization as its Inspector, retired in 1980. Schneider's replacement, Karl-Heinz Amft, a highly educated career police officer from West Germany's state police forces, took over as head of the organization even though he never served in the BGS. At the same time, BGS Commander Egon Schug became chief of the state riot police, a post he also assumed without coming up through its ranks. Schug, a legal scholar and licensed attorney, later returned to the BGS and succeeded Amft as Inspector. The leadership transfers reflected the ongoing project of integration between the state and federal police to the extent that by the late 1970s, the BGS became a key instrument in the Federal Republic's internal security program.

By the 1980s, however, the BGS faced yet another crisis of legitimacy when West Germany signed the Schengen Agreement, a step towards eliminating borders between European Member States. The opening of European Borders also brought with it a greater fear of crime and terrorism, because borders had been such an effective filter for capturing criminals. The rise of terrorism and illegal drug trafficking during the 1970s made open borders all the more concerning for the Interior Ministry. The BGS had to adapt to these new internal security demands. Gerhart Baum's prophetic warnings that right-wing terrorism should not be overlooked by the campaign against the RAF became clear on September 26, 1980, when a neo-Nazi detonated a bomb at the Octoberfest, killing thirteen people including himself. The horrific bombing was the deadliest attack on West German soil since the Olympic Games in Munich. The RAF's second and third generations also continued their campaign of bombings and assassinations. Despite his bodyguards and an armored Mercedes Benz, the RAF killed Deutsche Bank CEO Alfred Herrhausen with an armor-piercing rocket as he travelled to work in a convoy.[4] Thus West Germans remained

---

4   Ferdinand Protzman, "Head of Top West German Bank is Killed in Bombing by Terrorists," *New York Times*, December 1, 1989, 1.

uneasy about the stability of their democracy in the face of such political violence. Although European borders began to disappear, the BGS still functioned as an instrument for domestic security.

The Interior Ministry's effort to align the BGS with state police forces helped to end the ambiguity over its peculiar hybrid role and further solidified its place among the Federal Republic's law enforcement agencies. Because of this, it was more attractive to a newer generation of young professionals who joined because they wanted to be police officers rather than short-term recruits trying to avoid military service. During the 1980s, pressure for the Interior Ministry to hire women for the BGS also began to increase. To be sure, gender and family still defined how both postwar German states distinguished the other during the Cold War.[5] Yet West Germany's feminist movement, which emerged during the 1968 protests, still had to contend with conservative notions that a woman's place remained in the home raising children. Beginning in the 1980s, women began serving as enforcement officers in the state police, but the BGS remained a closed, male-dominated institution. Grassroots efforts by autonomous feminist movements in the 1970s began to challenge the status quo of the Federal Republic's conservative gender roles.[6] The Interior Ministry's Commission for Equal Rights and the close relationship of the BGS with state police forces helped to overcome internal resistance against admitting women. By 1987, the first thirty-two female recruits completed their training and performed better than their male colleagues on many of the exams and duties that came with their new profession. Nevertheless, female border police officers still faced misogyny from colleagues and the conservative press, which trivialized images of West German women carrying weapons and doing men's work.

In 1989 the surprising and sudden end to Germany's division and its rapid reunification forced the BGS to redefine its role yet again. The first challenge involved the vetting and integration of thousands of former East German border police officers into the BGS. Many of these men worked for the Ministry for State Security (MfS) as passport control officers and were hired on a probationary status pending the completion of background checks. By 1992, approximately 5,000 former East German police officers became civil servants in the BGS. Although the sudden collapse of the Inner-German border removed one of the organization's

---

5   Karen Hagemann, Donna Harsch, and Friederike Brühöfener, eds., *Gendering Post-1945 German History: Entanglements* (New York: Berghahn, 2019), 19.
6   Sarah E. Summers, "Finding Feminism: Rethinking Activism in the West German New Women's Movement of the 1970s and 1980s," *in Gendering Post-1945 German History: Entanglements*, ed. Karen Hagemann, Donna Harsch, and Friederike Brühöfener (New York: Berghahn, 2019), 290.

primary duties, because of its alignment and interchangeability with West Germany's state police forces, the loss of European and then internal borders did not affect its long-term survival. As Interior Minister Gerhart Baum aptly remarked: "The BGS would not have been able to survive if its only task had been to secure the Inner-German border."[7]

Aligning the BGS with State Police

Maihofer's resignation reflected the political consequences of trampling on the democratic rights of citizens in the process of trying to preserve them. To Maihofer's credit, however, his effort to advance the objectives of the 1972 legislative reforms helped to transform the BGS into a modern law enforcement agency. He accomplished this by pushing for a greater alignment of the BGS with West Germany's state police forces and oversaw the passage of a new Personnel Structure Act in 1976.[8] The law, which took effect on July 1, 1976, ended the practice of hiring short-term officers that contributed to such high turnover rates in the BGS. Henceforth, like their colleagues in the state police, border police officers could become civil servants for life, which afforded better career prospects because they could transfer to any number of other civil service professions. The law also required BGS members to receive training equivalent to the officers in the state police. The harmonization of training increased interchangeability and made it possible for border police officers to transfer into the state forces. Thus even though some stalwarts in the organization still promoted militarization, they could no longer ignore police training topics because the law now required it. More importantly, the new law outlined a five-year program to match the salaries of federal and state officers and the Conference of State Interior Ministers agreed to hire at least twenty percent of their personnel from the ranks of the BGS. Finally, border police officers who chose to transfer to the state police did not have to repeat examinations for promotions they had already achieved in the BGS.[9]

Although the law did not solve all of the personnel and salary problems in the BGS, it greatly improved the working conditions of its officers and pushed it closer to becoming a professional law enforcement

---

7   Gerhart Baum, "Neue Konzeption ist dem BGS gut bekommen/ Bundesinnenminister Baum in Coburg," *BGS Zeitschrift* 2 (February 1980): 13.

8   Dr. Reuter (BGS I 1) Interior Ministry to Conference of State Interior Ministers, "Entwurf einer Verwaltungsvereinbarung zur Regelung der Übernahme von Polizeivollzugsbeamten des BGS durch die Länder," 29. April 1975, BArch-K, B 106/115703.

9   "Das Gesetz über die Personalstruktur des Bundesgrenzschutzes: Tritt am 1. Juli 1976 in Kraft," *BGS Zeitschrift* 6 (June 1976): 2.

agency.[10] Thus when Gerhart Baum replaced Maihofer as Interior Minister, the BGS already made significant progress towards becoming a modern law enforcement agency that could be called upon by the states for support. In 1979, for example, BGS units reinforced the state police in 527 incidents to include hostage situations, fugitive searches, and large demonstrations.[11] Border police officers guarded government buildings during elections and took part in security operations at the controversial nuclear sites Brokdorf and Gorleben. BGS helicopter squadrons helped during manhunts and natural disasters, but the airships also played a humanitarian role by transporting accident victims and moving medical personnel and supplies wherever they were needed. In 1979, BGS helicopters flew 13,000 missions of which 11,000 included the medical evacuation of patients to regional hospitals. Moreover, many of these medical flights transported blood supplies and organs for patients in need of transplants.[12]

Baum brought a more progressive attitude to the Interior Ministry and promoted the principle of transparency to a greater extent than his predecessors. He made many of the conservative hardliners in Helmut Schmidt's administration uneasy and recalled that "Some didn't want me under any circumstances because of my political beliefs, and others had doubts as to whether I was up to the job, especially when dealing with the security authorities."[13] Baum was neither soft on crime nor a critic of the BGS when he took office, but he had to overcome the perceptions that he was. He believed West Germans misunderstood border police officers from the beginning because, still suffering from the shock of war, they did not trust armed forces of any kind. Yet at the same time, he recognized that the force needed equipment and training better suited for carrying out law enforcement duties. It helped that he had already worked in the ministry for almost seven years and developed strong working relationships with his colleagues, even those with opposing political views. He also worked closely with BKA Chief Herold because of their collaboration on counterterrorism operations and called him "a clever analyst" who also "kept an eye on social circumstances."[14]

Baum promoted a different approach to terrorism than Maihofer and in 1979 began raising the alarm about the rise in violence perpetrated by neo-Nazis and other radical right-wing militant groups. Barbara Manthe

10 "Anpassung des Stellenkegels des BGS an den Stellenkegel der Polizei der Länder," *BGS Zeitschrift* 6 (June 1976): 4.
11 Bundesinnenminister Baum legt den Tätigkeitsbericht des BGS für 1979 vor," *BGS Zeitschrift* (April 1980): 7.
12 Ibid.
13 Gerhart Baum, *Meine Wut ist jung: Bilanz eines politischen Lebens im Gespräch mit Matthias* Franck (Munich: Kössel, 2012), 110.
14 Ibid.

has argued that the end of the 1970s was "marked by a remarkable radicalization among right-wing terrorists …."[15] In his 1978 activity report, for example, Baum made a point of focusing on radical right-wing militants, citing a 93 percent increase in riot activity and a stark increase in violent crime attributed to neo-Nazi perpetrators.[16] Numerous police search operations revealed perpetrators in possession of weapons, ammunition, and Nazi propaganda. At one location, police seized 5 submachineguns, thousands of rounds of ammunition, and eight kilograms of explosive material. Investigators also recovered evidence that neo-Nazi perpetrators kept target or "hit lists" of prominent politicians they planned to assassinate. In one case, police disrupted a plot by a Nazi militant group to murder Schleswig-Holstein's Prime Minister, Gerhard Stoltenberg. Moreover, Baum pointed out that English writer and Holocaust-denier David Irving spoke at the Frankfurt Book Fair in 1978 where to prolonged applause he declared: "There is not a document and no proof that Hitler gave the order for the extermination of the Jews."[17] Yet Baum's warnings about these militant right-wing and neo-Nazi groups did not evoke the same visceral responses as the political violence perpetrated by the RAF. Historians have argued that Chancellor Brandt's *Ostpolitik* and the reduction of Cold War tensions angered conservatives on the far right in West Germany.[18] Since anti-communism still dominated the domestic politics of the Federal Republic, RAF terror reinforced hardline conservative beliefs about chaos and overthrow from Marxist insurgents. Baum later recalled that conservative politicians at the time were "blind in the right eye" and thus "concentrated fully on the acts of violence from the left and ignored the fact that there were quite a few acts of violence from the right at the same time."[19]

Baum recognized that to professionalize the BGS he had to advance the program begun with the revised Border Police Act of 1972 by further aligning the organization with West Germany's state police. Thus in 1980 he had to find a good replacement for the retiring Major General Kurt Schneider. Typical of the men that held the position before him, Schneider served in the Wehrmacht and ended the war as a POW. He joined the BGS in 1951 as one of its "men of the first hour" and worked his way up through its ranks, taking over as Inspector in 1973.[20] In a

15 Barbara Manthe, "On the Pathway to Violence," 61.
16 Gerhart Baum, "Tätigkeitsbericht des Bundesgrenzschutzes (BGS) 1978," 15, BA-MA, BH 28-2-887.
17 Ibid.
18 See Daniel Koehler, *Right-Wing Terrorism*; Barbara Manthe, "On the Pathway to Violence," 56–62.
19 Gerhart Baum, *Meine Wut ist jung*, 123.
20 Gerhart Baum, "Ansprache des Bundesministers des Innern, Gerhart Rudolf Baum, anläßlich der Verabschiedung des Inspekteurs des BGS Kurt

decision that reflected his philosophy of aligning the BGS with the state police, Baum appointed Karl-Heinz Amft, the head the State Riot Police to succeed Schneider. Although Amft also served in the Wehrmacht, he spent his entire career in the state police forces. At the change of command ceremony, Baum also announced that he selected BGS Commander Egon Schug to replace Amft as head of the Riot Police. Like Amft, Schug took over an organization as an outsider having never served in West Germany's state police forces. Baum emphasized that "Both personnel decisions make it clear to what extent the political goal of integrating the federal border guards into the police structure of the federal and state governments has been achieved ... [and] makes a significant contribution to implementing the basic concept of the BGS-Act and Personnel Structure Act as an administrative reality."[21]

Baum could not have selected a more capable leader to professionalize the BGS. Amft's educational background and years of experience with the state police helped accelerate the program to de-militarize border police officers and train them to the same level as their state counterparts. Upon his release from captivity in 1947, Amft joined the Lower Saxony Police in the British Occupation Zone. He transferred to the state police in North Rhine Westphalia and worked his way up through its ranks. Highly educated, he studied law and political science in Münster and taught at the prestigious Police Leadership Academy in Münster-Hiltrup, where he played a significant role in developing its curriculum and textbooks. Amft eventually took over as Chair of the Management Theory Department. He enjoyed the intellectual challenges of teaching and later recalled: "For me, what was special about the Police Institute was the climate of high motivation among the course participants, the familiarity of the teaching team and the freedom to expand my horizons."[22] Since 1973, Amft worked closely with BGS executives at the Interior Ministry as Chair of an advisory board to standardize its training programs. As a result of his work, Amft developed the entire training plan to harmonize border police officers with the rest of West Germany's state police forces.[23]

A particular challenge for West German law enforcement during the late 1970s and 1980s involved policing the massive and often violent anti-nuclear demonstrations at Brokdorf, Grohnde and the waste disposal site in Gorleben. West Germany's state police called on the BGS for support, but it was clear to Amft, who as head of the Riot Police responded

---

Schneider und der Amtseinführung des Inspekteurs des BGS Karl-Heinz Amft am 30. Januar 1980, Sankt Augustin," *BGS Zeitschrift* 2 (February 1980): 2–4.

21 Ibid.

22 Karl-Heinz Amft, "Wandervögel unterwegs: Heimat—Familie—Beruf," Deutsches Tagebucharchiv, Signatur: 2105-1 (1767-1), 136.

23 Ibid., 148.

to these early protests, that more training was needed to manage future large joint police operations. In November 1976, for example, the BGS sent two companies along with two helicopters to a large demonstration at the nuclear construction site in Brokdorf.[24] Despite the recommendations for more riot control training after the passage of the emergency laws in 1968, the Interior Ministry complained that its officers still "had no experience dealing with violent demonstrators." At Brokdorf, most of the 30,000 protestors demonstrated peacefully, but approximately 2,000 violent activists clashed with police when they attempted to storm the construction site. Some of the more radical protestors fired flare pistols and fireworks at low-flying BGS helicopters and also pelted officers with rocks, bottles, and Molotov cocktails. The heavy-handed response of the police to the troublemakers in the crowd escalated the violence and many of the peaceful protestors got caught in the mele. Several protestors and police officers suffered injuries in the clashes. Caught up in the chaos of the moment, some BGS units used unconventional or military-style methods to deal with the violent crowds such as using helicopters to "bomb" demonstrators with tear gas grenades—a sign that its personnel still needed more training despite the restraint it demonstrated during the 1968 student uprisings.[25]

Some SPD politicians and the West German press criticized the actions of border police officers and particularly their use of helicopters to drop tear gas on the crowds. The paramilitary BGS, they argued, escalated the violence. Moreover, their low flying helicopters stirred up rocks and other objects that injured many of the peaceful demonstrators. Archival video footage shows that BGS helicopters flew dangerously low to the ground towards the protestors, but also confirmed the statements of pilots that people fired flare guns at them.[26] Bundestag member Norbert Gansel (SPD) expressed sympathy for the injured border police officers, but criticized the practice of using helicopters for riot control. German Communist Party newspaper *Unsere Zeit* called the police response "Emphatically anti-democratic." The GdP, which began to recruit more BGS members after the passage of the Personnel Structure Act, complained to the Conference of Interior Ministers that it should provide officers with better equipment and defend them against what it called

---

24 "Bericht: des Bundesministers des Innern vor dem Innenausschuß des Deutschen Bundestages am 4. Mai 1977 über Zusammenarbeit BGS—Polizei, Einsatz Brokdorf 13. November, 1976," BArch-K, B 106/83927.

25 Dolores L. Augustine, *Taking on Technocracy: Nuclear Power in Germany, 1945 to the Present* (New York: Berghahn, 2018), 135.

26 Footage available online at https://www.ndr.de/geschichte/schauplaetz/brokdorfdemonstration101_page-2.html.

defamatory statements by the press.[27] The 1972 reforms and changing generational cohorts in the BGS did set it on a path towards becoming a modern police force, but remnants of its militarized organizational culture still created challenges for those who tried to overcome them.

As an observer of the events in Brokdorf and many other demonstrations, Amft analyzed the police responses and used these insights to improve how the BGS responded to them when he assumed command in 1980.[28] During the first large protest at Brokdorf, for example, he pointed to a lack of command and control and developed a model of unified leadership to coordinate future responses involving state and federal officers. Because officers who deployed from different departments experienced difficulties communicating with each other, he recommended the BGS telecommunications groups set up central networks for these larger joint operations. He explained that most of the protestors acted peacefully, but some arrived prepared to do battle with the police and thus armed themselves with Molotov cocktails, grappling hooks, protective clothing, flare pistols, and wire cutters. He also acknowledged that some of the officers overreacted and responded violently to peaceful protestors. Amft suggested that the scale and size of the protests required much more advanced planning and additional training for the officers deployed to police them. He emphasized de-escalation and argued against forceful confrontations with the crowds because, as he argued, "It is important to avoid broad solidarity among people against the state—deploying police officers cannot become the standard for this."[29]

For Amft and the members of BGS he led, the 1980s marked a period of increased deployment to support the state police in operations against civil unrest.[30] Activists rallied to protest against nuclear power plants and NATO polices that called for placing nuclear weapons in Western Europe. In 1980, for example, BGS officers supported police in Lower

---

27 Nobert Gansel (SPD) to Interior Minister Maihofer, "Einsatz von BGS-Hubschraubern in Brokdorf," November 16, 1976; "Polizeieinsatz ist demokratiefeindlich: Solidaritätsbeweise aus der ganzen Bundesrepublik," *Unsere Zeit*, November 16, 1976, 1; GdP Chairman Helmut Schirrmacher to Innenminister Dr. Burghard Hirsch, April 19, 1977, BArch-K, B106/83927.

28 Karl-Heinz Amft, "Wandervögel unterwegs," 152.

29 Karl-Heinz Amft, "Einsatz der Polizei aus Anlaß der Demonstrationen und gewalttätigen Aktionen am 13. November 1976 im Raume Brokdorf," BArch-K, B 106/83927.

30 Michael Sturm, "The Police," in *The Nuclear Crisis: The Arms Race, Cold War Anxiety, and theGerman Peace Movement of the 1980s*, ed. Christoph Becker-Schaum, Philipp Gassert, Martin Klimke, Wilfried Mausbach, and Marianne Zepp (New York: Berghahn, 2020), 275: see also Stephen Milder, *Greening Democracy: The Anti-Nuclear Movement and Political Environmentalism in West Germany and Beyond, 1969–1983* (Cambridge: Cambridge University Press, 2017), 234.

Saxony during ongoing demonstrations at the Gorleben nuclear waste facility. Activists staged several "sit-in" demonstrations and constructed an "anti-nuclear peace village" at the site they called the Free Republic of Wendland. Border police officers helped the state police clear the site and used non-violent means to remove passive resistors who refused to leave. Baum called the BGS response and its patience with protestors at Gorleben a "model example of the use and cooperation of the Federal Border Police with the states."[31]

Despite a court ordered ban against demonstrations at Brokdorf, on February 28, 1981, thousands of activists returned to the site to protest Schleswig-Holstein's renewal of the plant's construction permit. The state police once again called upon the BGS for support, and thousands of border police officers joined what was, at the time, the largest mass deployment of police forces in German history. The police cordoned off large areas around the plant, but still allowed people to protest. This time, however, officers set up checkpoints and searched many of the protestors as they arrived, yet still failed to stop all the agitators who smuggled weapons and Molotov cocktails into the site. The level of violence between the police and the crowds did not reach the same levels as the 1976 protest, but people still complained about the aggressive behavior of border police officers and their use of helicopters against the crowds. Many protestors reported being knocked to the ground by the low flying helicopters.[32] Nevertheless, because of efforts by both the police and organizers of the protest, far fewer people suffered injuries. Still, the violence, fear, and emotions of mass crowd control events often pushed police officers to their limits. Although the BGS had begun to make progress and were taking steps to demilitarize, it still had room for improvement. Critics seized upon its missteps at Brokdorf to revive the accusations that it was an army disguised as a police force, proving that its personnel needed much more training to handle these dynamic events. Baum acknowledged this need during a change of command ceremony after the protest by reminding the incoming officers that "the right to peaceful demonstrations is a fundamental right, whose protection is to be guaranteed by all constitutional organs, and which states that the use of force as a means of political dispute is to be rejected, and which calls for objectivity, moderation, and prudence."[33]

---

31 Gerhart Baum, "Gorleben—Modell für Zusammenarbeit BGS/Polizei," *BGS Zeitschrift* 2 (February 1980): 9–11.
32 Dolores L. Augustine, *Taking on Technocracy*, 149.
33 Gerhart Baum, "'Rede des Bundesministers des Innern, Gerhart Rudolf Baum," February 25, 1981, *BGS Zeitschrift* 3 (March 1981): 4.

The First Women in the BGS

On November 18, 1980, fifteen-year-old Astrid Eder wrote a personal letter to the Interior Ministry inquiring about a job in the BGS. Like other young women at her age, she had dreams about her future as she prepared to complete her Abitur and graduate from high school. In her neatly written letter, she explained "I would like some information about women at the Federal Border Police, (except as a cook or cleaning lady!) I am incredibly interested in the BGS, and I'd like to know if there are any opportunities for me. I hope to find a position in the BGS when I have my Abitur in three years." The Interior Ministry responded and told Astrid that she could not be employed in the border police because of its "special tasks" and instead, recommended she consider a career in the federal government's administrative services.[34] Unfortunately for Astrid and hundreds of other young West German women, law enforcement remained a male dominated profession. Although women had served in Germany's police forces since the Wilhelmine era, most of their work focused on child welfare, prostitution, or as investigators assigned to the Criminal Police. Otherwise, Germany's police women handled administrative or medical support tasks.[35]

Conservative West German society presented another obstacle to young Astrid's hopes and dreams, since feminist movements still faced challenges from the postwar male-breadwinner, female-homemaker gender order. Yet as Sarah Summers suggests, by the late 1970s and early 1980s a variety of autonomous feminists movements began exerting pressure against the postwar conservative gender order, which had been "a bulwark against communism and as a new form of civilized domestic masculinity to replace the militarized masculinity of the Third Reich."[36] In 1978, for example, West German feminist Alice Schwarzer used her magazine *Emma* as a platform to demand full admission for women in the army—including as combatants. Article 12(a) of the Basic Law, however, prohibited women from serving in armed conflicts. Schwarzer argued that banning women from the army was "the most extreme expression

---

34 Letter from Astrid Eder to Interior Minister, November 18, 1980; response by Department Director Hohmann, December 2, 1980, BArch-K, B 106/367613.

35 See for example, Ursula Nienhaus, "Einsatz für die 'Sittlichkeit': Anfänge der weiblichen Polizei im Wilhelminischen Kaiserreich und der Weimarer Republik," in *Sicherheit und Wohlfahrt: Polizei, Gesellschaft und Herrschaft im 19. und 20. Jahrhundert*, ed. Alf Lüdke (Frankfurt am Main: Suhrkamp, 1992), 243–66; Katharina Pluta, *Frauen in Führungsfunktionen von Polizei und Wirtschaft: Eine Bestandsaufnahme* (Hamburg: Diplomica, 2009).

36 Sarah E. Summers, "Rethinking Activism," 288.

of the division of labor between men and women."[37] Sibylle Plogstedt, Editor in Chief of the rival feminist magazine *Courage*, along with the DGB trade union, rejected the idea of women as soldiers. Plogstedt cited recent sexual harassment cases in US Army barracks as evidence against permitting women to serve in the German Army and argued: "Rather than racking our brains over what is progressive about pursuing a career as a female soldier, we should be doing everything in our power so that women are represented at disarmament negotiations."[38]

By the end of the 1970s, West Germany's police unions and other organizations began to pressure state and federal officials to fully open the police profession to women, including for enforcement jobs typically reserved for men. Moreover, anxiety among West Germany's conservatives about declining birth rates, which they blamed on the alleged widespread use of birth control pills—the so called "*Pillenknick*" (pill pause)—helped spread what turned out to be an urban myth that both the army and police forces needed women to make up for the looming deficit in male recruits. Minister of Defense Hans Apel (SPD), for example, caused a stir when he advocated hiring women for the army to make up for the perceived shortages.[39] Others argued that denying women full access to the police profession violated Article 3 Section 2 of the Basic Law, which mandated that "Men and women shall have equal rights." In January 1980, the German Section of the International Federation of Police Leaders (IOLP), a Non-Governmental Organization supported by the European Council, held its annual symposium in Bonn under the theme: "Women in the Police Force."[40] The IOLP had been studying the role of women in law enforcement for a number of years, and conducted in-depth studies on the extent to which they worked in the police forces of other nations. In the symposium report, German Section President Joachim Zimmermann argued that "gender equality in working life is a constitutional mandate ... the police as an institution should be a mirror of the sociological conditions of the community. The police can no longer turn a blind eye to the growing role played by women in business, administration, and politics." Moreover, he argued that the "constitution's offer

---

37 Alice Schwarzer, "Frauen ins Militär?," *Emma* 6, June 1978, 5.
38 Sibylle Plogstedt, "Frauen ins Militär?" *Emma* 12, December 1980, 18.
39 On the *Pillenknick*, see "'Bulletten' an die Front," *Der Spiegel* 25, June 15, 1987, 50–53; Hans Schueler, "Frauen in der Bundeswehr? Die Bonner Langzeitkommission rührt ein Tabu an," *Die Zeit*, May 21, 1982, 1–2; see also Dagmar Herzog, *Sex after Fascism*, 233.
40 Bericht über ein "Symposium der Internationalen Organisation Leitender Polizeibeamter (IOLP)—Deutsche Sektion—vom 18. bis 20. Januar 1980 unter dem Leitthema 'Frauen im Polizeidienst,'" BArch-K, B 106/367613.

of equal rights applies directly in the public sector." Zimmermann sent a copy of the IOLP report and its findings to BGS Inspector Amft.[41]

In 1980, several of West Germany's states began hiring women for pilot programs to evaluate bringing them into their police forces on an equal footing with their male colleagues. The Conference of Interior Ministers and Senators' Internal Security Branch (AK II) also established an ad-hoc committee to study the issue.[42] The ad-hoc committee used surveys and analyzed the status of current pilot programs in Hamburg, Hesse, and Berlin to make its recommendations for the rest of the federal states. The committee members suggested that most existing prejudices against women joining the police lacked foundation and expressed that in principle, women could be hired for the uniformed police service equal to males, but not with congruent duties. In fact, the committee found that based on what they had seen so far, women avoided violent conflict more than their male counterparts.[43] The majority of their findings, however, reinforced the ongoing unease of West Germany's conservatives over upending the Cold War gender order by including women in the closed masculine culture of policing. The report suggested, for example, that "Women are, on average, physically inferior to men and therefore not as well suited for violent situations."[44] More precisely, the committee's greatest concerns focused on the women's potential to disrupt West Germany's male-breadwinner gender order. Thus, the report concluded: "Due to their function and their current role in society, i.e., marriage, raising children, household and family roles, women are more likely to retire than men." The ministers decided to wait for all the results from the pilot programs before making a final decision.[45]

In spite of the promising results from West Germany's states, the BGS remained strictly off-limits to women unless they chose to work in administrative support jobs. The ongoing policy of aligning border police officers with West Germany's state police forces, however, became problematic for hardliners who resisted the recruitment and hiring of women. The proverbial pendulum swung both ways. On the one hand, the Interior Ministry recognized that preserving the organization relied upon integrating its training and duties with the states. On the other hand, one of the unintended consequences of aligning with the states meant that the BGS might lose some of its autonomy in the process. Thus when West

41 Ibid., 2–3; IOLP General Secretary Moser to BGS Inspector Karl-Heinz Amft, February 28, 1980, BArch-K, B 106/367613.
42 "Frauen im Vollzugsdienst der Schutzpolizei: Bericht des vom AK II eingesetzten ad-hoc-Ausschusses Bezug: Beschluß des AK II anläßlich der Sitzung am 24./25. September 1980," BArch-K, B 106/367613.
43 Ibid., 1–4.
44 Ibid., 1–2.
45 Ibid.

Germany's states opened the policing profession to women, the pressure on the Interior Ministry to do the same began to increase. Nevertheless, officials continued to resist the idea of women joining the border police even though in the state agencies they proved just as capable as their male colleagues. In 1981, the state of Hesse hired seventy-three women out of a class of five hundred officers who completed basic training for the riot police. Hessian Interior Minister Ekkehard Gries said the achievement of the female graduates reflected a "Socio-political task of the first order, which must be seen against the background of a changing understanding of the role of women." In 1983, police women from the state of North Rhine Westphalia joined their male colleagues in the closed formations at Krefeld to battle violent crowds protesting the visit of US President George H. W. Bush, ending lingering doubts about their ability to deal with physical violence.[46]

Pressure on the Interior Ministry to follow the lead of West Germany's states came from many sources and their resistance to women invoked a variety of excuses, which over time failed to hold up. Remarkably, both the Border Police Employees' Association and the GdP supported the full inclusion of women in the BGS. GdP Chairman Helmut Schirrmacher called on the Interior Ministry to stop using gender as a basis to discriminate against women. He argued that women serving in the state police forces had already proven themselves and should be hired in the BGS with the same rights and duties as their male colleagues. He emphasized that excluding female applicants violated their right to "choose their occupation freely." The President of the Border Police Employees' Association, Helmut Pfeffer, echoed Schirrmacher's arguments and also referred to the recent positive experiences with female officers reported by the state police. He also pointed out that the women performed well under stress during the violent riots in Krefeld.[47] Pressure to hire more women in the BGS also came from the Interior Ministry's Commission on Equal Rights, a governmental oversight board the Bundestag established in 1950 to guarantee the equal rights promised by the Basic Law in both public and private life. In 1980, after learning the BGS employed just a single female physician, they demanded that the Interior Ministry take immediate steps to hire more.[48] On March 19, 1982, Commission

---

[46] "Gleichwertige Berufsausbildung für Frauen Verfassungsgebot: Hessens erste Frauen in Polizeiuniform in Kassel," Bereitschaftspolizei heute (September 1982), 42; "Bulletten an die Front," *Der Spiegel* 25, June 15, 1987, 51.

[47] GdP Chairman Helmut Schirrmacher to Staatssekretär Fröhlich, "Frauen im Polizeiberuf," July 23, 1980; for Pfeffer's comments, see Bernd Hummel, "Verband: BGS für Fraüen öffnen," *Die Welt*, September 14, 1984, 1, BArch-K, B 106/367612.

[48] See Bundesministerium für Familie, Senioren, Frauen und Jugend, "20 Jahre Bundesfrauenministerium," 11, bmfsfj.de/resource/blob/83980/e7c35fc

Chairman Erdmenger wrote a blunt letter to Interior Minister Baum, calling the failure to hire women "intolerable and constitutionally questionable." Like the two police unions, Erdmenger pointed to the successes and commendable performance of the women working in state police forces. He concluded by demanding a written proposal adequate for equal rights that outlined the Interior Ministry's plans to begin hiring women as border police officers.[49]

Interior Minister Baum agreed with Erdmenger and, since 1980, had been trying to hire more women. Heinrich Boge, head of the Ministry's Police Branch, instructed his divisional staff to recruit more women for positions throughout the organization and explained that "female civil servants are to be given greater consideration." Eventually, more than 1,000 women worked in various administrative positions in support of the border police, but none of them served as law enforcement officers.[50] Changing the militarized, hyper-masculine culture of the BGS and its resistance to women proved far more difficult. In October 1982, West Germany's Social-Liberal Coalition collapsed, ending the Interior Ministry's progressive Baum era. Friedrich Zimmermann (CSU), a veteran solider and former member of the Nazi Party, replaced Baum, and his administration restored a more conservative vision in the ministry.[51] Thus hardliners in the organization found it easier to make excuses to explain why women could work as enforcement officers in the state police, but not in the BGS.

The West German press also exerted pressure by asking the Interior Ministry to explain why they banned women from the border police. An interoffice divisional memorandum provided staff members with a variety of responses that amounted to nothing more than a list of excuses or stall tactics that reinforced misogynistic attitudes and avoided the obvious violations of equal rights clauses in the Basic Law.[52] First of all, the government allegedly could not afford the cost of converting border police

---

a44fd0c99946f585c499ec7a/20-jahre-frauenministerium-data.pdf; Dr. Schiffer, Kommission für die Gleichberechtigung im Bundesministerium des Innern, to Gerhart Baum, December 16, 1980, BArch-K, B 106/367613.

49 Chairman Erdmenger to Interior Minister Gerhart Baum, "Frauen in der Abteilung P und im BGS," March 19, 1982, BArch-K, B 106/367613.

50 See Gerhart Baum, "Kabinettreferat Auszugsweise Mitteilung auf dem Kabinettsprotokol über die 179 Sitzung," May 27, 1980; see also Heinrich Boge to Ministerial Director Fischer, "Verwendung von Frauen im BGS," August 12, 1980, BArch-K, B 106/367613.

51 Franziska Kuschel and Dominik Rigoll, "Broschürenkrieg statt Bürgerkrieg: BMI und MdI im Deutsch-deutschen Systemkonflikt," in *Hüter der Ordnung*, ed. Frank Bösch and Andreas Wirsching, 376.

52 Memorandum: Referat P II 1—630 201/1, "Verwendung von Frauen im BGS—Presserefarat," September 18, 1984.

barracks to accommodate coeds. Then there was the violence that border police officers had to contend with during riots, where they claimed that "the physical and psychological conditions [made] women appear less suitable for assignments of this kind ... and that permanent and visible traces of physical injuries [were] even more serious for younger women than for younger men."[53] The ministry claimed that the operational usefulness of BGS units would decline, since women had no value for riot control. Last but not least, and its main justification against hiring women: border police officers had combatant status, and during a war, had to fight with the army.[54] Since 1965, the BGS had gone to great lengths justifying the need for combatant status, claiming it neither altered its police character nor transformed its personnel into soldiers. Yet in the face of growing pressure to hire women, the organization reversed course and argued that its "military duties" made them ineligible, since Article 12, Section 4 of the Basic Law prohibited their participation in combat.

In spite of the difficult questions posed by some members of the press, conservative newspapers reinforced gender discrimination by trivializing women who dared to take on police jobs. Since the 1950s, West Germany's print media promoted specific images that reinforced images of women as homemakers.[55] Women that challenged the gender order were mocked. Axel Springer's right-wing sensationalist *Bild Zeitung*, for example, published a story about the first women to join the North Rhine Westphalian State Police under the title "With Powder Compact and Pistol." The article described a day in the life of Beate Friesicke, a new police officer in Hamburg, who according to *Bild* Reporter Jürgen Schukar had "long curls under the service cap, a karate grip that leaves traces of perfume, and an interrogation that is both strict and soothing."[56] Springer's *Bild Hamburg* published a similar article about women in the Hamburg police under the headline *Das Fräulein Wunder*. The article profiled Officer Karin Marx as a "perky blond with wild curly hair, sky-blue eye shadow, a cherry mouth." The blatant sexualization of women in this manner fit West Germany's gendered division of labor, even though feminists were beginning to shift the boundaries.[57] As the Schwarzer—Plogstedt debate over women in the armed

53 Ibid., 2.
54 Ibid.
55 See for example, Jennifer Lynn, "Contested Representations of Women in the East and West German Illustrated Press of the 1950s," in *Gendering Post-1945 German History*, ed. Karen Hagemann, Donna Harsch, and Friederike Brühöfener, 515–16.
56 Jürgen Schukar, "Mit Puderdose und Pistole: Frauen sind bessere Polizisten," *Bild Zeitung*, July 24, 1986, 1.
57 Norbert Schubert und Lutz Jaffe, "Das Fräulein Wunder bei der Polizei," *Bild-Hamburg*, April 24, 1981, 1; Karen Hagemann, Donna Harsch, Friederike

forces made clear, for many West Germans the idea of equal rights in the labor market did not include arming women to confront criminals, guard borders, or use physical violence. Thus for the time being at least, BGS officials at the Interior Ministry could take advantage of a divided public to avoid hiring women.

By the mid-1980s, Interior Minister Zimmermann found himself caught between opposing forces in his own ministry regarding growing pressure to open border police careers to women. In 1985, Egon Schug, a conservative hardliner who promoted militarization, replaced the intellectual Karl-Heinz Amft as head of the BGS.[58] Schug and members of his staff tried to convince Zimmermann that women had no place as enforcement officers in their organization. On the other side, positive reports about the performance of women in the state police forces stood as strong evidence to refute the arguments of those who still denied they had something to offer the BGS. Zimmermann also faced growing pressure from police unions and the Commission for Equal Rights that demanded he give women more opportunities in law enforcement careers. Thus at the beginning of 1986 he began considering a pilot program to hire a limited number of women.

Those who opposed hiring women reacted immediately. Dieter Mechlinski, a BGS officer assigned to the Interior Ministry's Police Branch (P III 3), wrote a memorandum outlining every reason not to hire women for enforcement duties.[59] His justification reflected the misogyny facing any woman tempted to apply for the BGS. Mechlinski argued, without any empirical evidence, that because of "biological and gender reasons, more downtime is to be expected for women than for men, which can lead to a reduction in the operational capacity of the unit, or parts of it, at decisive moments." He went on to claim that women could not be deployed nationwide because of being limited by "mother-child relationships," which unfairly subjected their male colleagues to the hardships of covering their vacancies. He also explained that women had "less physical resiliency" and thus, "will instinctively react with more restraint, thereby reducing operational efficiency." Whereas West Germany's state police commended women for avoiding violence and found them better at de-escalation than their male counterparts, Mechlinski framed it as a weakness. He concluded his list of grievances about women by

---

Brühöfener, *Gendering Post-1945 German History*, 19.

58 Otto Diederichs, "In welcher Verfassung ist der BGS?" in "Schwerpunkt: Bundesgrenzschutz außerdem: Verfassungsschutz rassistische Polizei—Übergriffe Todesschüsse 1993," *Cilip* 47, 1(1994): 30.

59 Dieter Mechlinski to Referat P II 1, "Einstellung von Frauen in den Polizeivollzugsdienst der BGS-Verbände," April 25, 1986, 2, BArch-K, B 106/367612.

recommending that "the BGS should not take any pioneering role with its units" and fell back on its combatant status as an excuse for denying women full career rights.[60]

Nevertheless, Zimmermann pressed ahead with the pilot program and explained that the decisive factor in his decision "was the consistently positive experience of the federal states."[61] Yet to appease the hardliners, he promised that enforcement duties remained an exclusive job for men and thus planned to limit women to the GSE, where they could carry out passport control duties. Because GSE officers did not have combatant status, Zimmermann got around the objections of those that cited it as a reason against hiring women. In limiting women to the GSE, however, he reinforced the postwar conservative gender norms. Thus he claimed that the natural skill women demonstrated in dealing with children would contribute to the workload at the GSE because "In 1986 alone, 941 young runaways and missing persons were apprehended at the border."[62]

Thousands of women inquired about the new pilot program and 330 of them submitted applications. After an initial screening the staff from BGS-West in Hangelar disqualified 130 candidates for a variety of reasons. Overall, however, the selection committee found that almost half of the female applicant pool had better than average qualifications for the job and noted that the proportion of qualified candidates among the women exceeded that of their male counterparts. The training staff chose the barracks at Swisttal-Heimerzheim as the training site, because it could accommodate separate living quarters for the thirty women and sixty-one men who began their basic training on October 1, 1987.[63] Maike Paulsen, one of the first group of thirty women to join the BGS, explained that she was attracted to the idea of "breaking new ground." Her classmate Nadja Schubert remembered the challenges of enduring the militarized training that included night marches, rifles, and hand grenades. She recalled that the "tone of the trainers was very rough—you had to get used to it." Yet at the same time, as Officer Sigrid Tjaden recalled, members of the press took great interest in their class and the "constant media hype … disrupted the daily routine." From the perspective of the training staff, the women performed exceptionally. Michael Jäger, one of the training

---

60 Ibid., 3; for the perspective of state police forces, see "Gleichwertige Berufsausbildung für Frauen Verfassungsgebot: Hessens erste Frauen in Polizeiuniform in Kassel," *Bereitschaftspolizei Heute* (September 1982): 47.

61 Friederich Zimmermann, "Bundesinnenminister Dr. Friedrich Zimmermann eröffnet Frauen den Polizeidienst im BGS," *BGS Zeitschrift* 6 (June 1987): 2.

62 Ibid.

63 RD Runge, Referat P II 1, "Frauen im BGS: Einstellung von 30 Frauen als Anwärterinnen für den mittleren Polizeivollzugsdienst zum 1. Oktober, 1987," BArch-K, B 106/367612.

Figure 10.1. November 3, 1987: Four of the first thirty-one women to graduate BGS training at Swisttal-Heimerzheim. Photo by Bonn-sequenz, courtesy of IMAGO.

officers, recalled an initial reluctance on the part of the staff to deal with female recruits in the same way as the men. Nevertheless, he said many of the women outperformed their male colleagues and demonstrated a higher level of maturity. In their final exams, the female candidates also competed with and in some cases outscored the male officers.[64]

Due to the success of the pilot program, the Interior Ministry's Police Branch recommended hiring an additional thirty women in 1988 and deploying them in all organizational units rather than limiting them to the GSE. After all, in 1987, Interior Minister Zimmermann promised that "the women who are now hired should later be used for the same individual activities and have the same chances of success as male border police officers."[65] Director Runge in Police Branch Division P II 1 emphasized that all arguments against opening the organization lacked merit and violated women's constitutional rights to equal access. On March 11, 1988, Runge asked Dr. Markus Hellenthal, a lawyer assigned to the legal branch (V I 2) for an opinion on whether combatant status precluded women from law enforcement jobs in the BGS. According to Hellenthal, combatant status did not transform border police officers

64 Kati Frost, "Wo genau liegt Heimerzheim?" *Bundespolizei Kompakt* 5, May 2012: 6–10.
65 Friederich Zimmermann, *BGS Zeitschrift* 6 (June 1987): 2.

into soldiers during a war, but rather protected them from treatment as irregulars by enemy forces. Even in combat, BGS units carried out police rather than military missions. Thus Article 12, Section 4 applied to the Bundeswehr, not the BGS, and had no bearing on women serving as border police officers in its enforcement units.[66]

Inspector Egon Schug and Dieter Mechlinski in Division P III 1, however, pointed to an opposing legal analysis by Dr. Albert Bleckmann, a law professor from the Westfälische Wilhelm-Universität in Münster. Bleckmann explained his analysis during a lecture at the Police Leadership Academy in Münster, a transcript of which Schug sent to Police Branch Chief Dr. Wolfgang Schreiber. In essence, Bleckmann refuted Hellenthal's interpretation, because, among other things, Section 64 of the Border Police Act referred to the duty of its officers during a war to defend the state with "military means" thus making it a violation of the Basic Law to employ women in BGS enforcement units.[67] Schreiber disregarded Schug's opinions about women and did not give much weight to Bleckmann's findings. Schreiber wrote a lengthy memorandum to Interior Minister Zimmerman about Bleckmann's analysis, but called it fundamentally incorrect. According to Schreiber, Bleckmann's "false notion of an alleged 'military function' of the BGS is as old as the BGS itself."[68] He pointed out that the Ministry of Justice and the Ministry of Defense supported Hellenthal's legal opinion that "women have a constitutionally guaranteed right to be employed in the enforcement units of the BGS." Thus Schreiber recommended that Zimmermann implement Director Runge's proposal and begin hiring at least 150 female candidates per year.

Despite the positive experiences of the first thirty-one women to break open the doors of the BGS, navigating its militarized organizational culture proved more challenging. Although men retained their dominant role in both East and West Germany, the GDR encouraged women to work, and they had greater access to the labor market than their counterparts in the West. The resistance of the BGS to hiring women until the

66 RD Runge, Referat P II 1, "Frauen im BGS," March 25, 1988; Dr. Markus Hellenthal, Referat V I 2, to RD Runge, "Verwendung von Frauen im BGS," March 21, 1988, BArch-K, B 106/367614; see also Dr. Markus Hellenthal, *Frauen im Bundesgrenzschutz: Folge der Gleichberechtigung oder Verstoß gegen Art. 12a Abs. 4 Satz 2 GG?* (Berlin: Duncker & Humblodt, 1988), 25–26.

67 Egon Schug to Dr. Wolfgang Schreiber, "Verwendung von Frauen in der Kombattanten Verbänden des BGS," May 8, 1989; Dr. Albert Bleckmann, "Der Einsatz von Polizeiverbänden bei eskalierenden Lagen—Struktur und Aufgaben des Bundesgrenzschutzes im Konfliktfall, Vortrag in der Polizeiführungsakademie, Münster, 26. April 1989," 9–11, BArch-K, B 106/367614.

68 Abteilungsleiter P, Dr. Wolfgang Schreiber to Interior Minister Zimmermann, "Frauen im BGS," June 6, 1989, B 106/367614.

late 1980s thus shows the resiliency of the Federal Republic's Cold War gender order and points to one of the problems of framing its history as a success story.[69] Although men like Wolfgang Schreiber and Director Runge pushed for women to have the same promotional opportunities as men, others like Egon Schug and Dieter Mechlinski still insisted border policing was exclusively men's work. The experience of Nicole Bernstein, one of the first thirty-one women to join the BGS, reflected a more typical example of what women faced as pioneers in West Germany's law enforcement profession. At the beginning of her career, she experienced what she described as, "pure chauvinism" in her company and had to request reassignment. It took her fifteen years from the time she was hired before she was finally promoted to a higher management position.[70]

Imagining a Europe without Borders

The advent of women in the BGS was not the only challenge it faced as the 1980s drew to a close. On June 14, 1985, West Germany joined five European Member States (Belgium, France, Luxembourg, and the Netherlands) to sign the Schengen Agreement, a treaty that aimed to abolish Europe's internal borders and promote the concept of open movement.[71] For members of the BGS, the idea of abolishing borders called into question a role it had performed for the Federal Republic for the past 34 years. Dr. Horst Waffenschmidt, the Interior Ministry's Parliamentary Secretary, reported on the anticipated changes that came with the Schengen Agreement and reaffirmed the importance of border policing for keeping the Federal Republic's citizens safe. Borders still functioned like a filter to stop drug trafficking, illegal immigration, and terrorism. In 1985, the Interior Ministry reported that the BGS arrested more than 13,000 people for a variety of offenses, most of which involved illegal immigration and narcotics offenses.[72]

Effective January 1, 1990, border controls were supposed to shift from Europe's internal to its external borders. Dismantling the existing systems in each member country, however, took more time than

---

69 Karen Hagemann, Donna Harsch, Friederike Brühöfener, *Gendering Post-1945 History*, 29.

70 "Nicole Bernstein—erste BGS—Polizeirätin im Dienst," *Lausitzer Rundschau*, March 21, 2003, 1.

71 Schengen Agreement, available online at https://schengenvisainfo.com/Schengen-agreement/.

72 Horst Waffenschmidt, "Entschließung zur Vereinfachung der Personenkontrollen an den innergemeinschaftlichen Grenzen der Europäischen Gemeinschaft/Rede von Dr. Horst Waffenschmidt, Parlamentary Staatssekretär beim BMI, im Deutschen Bundestag am 24.4.1986," *BGS Zeitschrift* 6 (June 1986): 6.

the original signatories anticipated, and the decision by more Western European nations to join prolonged the process. Thus plans to end internal border controls did not take effect until 1995. Although BGS operations at the Inner-German border initially remained unchanged after the Schengen Agreement, it did expedite the Interior Ministry's goal to develop it into a multipurpose federal police agency. The agreement also enhanced cooperative efforts to fight crime among the European member states. Interior Minister Zimmermann took part in the initial negotiations with his European counterparts, all of which shared similar concerns about increases in crime and illegal immigration. In a message to BGS employees, he reported that "Together with my colleagues from the partner countries ... I am striving for compensatory measures to avoid security deficits ... the asylum policy is also to be further adjusted in order to effectively counteract the growing immigration pressure on the countries of Western Europe." He also pointed to recent statistics, including the arrest of 4,000 drug offenders at the Federal Republic's Western borders and warned that "It would not be possible to make up 100 percent of the loss of security associated with the lifting of all internal border controls."[73]

As the member states continued to debate how the Schengen Agreement might affect national security, events unfolding on the other side of the Iron Curtain changed the BGS in ways that none of its members could have anticipated. On November 9, 1989, Border Police Officer Josef Scheuring was driving home from a GdP event when he heard the news that East Germany had unexpectedly opened its borders. Scheuring recalled "For me, who had grown up very close to the Inner-German border, a deep joy spontaneously erupted ... not only in Berlin, but throughout Germany, a unique atmosphere of joy and confidence spread throughout these days."[74] When Wolfgang Schäuble (CDU) replaced Zimmermann as West Germany's Interior Minister in April 1989, he had no idea that in a matter of a few months his biggest challenge would be that he would be negotiating not the opening of Europe's borders but rather the reunification of Germany. Once the initial shock and euphoria subsided, the Interior Ministry had to consider the larger question of what this meant for the BGS—an organization justified by Germany's Cold War division—and its future as a law enforcement agency.

Yet because of its alignment with West Germany's state police forces, the BGS was well-prepared for the challenges of adapting to new roles

---

73   Dr. Friedrich Zimmermann, "Zum Stand der Verhandlungen im Zusammenhang mit dem Schengener Abkommen," *BGS Zeitschrift* 9 (September 1988): 1.

74   Josef Scheuring, *Den Menschen verpflichtet: Vom Bundesgrenzschutz zur Bundespolizei* (Hamburg: Tradition, 2020), 41.

before the Iron Curtain fell. Taking on internal security duties in the former GDR, and what to do with its border police personnel, however, proved to be one of the most immediate and significant problems. The BGS did not have enough police officers to cover the sudden addition of more than 100,000 square kilometers of territory. Soon, members of its command staff and officials at the Interior Ministry quickly realized they could not secure Germany's new external borders or provide for its internal security without incorporating former members of East Germany's border and passport control forces. Not everyone liked the idea of bringing East German border guards into the BGS. Afterall, GDR border troops had been part of its armed forces, and its passport control officers worked under the Ministry for State Security (MfS), the same organization that managed the Stasi secret police. East German border police officers also shot and killed hundreds of fleeing refugees and the MfS rewarded them with medals or commendations for their actions. BGS Officer Josef Scheuring recalled that many of his older colleagues balked at the prospect of bringing their former adversaries into the organization, but recognized that otherwise it would be impossible to hire enough staff to cover the new territories.[75]

In the months before officials agreed upon the final terms of reunification, East Germany's security forces faced an uncertain future. In January, GDR Interim Prime Minister, Hans Modrow, dissolved the border troops, which had been part of the armed forces under the Ministry of Defense. Modrow also reduced the strength of the force to 28,000 and transferred them to the Interior Ministry for use as a border police force. On April 2, 1990, East German Minister of Defense Theodor Hoffmann signed executive order number 46/90 establishing the East German Border Police. The West German Interior Ministry sent advisors from the BGS to guide the formation of the new force.[76] Interior Minister Schäuble and his East German counterpart Peter-Michael Diestel began negotiating the terms of a reunification treaty and agreed in principle to end internal identity and passport checks. Schäuble worried about increases in crime with the end of internal borders and called for a harmonization of visa policies, arguing that "the security needs of European Commission partners and the signatory states of the Schengen Agreement must be taken into account." Bernd Finger, former head of

---

75 Gerhard Sälter, *Grenzpolizisten: Konformität, Verweigerung und Repression in der Grenzpolizei und Grenztruppen der DDR, 1952 bis 1965* (Berlin: Ch. Links Verlag, 2009), 199.202; Josef Scheuring, *Den Menschen verpflichtet*,42–43.

76 Jürgen Ritter, Peter Joachim Lapp, *Die Grenze: Ein deutsches Bauwerk* (Berlin: Ch. Links, 1997), 140; Hans Ehlert, Hans-Joachim Beth, eds., *Armee ohne Zukunft: Das Ende der NVA und die deutsche Einheit; Zeitzeugenberichte und Dokumente* (Berlin: Ch. Links, 2002), 541; Josef Scheuring, *Den Menschen verpflichtet*, 43.

the Department of Public Safety and Order in Berlin recalled that "the fall of the Iron Curtain—happy as everyone was about it—also opened up free, largely uncontrolled entry and exit for perpetrators, means of crime and loot in a transnational dimension."[77]

On July 1, 1990, at the former border crossing that divided the towns of Neustadt/Coburg and Sonnenberg, Schäuble and Diestel signed the formal agreement ending identity checks at internal German borders. On the same day the Treaty on the Creation of a Monetary, Economic, and Social Union between East and West Germany took effect, making West Germany's Mark the legal form of currency for all of Germany.[78] Schäuble told thousands of Germans who gathered for the occasion that "What we have been dreaming of for forty years, something that many no longer dare to hope for, is becoming a reality: unhindered travel from Germany to Germany." Diestel echoed Schäuble's sentiments and called the former demarcation line "… a piece of a cruel past."[79] Schäuble also took a moment to reassure the employees of the BGS that reunified Germany still needed their services and that they could count on a secure future. He also told them he was "striving to transfer the tasks of the railway police and the search service to the Federal Police." Notably absent from his speech, however, was any mention or reassurance to members of East Germany's security forces that they might also expect a secure future. Many of the new border police officers worried about losing their jobs and some resented the BGS advisors who sometimes treated them as inferiors. One former GDR officer complained that the advisors ignored his rank as a captain and demoted him to the middle ranks even though he had studied for years to achieve the promotion. BGS Officer Josef Scheuring recalled good relations with his new colleagues, but also noted they remained skeptical about their fate despite his efforts to reassure them.[80]

In August 1990 Schäuble sent Commander Diethelm Brücker, former head of BGS-Coast, to establish Border Command East (*Grenzschutz*

---

77 Schäuble quoted from "Mit Personalausweis in die DDR/Wegfall der Paßflicht/Abbau der Personenkontrollen angestrebt," *BGS Zeitschrift* 6 (June 1990): 1; Bernd Finger, "Berliner Polizei-Einheit Berlins Magistrat und die Innere Sicherheit nach dem Mauerfall," *Zeitschrift für Deradikalisierung und demokratische Kultur* (January 2022): 2.

78 Konrad Jarausch and Volker Grasnow, eds., *Uniting Germany*, 154.

79 For Schäuble's and Diestel's comments see "Personenkontrollen an der innerdeutschen Grenzen aufgehoben: Abkommen von Bundesinnenminister. Dr. Schäuble und Minister Dr. Diestel unterzeichnet," *BGS Zeitschrift* 7 (July 1990): 1.

80 Alexandra Schwell, *Europa an der Oder: Die Konstruktion europäischer Sicherheit und der deutsch-polnischen Grenze* (Bielefeld: Transcript, 2015), 98–99; Josef Scheuring, *Den Menschen verpflichtet*, 46.

Ost) at Pätz, the headquarters of the GDR border troops. At Pätz he organized and managed the merging of thousands of former East German security and police officials into new border police units led by BGS advisors. At the time, the challenges of building and deploying these new units outweighed a closer scrutiny or investigation of the former GDR personnel.[81] By August 31, representatives from East and West Germany signed the Unification Treaty, setting October 3, 1990 as the official day of German reunification. As a result, East Germany's Minister for Disarmament and Defense, Rainer Eppelmann, issued order number 49/90 disbanding the GDR border troops, according to the terms of the Unification Treaty. At midnight on October 3, Brücker ordered federal service flags raised at the former East German border command centers in Pätz, Wilhelmshagen, Neustrelitz, and Chemnitz.[82] As thousands of Germans surged into Berlin to celebrate the official reunification, BGS-Ost, the Berlin Police, and members of the People's Police all worked together to protect politicians and government buildings, control traffic, and deal with the large crowds. The officers recognized the significance of the moment and also got caught up in the euphoria. Border Police Officer Rolf Lumack, for example, realized he was part of something momentous and thought to himself "The BGS in Berlin! Who would have dared to think that a year ago? Now we can say that we were the first at a historical time!"[83]

When the Unification Treaty took effect, the BGS employed approximately 3,500 members of the former East German border police, a further 1,800 officers from the transport police, 1,200 members of the Passport Control Unit, and 200 officers from other MfS units.[84] In an organizational address recognizing German reunification, Schäuble made a point to finally welcome these former East German police officers to the BGS. He explained, "With you, we want to create a federal border guard as the federal police force in the area of the new five states and in Berlin ... I am confident that this will succeed soon [and] we will simultaneously grow

---

81 Ronny von Bresinski, "Aus den Erinnerungen des ersten Kommandeurs Der Aufbau des Grenzschutzkommandos," *Bundespolizei Kompakt* 4 (April 2020): 16–17.

82 See "Unification Treaty, August 31, 1990," Document 3, in Konrad Jarausch and Volker Grasnow, *Uniting Germany*, 188–99; Hans Ehlert and Hans Joachim-Beth, *Armee ohne Zukunft*, 505; Ronny von Bresinski, "Aus den Erinnerungen," 17.

83 Rolf Lumack, "Wir waren die ersten! Eindrücke eines Hundertschaftsführers vom ersten Berlin-Einsatz den Bundesgrenzschutz vom 1. bis 4. Oktober 1990 durchführen hatte," *BGS Zeitschrift* 11 (November 1990): 10.

84 Josef Scheuring, *Den Menschen verpflichtet*, 52.

into a single Federal Border Police."[85] Yet the excitement over reunification soon turned bitter as thousands of former East German border police officers faced immediate dismissal because of their service in the security agencies of the former East German state. The Stasi employed thousands of East Germans over the course of its lifespan either as secret police officials or informers (*inoffizielle Mitarbeiter*—IM); thousands more worked as civilians in the MfS or collaborated in one form or another with the GDR's repressive security system. According to historian John Miller, the Stasi made up "2 percent of the adult population" and "accumulated records said to cover between 180 and 200 km of shelving and to include reports on six million persons." Moreover, John Koehler estimated that at its zenith "it would not have been unreasonable to assume that at least one Stasi informer was present in any party of ten or twelve dinner guests." When Schäuble learned about the mass volumes of secret files, he considered destroying them all.[86] Thus finding East Germans who had not collaborated with the MfS in one form or another proved difficult.

As a GdP representative, BGS Officer Josef Scheuring and his colleagues played a key role in the initial round of interviews and hearings to evaluate the suitability of integrating the new East German border police officers into the BGS. Similar vetting processes took place in Germany's state police forces. Probing into personnel files of the new officers, however, produced accusations of hypocrisy and evoked comparisons to the Nuremberg trials or the reviled denazification hearings. Article 103, Section 2 of the Basic Law prohibited retroactive punishment.[87] On December 20, 1991, the Bundestag passed the Law on the Documents of the State Security Service of the Former GDR (*Stasi-Unterlagen-Gesetz*—StUG), which established a Federal Commissioner for the Stasi records—known later as the "Gauck Authority" after its first Commissioner, Joachim Gauck. Gauck, a Protestant minister, played a key role in the East German movement that toppled the SED regime. The law allowed employers like the BGS to request information from the archives concerning the extent of an employee's complicity with the Stasi. According to Gauck, the intent of what he called "a judicial reckoning

---

85 "Grußwort des Bundesministers des Innern, Dr. Wolfgang Schäuble, an die Angehörigen des Bundesgrenzschutzes aus Anlaß der Vereinigung der beiden deutschen Staaten am 3. Oktober 1990," *BGS Zeitschrift* 10 (October 1990): 2.

86 John Miller, "Settling Accounts with a Secret Police: The German Law on the Stasi Records," *Europe-Asia Studies* 50, no. 2 (March 1998): 305, 307–8; John O. Koehler, *Stasi*, 9; Mary Fulbrook, *Anatomy of a Dictatorship*, 45–56; Jens Gieseke, *The History of the Stasi: East Germany's Secret Police, 1945–1990* (New York: Berghahn, 2014), 202–3.

87 Peter R. Quint, "The Border Guard Trials and the East German Past—Seven Arguments," *American Journal of Comparative Law* 48, no. 4 (2000): 541.

with the past" was for Germans to confront their past in a much more introspective manner than had been the case after the Second World War. He argued, "This time, collaboration, failure and guilt would not be suppressed; it would be acknowledged, faced up to."[88] Certainly, if the BGS had implemented a similar vetting process to investigate the Nazi pasts of its founding members in 1951, the hiring authority would have dismissed many of them.

Since the Gauck Authority had to screen all former GDR personnel employed in BGS-Ost, the Interior Ministry hired these officers on probationary status pending the outcome of their individual investigations. As a consequence of the findings, it dismissed many officers. Scheuring, who represented many of these new East German employees during the BGS hearing committees said he was not always convinced of the guilt for everyone the ministry chose to dismiss. He said that over time, his reservations about working with former GDR officers eased and he often asked himself "How would I have behaved if I had grown up in the GDR—would I have opposed the system … would I really have refused to take on the tasks for this state?" Bernd Finger expressed similar sentiments from his experience integrating East Germans into the Berlin Police, recalling that he was "firmly convinced that the People's Police should not be excluded from the democratic renewal process."[89] In some cases the hearing committees appealed the dismissals and succeeded in retaining officers, which, according to Scheuring showed that "a bit of humanity made its way through a problematic path." Moreover, in order to speed up the process, the Interior Ministry also assigned special BGS representatives to act as liaison officers with the Gauck authority. By 1992, approximately 5,000 officers made it through the vetting process and achieved civil servant status. BGS-Ost, however, dismissed a further 650 employees who had worked in the passport control division of the MfS.[90]

By far the most controversial cases involved the criminal prosecution of former border police officers who shot and killed or wounded East Germans attempting to flee to the West.[91] Although the precise num-

88 Joachim Gauck and Matin Fry, "Dealing with a Stasi Past," *Daedalus* 123, no. 1 (Winter 1994): 280.

89 Josef Scheuring, *Den Menschen Verpflichtet*, 51; Bernd Finger, "Berliner Polizei-Einheit: Berlins Magistrat und die Innere Sicherheit nach dem Mauerfall," Deutschland Archiv (October 11, 2021), 9, https://www.bpb.de/themen/deutschlandarchiv/341583/berliner-polizei-einheit/.

90 Josef Scheuring, *Den Menschen verpflichtet*, 56; "Erste Verbeamtungen beim Bundesgrenzschutz Ost," *BGS Zeitschrift* 10 (October 1991): 15.

91 There is an extensive debate and body of legal scholarship covering these cases, see for example, Roman Grafe, *Deutsche Gerechtigkeit: Prozesse gegen DDR-Grenzschützen und Ihre Befehlsgeber* (Munich: Siedler Verlag, 2009); Jörg Arnold, Nora Karsten, and Helmut Kreicker, "The German Border Guard Cases before

ber of victims of the so called "shoot to kill order" (*Schießbefehl*) is still largely unknown, some estimates claim that GDR border troops killed or wounded at least 600 people and probably many more.[92] Besides the contradiction with the Basic Law's prohibition of retroactive punishment, lawyers for the individuals charged argued that they acted in accordance to the laws of the GDR and followed orders that were valid at the time. Prosecutors argued, however, that the brutal killings violated human rights and dignity to the extent that their "actions were so reprehensible that the principle of non-retroactivity is outweighed." Or, as Peter Schneider put it "No one who has invoked orders or higher authority to trample on human rights should feel confident, now or in the future, that he will go unscathed."[93]

Thus between 1992 and 2004 the state prosecuted approximately 145 officers, of whom eighty received suspended sentences or probation; the court declared the remaining sixty-five defendants innocent.[94] Some of the defendants appealed to the European Court of Human Rights (ECHR), claiming their convictions violated Article 7, Section 1 of the Convention for Human Rights and Fundamental Freedoms, which prohibited punishment for offenses that, when committed, did not constitute criminal offenses under national or international law. In 1997, for example, an officer applied to the ECHR in the case *K.-H. W. v. Germany*, arguing that his conviction for the 1972 killing of Manfred Weylandt, a 29-year-old trying to flee to West Germany, should be overturned since it did not violate valid GDR laws in effect at the time. The Court disagreed, however, and confirmed his conviction, on the basis, among other facts, that "although the event in issue took place in 1972, before the ratification of the International Covenant, he should have known, as an ordinary citizen, that firing on unarmed persons who were merely trying to leave their country infringed fundamental and human rights."[95]

---

the European Court of Human Rights," *European Journal of Crime, Criminal Law and Criminal Justice* 11, no. 1 (2003): 67–92.

92 An online archive project tracks the biographies of many of these victims, see website: "Eiserner Vorhang: Tödliche Flüchten und Rechtsbeugung," http://todesopfer.eiserner-vorhang.de/article/.

93 Peter R. Quint, "The Border Guard Trials," 543–44; Peter Schneider, "Facing Germany's Newer Past," *New York Times*, September 30, 1991, 17.

94 Andreas Tzortzis, "Shooting Germans," *Deutsche Welle*, November 11, 2004, http://dw.com/en/when-germans-shot-germans/a-1391426.

95 Convention for the Protection of Human Rights and Fundamental Freedoms, September 3, 1953, University of Minnesota Human Rights Library, http://hrlibrary.umn.edu/instree/z17euroco.html; Judgment: *K.-H. W. v. Germany*, European Court of Human Rights, Strasbourg, France, March 22, 2001, https://hudoc.echr.coe.int/eng?i=001-59352.

From Paramilitary Border Guard to Multipurpose Law Enforcement Agency

The reunification of Germany, a development that no one anticipated, completed transforming the BGS into a national law enforcement agency, a process that began with the 1972 revision of the Border Police Act. The disappearance of the Inner-German border and the Schengen Agreement ended the German "Cold Civil War" and the lingering focus on militarization promoted by its earlier generations of leaders. By the end of 1990, the border police officers graduating from basic training at Swisttal-Heimerzheim included more women and East Germans such that they earned the nickname: "Ossis, Wessis and Tussis"—or, Easties, Westies, and Broads.[96] Nevertheless, women still faced challenges and had to file legal actions with the support of their trade unions to finally overturn the rule restricting them to service in the GSE. During the 1990s, the organization began treating women on more of an equal footing with their male colleagues and ended the use of separate female liaison officers during basic training. In 1992, Michaela Busemann, one of the first thirty-three women to join the BGS, was promoted to the rank of sergeant. The opening of the Inner-German border also made thousands of officers available for other duties such as security operations and passport control duties at Germany's airports and train stations.[97]

Finally, in 1994 the Bundestag passed new legislation further revising the Border Police Act to reflect that the BGS carried out law enforcement duties, ending decades of ambiguity over its peculiar hybrid role between a police and military force. The disappearance of the Inner-German border negated the need for combatant status granted to its personnel in 1965 under Section 64 of the Act. Petra Hoyer, a Director in the Interior Ministry's legal division who worked on the revisions, argued that the end of combatant status made it clear once and for all that the BGS was a police force. Previous fears that enemy soldiers might treat border police officers as irregulars no longer stood up against new concerns that they might justify attacking civilian sites guarded by police officers confused as soldiers.[98] Yet the new law also increased the police powers of BGS personnel and codified some of its more controversial surveillance and data

---

96 Katie Frost, Kati Frost, "Wo genau liegt Heimerzheim," 9.

97 Kati Frost, "Wo genau liegt Heimerzheim," 9; Bernd-Michael Schuman, "Integrierte Ausbildung von Frauen und Männern im BGS," *BGS Zeitschrift* 1 (January 1991): 8–9; "erste Polizeimeisterin beim Grenzschützpräsidium West," *BGS Zeitschrift* 3 (March-April 1992): 33; "Bundesgrenzschutz soll die Bahnpolizei und Schutzaufgaben für Sicherheit des Luftverkehrs auf den Flughäfen übernommen," *BGS Zeitschrift* 6 (June 1991): 12.

98 Petra Hoyer, "Neues Bundesgrenzschutz-gesetz in Kraft getreten," *BGS Zeitschrift* 11 (October-November 1994): 5.

collection policies. Data collected at the borders, for example, could still be shared with Germany's intelligence agencies, but not without informing the Parliamentary Control Council. In response to the violent demonstrations of the 1980s, it also gave border police officers broad powers to detain subjects in "preventative custody for up to four days before violent demonstrations," but failed to define what constituted a violent demonstration. The new law also transferred the legal basis for BGS covert Group-F, which had none prior to 1994, to the Federal Protection of the Constitution Act under the Parliamentary Control Council. Since the Bundestag never even knew the unit existed until 1994, it was a proverbial case of asking for forgiveness rather than permission; its records remained classified, leaving many open questions about the extent to which its activities may have violated Germany's rule of law (*Rechtsstaat*) during nearly forty years of clandestine operations.

At the start of the new millennium, few, if any, traces of the old militarized BGS remained, and the force reached a combined strength of 30,000 officers. Its personnel had become an integral part of modern Germany's national security infrastructure, and other than the color of their uniforms, they were indistinguishable from state police officers. In 2001 the BGS was once again called upon to fight terrorism in the aftermath of the 9/11 attacks in New York and Washington, DC. Border police officers intensified passenger and baggage screening at all of Germany's airports and deployed officers abroad to guard its embassies and their staffs.[99] On April 7, 2004, during the US war in Iraq, GSG 9 members Tobias Retterath and Thomas Hafenecker were killed in an ambush outside the city of Fallujah while travelling to Baghdad to provide security at Germany's embassy.[100] At the end of 2004, Interior Minister Otto Schily announced the renaming of the BGS to the Bundespolizei and the changing of its uniform color from green to blue matching those of other European national police forces.[101] Schily's decision reflected an important, albeit largely symbolic recognition of the fact that the BGS had become what for decades its leaders had always claimed it to be, but at times struggled to fully realize: a national law enforcement agency.

---

99 Interior Minister Otto Schily, "Der Bundesgrenzschutz in den Jahren 2001/2002—Rückblick und Ausblick," *BGS Zeitschrift* 4 (December 2001), 1.

100 "Germany Pays Tribute to Officers Killed in Iraq," *Deutsche Welle*, June 29, 2004,1; "GSG 9 Beamte bei Falludscha verscharrt," *FAZ*, April 18, 2004, 1.

101 Otto Schily, "Vorwort: Umbenennung des Bundesgrenzschutzes in "Bundespolizei," BGS Zeitschrift 4 (December 2004): 1.

CONCLUSION: GERMANY'S POLICE: A MODEL FOR DEMOCRATIC POLICING?

THIS BOOK BEGAN as a project to explore Germany's democratization through an analysis of the *Bundesgrenzschutz*, a militarized border guard that over time evolved into Germany's modern national police force. Over the course of researching, writing, and revising the final draft, many of the historical issues it raised about the Federal Republic's law enforcement institutions re-emerged as topics of current events. In the United States, journalists often invoked Germany's police as an ideal model for de-militarizing and reforming America's police departments, citing stark differences in the levels of police violence between the two countries. Yet propping up Germany's police as a model for law enforcement without also recognizing its own problematic legacies forms another layer of the success narrative this book set out to question. In the aftermath of George Floyd's brutal murder by Minneapolis police officers, for example, the *New York Times* published an article citing Germany as a country that got policing right and learned from its mistakes. According to the article's subtitle: "In the postwar era, Germany fundamentally redesigned law enforcement to prevent past atrocities from ever repeating. Its approach may hold lessons for police reform everywhere." For support, the article claimed that in postwar Germany "the privacy of citizens was rigorously protected, and the police and military were strictly separated," neither of which is really true.[1]

As my analysis of the BGS has shown, the Federal Republic struggled, and still does, with the question of how to tame its coercive forces of legitimate violence. As the government tried to weigh how to keep citizens safe without eroding the rule of law in the process, it faced some of the same challenges and considered similar authoritarian responses that corrupted its police institution in 1933. During its response to domestic terrorism in the 1970s, for example, border police officers recorded the personal data of unsuspecting individuals and transmitted it to the Federal Republic's intelligence agencies. Moreover, the BGS established a

---

[1] Katrin Bennhold and Melissa Eddy, "In Germany, Confronting Shameful Legacy is Essential Part of Police Training," *New York Times*, June 23, 2020; http://www.nytimes.com/2020/06/23/world/europe/germany-police.html.

top-secret telecommunications unit, Group-F, which clandestinely monitored West German citizens without their knowledge or consent, and concealed its existence and activities from parliament for almost forty years. The true scope of its surveillance operations is still largely unknown, because its records remain classified.

While East Germany's Stasi has become synonymous, and deservedly so, with pervasive surveillance, the Federal Republic was not above deploying similar methods against those it perceived to be its internal enemies. Although there is no comparison to the scale and insidiousness of the Stasi, West Germany's covert police surveillance operations also ruined lives and reputations. The forgotten case of Iain Macleod, the British expat shot and killed by the Stuttgart Police acting on faulty intelligence, and Maihofer's secret wiretapping operation against Dr. Klaus Traube are but two examples of the consequences that came with its militant democracy. It is important to remember, however, that other Western democracies like Great Britain and the United States also used invasive surveillance operations against their citizens in the name of national security. Matt Foot's recent article about the activities of the London Metropolitan Police's Special Demonstration Squad (SDS), which infiltrated alleged "subversive" groups in the name of national security, shows how democracies are not above deploying surveillance tactics more commonly associated with totalitarian regimes.[2]

Since the BGS was the Federal Republic's first postwar attempt to reestablish policing at the national level, the organization sheds light on the course of its democratization. As Berlin's Public Safety Officer Bernd Finger put it, "The more democracy within the police means more democracy for the citizen."[3] From the beginning, however, Chancellor Adenauer and his first Interior Minister Robert Lehr never intended the BGS to become a law enforcement agency in the traditional sense. From this perspective, it is important to contextualize their approach to security as a manifestation of their legitimate concerns about the potential for Soviet aggression at the Inner-German border. In 1949 West Germany sat on the frontlines of a battle between East and West that was both ideaological and physical. The behavior of Soviet troops in the final months of the war, their blockade of Berlin in 1948, and the Korean War in 1950 underscored Adenauer's pleas for more security.

Both Adenauer and Lehr harbored a pathological fear of Bolshevism that was forged by their Christian conservatism and their similar experiences dealing with political violence during the interwar years. East Germany's paramilitary police units evoked their worst fears of

---

2 Matt Foot, "Children of the Spied-On," *London Review of Books* 45, no. 13 (June 29, 2023): 41.
3 Bernd Finger, "Berliner Polizei," 13.

communist revolution and civil war. Adenauer blamed the collapse of the Weimar Republic on the failure of its government to forcefully quell violent unrest and communist strikers in particular. And so, to prevent Bonn from following in the path of Weimar, they established the BGS, not as a border guard, but rather as an instrument of state violence that they could deploy against the Federal Republic's internal enemies. More than 15,000 men applied for its 650 commanding officer positions, but Lehr's Interior Ministry overwhelmingly selected tough, battle-hardened veterans, including members of the Waffen-SS, to lead the new force. If Adenauer or Lehr truly wanted a police organization, as both repeatedly claimed, they chose the wrong men.

Gerhard Matzky, Anton Grasser, Kurt Andersen, Heinrich Müller, and countless other veteran soldiers made the BGS into a fighting force and shaped its organizational culture for years to come. For these men, one war against the Soviets had just ended, and they had to be ready for the next one to begin. And in the BGS they found a profession in which they could apply their training and experience in the defense of their homeland, albeit under a completely different political regime. Their quick return to prominent positions as armed servants of the state helped to ease the personal shame that they and many of their colleagues endured at the end of the war. Heinrich Müller's daughter Irmgard, for example, recalled that he returned home from the war jobless and emaciated from dysentery after nearly starving to death in an Allied POW camp outside Heidelberg. Müller, the talented intellectual who served on Field Marshall Erwin Rommel's staff and taught at the Nazi war academy had no other option but to begin an apprenticeship as a carpenter to support his family.[4] Donning a new uniform as an official of the Federal Republic restored his dignity and bound him to its democracy, even if ideologically he and many of his colleagues remained politically conservative militarists. The pragmatic realities of earning a living in a familiar profession outweighed the alternatives that included unemployment or having to work in manual labor. Better to keep one's political ideology in the private sphere.

Nevertheless, over the first twenty-five years of its existence, the BGS struggled to overcome an internal identity crisis, caught as it was between the forces of continuity and change, between its connections to the old Wehrmacht and its efforts to become a law enforcement agency. Thus its personnel were "border hunters" (*Grenzjäger*) instead of police officers, held military ranks, lived in barracks, trained for combat, and wore the trademark steel helmets of Nazi Germany's armed forces, as well as similar uniforms. Its units were equipped with mortars, machine guns, hand

---

[4] Email from Frau Dr. Professorin Irmgard Müller to author, September 21, 2022.

grenades, and armored vehicles. When deployed to the borders to deal with smugglers, its officers revived the Wehrmacht's *Grossunternehmen* (large-scale operations) and *Bandenbekämpfung* (bandit-fighting) tactics.[5] After West Germany established a new army in 1956, the BGS lost more than half of its personnel, who became soldiers. The federal government refused to disband it and transfer its remaining officers to West Germany's state police because, as they argued at the time, it was the only instrument and source of its executive powers. The army was bound by NATO and could not be deployed for domestic security: otherwise, police power in the Federal Republic remained with its state governments.

During the 1950s, 1960s, and early 1970s, the majority of training and education in the BGS still emphasized military rather than law enforcement topics. With few exceptions, xenophobic and ethno-chauvinistic themes, grounded in Western anti-communism and racist stereotypes of foreign enemies, permeated its organizational training, professional ethics seminars, and institutional literature. At the same time, the Catholic and Protestant chaplains who taught professional ethics employed innovative methods to engage their students in serious discussions about race, the Nazi past, and other topics they believed would help the men make good decisions and live according to the moral principles of western Christianity. As Paul Betts has recently argued, the Churches "led the charge in reasserting their role in redrawing the cultural geography of Cold War Europe around the frontiers of faith ... Conservative Western European ideas of the revival of a neomedieval *Abendland*, or land of the West, helped to overcome confessional divides between Catholics and Protestants in the fight against 'godless' communism."[6] Border police officers guarded what was, for Christian Europe, one of its most dangerous "frontiers of faith"—the Iron Curtain. It is difficult to assess the effect of these courses on the men and how they reacted to them. Still, many of the themes reinforced negative stereotypes about non-Christians or explained National Socialism as the work of one man—Hitler—and a small minority of fanatical followers.

Border police officers also participated in massive NATO war games and in 1964, took part in a controversial counterinsurgency exercise (Operation South-Bavaria) with US Special Forces units, during which many of its officers complained, to no avail, about harsh treatment and even torture. The Bundestag's 1965 decision to designate border police officers as military combatants renewed public debate about the ambiguous role of the BGS, in which both sides used Germany's military past to justify their position. By far, until at least the early 1970s, most of its

---

5   Ben Shepherd, *Hitler's Soldiers*, 290.
6   Paul Betts, *Ruin and Renewal: Civilizing Europe after World War II* (New York: Basic, 2020), 23.

senior staff and instructors were military veterans, many of whom had fought with Nazi Germany's armed forces and been held as POWs before joining the BGS. Senior Pilot Erwin Knorr, a Luftwaffe ace accused of abusing trainees, and Colonel Hans-Jürgen Pantenius, a veteran of Nazi Germany's motorized infantry divisions who instructed border police officers about the finer points of "street fighting" from his experiences during the Warsaw Uprising, are just two among many examples of how the organization consistently blurred the division between police and military duties.

Nothing changed for the BGS until 1968, when the Bundestag passed emergency legislation assigning additional security duties to it and turning it into a police reserve for the states. The organization still suffered from a lack of adequate staffing, and most of its personnel consisted of short-term conscripts. The Interior Ministry recognized that they either had to completely overhaul and reform the BGS or disband it altogether—they chose the former. In 1972, as part of Brandt's Program for Internal Security, the Bundestag passed the first comprehensive revision of the Border Police Act since 1951 and began the process of aligning the BGS to West Germany's state police forces. The revisions, coupled with the retirement of its Wehrmacht generation, finally began to transform the organization into a law enforcement agency. By 1976, border police officers received the same pay and training as their state police counterparts and could transfer between the forces after a specified term of service. The incentive of a job with the state police made the BGS more attractive as a career choice and ended its long-term staffing problems.

In spite of the legislative changes and reforms, however, the BGS still promoted a hyper-masculine organizational culture and struggled with the legacies of its militarization. During the anti-nuclear demonstrations at Brokdorf, for example, border police pilots dropped tear gas canisters on the crowds and deliberately flew their helicopters dangerously low to the ground, injuring people with flying debris in the process. During the 1980s, West German civil rights groups complained about a "progressive militarization" in the BGS.[7] The organization's resistance to hiring women, and the misogynistic justifications given by some if its staff to avoid it, reflected the strength of West Germany's conservative gender order and calls into question the narrative of its progressive liberalization. The first women to join the BGS often outperformed their male colleagues, but they still had to struggle to gain equal recognition. Despite Interior Minister Zimmermann's promise that they would have the same opportunities for advancement, the first women had to take legal action to end the organizational practice of limiting them to passport control duties. The reunification of Germany in 1990 followed by the revisions

7   Otto Diederichs, "In welcher Verfassung ist der BGS?" 30.

to the Border Police Act in 1994 finally terminated the status of border police officers as military combatants ending decades of ambiguity over its peculiar hybrid role in between a police force and an army. Thus Interior Minister Otto Schily's 2004 decision to rename the BGS and eliminate its green uniforms was largely symbolic, because it had already become a federal police force in all but name.

Unlike their predecessors in the BGS, the men and women who donned the blue uniforms of the *Bundespolizei* came to their new profession after years of intense study and with advanced university degrees. Nevertheless, if recent events tell us anything, despite all the education, training, and emphasis on lessons from the Nazi past, Germany's police institution is still contending with systemic racism and militarization. Between 2000 and 2007, for example, investigators failed to link the murders of eight Turkish immigrants by neo-Nazis from the National Socialist Underground, even though the perpetrators killed the victims with the same firearm. The investigating officers, influenced by bias and stereotyping, dismissed the murders as the work of the Turkish Mafia, missed vital clues, and tried to intimidate family members of the victims to falsely admit their relatives participated in organized crime.[8] In August 2022, German police officers armed with submachineguns shot and killed a knife-wielding Senegalese teenager suffering from a mental health emergency, setting off nationwide protests and calls for reform.[9] German authorities have also reported an alarming rise in the number of its police officers that support and promote radical right-wing groups. In some cases, officers conspired to assassinate politicians and start a race war to overthrow the democratic government. An officer from Saxony reported that during tactical training at the firing range his academy instructor told the class "We have to shoot well, because there are many refugees coming to Germany." As evidence of these behaviors and plots surfaced, Interior Minister Horst Seehofer dismissed them and claimed "We are dealing with a small number of cases, meaning we have no structural problem with right-wing extremism in the security forces." Investigators, however, discovered at least 300 members of the *Bundespolizei* who had joined various extremist groups and hundreds more who subscribed to and/or followed radical right-wing social media sites.[10]

---

8   Thomas Meaney and Saskia Schäfer, "The neo-Nazi murder trial revealing Germany's darkest secrets," *Guardian*, December 15, 2016, http://theguardian.com/world/2016/dec/15.

9   Ralf Bosen, "Killing of Youth Sparks Debate About German Police Brutality," *Deutsche Welle* (August 12, 2022), http://dw.com/en/police-brutality-in-germany-killing-of-16-year-old-sparks-debate/a-62791336.

10   Katrin Bennhold, "Body Bags and Enemy Hit Lists: How Far-Right Police Officers and Ex-Soldiers Planned for Day X," *The New York Times* (August 1, 2020), 1; Rob Schmitz, "With Far-Right Extremism on the Rise,

Seehofer's refusal to acknowledge that a problem even existed is a striking example of how police organizations fail, even those like Germany's with its high educational standards and culture of liberalism. As my analysis of the BGS has shown, organizations and the people in them can and do change, but the process is far from linear and requires constant vigilance and oversight. There is no simple solution. The BGS shows how even in a new, post-dictatorial democracy, militarized training and organizational culture can be difficult to root out—forces of continuity often exist in tension with calls for change and reform. Germany's modern police institution does indeed hold lessons for other Western democracies—that without "discursive contestation, democratic scrutiny, and constitutional control," all law enforcement agencies and their personnel remain vulnerable to the same darker, authoritarian impulses that in 1933 led its democratic police institution down the path of dictatorship and war.[11]

Germany Investigates its Police, *NPR* (December 10, 2020), http://npr.org/2020/12/10/943823021/.

11 Ian Loader and Neil Walker, *Civilizing Security*, 7.

BIBLIOGRAPHY

Archival Sources

Amherst College Library Archives and Special Collections

The John J. McCloy Papers
    Box +HC5
    Box +HC6
    Box GYI
    Box SP 1

Bundesarchiv Koblenz (BArch-K)

B 106—Bundesministerium des Innern—Hauptgruppe 6 Innere Sicherheit/ Polizei/Bundespolizei
B 136—Bundeskanzleramt 1949–69
B 144—Bundesministerium für Angelegenheiten des Bundesrates und der Länder,
B 145—Presse- und Informationsamt der Bundesregierung (BPA)
B 273—Bundespolizeipräsidium—Grenzpolizeilichen Aufgaben des BGS, 1951–57
B 443—Bundesamt für Verfassungsschutz

Bundesarchiv Militärarchiv Freiburg (BA-MA)

BH28—Wehrbereichskommando II, 1955–94
BW 1—Bundesministerium der Verteidigung Abteilung Verwaltung und Recht.
BW 9—Deutsche Dienststellen zur Vorbereitung der Europäischen Verteidigungsgemeinschaften zusammenhängenden Fragen
DVW 1—DDR Ministerium für Nationale Verteidigung
N245—Nachlass Hans-Georg Reinhardt
N848—Nachlass Heinrich Müller
N181—Nachlass Gerhard Matzky
PERS/6—Personalunterlagen von Angehörigen der Reichswehr und Wehrmacht.

Bundesarchiv Ludwigsburg (BArch-LW)

B 162—Zentrale Stelle der Landesjustizverwaltungen zur Aufklärung nationalsozialistischer Verbrechen 1958–2003.
409 AR 1657/64—Otto Dippelhofer
    Karte nos. 1 and 2—10 AR 932/64

Deutscher Bundestag Archiv

Drucksachen und Plenarprotokolle des Bundestages—ab 1949. Available online at https://dip.bundestag.de/

Deutsche Hochschule der Polizei—Hochschulbibliothek (DHPol)

Der Grenzjäger, Zentralorgan des Bundesgrenzschutz-Verbandes e.V.
Die Parole, illustrierte Zeitschrift für den Bundesgrenzschutz
Polizei Kurrier

Dwight David Eisenhower Presidential Library

White House Office, National Security Council Staff: Papers, 1948–1961, Disaster File
    Box 48
Papers, Pre-Presidential, 1916–1952
    Box 116
Papers as President, 1953–1961 (Ann Whitman File), Dulles-Herter Series.
    Box 5

Harry S. Truman Presidential Library

McKinzie, Richard. Oral History Interview with Special Assistant to director, Bureau of German Affairs, Department of State, Perry Laukhuff. Norwalk: Connecticut, 23 July 1974.

Harvard University Archives

Papers of James Bryant Conant
    Box 139—Germany

Niedersächsiches Landesarchiv Hannover (NLA-HA)

ds. 220—Oberfinanzdirektion Hannover

Staatsarchiv München (StArch-M)

35279—Ermittlungsverfahren gegen Radtke, Wilhelm, wegen Verdachts des Mordes (NSG) (Gedacht 1 Oktober 1969), Bd. Nos. 1–3.

Staatsbibliothek zu Berlin—Zeitungsabteilung (StB-Z)

Frankfurter Allegemeine Zeitung (*FAZ*) Collection

The National Archives—United Kingdom (TNA)

FO 371—Foreign Office: Political Departments: General Correspondence from 1906 to 1966.
FO 371/85324—Formation of a German Federal Police Force, papers 1 to 4414, 1950.
FO 371/104138—Arming and proposed increase in size of Federal Frontier Police (Bundesgrenzschutz), papers 1–14, 1953.
FO 371/104139—Arming and proposed increase in the size of the Federal Frontier Police (Bundesgrenzschutz), papers 15–29, 1953.
FO 371/104140—Arming and proposed increase in the size of the Federal Frontier Police (Bundesgrenzschutz), papers 30 to end, 1953.
FO 371/109719—Expansion of Federal Frontier Police (Bundesgrenzschutz), 1954.
FO 371/118418—Expansion of Federal Frontier Police (Bundesgrenzschutz), 1955.

The United States National Archives and Records Administration (NARA)

Record Group 466—Records of the US High Commission for Germany.
John J. McCloy, General Classified Records.
    Box 9
    Box 11
    Box 12
Office of the Executive Director, Miscellaneous Files Maintained by Colonel H. A. Gerhardt.
    Box 1
    Box 2
Office of the Executive Director, General Hays's Executive Files, 1949–1951.
    Box 1
    Box 2
Military Security Board: Military Division, Secret General Records, 1949–1955.
    Box 2
Industrial Division (US Element), Correspondence and Other Records Relating to the Regulation of German Industrial Companies, 1949–1955.
    Box 8—"Bundesgrenzschutz thru Stahlbau Rheinhausen."
Record Group 218—Records of the US Joint Chiefs of Staff to Secretary of Defense.

Geographic File, 1948–1950.
 Box 25
German Army and Luftwaffe Personnel "201" Files, 1900–1945.
 Box 237, Microfilm Publication A3356—Grasser, Anton

Films and Media

Andelfinger, Fritz, and K. Richter. *Zum Schutz der Heimat*. Deutsche Industrie und Auftragsfilm, 1956.
Erras, Carl. *Für Frieden und Freiheit*. Munich: DIA Film, 1960.
Koshofer, Nina. *Adenauers letzte Reise*. Phoenix—ZDF, 2016.

Newspapers and Magazines

Bild am Sonntag
Bild Hamburg
Bonnischer Anzeiger
Bremer Nachrichten
Cleveland Plains Dealer
Christ und Welt
Der Spiegel
Deutsches Allgemeines Sonntagsblatt
Deutsche Welle (DW)
Die Welt
Frankfurter Allgemeine Zeitung (FAZ)
Hamburger Morgen Post
Hannoversche Allgemeine Zeitung
Hannoversche Presse
Life Magazine
New York Times
Oxnard Currier
St. Petersburg Times
Stuttgart Christ und Welt
Stuttgarter Zeitung
Süddeutsche Zeitung
The Atlantic
US News and World Report
Vörwarts
Welt an Sonntag
Weser-Kurier
Zeitschriften des BGS (1974–2004)

Secondary Sources

Abenheim, Donald. *Reforging the Iron Cross: The Search for Tradition in the West German Armed Forces*. Princeton, NJ: Princeton University Press, 1988.

Adenauer, Konrad, and Hans-Peter Mensing, eds. *Briefe, 1951–1953*. Berlin: Siedler, 1987.

Allen, Jennifer L. "Against the 1989–1990 Ending Myth." *Central European History* 52, no. 1 (2019): 125–47.

Ameri-Siemens, Anne. *Ein Tag im Herbst: Die RAF, der Staat und der Fall Schleyer*. Berlin: Rowohlt, 2017.

Amft, Karl-Heinz. *Wandervogel Unterwegs: Heimat-Familie-Beruf*. Meckenheim, 2008.

Appelgate, Celia. *A Nation of Provincials: The German Idea of Heimat*. Berkeley: University of California Press, 1990.

Aronson, Shlomo. *Reinhard Heydrich und die Frühgeschichte von Gestapo und Sd*. Stuttgart: DeutscherVerlag, 1971.

Augustine, Dolores L. *Taking on Technocracy: Nuclear Power in Germany, 1945 to the Present*. New York: Berghahn Books, 2018.

Aust, Stefan. *Baader-Meinhof: The Inside Story of the R.A.F.* New York: Oxford University Press, 2008.

Badura, Peter. "Arnold Köttgen (1902–1967)." In *Staatsrechtslehrer des 20. Jahrhunderts*, edited by Peter Häberle, Michael Kilian, and Heinrich Amadeus Wolff, 628–38. Boston: De Gruyter, 2013.

Bald, Detlef. *Militär und Gesellschaft, 1945–1990: Die Bundeswehr der Bonner Republik*. Baden Baden: Nomos, 1994.

Balko, Radley. *Rise of the Warrior Cop: The Militarization of America's Police Forces*. New York: Public Affairs, 2013.

Baranowski, Shelley. *The Confessing Church, Conservative Elites, and the Nazi State*. Texts and Studies in Religion, vol. 28. Lewiston: Edwin Mellen, 1986.

Barrie, David G., and Susan Broomhall, eds. *A History of Police and Masculinities, 1700–2010*. New York: Routledge, 2012.

Bartov, Omer. *Hitler's Army: Soldiers, Nazis, and War in the Third Reich*. Oxford: Oxford University Press, 1992.

Bartov, Omer, and Phyllis Mack, eds. *In God's Name: Genocide and Religion in the Twentieth Century*. New York: Berghahn, 2001.

Baum, Gerhart. *Meine Wut ist jung: Bilanz eines politischen Lebens im Gespräch mit Matthias Franck*. Munich: Kössel, 2012.

Bayley, David H. *Patterns of Policing: A Comparative International Analysis*. New Brunswick: Rutgers, 1985.

Beaujon, Danielle. "Policing Colonial Migrants: The Brigade Nord-Africaine in Paris, 1923–1944." *French Historical Studies* 42, no. 4 (October 2019): 655–80.

Becker-Schaum, Christoph, Philipp Gassert, Martin Klimke, Wilfried Mausbach, and Marianne Zepp, eds. *The Nuclear Crisis: The Arms Race, Cold*

War Anxiety, and the German Peace Movement of the 1980s. New York: Berghahn, 2020.

Beese, Dieter. "Polizei Berufsethik." In *Berufsethik—Glaube—Seelsorge: Evangelische Seelsorge im Bundesgrenzschutz Polizei des Bundes, Festschrift für Rolf Sauerzapf*, edited by Joachim Heubach and Klaus-Dieter Stephan, 10–24. Leipzig: Evangelische Verlagsanstalt, 1997.

Bellers, Jürgen, and Maren Königsberg. *Skandal oder Medienrummel?* Münster: LIT, 2004.

Bennewitz, Inge, and Rainer Potratz. *Zwangsaussiedlungen an der innerdeutschen Grenze: Analysen und Dokumente.* Berlin: Ch. Links, 2012.

Berkley, George E. *The Democratic Policeman.* Boston: Beacon, 1974.

Berlin, M. "An Overview of Police Training in the United States; Historical Development, Current Trends and Critical Issues: The Evidence." In *International Perspectives on Police Education and Training*, edited by Peter Stanislas, 23–42. New York: Routledge, 2014.

Bernhard, Gotto. "Von enttäuschten Erwartungen: Willy Brandt's 'Mehr Demokratie Wagen' und Valéry Giscard d'Estaing's 'Démocratie française.'" In *Nach "Achtundsechzig": Krisen und Krisenbewusstsein in Deutschland und Frankreich in den 1960er Jahren*, edited by Gotto Bernhard, Horst Möeller, Jean Mondot, and Niccole Pelletier, 31–44. Munich: Oldenbourg Wissenschaftsverlag, 2013.

Bernhard, Gotto, Horst Möeller, Jean Mondot, and Niccole Pelletier, eds. *Nach "Achtundsechzig": Krisen und Krisenbewusstsein in Deutschland und Frankreich in den 1960er Jahren.* Munich: Oldenbourg Wissenschaftsverlag, 2013.

Bessel, Richard. *Germany 1945: From War to Peace.* New York: Harper Perennial, 2010.

———. "Policing, Professionalization and Politics in Weimar Germany." In *Policing Western Europe: Politics, Professionalism and Public Order, 1850–1940*, edited by Clive Emsley and Barbara Weinberger, 187–218. New York: Greenwood, 1991.

Biess, Frank. *Homecomings: Returning POWs and the Legacies of Defeat in Postwar Germany.* Princeton, NJ: Princeton University Press, 2006.

Biess, Frank, and Astrid M. Eckert. "Why Do We Need New Narratives for the History of the Federal Republic?" *Central European History* 52, no. 1 (2019): 1–18.

Biess, Frank, and Robert G. Moeller, eds. *Histories of the Aftermath: The Legacies of the Second World War in Europe.* New York: Berghahn, 2010.

Biess, Frank, Mark Roseman, and Hanna Schissler, eds. *Conflict, Catastrophe and Continuity: Essays in German History*, 2007.

Boa, Elizabeth, and Rachel Palfreyman. *Heimat: A German Dream: Regional Loyalties and National Identity in German Culture 1890–1990.* New York: Oxford University Press, 2000.

Bohlander, Michael. *The German Criminal Code: A Modern English Translation.* Oxford: Hart, 2008.

Borodziej, Włodzimierez. *The Warsaw Uprising of 1944*. Madison: University of Wisconsin Press, 2001.
Bösch, Frank, and Andreas Wirsching, eds. *Hüter der Ordnung: Die Innenministerien in Bonn und Ost Berlin nach dem Nationalsozialismus*. Göttingen: Wallstein, 2018.
Brandt, Willi. *My Life in Politics*. New York: Viking, 1992.
Braunschweig: Gersbach & Sohn, 1955.
Braunthal, Gerard. *Political Loyalty and Public Service in West Germany: The 1972 Decree against Radicals and Its Consequences*. Amherst: University of Massachusetts Press, 1990.
Breiting, Otto, and Kurt M. Hoffmann. *Lehr und Lesebuch für die politische Bildung und Staatsbürgerliche Erziehung im Bundesgrenzschutz*.
Breitman, Richard. "Hitler and Genghis Khan." *Journal of Contemporary History* 25, no. 2/3 (1990): 337–51.
Brill, Heinz. *Bogislaw von Bonin im Spannungsfeld zwischen Wiederbewaffnung—Westintegration—Wiedervereinigung: Ein Beitrag zur Entstehungsgeschichte der Bundeswehr 1952–1955, Band II Dokumente und Materialien*. Baden-Baden: Nomos Verlagsgesellschaft, 1987.
Brown, Timothy Scott. *West Germany and the Global Sixties: The Antiauthoritarian Revolt, 1962–1978*. Cambridge: Cambridge University Press, 2013.
Browning, Christopher. *Ordinary Men: Reserve Police Battalion 101 and the Final Solution in Poland*. New York: Harper Perennial, 1998.
Brühöfener, Friederike. "Defining the West German Soldier: Military, Masculinity and Society in West Germany, 1945–1989." PhD diss., University of North Carolina, 2014.
Buchstab, Günter, Brigitte Kaff, and Hans-Otto Kleinmann, eds. *Christliche Demokraten gegen Hitler: Aus Verfolgung und Widerstand zur Union*. Freiburg im Breisgau: Herder, 2004.
Burleigh, Michael. *Small Wars, Faraway Places: Global Insurrection and the Making of the Modern World, 1945–1965*. New York: Penguin Books, 2014.
Campion, David A. "Policing the Peelers: Parliament, the Public, and the Metropolitan Police, 1829–33." In *London Politics, 1760–1914*, edited by Matthew Cragoe and Anthony Taylor, 38–54. London: Palgrave Macmillan, 2005.
Canoy, Jose Raymund. *The Discreet Charm of the Police State: The Landpolizei and the Transformation of Bavaria, 1945–1965*. Studies in Central European Histories. Edited by Thomas A. Brady Jr. and Roger Chickering, vol. 41. Leiden, Netherlands: Koninklijke Brill NV, 2007.
Carr, James G. "Wiretapping in West Germany." *American Journal of Comparative Law* 29, no. 4 (1981): 607–45.
Cashner, Bob. *The Fn Fal Battle Rifle*. Oxford, Bloomsbury Publishing, 2013.
Chin, Rita and Heide Fehrenbach. "Introduction: What's Race Got to Do with It? Postwar German History in Context." In *After the Nazi Racial*

State: Difference and Democracy in Germany and Europe, edited by Rita Chin, Heide Fehrenbach, Geoff Eley, and Atina Grossmann, 1–29. Ann Arbor: University of Michigan Press, 2009.

Chin, Rita, Heide Fehrenbach, Geoff Eley, and Atina Grossmann, eds. *After the Nazi Racial State: Difference and Democracy in Germany and Europe*. Ann Arbor: University of Michigan Press, 2009.

Christoph-Müller, Hendrik. *West Germans against the West: Anti-Americanism in the Media and Public Opinion in the Federal Republic of Germany, 1949–1968*. New York: Palgrave-Macmillan, 2010.

Churchill, Winston. *The World Crisis: The Aftermath*. London: Thornton Butterworth, 1929.

Citino, Robert. *The German Way of War: From the Thirty Years War to the Third Reich*. Lawrence: University Press of Kansas, 2005.

Clark, Christopher. *Iron Kingdom: The Rise and Downfall of Prussia, 1600–1947*. Cambridge, MA: Harvard University Press, 2006.

Cohen, Stanley. *Folk Devils and Moral Panics: The Creation of the Mods and Rockers*. 3rd ed. New York: Routledge, 2002.

Cole, Wayne S. *Charles A. Lindbergh and the Battle against American Intervention in World War Two*. New York: Harcourt, 1974.

Collings, Justin. *Democracy's Guardians: A History of the German Federal Constitutional Court, 1951–2001*. Oxford: Oxford University Press, 2015.

Collings-Wells, Sam. "Policing the Windrush Generation: Police Brutality and Stop-and-Search Are Yet Another Legacy of Empire." *History Today* 69, no. 11 (2019): historytoday.com/archive/history-matters/policing-windrush-generation.

Commager, Henry Steele, Günther Doeker, Ernst Fraenkel, Ferdinand Hermes, William C. Harvard, and Theodor Manz, eds. *Festschrift für Karl Loewenstein: Aus Anlass seines achtzigsten Geburtstages*. Tübingen: J. C. B. Mohr, 1971.

Confino, Alon. *Germany as a Culture of Remembrance: Promises and Limits of Writing History*. Chappel Hill: University of North Carolina Press, 2006.

Cornils, Ingo. *Writing the Revolution: The Construction of "1968" in Germany*. Studies in German Literature, Lingusitics, and Culture. Rochester: Camden House, 2016.

Corum, James S., ed. *Rearming Germany*. Leiden, Netherlands: Brill, 2011.

Cragoe, Matthew, and Anthony Taylor, eds. *London Politics, 1760–1914*. London: Palgrave Macmillan, 2005.

Crawford, James, Alain Pellet, Simon Olleson, and Kate Parlett, eds. *The Law of International Responsibility*. New York: Oxford University Press, 2010.

Creuzberger, Stefan, and Dierk Hoffmann, eds. *Geistige Gefahr und Immunisierung der Gesellschaft: Antikommunismus und politische Kultur in der frühen Bundesrepublik*. Munich: Oldenbourg, 2014.

David, Saul. *Operation Thunderbolt: Flight 139 and the Raid on Entebbe Airport, the Twentieth Century's Greatest Special Forces Mission*. New York: Hachette Book Group, 2015.

Davidson, John, and Sabine Hake. *Framing the Fifties: Cinema in Divided Germany*. New York: Berghahn Books, 2007.
Davis, Belinda. "Polizei und Gewalt auf der Strasse: Konfliktmuster und ihre Folgen im Berlin des 19. und 20. Jahrhunderts." In *Polizei, Gewalt und Staat im 20. Jahrhundert*, edited by Alf Lüdtke, Herbert Reinke, and Michael Sturm, 81–103. Wiesbaden: Springer, 2011.
Detter, Ingrid. *The Law of War*. 2nd ed. Cambridge: Cambridge University Press, 2000.
Dickinson, Edward Ross. *The Politics of German Child Welfare from the Empire to the Federal Republic*. Cambridge: Cambridge University Press, 1996.
Diebel, Martin. *Die Stunde der Exekutive: Das Bundesinnenministerium im Konflikt um die Notstandsgesetzgebung, 1949–1968*. Göttingen: Wallstein, 2019.
Diederichs, Otto. "In welcher Verfassung ist der BGS?" *Bürgerrechte & Polizei Cilip* 47, no. 1 (1993): 30–36.
Dierske, Ludwig. *Der Bundesgrenzschutz: Geschichtliche Darstellung seiner Aufgabe und Entwicklung von der Aufstellung bis zum 31. März 1963*. Munich: Walhalla & Praetoria, 1967.
Dietze, Carola. *Nachgeholtes Leben: Helmuth Plessner 1892–1895*. Göttingen: Wallstein, 2013, 2013.
Dobson, Andrew. *An Introduction to the Politics and Philosophy of José Ortega y Gasset*. New York: Cambridge University Press, 1989.
Doering-Manteuffel, Anselm. *Wie westlich sind die Deutschen? Amerikanisierung und Westernisierung im 20. Jahrhundert*. Göttingen: Vandenhoeck & Ruprecht, 1999.
Doerry, Martin, and Hauke Janssen, eds. *Die Spiegel-Affäre: Ein Skandal und seine Folgen*. Munich: Deutsche Verlags-Anstalt, 2013.
Donner, Frank J. *Protectors of Privilege: Red Squads and Police Repression in Urban America*. Berkeley: University of California Press, 1990.
Dörfler-Dierken, Angelika, and Christian Göbel, eds. *Charakter—Haltung—Habitus: Persönlichkeit und Verantwortung in der Bundeswehr*. Wiesbaden: Springer, 2022.
Dunnage, Jonathan. "Policing Right-Wing Dictatorships: Some Preliminary Comparisons of Fascist Italy, Nazi Germany and Franco's Spain." *Crime, Histoire & Sociétés* 10, no. 1 (2006): 93–122.
Eckardt, Felix von. *Ein unordentliches Leben: Lebenserrinerungen*. Düsseldorf: Econ-Verlag, 1967.
Ehlert, Hans, and Hans-Joachim Beth, eds. *Armee ohne Zukunft: Das Ende der NVA und die deutsche Einheit: Zeitzeugenberichte und Dokumente*. Berlin: Ch. Links, 2002.
Ehlert, Hans, Christian Greiner, Georg Meyer and Bruno Thoß. *Anfänge Westdeutscher Sicherheitspolitik 1945–1956, Bd. 3, Die Nato-Option*. Munich: R. Oldenbourg, 1993.
Eley, Geoff. *Forging Democracy: The History of the Left in Europe, 1850–2000*. Oxford: Oxford University Press, 2002.

Elkins, Caroline. *Legacy of Violence: A History of the British Empire.* New York: Knopf, 2022.
Emmerich, Klaus. *Die Grenzkommission beider deutscher Staaten: Aufgaben, Tätigkeit und Dokumente.* Norderstedt: Books on Demand, 2014.
Emsley, Clive. *Gendarmes and the State in Nineteenth-Century Europe.* Oxford: Oxford University Press, 1999.
Emsley, Clive, and Barbara Weinberger, eds. *Policing Western Europe: Politics, Professionalism, and Public Order, 1850–1940.* New York: Greenwood, 1991.
Eppe, Heinrich, ed. *Sozialistische Jugend im 20. Jahrhundert: Studien zur Entwicklung und politischen Praxis der Arbeiterjugendbewegung in Deutschland.* Munich: Juventa, 2008.
Erlichman, Camilo, and Christopher Knowles, eds. *Transforming Occupation in the Western Zones of Germany: Politics, Everyday Life and Social Interactions.* London: Bloomsbury Academic, 2019.
Etzemüller, Thomas. *1968—Ein Riss in der Geschichte? Gesellschaftlicher Umbruch und 68er-Bewegungen in Westdeutschland und Schweden.* Konstanz: UVK, 2005.
Fairchild, Erika S. *German Police: Ideals and Reality in the Post-War Years.* Springfield, Illinois: Charles C. Thomas, 1988.
Fehrenbach, Heide. *Cinema in Democratizing Germany: Reconstructing National Identity after Hitler.* Chapel Hill: University of North Carolina Press, 1995.
Fenner, Angelica. *Race under Reconstruction in German Cinema: Robert Stemmle's Toxi.* Toronto: University of Toronto Press, 2011.
Fingerle, Stephan. *Waffen in Arbeiterhand? Die Rekrutierung des Offizierkorps der Nationalen Volksarmee und ihrer Vorläufer.* Berlin: Ch. Links, 2001.
Fischer, Bernhard. "Die Olympischen Spiele in München: Sicherheitskonzept und Attentat im Spiegel der Akten des Sicherheitsbeuftragten im Bayerischen Staatsministerium des Innern und der Staatsanwaltschaft München I." PhD, Bundeswehr Universität, 2006.
Flex, Walter. *Der Wanderer zwischen beiden Welten: Ein Kriegserlebnis.* Munich: C. S. Beck, 1920.
Foot, Max. "Children of the Spied-On." *London Review of Books* 45, no. 13 (2023): 41.
Forner, Sean A. *German Intellectuals and the Challenge of Democratic Renewal.* Cambridge: Cambridge University Press, 2014.
Frei, Norbert. *Adenauer's Germany and the Nazi Past: The Politics of Amnesty and Integration.* New York: Columbia University Press, 2002.
———, ed. *Hitlers Eliten nach 1945.* Frankfurt am Main: Campus, 2012.
Frevert, Ute. *A Nation in Barracks: Modern Germany, Military Conscription, and Civil Society.* New York: Berg, 2004.
Freytag, Ulrich. "Warum ich Soldat wurde!" *Internationales Magazin für Sicherheit,* 2006, 58.

Fulbrook, Mary. *Anatomy of a Dictatorship: Inside the GDR, 1949–1989.* New York: Oxford University Press, 1994.

———. *A Small Town near Auschwitz: Ordinary Nazis and the Holocaust.* Oxford: Oxford University Press, 2012.

Gaddis, John Lewis. *Strategies of Containment: A Critical Appraisal of Postwar American National Security Policy.* New York: Oxford University Press, 1982.

———. *The United States and the End of the Cold War: Implications, Reconsiderations, Provocations.* New York: Oxford University Press, 1992.

Gailus, Manfred, and Armin Nolzen, eds. *Zerstrittene "Volksgemeinschaft"; Glaube, Konfession und Religion im Nationalsozialismus.* Göttingen: Vandenhoeck & Ruprecht, 2011.

Gauck, Joachim, and Martin Fry. "Dealing with the Stasi Past." *Daedalus* 123, no. 1 (1994): 277–84.

Genscher, Hans-Dietrich. *Erinnerungen.* Munich: Siedler, 1995. Gerwarth, Robert, and John Horne, eds. *War in Peace: Paramilitary Violence in Europe after the Great War.* Oxford: Oxford University Press, 2013.

Gerwarth, Robert. "Fighting the Red Beast: Counter-Revolutionary Violence in the Defeated States of Central Europe." In Gerwarth and Horne, *War in Peace: Paramilitary Violence in Europe after the Great War,* e52–71. Geuter, Ulfried. *The Professionalization of Psychology in Nazi Germany.* Cambridge: Cambridge University Press, 1992.

Geyer, Michael. "Cold War Angst: The Case of West German Opposition to Rearmament and Nuclear Weapons." In *The Miracle Years: A Cultural History of West Germany, 1949–1968,* edited by Hanna Schissler, 376–408. Princeton, NJ: Princeton University Press, 2001.

Gibbons, Floyd. *The Red Napoleon.* Carbondale: Southern Illinois University Press, 1976.

Gieseke, Jens. *The History of the Stasi: East Germany's Secret Police, 1945–1990.* New York: Berghahn Books, 2014.

Giessen, Rolf. *Nazi Propaganda Films: A History and Filmography.* Jefferson, NC: McFarland, 2003.

Glovka Spencer, Elaine. "Police-Military Relations in Prussia, 1848–1914." *Journal of Social History* 19, no. 2 (1985): 305–17.

Go, Julian. "The Imperial Origins of American Policing: Militarization and Imperial Feedback in the Early 20th Century." *American Journal of Sociology* 125, no. 5 (2020): 1193–254.

Goedde, Petra. *The Politics of Peace: A Global Cold War History.* Oxford: Oxford University Press, 2019.

Goschler, Constantin, and Michael Wala. *Keine neue Gestapo: Das Bundesamt für Verfassungsschutz und die NS-Vergangenheit.* Hamburg: Rowohlt, 2015.

Granieri, Ronald J. *The Ambivalent Alliance: Konrad Adenauer, the CDU/CSU, and the West, 1949–1966.* New York: Berghahn Books, 2002.

Greener, B. K., and W. J. Fish. *Internal Security and Statebuilding: Aligning Agencies and Functions.* Routledge Studies in Intervention and

Statebuilding. Edited by David Chandler. Vol. 16. New York: Routledge, 2015.
Grützner, Kurt, Wolfgang Gröger, Claudia Kiehn, and Werner Schiewek, eds. *Handbuch Polizeiseelsorge*. Göttingen: Vandenhoeck & Ruprecht, 2012.
Gunnarsson, Robert L. Sr. *American Military Police in Europe, 1945–1991: Unit Histories*. Jefferson, NC: McFarland, 2011.
Hagemann, Karen, Donna Harsch, and Friederike Brühöfener, eds. *Gendering Post-1945 German History: Entanglements*. New York: Berghahn, 2019.
Hall, Sara F. "Moving Images and the Policing of Political Action in the Early Weimar Period." *German Studies Review* 31, no. 2 (2008): 285–302.
Hamilton, Charles. *The Hitler Diaries: Fakes That Fooled the World*. Lexington: University Press of Kentucky, 1991.
Hannah, Matthew G. *Dark Territory in the Information Age: Learning from the West German Census Controversies of the 1980s*. London: Routledge, 2010.
Hanshew, Karrin. *Terror and Democracy in West Germany*. Cambridge: Cambridge University Press, 2012.
Harsch, Donna. *German Social Democracy and the Rise of Nazism*. Chapel Hill: University of North Carolina Press, 1993.
Hayse, Michael. *Recasting West German Elites: Higher Civil Servants, Business Leaders, and Physicians in Hesse between Nazism and Democracy, 1945–1955*. New York: Berghahn Books, 2003.
Heale, M. J. "Red Scare Politics: California's Campaign against Un-American Activities, 1940–1970." *Journal of American Studies* 20, no. 1 (1886): 5–32.
Heer, Hannes, and Klaus Naumann, eds. *War of Extermination: The German Military in World War II, 1941–1944*. New York: Berghahn Books, 2000.
Heinemann, Winfried. *Operation Valkyrie: A Military History of the July 20, 1944 Plot*. Oldenbourg: De Gruyter, 2021.
Hellenthal, Markus Daniel. *Frauen im Bundesgrenzschutz: Folge der Gleichberechtigung oder Verstoss gegen Art. 12a Abs. 4 Satz 2 Gg?* Schriften zum öffentlichen Recht, vol. 537. Berlin: Duncker & Humblot, 1988, 1988.
Henzler, Christoph. *Fritz Schäffer (1945–1967): Eine biographische Studie zum ersten bayerischen Nachskriegs-Ministerpräsidenten und ersten Finanzminister der Bundesrepublik Deutschland*. Munich: Hans-Seidel-Stiftung, 1997.
Herf, Jeffrey. *Divided Memory: The Nazi Past in the Two Germanys*. Cambridge, MA: Harvard University Press, 1997.
Herzog, Dagmar. "Pleasure, Sex, and Politics Belong Together: Post-Holocaust Memory and the Sexual Revolution in West Germany." *Critical Inquiry* 24, no. 2 (1998): 393–444.
———. *Sex after Fascism: Memory and Morality in Twentieth-Century Germany*. Princeton, NJ: Princeton University Press, 2005.

Hett, Benjamin Carter. *Burning the Reichstag: An Investigation into the Third Reich's Enduring Mystery.* Oxford: Oxford University Press, 2014.

Heubuch, Joachim, and Klaus-Dieter Stephan, eds. *Berufsethik—Glaube—Seelsorge: Evangelische Seelsorge im Bundesgrenzschutz Polizei des Bundes; Festschrift für Rolf Sauerzapf.* Leipzig: Evangelische Verlagsanstalt, 1997.

Hilger, Andreas, Milke Schmeitzner, and Ute Schmidt, eds. *Sowjetische Militärtribunale Band 2: Die Verurteilung deutscher Zivilisten 1945–1955.* Cologne: Böhlau Verlag, 2003.

Hinz, Wolfgang. "Geschichtliche Entwicklung der Polizeiseelsorge." In *Handbuch Polizeiseelsorge*, edited by Kurt Grützner, Wolfgang Gröger, Claudia Kiehn, and Werner Schiewek. 50–60. Göttingen: Vandenhoeck & Ruprecht, 2012.

Hitchcock, William I. *The Age of Eisenhower: America and the World in the 1950s.* New York: Simon and Schuster, 2018.

———. *France Restored: Cold War Diplomacy and the Quest for Leadership in Europe, 1944–1954.* Chapel Hill: University of North Carolina Press, 1998.

Holmes, Richard. *Firing Line.* London: Jonathan Cape, 1985.

Hong, Young-Sun. *Cold War Germany, the Third World, and the Global Humanitarian Regime.* Cambridge: Cambridge University Press, 2015.

Horbrügger, Anja. *Aufbruch zur Kontinuität, Kontinuität im Aufbruch: Geschlechterkonstruktionen im West und Ostdeutschen Nachkriegsfilm von 1945 bis 1952.* Marburg: Schüren, 2007.

Horn, Bernd J., Paul de B. Taillon, and David Last, eds. *Force of Choice: Perspectives on Special Operations.* Montreal: Queens University School of Policy Studies, 2004.

Horne, John, and Alan Kramer. *German Atrocities 1914: A History of Denial.* New Haven, CT: Yale University Press, 2001.

House, Jim, and Neil Macmaster. *Paris 1961: Algerians, State Terror, and Memory.* 2006.

Hughes, Michael L. *Embracing Democracy in Modern Germany: Political Citizenship and Participation, 1871–2000.* London: Bloomsbury Academic, 2021.

Iacopino, Vincent, and Rohini J. Haar. "Lethal in Disguise: The Health Consequences of Crowd-Control Weapons." *Physicians for Human Rights* (2016). phr.org/our-work/resources/lethal-in-disguise/.

Invernizzi, Carlo, and Ian Zuckerman. "What's Wrong with Militant Democracy?" *Political Studies* 65 (IS) (2017): 182–99.

Jähner, Harald. *Aftermath: Life in the Fallout of the Third Reich.* New York: Knopf, 2022.

Jarausch, Konrad. *After Hitler: Recivilizing Germans, 1945–1995.* Oxford: Oxford University Press, 2006.

———. "The Federal Republic at Sixty: Popular Myths, Actual Accomplishments and Competing Interpretations." *German Politics and Society* 28, no. 1 (2010): 16–18.

Jarausch, Konrad, and Volker Grasnow, eds. *Uniting Germany: Documents and Debates, 1944–1993.* New York: Berghahn, 1994.
Johnson, James Turner. *The Ashgate Research Companion to Military Ethics.* New York: Routledge, 2016.
Johnston, Douglas, and Cynthia Sampson, eds. *Religion, the Missing Dimension of Statecraft.* New York: Oxford University Press, 1994.
Jones, Howard. *The Bay of Pigs.* Oxford: Oxford University Press, 2008.
Jones, Mark. *Founding Weimar: Violence and the German Revolution of 1918–1919.* Cambridge: Cambridge University Press, 2018.
Judt, Tony. *Postwar: A History of Europe since 1945.* New York: Penguin Books, 2005.
Kaff, Brigitte. "Robert Lehr (1883–1956)." In *Christliche Demokraten gegen Hitler: Aus Verfolgung und Widerstand zur Union,* edited by Günter Buchstab, Brigitte Kaff, and Hans-Otto Kleinmann, 191–207. Freiburg im Breisgau: Herder, 2004.
Kallis, Aristotle A. *Nazi Propaganda and the Second World War.* New York: Palgrave Macmillan, 2005.
Kannapin, Detlef. *Dialektik der Bilder: Der Nationalsozialismus im deutschen Film: Ein Ost-West-Vergleich.* Berlin: Karl Dietz, 2005.
Kehoe, Thomas J., and James E. Kehoe. "Civilian Crime during the British and American Occupation of Western Germany." *European Journal of Criminology* 19, no. 2 (November 15, 2019): 3–28.
Keßelring, Agilolf. *Die Organisation Gehlen und die Neuformierung des Militärs in der Bundesrepublik.* Berlin: Ch. Links, 2017.
Kesselring, Albert. *Soldat bis zum letzten Tag.* Bonn: Anthenaum, 1953.
Kießling, Günter. *Staatsbürger und General.* Düsseldorf: Blazek & Bergmann, 2000.
———. *Versäumter Widerspruch.* Mainz: Hase & Koehler, 1993.
Kilian, Michael, Heinrich Amadeus Wolff, and Peter Häberle, eds. *Staatsrechtslehrer des 20. Jahrhunderts.* Boston: De Gruyter, 2018.
Kim, Dong Choon. "Forgotten War, Forgotten Massacres: The Korean War (1950–1953) as Licensed Mass Killings." *Journal of Genocide Research* 6, no. 4 (2004): 523–44.
Klimke, Martin. *The Other Alliance: Student Protest in West Germany and the United States in the Global Sixties.* Princeton, NJ: Princeton University Press, 2010.
Knüsel, Ariane. *Framing China: Media Images and Political Debates in Britain, the USA and Switzerland, 1900–1950.* Surrey, UK: Ashgate, 2012.
Koch, Lars. *Der erste Weltkrieg als Medium der Gegenmoderne: Zu Werken von Walter Flex und Ernst Jünger.* Würzburg: Königshausen & Neumann, 2006.
Koehler, Daniel. *Right-Wing Terrorism in the 21st Century:"The 'National Socialist Underground" and the History of Terror from the Far Right in Germany.* London: Routledge, 2017.
Koehler, John O. *Stasi: The Untold Story of the East German Secret Police.* Oxford: Westview, 1999.

Kommers, Donald P. "West German Constitutionalism and Church-State Relations." *German Politics and Society* 19 (1990): 1–13.

Komska, Yuliya. *The Icon Curtain: The Cold War's Quiet Border.* Chicago: University of Chicago Press, 2015.

Kosthorst, Daniel, and Michael F. Feldkamp, eds. *Akten zur auswärtigen Politik der Bundesrepublik Deutschland, 1949–1950.* Munich: Oldenbourg Wissenschaftverlag, 2013.

Kramer, Alisa Sarah. "William H. Parker and the Thin Blue Line: Politics, Public Relations and Policing in Postwar Los Angeles." PhD diss, American University, 2007.

Kramer, Mark. "International Politics in the Early Post-Stalinist Era: A Lost Opportunity, a Turning Point, or More of the Same?" In *The Cold War after Stalin's Death: A Missed Opportunity for Peace?*, edited by Klaus Larres and Kenneth Alan Osgood, xiii–xxxiv. Lanham, MD: Rowan & Littlefield, 2006.

Krüger, Dieter, and Volker Bausch, eds. *Fulda Gap: Battlefield of the Cold War Alliances.* New York: Lexington, 2018.

Kuhn-Osius, K. Eckhard. "Germany's Lessons from the Lost 'Great War': Pacifist Andreas Latzko and Bellicist Walter Flex." *Peace Research* 42, no. 1/2 (2010): 23–51.

Kühne, Thomas. *The Rise and Fall of Comradeship: Hitler's Soldiers, Male Bonding and Mass Violence in the Twentieth Century.* Cambridge: Cambridge University Press, 2017.

Kuschel, Franziska, and Dominik Rigoll. "Broschürenkrieg statt Bürgerkrieg: BMI und MDI im Deutsch-Deutschen Systemkonflikt." In *Hüter der Ordnung: Die Innenministerien in Bonn und Ost Berlin nach dem Nationalsozialismus*, edited by Frank Bösch and Andreas Wirsching. Göttingen: Wallstein, 2018.

Lagrou, Pieter. "The Age of Total War." In *Histories of the Aftermath: The Legacies of the Second World War in Europe*, edited by Frank Biess and Robert G. Moeller. New York: Berghahn, 2010.

Lange, Hans-Jürgen, ed. *Polizei der Gesellschaft: Zur Sociologie der inneren Sicherheit.* Wiesbaden: Springer, 2003.

Langenbacher, Erich, and David P. Conradt. *The German Polity.* 11th ed. New York: Rowan & Littlefield, 2017.

Large, David Clay. *Germans to the Front: West German Rearmament in the Adenauer Era.* Chapel Hill: University of North Carolina Press, 1996.

———. *Munich 1972: Tragedy, Terror, and Triumph at the Olympic Games* New York: Rowan & Littlefield, 2012.

Larres, Klaus, and Kenneth Osgood, eds. *The Cold War after Stalin's Death: A Missed Opportunity for Peace?* Lanham, MD: Rowan & Littlefield, 2006.

Leffler, Melvyn P. *For the Soul of Mankind: The United States, the Soviet Union and the Cold War.* New York: Hill & Wang, 2008.

Lehman, Brittany. *Teaching Migrant Children in West Germany and Europe, 1949–1992.* London: Palgrave Macmillan, 2019.

Levsen, Sonja, and Cornelius Torp. *Wo liegt die Bundesrepublik?* Göttingen: Vandenhoeck & Ruprecht, 2016.

Levy, Daniel, and Nathan Sznaider. *The Holocaust and Memory in the Global Age*. Philadelphia: Temple University Press, 2006.

Liang, Hsi-Huey. *The Berlin Police Force in the Weimar Republic*. Berkeley: University of California Press, 1970.

Library, Ike Skelton Combined Arms Research. *Supreme Headquarters Allied Expeditionary Force, Public Safety Manual of Procedures*. Fort Leavenworth, Kansas: US Army Command and Staff College, 1944.

Lipski, Steven von, ed. *Dokumentation zur Geschichte der Stadt Düsseldorf während der Revolution 1918–1919 (November 1918 bis März 1919), Quellensammlung*. Düsseldorf: Pädagogisches Institut der Landeshauptstadt Düsseldorf: June 1983.

Little, Douglas. *American Orientalism: The United States and the Middle East since 1945*. 3rd ed. Chapel Hill: University of North Carolina Press, 2008.

Liulevicius, Vejas Gabriel. *The German Myth of the East: 1800 to the Present*. Oxford: Oxford University Press, 2009.

———. *War Land on the Eastern Front: Culture, National Identity, and German Occupation in Word War I*. London: Cambridge University Press, 2000.

Loader, Ian, and Neil Walker. *Civilizing Security*. New York: Cambridge University Press, 2007.

"Local Police Departments, 2016 Personnel." US Department of Justice, 2019, accessed June 1, 2022. https://bjs.ojp.gov/library/publications/local-police-departments-2016-personnel.

Lowe, Keith. *Savage Continent: Europe in the Aftermath of World War Two*. New York: St. Martin's, 2012.

Ludtke, Alf, ed. *Police and State in Prussia, 1815–1850*. New York: Cambridge University Press, 1989.

———. *Sicherheit und Wohlfahrt: Polizei, Gesellschaft und Herrschaft im 19. und 20. Jahrhundert*. Frankfurt am Main: Suhrkamp, 1992.

Lüdtke, Alf, Herbert Reinke, and Michael Sturm, eds. *Polizei, Gewalt und Staat im 20. Jahrhundert*. Wiesbaden: Verlag für Sozialwissenschaften, Springer Fachmedien, 2011.

Luttwak, Edward. "Franco-German Reconciliation: The Overlooked Role of the Moral Re-Armament Movement." In *Religion, the Missing Dimension of Statecraft*, edited by Douglas and Cynthia Sampson Johnston, 37–57. New York: Oxford University Press, 1994.

Lynn, Jennifer. "Contested Representations of Women in the East and West German Illustrated Press of the 1950s." In *Gendering Post-1945 German History: Entanglements*, edited by Karen Hagemann, Donna Harsch, and Friederike Brühöfener, 337–61. New York: Berghahn Books, 2019.

Major, Patrick. *The Death of the KPD: Communism and Anti-Communism in West Germany, 1945–1956*. Oxford: Clarendon, 1998.

Manig, Bert-Oliver. *Die Politik der Ehre: Die Rehabilitierung der Berufssoldaten in der frühen Bundesrepublik*. Göttingen: Wallstein Verlag, 2004.

Manthe, Barbara. "On the Pathway to Violence: West German Right-Wing Terrorism in the 1970s." *Terrorism and Political Violence* 33, no. 1 (2021): 49–70.

Mausbach, Wilfried. "Wende um 360 Grad? Nationalsozialismus und Judenvernichtung in der 'Zweiten Gründungsphrase' der Bundesrepublik." In *Wo "1968" liegt: Reform und Revolte in der Geschichte der Bundesrepublik*, edited by Christina von Hodenberg and Detlef Siegfried, 15–47. Göttingen: Vandenhoek & Ruprecht, 2006.

Mawby, Spencer. *Containing Germany: Britain and the Arming of the Federal Republic*. London: Macmillan, 1999.

McCloy, John J. *Report on Germany: September 21, 1949–July 31, 1952, Office of the US High Commission for Germany*. Cologne: Greven & Bechtold, 1952.

McCormack, Matthew. "A Species of Civil Soldier: Masculinity, Policing and the Military in 1780s England." In *A History of Police Masculinities, 1700–2010*, edited by David G. Barrie and Susan Broomhall, 55–71. London: Routledge, 2012.

McDougall, Alan. *Youth Politics in East Germany: The Free German Youth Movement, 1946–1968*. Oxford: Clarendon, 2004.

McNab, Chris. *The Mg 34 and 42 Machineguns*. Oxford: Osprey, 2012.

Michels, Eckard. *Schahbesuch 1967: Fanal für die Studentenbewegung*. Berlin: Ch. Links, 2017.

Milcher, Manfred. *Der Bundesgrenzschutz: Ein Bildband*. Cologne: Markus-Verlag, 1966.

Milder, Stephan. *Greening Democracy: The Anti-Nuclear Movement and Political Environmentalism in West Germany and Beyond, 1969–1983*. Cambridge: Cambridge University Press, 2017.

Miller, John. "Settling Accounts with a Secret Police: The German Law on the Stasi Records." *Europe-Asia Studies* 50, no. 2 (1998): 305–30.

Moeller, Robert G. *Protecting Motherhood: Women and the Family in the Politics of Postwar West Germany*. Berkeley: University of California Press, 1993.

———. *War Stories: The Search for a Useable Past in the Federal Republic of Germany*. Berkeley: University of California Press, 2003.

———, ed. *West Germany under Construction: Politics, Society, and Culture in the Adenauer Era*. Ann Arbor: University of Michigan Press, 1997.

Molt, Matthias. "Von der Wehrmacht zur Bundeswehr: Personelle Kontinuitat und Diskontinuitat beim Aufbau der deutschen Streitkrafte 1955–1966. PhD diss., University of Heidelberg, 2007.

Mosse, George L. *Fallen Soldiers: Reshaping the Memory of the World Wars*. Oxford: Oxford University Press, 1991.

Muehlenbeck, Philip E., ed. *Religion and the Cold War: A Global Perspective*. Nashville: Vanderbilt University Press, 2012.

Müller, Jan-Werner. *A Dangerous Mind: Carl Schmitt in Post-War European Thought*. New Haven, CT: Yale University Press, 2003.

Murray, Williamson and Alan R. Millet. *A War to Be Won: Fighting the Second World War*. Cambridge, MA: Belknap, 2000.

Naimark, Norman. *The Russians in Germany: A History of the Soviet Zone of Occupation, 1945–1949*. Cambridge, MA: Belknap, 1995.

Nakata, Jun. *Der Grenz- und Landesschutz in der Weimarer Republik, 1918 bis 1933: Die geheime Aufrüstung und die deutsche Gesellschaft*. Einzelschriften zur Militärgeschichte, vol. 41. Freiburg im Breisgau: Rombach, 2002.

Nasution, Abdul. *The Fundamentals of Guerilla Warfare and the Indian Defense System Past and Future*. Djakarta: Indonesian Army Information Service, 1953.

Nationes, Inter. *Films of the Federal Republic of Germany*. Vol. 1. Bonn: Press and Informations Office of the Federal Republic of Germany, 1986.

Naumann, Klaus. "The Unblemished Wehrmacht: The Social History of a Myth." In *The German Military in World War II, 1941–1944*, edited by Hannes Heer and Klaus Naumann, 417–29. New York: Berghahn, 2000.

Nehring, Holger. *Politics of Security: British and West German Protest Movements and the Early Cold War, 1945–1970*. Oxford: Oxford University Press, 2013.

Nienhaus, Ursula. "Einsatz für die 'Sittlichkeit': Anfänge der weiblichen Polizei im Wilhelminischen Kaiserreich und der Weimarer Republik." In *Sicherheit und Wohlfahrt: Polizei, Gesellschaft und Herrschaft im 19. und 20. Jahrhundert*, edited by Alf Ludtke, 243–66. Frankfurt am Main: Suhrkamp, 1992.

Niven, Bill. *Facing the Nazi Past: United Germany and the Legacy of the Third Reich*. New York: Routledge, 2002.

Noethen, Stefan. *Alte Kameraden und neue Kollegen: Polizei in Nordrhein-Westfalen, 1945–1953*. Essen: Klartext, 2003.

———. "Polizei in der Besatzungszeit—Vorstellungen und Einflüsse der Alliierten." In *Die Polizei der Gesellschaft: Zur Soziologie der inneren Sicherheit*, edited by Hans-Jürgen Lange, 77–90. Wiesbaden: Springer, 2003.

Nowack, Sabrina. *NS-Belastung: Personalüberprüfungen im Bundesnachrichtendienst in den 1960er Jahren*. Berlin: Ch. Links, 2016.

Nübel, Christoph, ed. *Dokumente zur deutschen Militärgeschichte 1945–1990: Bundesrepublik und DDR im Ost-West-Konflikt*. Berlin: Ch. Links, 2019.

Oliver, Willard. *August Vollmer: The Father of American Policing*. Durham, NC: Carolina Academic Press, 2017.

Ortega y Gasset, José. *The Revolt of the Masses*. New York: W. W. Norton, 1993.

Ostermann, Christoph, ed. *Uprising in East Germany, 1953: The Cold War, the German Question, and the First Major Upheaval behind the Iron Curtain*. New York: Central European University Press, 2001.

Paddock, Troy R. E. *Creating the Russian Peril: Education, the Public Sphere, and National Identity in Imperial Germany.* Rochester, NY: Camden House, 2010.

Parma, David. *Installation und Konsolidierung des Bundesgrenzschutzes 1949 bis 1972: Eine Untersuchung der Gesetzgebungsprozesse unter besonderer Betrachtung der Inneradministrativen und politischen Vorgänge.* Munich: Springer, 2016.

Pasley, James F. "Chicken Pax Atomica: The Cold War Stability of Nuclear Deterrence." *Journal of International and Area Studies* 15, no. 2 (2008): 21–39.

Peukert, Detlev. *The Weimar Republik: The Crisis of Classical Modernity.* New York: Hill & Wang, 1989.

Pluta, Katharina. *Frauen in Führungsfunktionen von Polizei und Wirtschaft: Eine Bestandsaufnahme.* Hamburg: Diplomica, 2009.

Poiger, Uta G. "A New Western Hero? Reconstructing German Masculinity in the 1950s." In *The Miracle Years: A Cultural History of West Germany, 1949–1968*, edited by Hanna Schissler, 412–27. Princeton, NJ: Princeton University Press, 2001.

———. "Rock 'N' Roll, Female Sexuality, and the Cold War Battle over German Identities." *Journal of Modern History* 68, no. 3 (1996): 577–616.

Poncet, André François. *Les rapports mensuels d'André François-Poncet: Haut-Commissaire français en Allemagne, 1949–1955: Les débuts de la République fédérale d'Allemagne / puliés et annotés par Hans Manfred Bock.* Vol. 2. Paris: Imprimerie Nationale, 1996.

Pöpping, Dagmar. "Die Wehrmachtseelsorge im Zweiten Weltkrieg: Rolle und Selbstverständnis von Kriegs- und Wehrmachtspfarren im Ostkrieg, 1941–1945." In *Zerstrittene "Volksgemeinschaft": Glaube, Konfession und Religion im Nationalsozialismus*, edited by Manfred Gailus and Armin Nolze, 257–86. Göttingen: Vandenhoeck & Ruprecht, 2011.

Poske, Fritz. *Der Seegrenzschutz, 1951–1956: Erinnerung, Bericht, Dokumentation.* Munich: Bernard & Graefe, 1982.

Powers, Francis Gary, and Curt Gentry. *Operation Overflight: A Memoir of the U-2 Incident.* Washington, DC: Potomac, 2004.

Prätorius, Rainer. "Polizei in der Kommune." In *Die Polizei der Gesellschaft: Zur Soziologie der inneren Sicherheit*, edited by Hans-Jürgen Lange, 303–319. Wiesbaden: Springer, 2003.

Prawdin, Michael. *The Mongol Empire: Its Rise and Legacy.* 4th ed. New Brunswick: Transaction, 2009.

Quint, Peter R. "The Border Guard Trials and the East German Past—Seven Arguments." *American Journal of Comparative Law* 48, no. 4 (2000): 541–72.

Rahden, Till van. "Fatherhood, Rechristianization, and the Quest for Democracy in Postwar West Germany." In *Raising Citizens in the Century of the Child: The United States and German Central Europe in Comparative Perspective*, edited by Dirk Schumann, 141–64. New York: Berghahn, 2010.

Raible, Eugen. *Geschichte der Polizei, Ihre Entwicklung in den alten Ländern Baden und Württemberg und in dem neuen Bundesland Baden-Württemberg, unter besonderer Berücksichtigung der kasernierten Polizei (Bereitschaftspolizei)*. Stuttgart: R. Boorberg, 1963.

Reeve, Simon. *One Day in September: The Full Story of the 1972 Munich Olympics Massacre and the Israeli Revenge Operation 'Wrath of God.'* London: Faber & Faber, 2005.

Rehg, William. *Insight and Solidarity: A Study in the Discourse Ethics of Jürgen Habermas*. Berkeley: University of California Press, 1997.

Reinke, Herbert. "Armed As If for a War: The State, the Military and the Professionalization of the Prussian Police in Imperial Germany." In *Policing Western Europe: Politics, Professionalization, and Public Order, 1850–1940*, edited by Clive Emsley and Barbara Weinberger, 55–73. Westport: Greenwood, 1991.

Reitter, Paul, and Chad Wellmon, eds. *Charisma and Disenchantment: Max Weber: The Vocational Lectures*. New York: New York Review of Books, 2020.

Rentschler, Eric. *The Ministry of Illusion: Nazi Cinema and Its Afterlife*. Cambridge, MA: Harvard University Press, 1996.

Riesman, David, , Reuel Denney, and Nathan Glazer. *The Lonely Crowd: A Study of the Changing American Character*. New Haven, CT: Yale University Press, 1950.

Rigoll, Dominik. "From Denazification to Renazification? West German Government Officials after 1945." In *Transforming Occupation in the Western Zones of Germany*, edited by Camilo Erlichman and Christopher Knowles, 251–70. London: Bloomsbury Academic, 2018.

———. "Kampf um die innere Sicherheit: Schutz des Staates oder Demokratie?" In *Hüter der Ordnung: Die Innenministerien in Bonn und Ost Berlin nach dem Nationalsozialismus*, edited by Frank Bösch and Andreas Wirsching, 454–97. Göttingen: Wallstein Verlag, 2018.

———. *Staatsschutz in Westdeutschland: Von der Entnazifizierung zur Extremistenabwehr*. Göttingen: Wallstein, 2013.

Ritchie, Alexandra. *Warsaw 1944: Hitler, Himmler, and the Warsaw Uprising*. New York: Farrar, Straus & Giroux, 2013.

Ritter, Jürgen, and Peter Joachim Lapp. *Die Grenze: Ein deutsches Bauwerk*. Berlin: Ch. Links, 1997.

Rosenbaum, Robert A. *Walking to Danger: Americans and Nazi Germany, 1933–1941*. Oxford: Praeger, 2010.

Rossi, Lauren Faulkner. *Wehrmacht Priests: Catholicism and the Nazi War of Annihilation*. Cambridge, MA: Harvard University Press, 2015.

Röw, Martin. *Militärseelsorge unter dem Hakenkreuz: Die katholische Feldpastoral 1939–1945*. Paderborn: Ferdinand Schöningh, 2014.

Ruff, Mark Edward. "Catholic Elites, Gender, and Unintended Consequences in the 1950s: Toward a Reinterpretation of the Role of Conservatives in the Federal Republic." In *Conflict, Catastrophe, and Continuity: Essays*

on Modern German History, edited by Frank Biess, Mark Roseman, and Hanna Schissler, 252–72. New York: Berghahn, 2007.
———. *The Wayward Flock: Catholic Youth in Postwar West Germany, 1945–1965*. Chapel Hill: University of North Carolina Press, 2005.
Said, Edward. *Orientalism*. New York: Random House, 1978.
Sälter, Gerhard. *Grenzpolizisten: Konformität, Verweigerung und Repression in der Grenzpolizei und Grenztruppen der DDR, 1952 bis 1965*. Berlin: Ch. Links Verlag, 2009.
Sammartino, Annemarie H. *The Impossible Border: Germany and the East, 1914–1922*. Ithaca, NY: Cornell University Press, 2010.
Schaefer, Karen. *German Military and the Weimar Republik: General Hans von Seeckt, General Erich Ludendorff and the Rise of Hitler*. Haverton, PA: Pen & Sword, 2020.
Schaefer, Sagi. *States of Division: Borders and Boundary Formation in Cold War Rural Germany*. Oxford: Oxford University Press, 2014.
Schenk, Dieter. *Der Chef: Horst Herold und das BKA*. Hamburg: Spiegel-Buchverlag, 1998.
Scheuring, Josef. *Den Menschen verpflichtet: Vom Bundesgrenzschutz zur Bundespolizei*. Hamburg: Tredition, 2020.
Schildt, Axel, and Arnold Sywottek "Reconstruction and Modernization: West German Social History during the 1950s." In *West Germany under Construction: Politics, Society, and Culture in the Adenauer Era*, edited by Robert G. Moeller, 413–43. Ann Arbor: University of Michigan Press, 1997.
Schiller, Kay, and Christopher Young. *The 1972 Munich Olympics and the Making of Modern Germany*. Berkeley: University of California Press, 2010.
Schissler, Hanna, ed. *The Miracle Years: A Cultural History of West Germany, 1949–1968*. Princeton, NJ: Princeton University Press, 2001.
Schmidtke, Michael. *Der Aufbruch der jungen Intelligenz: Die 68er Jahre in der Bundesrepublik und der USA*. Frankfurt am Main: Campus Verlag, 2003.
Schmitt, Carl. *The Crisis of Parliamentary Democracy*. Cambridge, MA: MIT Press, 1985.
———. *The Leviathan in the State Theory of Thomas Hobbes: Meaning and Failure of a Political Symbol*. Translated by George Schwab and Erna Hilfstein. Chicago: University of Chicago Press, 2008.
Schneider, Michael. *Demokratie in Gefahr? Der Konflikt um die Notstandsgesetze: Sozildemokratie, Gewerkschaften und intellektueller Protest*. Bonn: Neue Gesellschaft, 1986.
Scholten, Jens. "Offiziere: Im Geiste unbesiegt." In *Hitlers Eliten nach 1945*, edited by Norbert Frei. Frankfurt am Main: Campus, 2012.
Schrader, Stuart. *Badges without Borders: How Global Counterinsurgency Transformed American Policing*. Oakland: University of California Press, 2019.

Schreiber, Hermann. *Henri Nannen: Drei Leben.* Munich: Bertelsmann Verlag, 1999.

Schumann, Dirk. *Political Violence in the Weimar Republic, 1918–1933.* New York: Berghahn Books, 2012.

———, ed. *Raising Citizens in the Century of the Child: The United States and German Central Europe in Comparitive Perspective.* New York: Berghahn Books, 2010.

Schütte-Bestek, Patricia M. *Aus Bundesgrenzschutz wird Bundespolizei: Entwicklung einer deutschen Polizeiorganisation des Bundes aus organisationssoziologischer Perspektive.* Wiesbaden: Springer VS, 2015.

Schwarz, Hans-Peter. *Konrad Adenauer: A German Politician and Statesman in a Period of War, Revolution and Reconstruction, Vol. 1: From the German Empire to the Federal Republic, 1876–1952.* Translated by Louise Willmot. New York: Berghahn, 1995.

Schwell, Alexandra. *Europa an der Oder: Die Konstruktion europäischer Sicherheit an der deutsch-polnischen Grenze.* Bielefeld: Transcript Verlag, 2015.

Scott, Joan. "Gender: A Useful Category of Historical Analysis." *American Historical Review* 91, no. 5 (1986): 1053–75.

Searle, Alaric. "Internecine Secret Service Wars Revisited: The Intelligence Career of Count Gerhard von Schwerin, 1945–1956." *Militärgeschichtliche Zeitschrift* 71, no. 1 (2012): 25–55.

———. *Wehrmacht Generals, West German Society, and the Debate on Rearmament, 1949–1959.* Westport, CT: Praeger, 2003.

Seed, David. "Constructing America's Enemies: The Invasions of the USA." *Yearbook of English Studies* 37, no. 2 (2007): 64–84.

Settle, David E. *Faith and War: How Christians Debated the Cold and Vietnam Wars.* New York: New York University Press, 2011.

Sheehan, James J. *Where Have All the Soldiers Gone? The Transformation of Modern Europe.* Boston: Mariner, 2009.

Sheffer, Edith. *Burned Bridge: How East and West Germans Made the Iron Curtain.* Oxford: Oxford University Press, 2014.

Shepherd, Ben H. *Hitler's Soldiers: The German Army in the Third Reich.* New Haven, CT: Yale University Press, 2016.

Siemens, Daniel. *The Making of a Nazi Hero: The Murder and Myth of Horst Wessel.* London: I. B. Tauris, 2009.

Slobodian, Quinn. *Foreign Front: Third World Politics in Sixties West Germany.* Durham, NC: Durham University Press, 2012.

Smith, J., and André Moncourt, eds. *The Red Army Faction: A Documentary History, Vol. I: Projectiles for the People.* Montreal: Kersplebedeb, 2009.

Smith, Jean Edward, ed. *The Papers of General Lucius G. Clay: Germany, 1945–1949.* Vol. 2. Bloomington: Indiana University Press, 1974.

Soukoup, Uwe. *Ein Schuss der die Republik veränderte: Der 2. Juni 1967.* Berlin: Transit, 2017.

Spernol, Boris. *Notstand der Demokratie: Der Protest gegen die Notstandsgesetze und die Frage der NS-Vergangenheit.* Essen: Klartext, 2008.

Sprigboard, Patricia. "Hobbes and Schmitt on the Name and Nature of Leviathan Revisited." In *Thomas Hobbes and Carl Schmitt: The Politics of Order and Myth*, edited by John Tralau, 297–315. New York: Routledge, 2011.

Stacy, William. *US Army Border Operations in Germany, 1945–1983*. Heidelberg: Headquarters US Army, Europe and 7th Army, 1984.

Stanislas, Peter, ed. *International Perspectives on Police Education and Training*, Routledge Frontiers of Criminal Justice. New York: Routledge, 2014.

Steininger, Rolf. *The German Question: The Stalin Note of 1952 and the Problem of Reunification*. New York: Columbia University Press, 1990.

Stern, Sheddon M. *The Cuban Missile Crisis in American Memory: Myth versus Reality*. Stanford: Stanford University Press, 2012.

Stoklosa, Katarzyna. *Polen und die deutsche Ostpolitik, 1945–1990*. Göttingen: Vandenhoeck & Ruprecht, 2011.

Stolberg-Werinigerode, Otto. *New German Biography, vol. 17: Melander-Moller*. Berlin: Duncker & Humblot, 1994.

Stolleis, Michael. *Geschichte des öffentlichen Rechts in Deutschland, vierter Band: Staats- und Verwaltungsrechtwissenschaft in West und Ost, 1945–1990*. Munich: C. H. Beck, 2012.

Strong, Tracy B. "Carl Schmitt and Thomas Hobbes: Myth and Politics." In Carl Schmitt, *The Leviathan in the State Theory of Thomas Hobbes: Meaning and Failure of a Political Symbol*, vii–xxviii. Chicago: University of Chicago Press, 2008.

Sturm, Michael. "The Police." In Christoph Becker-Schaum, Philipp Gassert, Martin Klimke, Wilfried Mausbach, and Marianne Zepp," *The Nuclear Crisis: The Arms Race, Cold War Anxiety, and the German Peace Movement of the 1980s*, 274–89. New York: Berghahn Books, 2020.

Summers, Sarah E. "Finding Feminism: Rethinking Activism in the West German New Women's Movement of the 1970s and 1980s." In *Gendering Post-1945 German History: Entanglements*, edited by Karen Hagemann, Donna Harsch, and Friederike Brühöfener, 184–206. New York: Berghahn Books, 2019.

Taillon, Paul de B. *Hijacking and Hostages: Government Responses to Terrorism*. Westport: Praeger, 2002.

Taylor, Clarence. *Fight the Power: African Americans and the Long History of Police Brutality in New York City*. Oxford: Oxford University Press, 2019.

Thacker, Toby. *Music after Hitler*. Burlington, VT: Ashgate, 2007.

Thomas, Martin. *Violence and Colonial Order: Police, Workers and Protest in the European Colonial Empires, 1918–1940*. London: Cambridge University Press, 2012.

Thomas, Nick. *Protest Movements in 1960s West Germany: A Social History of Dissent and Democracy*. Oxford: Berg, 2003.

Thoß, Bruno. *NATO-Strategie und nationale Verteidigungsplanung: Planung und Aufbau der Bundeswehr unter den Bedingungen einer massiven*

atomaren Vergeltungsstrategie 1952 bis 1960. Munich: R. Oldenbourg Verlag, 2006.
Trachtenberg, Marc. *A Constructed Peace: The Making of the European Settlement, 1945–1963*. Princeton, NJ: Princeton University Press, 1999.
Tralau, John, ed. *Thomas Hobbes and Carl Schmitt: The Politics of Order and Myth*. New York: Routledge, 2011.
Trauschweizer, Ingo. *The Cold War US Army: Building Deterrence for Limited War*. Lawrence: University Press of Kansas, 2008.
Verheyen, Nina. *Diskussionslust: Eine Kulturgeschichte des "besseren Arguments" in Westdeutschland*. Göttingen: Vandenhoeck & Ruprecht, 2010.
von Hodenberg, Christina. *Konsens und Krise: Eine Geschichte der Westdeutschen Medienöffentlichkeit*. Göttingen: Wallstein Verlag, 2006.
von Hodenberg, Christina, and Detlef Siegfried, eds. *Wo "1968" liegt: Reform und Revolte in der Geschichte der Bundesrepublik*. Göttingen: Vandenhoeck & Ruprecht, 2006.
von Lingen, Kerstin. *Kesselring's Last Battle: War Crimes Trials and Cold War Politics, 1945–1960*. Lawrence: University Press of Kansas, 2009.
Waddington, P. A. J. *Policing Citizens: Authority and Rights*. New York: Routledge, 1999.
Wagener, Ulrike. "Berufsethische Bildung für staatliche Sicherheitskräfte: Das Beispiel Polizei." In *Charakter—Haltung—Habitus: Persönlichkeit und Verantwortung in der Bundeswehr*, edited by Angelika Dörfler-Dierken and Christian Göbel, 9–27. Wiesbaden: Springer, 2022.
Weber, Leanne, and Ben Bowling, eds. *Stop and Search: Police Power in Global Context*. New York: Routledge, 2013.
Weber, Werner. *Weimarer Verfassung und Bonner Grundgesetz*. Göttingen: Fleischer, 1949.
Wegener, Ulrich. "The Evolution of Grenzschutzgruppe (GSG) 9 and the Lessons of 'Operation Magic Fire' in Mogadishu." In *Force of Choice: Perspectives on Special Operations*, edited by Bernd J. Horn, Paul de B. Taillon, and David Last, 107–18. Montreal: Queens University School of Policy Studies, 2004.
Wegener, Ulrich, Ulrike Zander, and Harald Biermann. *GSG 9: Stärker als der Terror*. Berlin: Lit Verlag Dr. W. Hopf, 2017.
Weigley, Russell Frank. *The Age of Battles: The Quest for Decisive Warfare from Breitenfeld to Waterloo*. Bloomington: Indiana University Press, 1991.
Weikop, Christian. *New Expressions on Brücke Expressionism: Bridging History*. Burlington, VT: Ashgate, 2011.
Weinhauer, Klaus. *Schutzpolizei in der Bundesrepublik: Zwischen Bürgerkrieg und innerer Sicherheit: Die turbulenten sechziger Jahre*. Munich: Ferdinand Schoningh, 2003.
Weitz, Eric. *Creating German Communism, 1890–1990: From Popular Protests to Socialist State*. Princeton, NJ: Princeton University Press, 1997.
———. *Weimar Germany: Promise and Tragedy*. Princeton: Princeton University Press, 2007.

Weitz, Eric D. "The Ever Present Other: Communism in the Making of West Germany." In *The Miracle Years: A Cultural History of West Germany, 1949–1968*, edited by Hanna Schissler, 219–32. Princeton, NJ: Princeton University Press, 2001.
Wengst, Udo. *Thomas Dehler: 1897–1967; Eine politische Biographie*. Munich: R. Oldenbourg, 1997.
Werkentin, Falco. *Die Restauration der deutschen Polizei: Innere Rüstung von 1945 bis zur Notstandsgesetzgebung*. Frankfurt am Main; New York: Campus, 1984.
Westermann, Edward. *Hitler's Police Battalions: Enforcing Racial War in the East*. Lawrence: University Press of Kansas, 2010.
Wette, Wolfram. *The Wehrmacht: History, Myth, Reality*. Translated by Deborah Lucas Schneider. Cambridge, MA: Harvard University Press, 2006.
Wildenthal, Lora. *Human Rights Discourse in West Germany* Philadelphia: University of Pennsylvania Press, 2013.
Wildt, Michael. *An Uncompromising Generation: The Nazi Leadership of the Reich Security Main Office*. Translated by Tom Lampert. Madison: University of Wisconsin Press, 2009.
Wilke, Manfred, and Sophie Perl. *The Path to the Berlin Wall: Critical Stages in the History of Divided Germany*. New York: Berghahn Books, 2014.
Wilson, O. W., ed. *Parker on Police*. Springfield: Charles C. Thomas, 1957.
Winkler, Heinrich August. *Germany: The Long Road West, Vol. 1, 1789–1933*. New York: Oxford University Press, 2006.
———. *Germany: The Long Road West, Vol. 2, 1933–1990*. New York: Oxford University Press, 2007.
Wohl, Robert. *The Generation of 1914*. Cambridge: Cambridge University Press, 1979.
Wolf, Thomas. *Die Entstehung des BND: Aufbau, Finanzierung, Kontrolle*. Berlin: Ch. Links, 2018.
Wolff, Michael, ed. *The Collected Essays of Sir Winston Churchill*, vol. 1. London: Library of Imperial History, 1976.
Woodman, Connor. "The Imperial Boomerang: How France Used Colonial Methods to Massacre Algerians in Paris." *Verso Books Blog* (2020). https://www.versobooks.com/blogs/news/4418-the-imperial-boomerang-how-france-used-colonial-methods-to-massacre-algerians-in-paris.
Wyneken, David K. "The Western Allies, German Churches, and the Emerging Cold War in Germany, 1948–1952." In *Religion and the Cold War: A Global Perspective*, edited by Philip E. Muehlenbeck, 18–43. Nashville: Vanderbilt University Press, 2012.
Zimmermann, John. *Ulrich de Maizière: General der Bonner Republik, 1912 bis 2006*. Munich: Oldenbourg, 2012.
Zitzlsperger, Ulrike. *Gender, Agency and Violence: European Perspectives from Early Modern Times to the Present Day*. Newcastle upon Tyne: Cambridge Scholars, 2013.

INDEX

Abenheim, Donald, 86
Acheson, Dean, 32, 34
"Action Vermin," 76, 148
Adenauer, Konrad, 1–2, 17–43, 48–49, 51, 59, 71–72, 99, 101, 225, 244; Bolshevism fears of, 12, 18, 21, 28–29, 31, 58, 63, 286–87; death of, 203; EDC treaty and, 73, 75, 77, 83; expansionist plans for BGS by, 74–82, 92; Korean War and, 31–34; reelection of, 81–82; watch battalion of, 61–62
airport security, 204, 222, 241, 242, 249–50, 284
Allen, Jennifer, 11
Allied High Commission for Germany (HICOG), 7, 20, 22, 23, 25–29, 31, 42, 47, 78–79, 81, 124–25, 225
Allied-occupied Germany, policing in, 4–8
Amft, Karl-Heinz, 256, 261, 263, 267, 271
Andelfinger, Fritz, 111–15
Anders, Artur, 189
Andersen, Dieter, 173
Andersen, Kurt, 45–46, 64–71, 125, 287; photograph of, 140; rebuilding of BGS by, 102–3, 136–37, 145; retirement of, 146
Anti-radical decree (*Radikalenerlaß*), 238
anti-Semitism, 151, 153, 157, 173
Apel, Hans, 266
Apel, Karl-Otto, 172
Association of German Soldiers, 53–54
Association of Social Democratic Police Officers, 187
Axel Springer Verlag, 211, 247, 270

Baader, Andreas, 228, 251, 253
Baader-Meinhof Gang. *See* Red Army Faction
Bachmann, Josef, 211
"bandit fighting" (*Bandenbekämpfung*), 101, 135, 141–42, 188, 288
Baranowski, Shelley, 152
Bargatzky, Walter, 59–60, 102–3
Barth, Eberhard, 198–99
Bartov, Omer, 131, 151
Basic Law (West German constitution), 18, 26, 30, 36–37, 39, 60, 63, 118; Article 3, 266, 268, 269; Article 12, 186, 188, 189, 191, 265, 270, 274; Article 16, 162; Article 5, 207; Article 48, 205–6; Article 73, 62; Article 87, 19–20, 41–42, 216, 225–26; Article 91, 207; Article 103, 280, 282; Article 115, 207; Article 131, 43; religion and, 150
Basic Treaty, 204
Baudissin, Wolf von, 12, 88, 90; *Innere Führung* philosophy of, 84–85, 86
Baum, Gerhart, 255, 256, 258–61, 264, 269
Bavaria, 38, 39–40, 42, 43, 76–77, 249; border security in, 58, 59, 60, 226–27; Munich Olympics and, 236–37
Bavarian Party, 78
Bavarian Peoples Party, 24
Becker, Max, 42
Beermann, Friederich, 84, 100, 101, 102, 135–36
Belgium, invasion of (1914), 183–84
Benda, Ernst, 220

Ben-Horin, Eliashiv, 234
Bérard, Armand, 78, 82
Berber, Friederich, 183, 185
Bereitschaftspolizei (BePo), 7, 36–37, 39, 50, 213, 261
Berkley, George E., 123–24
Berlin, Soviet blockade of, 7, 286
Berlin Agreement, 204
Berlin Police Department, 210, 213–14, 279, 281
Berlin Wall, 148, 177, 193, 206; fall of, 257, 276
Bernstein, Nicole, 275
Betts, Paul, 288
Beyerhaus, Peter, 166
Bidault, Georges, 81
black marketeering, 7, 20, 64–71, 135
Black September Organization, 228, 239, 241. *See also* Munich Olympic Games
Blank, Theodor, 136
Blank Office, 74, 83–84, 85–87, 91
Blankenhorn, Herbert, 25, 27
Bleckmann, Albert, 274
Boge, Heinrich, 269
Bolshevism, opposition to, 153, 155, 157–60. *See also* communists; *and under* Adenauer, Konrad; Weimar Republic
Bonin, Bogislaw von, 135–36, 196
Border Police Act, 94–95; revision of, 184–90, 205, 220–23, 229, 236–37, 256, 260, 274, 282, 289–90
Border Police Individual Service (GSE), 147, 149; women in, 272–73, 283
border policing, 12, 13, 17, 19–21, 24–26, 56–60, 62, 66; new challenges of, 100–101, 103–5, 193–94, 217–18, 275–76. *See also Bundesgrenzschutz*
Boysen, Carl, 226
Brandt, Willy, 13, 204, 216–17, 220, 229, 236–37, 260, 289
Breiting, Otto, and Kurt M. Hoffmann, 150
Breitman, Richard, 159–60
Brentano, Heinrich von, 61

Brill, Heinz, 136
Brooks, Rosa, 130
Brücker, Diethelm, 278–79
Bruhn, Johannes, 52
Brühöfener, Friederike, 107, 110
Brundage, Avery, 233
Buback, Siegfried, 250
Bundesgrenzschutz (BGS): background and creation of, 2, 11–12, 17–44, 47–48; as Bonn's "problem child," 203; command centers of, 1, 52, 192; crowd control and, 212–14, 284; Employees Association of, 92, 93–94, 110, 168, 209, 215–16, 218, 223, 268; marine component of (see *Seegrenzschutz*); marriage regulations in, 106–8, 167; militaristic aspects of, 3–4, 9, 12, 27, 46, 51, 55–59, 62, 64–67, 83, 88, 100, 123–49, 176, 190–91, 204, 214–15, 218–19, 287–89; modernization of, 13, 203–27, 255–84; press scrutiny of, 195–200, 214; suicides in, 167–68; termination of, 3, 14, 285, 290; uniforms of, 1, 47–48, 52, 61, 76, 106, 218, 231, 253, 284, 287, 290; war games by, 191–92, 247, 288; watch battalion of, 61–62, 212; women in, 166, 191, 257, 265–75, 283, 289. *See also* combatant status debate; ethics programs; Group F; GSG 9; protest policing; recruitment and rebuilding programs; training and education programs
Bundeskriminalamt (BKA), 43, 52, 224, 238, 241
Bundesnachrichtendienst (BND), 43, 241
Bundespolizei (BPOL), 11, 13, 284, 290
Bundeswehr: American Army model for, 191; ideological foundation of, 84; marriage policy in, 110; NATO control of, 124; SPD and, 75–76, 78, 84, 91–92, 95; transfers from BGS to, 73–76, 86, 91–95, 99

Busemann, Michaela, 283
Bush, George H. W., 268
Byroade, Henry A., 26

Castro, Fidel, 188, 195
Chin, Rita, and Heide Fehrenbach, 163
Christian Democratic Party (CDU), 52, 75, 82, 206-7
Christian Social Party (CSU), 24, 76-77, 80-81, 206
Christianity, 150-61, 164-66, 174, 195, 286, 288
Christophe-Müller, Hendrik, 41
Churchill, Winston, 158-59
Civil Service Remuneration Act, 94, 95
Clark, Christopher, 130
Clay, Lucius, 7
Cohen, Stanley, 57
"cold civil war," 193-94, 217, 283
colonialism, 13
combatant status debate, 13, 175-95, 270, 272, 273-74, 283, 288
Communist Party of Germany (KPD), 41, 156, 262
communists: Christian opposition to, 157-58, 164; fear of, 5, 13, 18, 21, 22, 28-29, 31-33, 37, 41, 42, 45, 51, 55, 57-58, 60, 63, 74, 85, 100-102, 137, 149, 176, 260; in *Zum Schutz der Heimat*, 113
Conant, James, 78-80
concentration camps, 25-26, 55, 119, 176
conscription, 122, 126, 207-9, 219-20, 256, 289; compulsory service legislation, 203, 207
Cry the Beloved Country (film), 170, 171
Cuban Missile Crisis, 148, 177

Dahms, Alexander, 163
Daume, Willy, 232, 233
death strip (*Todesstreifen*), 115, 218
decolonization, 11, 13, 195
Dehler, Thomas, 18-19, 24, 41
denazification process, 43, 46-47, 181, 280

détente, 13, 82, 194n93, 204, 217
Deutsche Gewerkschaft Bund (DGB), 206, 223, 266
Deutschland Lied, Das, 51
Dierske, Ludwig, 50-51, 102, 134, 145, 146
Diestel, Peter-Michael, 277-78
Dietze, Carola, 26
Dippelhofer, Otto, 1, 128-29, 133, 137, 137
Diskussionslust, 172
Döge, Eberhard, 105
Döring, Ralf, 197-98
drug trafficking, 162, 256, 275, 276
Dulles, Allen, 33, 81
Dulles, John Foster, 78, 81
Duncan, David Douglas, 123
Dutschke, Rudi, 211, 213
Dylan, Bob, 200

East German Border Police (1990), 277
East Germany (GDR): evaluation of BGS by, 194, 214; policing in, 6-7; propaganda from, 56; Soviet atrocities in, 28-29, 157; uprising of 1953 in, 80. See also People's Police
Easter Riots, 211-14, 215
Eckardt, Felix von, 83
"economic miracle" (*Wirtschaftswunder*), 82, 99, 122, 164, 203
Eder, Astrid, 265
Egidi, Hans, 24-26, 52-53, 59, 76, 141
Ehlers, Hermann, 77
Einwag, Alfred, 191
Eisenhauer, Dwight D., 24, 34, 40
Elkins, Caroline, 48n8
emergency laws, 13, 178, 205-9, 213, 214, 215-16, 220-21, 289
ENERGA anti-tank rifle grenade, 137, 138
Ensslin, Gudrun, 251, 253
Entebbe raid (Operation Thunderbolt), 252, 253
Eppelmann, Rainer, 279

Erdmenger, Chairman, 269
Erhard, Ludwig, 203, 206
Ermacora, Felix, 185–86
Erras, Carl, 117–18
ethics programs, 13, 150–74, 288
Etzemüller, Thomas, 215
"European Bridge" checkpoint, 103–4
European Court of Human Rights, 282
European Defense Community (EDC) Treaty, 73, 74, 75, 76–83, 139; Interim Committee of, 85

Fanon, Frantz, 248
Federal Police Academy, 103
Federal Police Act, 106, 110, 220
Fehrenbach, Heide, 111
feminist movement, 257, 265
films: in ethics programs, 169–72, 174; in recruitment programs, 111–18
Finger, Bernd, 277–78, 286
"flash-bang" grenades, 252n102
Flecken, Adolf, 61–62, 67–68
Flex, Walter, 131–32
Floyd, George, 285
Foot, Matt, 286
France, German relations with, 82
François-Poncet, André, 21, 37, 48, 79, 82, 139
Frederick the Great, 192
Free German Youth (FDJ), 29, 33, 51, 60, 63, 65, 66; World Youth Festival and, 56–59, 74, 130
Frei, Norbert, 129
Freikorps, 5, 23, 45, 53
Freytag, Ulrich, 52
Friedrichs, Reinhold, 153n12
Friesicke, Beate, 270
Frings, Klaus, 211–12
Fröhlich, Siegfried, 117, 181–82, 222–23, 225
Für Frieden in Freiheit (recruitment film), 117–18

Gansel, Norbert, 262
Gauck, Joachim, 280–81
Gehlen, Reinhard, 33

Gehlen Organization, 43, 50, 53, 240
Geis, Bernd, 218
gender roles and relationships, 107–9, 113, 152, 166, 168–69, 257, 265–70
Geneva Conventions, 180–81, 183, 184, 186
Genscher, Hans Dietrich, 217, 219–22, 224, 226–27, 228–30, 234–38, 241–47, 255
Gerhardt, H. A., 26
Gestapo, 179
Gewerkschaft der deutschen Polizei (GdP), 130, 183, 185, 223–24, 226, 230, 247–48, 262, 268, 280
Gewerkschaft Öffentliche Dienste, Transport und Verkehr (ÖTV), 130, 145, 183, 189, 217–19, 223
Gibbons, Floyd, 158
Giese, Herbert, 52
Grapes of Wrath, The (film), 171
Grasser, Anton, 49–53, 125, 127–28, 287
Greener, B. K., and W. J. Fish, 132–33
Grenzjäger (term), 3, 106, 287
Grenzjäger, Der (BGS journal), 91, 106, 160, 195
Gries, Ekkehard, 268
Groener, Wilhelm, 53
Group F (*Gruppefernmeldewesen*), 240–41, 242–43, 284, 286
Grüner, Rudolf, 241, 244
GSG 9 (BGS counterterrorism unit), 13, 230, 238, 243–44, 245–46, 247, 248–54, 255; foreign models for, 238, 248, 249; Iraq War and, 284
Guderian, Heinz, 56
guerilla warfare, 3, 50, 100, 135, 142, 149, 183n32, 190, 192–95, 248
Guevara, Che, 192, 195
Gumbel, Karl, 74–75, 209, 213, 220
Günther, Herbert, 250

Habermas, Jürgen, 172
Hafenecker, Thomas, 284
Hahn, Ulrich, 166
Halder, Franz, 33

Halt, Adalbert, 224
Hamann, Andreas, 185–86
Hancock, Patrick, 81
Hanshew, Karrin, 205, 241, 253
Hays, George P., 25, 26, 33, 38
Heimat film genre, 112
Heineman, Dane, 32
Heinemann, Gustav, 35, 52–53
Heinlein, Robert, 158
Hellenthal, Markus, 273–74
Herold, Horst, 239, 240, 241, 246, 259
Herrhausen, Alfred, 256
Heusinger, Adolf, 33, 85, 86–88
Himmerod Memorandum, 84
Himmler, Heinrich, 4, 159, 188
Hitler, Adolf, 19, 26, 34, 36–37, 55, 91–92, 152, 159–60, 169, 173, 260, 288; photograph of, 54; plot to assassinate, 173–74
Höcherl, Hermann, 182, 183, 198–99, 206, 255
Hodenberg, Christina von, 196
Hoegner, Wilhelm, 39–40
Hoffmann, Theodor, 277
Höffner, Hans, 71, 139
Holmes, Richard, 130
Horne, John, and Alan Kramer, 183–84
"Horst Wessel-Lied," 60n46
Hoyer, Petra, 283
Hudak, Adalbert, 166
Hughes, Michael, 63
Hungarian uprising, 104

immigrants (and asylum-seekers), 10, 162–63, 290
Innsbruck Olympics, 249
International Federation of Police Leaders, 266–67
Irving, David, 260

Jaeger, Richard, 76–77
Jäger, Michael, 272–73
Jansch, Siegfried, 193
Jarausch, Konrad, 3–4
Jentsch, Werner, 161
Jess, Hans, 182

Junker, Heinrich, 185
juvenile delinquency, 65

Kallis, Aristotle, 160
Keitel, Wilhelm, 54, 187
Kennedy, John F., 148
Kesselring, Albert, 180n17
Khrushchev, Nikita, 148, 161
Kielmansegg, Johann von, 83–84
Kiesinger, Kurt Georg, 206–7
Kirkpatrick, Ivone, 27, 81
Knackstedt, Heinz, 184
Knorr, Erwin, 244–48, 289
Koehler, John, 280
Kohl, Helmut, 162, 251
Kollreutter, Otto, 25
Kommers, Donald, 150
Korean War, 31–34, 36, 82, 120, 225, 286
Köttgen, Arnold, 25–26
Krannhals, Hanns von, 190
Krekeler, Heinz, 37
Kruge, Günther von, 21
Küffner, Hanns, 105
Kuhlmann, Werner, 143, 185–86, 188–89, 204, 223–26, 230, 243–45, 247, 248
Kuhlwein, Eckart, 255
Kurras, Karl Heinz, 210

Labor Service Units (*Dienstgruppen*), 35
Langkeit, Willy, 1
Laniel, Joseph, 82
Large, David Clay, 28n37, 235, 237
Lehman, Brittany, 162
Lehr, Robert, 17, 35, 38–42, 49–52, 55–56, 61–63, 68, 71–72, 73, 95, 101, 219, 286–87; background of, 22–23; expansionist plans of, 74–82, 85, 126
Lenden, Gerhard, 250
Lenz, Otto, 74
Liddel Hart, Basil, 86
Life magazine, 83, 123
Lindbergh, Charles, 120, 158
Loader, Ian, and Neil Walker, 229, 242, 243, 246, 247–48

Loßberg, Bernhard von, 87
Lost Boundaries (film), 170
Lübeck-St. Hubertus, BGS school in, 50, 102, 125, 127, 133, 136, 148, 167, 190
Lücke, Paul, 199, 206
Lufthansa Flight 181 hijack, 230, 251–54, 255
Lumack, Rolf, 279
Luttwak, Edward, 152–53

Maasen, Hermann, 244–45, 246
Mack, Phyllis, 151
Macleod, Iain, 242–43, 286
Maier, Friedrich, 76
Maihofer, Werner, 251, 253, 254, 255, 258, 259, 286
Mangelsdorf, Georg, 144
Manig, Bert-Oliver, 128
Manthe, Barbara, 259–60
Manz, Rudi, 250
Mao Zedong, 161, 192
"March on Bonn," 214–15
Marighella, Carlos, 248
Marx, Karin, 270
masculinity, ideals of, 12, 105–11, 118, 122, 152, 166, 169, 248, 289
Matzky, Gerhard, 53–56, 58, 65–66, 71, 85–87, 90, 99, 102, 125, 135, 136, 139, 287; photograph of, 140
McCloy, John J., 19, 26, 29–31, 34, 36, 58, 78, 80
McCormack, Matthew, 105, 106n27
McKay, Jim, 228, 237
Mechlinski, Dieter, 271–72, 274, 275
Meder, Johann, 68
Meinhof, Ulrike, 228, 248
Meins, Holger, 249
Meir, Golda, 234
Meister, Michael, 208
Mellies, Wilhelm, 95
memory culture, 173, 176
"men of the first hour" designation, 46, 47, 71, 146, 164, 253, 260
Menzel, Walter, 39, 41–42, 61–63, 78
Merk, Bruno, 230–31, 234

Merkel, Angela, 163
Meurer, Christian, 183–84
MG-42 ("Hitler's buzzsaw"), 126
Michels, Eckard, 214n43
Militärgeschichtliches Forschungsamt, 187
militarized policing, 9–10, 12, 26–31, 35, 41, 48, 51; SPD opposition to, 42, 55–56, 61–62, 72. *See also* training and education programs
Millar, Frederick Hoyer, 139, 141
Miller, John, 280
Ministry for State Security (MfS), 75, 277, 280, 281, 286
Mobilwerbung GmbH, 116–17
Modrow, Hans, 277
Moeller, Robert, 173
Mogadishu hijack. *See* Lufthansa Flight 181 hijack
Moltke, Helmuth von, 192
Monnet, Jean, 73
"moral panic," 57, 192
Mosse, George L., 132
Müller, Heinrich, 1–2, 88, 125–27, 131–32, 133, 146; background and views of, 90, 125, 155–57, 159–60, 165, 166, 173–74, 192, 195, 287; photographs of, 2, 89, 126, 140; promotion (1963) and later career of, 148–49, 190, 191–92, 196, 213, 214
Müller, Irmgard, 287
Munich Olympic Games, 13, 210n29, 227, 228–39, 241, 244–45, 246

Nannen, Henri, 197–98
Nasution, Abdul, 192–93, 195
National People's Army (NVA), 177, 178, 193
National Police Leadership Academy, 151, 261
NATO, 30–31, 74, 83, 90, 95, 100–101, 123–24, 137, 144, 156, 178, 194, 196, 204, 263, 288
Nazi Germany, 25–26, 39, 131, 141–42, 163, 169, 247; Federal Republic and, 8–9, 189; Germans as "victims" of, 172–73; policing

under, 4, 9, 18, 30, 37, 41, 56, 120, 123, 179, 187–88; religious support for, 151, 152, 155; songs of, 51, 60–61, 71; war criminal trials after, 176, 179–80, 181, 280. *See also* Hitler, Adolf; Waffen-SS; Wehrmacht
Nehring, Holger, 177–78
neo-Nazis, 21, 239, 256, 259–60, 290
Neumann, Werner, 113–14
Niemöller, Martin, 35
Nine-Power Conference, 83
Noftke, Siegfried, 197, 198–99
nuclear war, threat of, 100–101, 148, 156, 158, 177–78; anti-nuclear demonstrations, 261–64, 289

Oberle, Helmut, 172–73
Occupation Statute, 38, 42, 47
Ochquvist, Harald, 54
Office of Constitutional Protection (BfV), 47, 52, 58, 231, 241
Ohnesorg, Benno, 210, 213
Olympia (propaganda film), 197
Operation Blue, 138–39
Operation Danube, 139, 143
Operation Magic Fire, 252–53
Operation Martha, 45, 64–71
Operation South Bavaria, 141–43, 243, 245, 288
Ordnungsdienst (Munich Security Service), 231–33, 235
Ordnungspolizei (OrPo), 46
Ortega y Gasset, José, 156
Osborne, Robert, and Donald Bogle, 170
Ostpolitik, 13, 204, 217, 260
ÖTV. *See Gewerkschaft Öffentliche Dienste, Transport und Verkehr*

Pantenius, Hans-Jürgen, 46, 175, 289
Papon, Maurice, 10–11
Paris Treaties, 205
Parker, William H., 6
Parma, David, 27
Parole, Die (BGS journal), 61–62, 63, 85, 108, 109, 113, 160–61, 195, 216

passport control, 3, 20, 59–60, 62, 93, 257; renaming of, 147; reunification changes to, 277, 279
paternalism (political), 243, 246, 247
Paulsen, Maike, 272
Peel, Robert, 10
People's Police (*Volkspolizei*), 7, 29, 31, 34, 57, 59–60, 76, 80, 88, 100; in recruitment films, 113–14, 118; reunification adjustments to, 279, 281; superiority of, 139; training for, 134
Persilscheine, 47
Personal Advisory Committee (PGA), 91, 92, 93, 102
personal data and privacy concerns, 240–41, 255, 280, 284, 285–86
Personnel Structure Act, 256, 258–59, 261
Pfeffer, Helmut, 268
Pioch, Hans-Hugo, 187–88
Platen, Detlev von, 1, 214, 216, 218–19
Pleven, René, 73
Plogstedt, Sibylle, 266, 270
Pohlmann, Herr, 117
Poiger, Uta, 113
Poland, invasion and atrocities in, 25–26, 175–76, 190. *See also* Warsaw Uprising
Ponto Jürgen, 251
Popular Front for the Liberation of Palestine (PFLP), 222, 227, 251–52
Poske, Fritz, 55
Protestant Academy, 131, 148, 160–61, 173
Potsdam Agreement, 4, 112
Prague Spring crackdown, 157, 209
Prawdin, Michael, 159
protest policing, 209–15, 261–64
Prussian militarism, 4, 12, 61, 83, 86, 102, 130, 131, 192

Quirini, Helmut, 246–47

racism and xenophobia, 10–11, 12–13, 155, 156–63, 171, 174,

racism and xenophobia (*continued*), 288; Genscher's anti-Arabism, 241–42; recent examples of, 290
Radtke, Wilhelm, 204n4
Rahden, Till van, 132
Raspe, Jan-Carl, 253
Raymond, Jack, 32
Reber, Samuel, 34
recruitment and rebuilding programs, 12, 99–122
Red Army Faction (RAF), 13, 227, 228, 229, 238–42, 250–54, 255, 256, 260
"red scare," 31, 158
Rehg, William, 172
Reichsarbeitdienst (RAD), 184, 185
Reichstag fire, 179
Reichswehr, 5, 28, 85, 87, 136
Reinfarth, Heinz, 190
Reischle, Günther, 160
Renthe-Fink, Leonhard von, 133–35, 144
Retterath, Tobias, 284
reunification challenges, 257–58, 276–84, 289–90
Reza Pahlavi, Mohammad, 210–11
Rhee, Syngman, 33
Ribbentrop, Joachim von, 54, 183
Richter, K., 111
Riedl, Karl, 60
Riesman, David, 164–65
Riot Police. See *Bereitschaftspolizei*
Ritter von Lex, Hans, 19, 24–26, 50, 51, 52, 55–56, 59, 60
Roberts, Frank, 78
Robertson, Brian, 27
Roemer, Walter, 180–81
Rohrbach, Oskar, 169–71
Rombach, Wilhelm, 92
Ruff, Mark Edward, 164
Ruhnau, Heinz, 247
Runge, Director, 273–75
Russia (USSR), opposition to, 156–61
Rust, Josef, 91

Saar dispute, 82
Said, Edward, 161
Samlowski, Alfred, 146–47, 148

Saurzapf, Rolf, 165
Sauvagnargues, Jean, 78
Schäffer, Fritz, 24–25, 40, 59
Schäuble, Wolfgang, 276, 277–78, 279–80
Schengen Agreement, 256, 275–76, 277, 283
Scheuring, Josef, 276, 277, 278, 281
Schildt, Axel, and Arnold Sywottek, 160
Schiller, Kay, and Chris Young, 233
Schily, Otto, 284, 290
Schirrmacher, Helmut, 268
Schleiffen, Alfred, 192
Schleyer, Hanns-Martin, 251, 253, 255
Schmidt, Gerhard, 217, 218–20
Schmidt, Helmut, 186–87, 251–52
Schmitt, Carl, 40–41, 206
Schneider, Kurt, 256, 260–61
Schneider, Peter, 282
Schneppel, Hans, 178–80, 182, 214–15
Schreck, Rudiger, 212
Schreiber, Manfred, 210, 211, 214, 229, 231–35, 237
Schreiber, Wolfgang, 274–75
Schröder, Gerhard, 73, 82, 94–96, 99, 146, 148, 206
Schubert, Nadja, 272
Schuchardt, Fritz, 59
Schug, Egon, 256, 261, 271, 274, 275
Schumacher, Kurt, 55–56, 75
Schumann, Jürgen, 252
Schütte-Bestek, Patricia, 216
Schutzpolizei, 9, 22, 45, 125, 146, 197
Schwartz, Hans-Peter, 21, 27
Schwarz, Heinz, 227
Schwarzer, Alice, 265, 270
Schwerin, Gerhard von, 27–28, 32, 33–34, 35, 49, 83, 141
Seeckt, Hans von, 85, 86n52, 102, 192
Seegrenzschutz, 2, 54–55
Seehofer, Horst, 290–91
Seelsorge, 13, 153

Settle, David E., 164
Severing, Carl, 9–10, 39
Sheehan, James, 106, 114
Shepherd, Ben, 153
"shoot to kill order" (*Schießbefehl*), 282
Simpson, Joseph, 10
Sleik, Franz, 141–43, 244, 245
smuggling. *See* black marketeering
Social Democratic Party (SPD), 38–39, 41–42, 55–56, 61, 62–63, 72, 137, 139; during modernization period, 205–6, 239. *See also Bundeswehr*
Socialist German Student Union, 211
Socialist Reich Party (SRP), 21, 23–24
Socialist Union Party (SED), 29, 280
Sondersicherheitsgruppe, 239
Sozialistische Jugend Deutschlands (SJD), 185
Spartacus League demonstration, 23
Speidel, Hans, 33, 85, 87
Spengler, Oswald, 156
Spezialeinsatzkommandos (SEKs), 249
Spiegel Affair, 196–97
Spitzer, Kurt, 85, 100–101, 135–36
Stahel, Rainer, 190
Stahl, Friedrich Cristian, 187–88
Stalin, Joseph, 82
"Stalin Notes," 75
Stasi. *See* Ministry for State Security
Steele, Christopher, 27
Stemmle, Robert A., 65
Stern, Hans, 46
Stern photo-essay scandal, 196–200, 214
Stöcker, Otmar, 164–65
Stoltenberg, Gerhard, 260
Strauss, Franz Josef, 77–78, 136, 180, 197, 206
"Street Fighting Manual," 190–91
student protests, 203, 209–15, 224, 257, 262
Stülpnagel, Friedrich von, 92, 102n8
Stülpnagel, Joachim von, 101
Summers, Sarah, 265
sündige Grenze, Die (film), 65
SWAT teams, 249n85

Teichmann, Alex B., 191
terrorism, 13, 222, 228–54, 256, 259–60, 284, 285
Thadden, Adolf von, 42
Third Reich. *See* Nazi Germany
Thompson, Kenneth, 57–58
Tjaden, Sigrid, 272
To Kill a Mockingbird (film), 170
training and education programs, 12, 50, 123–49, 258, 288; criminal complaints about, 243–47; legal coursework and, 128, 134, 144–47; public scrutiny of, 145, 195–96
Traube, Klaus, 255, 286
Treaty of Versailles, 4

Ulbrich, Fritz, 151, 157
Ulbricht, Walter, 161
Unification Treaty, 279
US Constabulary, 20, 58
US culture, 164–66
US Naval Historical Team (NHT), 55
US troops stationed in Germany, 143–44, 205, 209, 243–45, 266

Verheyen, Nina, 172
"victors justice" complaint, 181
Vietnam War, 13, 82, 147–48, 176, 192, 195, 209
Vietor, Jürgen, 252
Voigt, Kurt, 161
Vollmer, Sergeant, 70
Völzke, Hans, 197

Waffenschmidt, Horst, 275
Waffen-SS, 126, 184, 287
Ward, Jack, 80
Warner, Christopher F. A., 81
Warren, Earl, 158
Warsaw Uprising, 13, 46, 175, 187, 190, 217, 289
We Are All Murderers (film), 171
Weber, Leanne, and Ben Bowling, 240
Weber, Max, 17
Weber, Werner, 40–41
Wechmar, Rüdiger, 77
Wegener, Ulrich, 230, 232, 235, 237–38, 248–50, 251, 253, 254, 255

Wehrmacht: in Nazi era, 13, 34, 45–46, 53, 87, 91–92, 119, 152–53, 155, 173–74, 175, 190; presence in BGS of, 1, 12, 27, 31, 33–35, 45–56, 61, 73–74, 83, 85, 106, 124–25, 130, 141, 144, 147, 149, 151, 191, 256
Wehrsportgruppe Hoffmann, 238
Weimar Republic: Bolsheviks and, 28–29, 53; border guarding in, 101; policing in, 5, 9–10, 21–23, 133, 285; as warning example, 205–6, 247, 291. *See also* Reichswehr
Weitz, Eric, 9, 63
Weyer, Willi, 247
Weylandt, Manfred, 282
Wildenthal, Lora, 186, 195
Winkelbrandt, Karl, 190
Winterle, Franz, 46

Wir tragen Gewehre (recruitment film), 114
Wirtz, Anton, 153, 169
World Youth Festival, 56–59, 74

xenophobia. *See under* racism

"yellow peril," 158–61

Zamir, Zvi, 234, 236
Zeitschrift des Bundesgrenzschutzes (BGS journal), 162, 163, 195
Zimmerman, Friedrich, 269, 271–74, 276, 289
Zimmermann, Joachim, 266–67
Zollgrenzdienst, 20, 24, 25, 58, 59, 147; Operation Martha and, 64–70
Zum Schutz der Heimat (recruitment film), 111–18, 119

Printed in the United States
by Baker & Taylor Publisher Services